Learning to Read Naturally

Margaret Greer Jewell
University of Alaska, Anchorage
Miles V. Zintz
University of New Mexico

Kendall/Hunt
Publishing Company
Dubuque, Iowa

Library of Congress Catalog Card Number: 85–82032

ISBN: 0–8403–3838–4

Printed in the United States of America

C 403838 01

To Allen Jewell
Lillie Smith
And Mary Hatley Zintz

One of the greatest delights of adult life is watching a child "discover" reading.

Contents

List of Figures

List of Tables

List of Your Turn Activities

Preface

This book has been written for those people who work with children in nursery school, kindergarten, and primary grades. It discusses the child from infancy to age eight. It can be studied by preservice teachers prior to their student teaching experience, but it will also be useful to all in-service teachers who are not already acquainted with the whole-language approach to teaching reading. The book will also be of interest to many parents who wish to understand the process by which their child may most naturally learn to read and write.

Our Views on Teaching Reading

The concern herein is with the way children master the process of reading and then use reading for both its utility and its enjoyment. We believe that the great majority of boys and girls can learn to read as easily and as naturally as they have learned to talk.

In *Psycholinguistics* . . . Constance Weaver wrote:

> Learning to read naturally happens when the child works from whole language back to parts; from memorized stories to words; and from words to the letters and their sounds. The prime feature of the natural reading is the comprehending of meaning as it is expressed in whole language. Many natural readers have been immersed in the written language—and they have usually had someone to assist them in their individual exploration of the relationship between spoken language and written language. But, they have learned to read without really being "taught" (1980, 150, 261).

Learning to read is a means to an end—not an end in itself. That end is permanent reading interests for all children who then will read because they want to for both information and pleasure. Successful teaching of reading requires that the learners come to know that reading is personally valuable to them. They internalize reading as a value that they cherish.

We believe that much present teaching makes learning to read an end in itself. Mastering enough decoding skills and word recognition abilities to pronounce the words correctly does not constitute reading as we view it.

A kindergarten teacher sat down to dinner with her parents and related the following anecdote:

> Something very interesting happened at school today. Sarah is in my afternoon kindergarten. She is a lovely child and I have enjoyed her a lot. I have never noticed anything particular about her, though, when I read to the group. And I can't remember any specific times when I've read with her alone. Today, she came up to me and said, "May I read you a book?" I told her as soon as I got the groups working I'd be glad to read with her. In a few minutes, she and I sat down in one corner and she opened the preprimer of a reading series to the first page. She read exactly what the few words said (I'd supposed she would look at the pictures and tell me a story). Then, page by page, she read the entire little book and pronounced every word correctly. There were

> perhaps twenty-five different words in the book. I told her how pleased I was that she'd read so well and thanked her for asking to read to me. I didn't tell her how surprised I was that she would really be able to read. (Murphy and Zintz, 1981, p. 4.)

We believe that the best way to teach reading will be not to teach it in the traditional sense but to engage youngsters in many learning activities in which reading is necessary. Then the teacher must provide all the help possible to enable youngsters to "make use of reading."

Teachers and administrators face criticism daily because there are too many children not making progress in reading in primary classrooms. The rationale presented in this text is a response to that failure with suggestions for curricular changes that utilize an enriched classroom learning environment and for many activities that provide opportunities for children to explore, experiment, and solve problems. Timing is also an important factor and provisions are made for students to progress at the rate at which they optimally grow.

Having visited innumerable elementary classrooms through the years and having become painfully aware that there is some truth to what our critics say about us, we are burdened with helping teachers and parents who must struggle with the simplistic, narrow views espoused by critics of education. The half-truths, the limited perspectives, and the complexity of changing human behavior explain why improvement of instruction moves slowly.

Teachers must discover the children who, too often, *sit* behind basal readers and their accompanying workbooks. If we can discover *the children*—their sensitivity, their quality, their interests, their motives, and their tastes and talents—they will help us create relevant reading materials for all children.

We are concerned about the individual differences in rates of growth and development. A child is not *deficient* just because he happens to perform tasks at a level that is not equivalent to many of his agemates. We must accept the different rates of acquisition of all the skills of communication: speaking, listening, reading, and writing. The tradition of starting all children to school at age six has cemented us into unreasonable expectations that do damage daily to some children. When a society elects to educate all of the children of all the people, schools must provide proper cognitive and affective environments for the complete range of abilities.

About This Text

A process by which young children will be able to grow into reading and writing is presented here. Acquiring language and then developing an enriched oral competence should enable many children, at their own rates, to pursue reading and writing activities in ways that are relevant to their lives. The practical aspects of what we have written respond to the research on the theory of language acquisition and development and to the research on the nature of children and the forces that impinge on their lives as they grow up. The language-experience approach and the shared-book experience provide an avenue for demonstrating the meaningfulness, relevance, and utility of reading in the child's world.

In this text, the three important elements that are interrelated when a child learns to read naturally are described: (1) the nature of language, how it is acquired, and how it is extended into a rich store of meanings; (2) the nature of childhood and how children grow and develop; and (3) the nature of the reading process and how it is mastered by effective readers. This process develops through three distinguishable stages: (1) building a support system for reading; (2) focusing on print; and (3) functioning as a reader. Meaning is the entry point for the development of literacy. The major emphasis is on meanings, and in the process of arriving at meanings, the learner develops a perceived need for skills. *It is not natural to begin with segments of the language that are meaningless; it is natural to begin with whole language.*

The book is organized in three parts: Part one provides a theoretical base for the methodology to follow. It consists of three chapters. Chapter 1 is an overview of the development of natural readers. Chapter 2 contains a discussion of the language process: how and why children learn language; the components of language; oral, written, and nonverbal language; and a comparison of the learning to speak with the learning to read process. Chapter 3 contains a discussion of children and how they grow and develop.

Part two includes chapters 4 and 5. Chapter 4 evaluates our present status and the need for changes in the teaching of reading, and chapter 5 discusses the application of psycholinguistic theory to the teaching of reading.

Part three, chapters 6 through 9, presents ways to make informal assessments of children's progress as they grow into reading and a methodological approach for guiding children into reading through meaningful activities. Chapter 9 is a concluding statement to the text.

Terminology

Because the content of this text presents many concepts that may be new to its readers, we have included a list of terms at the beginning of each chapter. An inclusive glossary at the end of the book contains concise definitions of these terms.

Guide Questions

Guide questions are provided to aid the student in the directed study of each chapter. These questions are designed to assess understanding of chapter content.

Your Turn

Your turn activities provide a series of assignments that require application of the theoretical base of the text to practical problems in classrooms. The *Your Turn* activities can also be used by the instructor as examination material for the course.

Appendixes

The fourteen appendixes provide a wide range of helps to teachers. The several lists will help teachers find the kinds of materials and books they seek. These appendixes should provide a "hands-on" ready reference for everyday use. Of course, teachers will need to continually search out the new items to be added to such bibliographies each year.

We believe that this program should be followed through the primary years of school, while the emphasis on whole language should continue all the way through school. Primary is typically through the third grade, although it is clear in our writing that we wish to consider levels at which children can perform and not "to what grade they are assigned." Of course, as children discover reading and gain confidence in their ability to handle print, they should have access to many basal readers and quantities of children's literature to give them the opportunity to practice reading in materials of interest to them. This means that reading stories in the basals should be pleasurable, interesting experiences. Attention to skills will be given when the children, individually or in small groups, give evidence of needing help in specific situations.

We would argue that the methodology presented here can be used by many beginning teachers. Of course, beginning teachers should have supervisory help from master teachers over an extended period of time. The absence of such supervision, however, does not alter the circumstance that the kind of experiences which lead children in becoming thoughtful, critical readers are necessary if education as a process is to succeed. Master teachers need to guide the work of beginning teachers in individualizing instruction, in teaching each child where he is on a continuum of learning, and making the atmosphere in which twenty-five or thirty children work all day as nongraded as possible. Becoming a competent teacher is a developmental process and requires years of diligent effort. Laura Zirbes, when she was a professor at Ohio State University, chided us once in a lecture to teachers not to be like the teacher she knew who had taught thirty years and had had *one* experience *thirty* times!

The concerns that prompted the writing of this text are the same concerns expressed by Moira McKenzie when she asked:

> Are we wise to spend so much time, in the early years in school, teaching reading as a "head-on" activity? . . . Could reading be more significant in upper grades for the many children who can but don't read if, from the very beginning, reading is seen as functional, pleasurable, and relevant to the child himself (Williams 1976, 55)?[1]

And Denny Taylor committed herself to the whole-language approach to reading:

> My findings emphasize that a skills approach to literacy runs counter to the natural development of reading and writing as complex cultural activities. . . . If one subscribes to the position that the activities of young children must have some intrinsic relationship to their immediate situation, then the idea that reading and writing should be taught as a series of skills (the traditional approach) becomes less palatable. Children in the present study learned of print through a whole language process. . . . (1983, 90–91).

We believe that by reordering the "time-line" for tasks asked of young children when they first enter school, boys and girls can be given as much time as they need to "arrive at" the occasion where they are asked to read a textbook. We have presented a way to introduce children to reading that will permit each learner to experience success in his or her own time and avoid much of the failure and deadening of motivation.

1. Moira McKenzie, "Schematic Learning and Reading," in Robert T. Williams, editor, *Insights into Why and How to Read* (Newark, Del.: International Reading Association, 1976), p. 55.

If children are given the many experiences to enable them to learn to read print in ways that seem purposeful to them, then they will be ready to read from a variety of basals, but without the consumate exercises to learn all the skills of reading. And an abundance of children's literature will make reading fun, interesting, and self-motivating.

Figure P.1 is a graphic portrayal of the interrelated components of the program that has been described in this text.

In concluding our preface, we would like to add that we made every effort to avoid sexist language. We used masculine pronouns in odd-numbered chapters and feminine pronouns in even-numbered chapters. The only exceptions occurred when quoted materials sometimes required a departure from this practice.

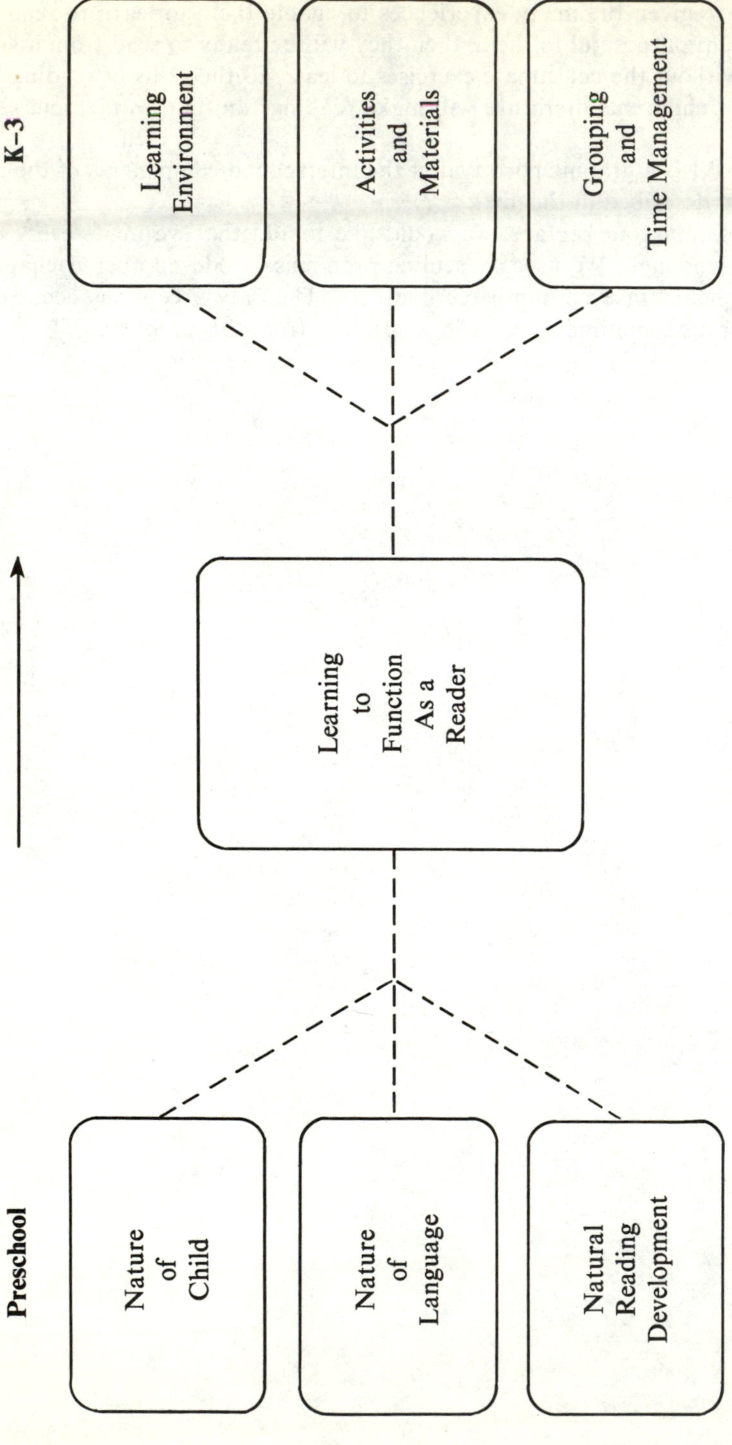

Figure P.1. Learning to read naturally: program components.

Part One

Growing into Literacy

The kind of environment that encourages the child to read is discussed in chapter 1. The parent reading either to the child or acting as a "model of reading," the parent responding to a child's need, and the presence of reading and writing materials are all parts of this reading environment. Other vital ingredients in the reading environment are the child's growing ability to recognize print as meaningful, understand the relationship between speech and writing, and to acquire "print awareness." The affective dimension of the child's life is also a key factor.

In chapter 2, the rationale for a new methodology is discussed: why children learn language; how children learn it; the incorporation of the phonetic, syntactic, and semantic cues in language use; and the presence of nonverbal language.

The nature of childhood is discussed in Chapter 3. Natural curiosity and its nurture, cognitive development during the earliest years, and the affective dimension in learning are described.

1

Learning to Read Naturally

Outline

The World of Natural Readers: Factors Associated with Learning to Read Naturally
- Reading to Children
- Availability of Reading Materials in the Environment
- Parents as Reading Models
- Availability of Writing Materials
- Responsive Persons in the Environment

The Payoff from a Reading Environment
- Recognizing Print as Meaningful
- Distinguishing between Print and Speech
- Developing Reading-Like Behaviors
- Developing Affect: Feelings, Sensitivities, and Empathy
- Acquiring Book and Print Awareness

Summary
References

Guide Questions

1. What is a natural reader?
2. What factors are associated with learning to read naturally?
3. How did you learn to read? If you were not a natural reader, compare the way you learned to read with that of the natural readers described in this chapter.
4. What do children learn in a reading environment that enables them to become natural readers?
5. Why are these insights important in learning to read?

Terminology

natural readers	cumulative sequence
modeling behavior	reading-like behaviors
invented spelling	assisted reading
reading environment	print awareness
environmental print	literacy
body language	emergent reading behaviors
repetitive sequence	

David sits on his potty reading a book. At three years his chubby legs, bent to accommodate the low seat, form a comfortable lap for holding a book. He alternately examines the pictures by touching different parts of them and then carries on a "conversation" with the characters shown. Then he "reads" the page. His version is a fairly accurate rendition of the actual words printed. The sense of the story is completely intact. Before he turns the page, he sometimes plays a little guessing game with a character illustrated by saying, "I'll bet you don't know what's gonna happen next . . . , but I do!" Then he turns the page and continues with the story.

David's mother has wished a thousand times that he would take care of learning "first things first." After all, whoever heard of a body reading in wet training pants? David seems to be perfectly satisfied with the way things are. David is a natural reader.

From infancy Jill has accompanied her mother on errands about town. Her favorite route to the grocery is lined with a number of fast food chains. Now at age three, Jill sits in her car seat and supplies her mother with a running travelogue of establishments along the way. " 'At's McDonald's. 'At's Tucky Fried. 'At's Pizza, and Dunkin Donuts, and Tasty Freeze."

Inside the supermarket, Jill sits in the grocery cart and continues her travelogue up and down the aisles. " 'At's Pop Tarts. 'At's Cheerios. 'At's Tide. 'At's Oreos. 'At's Coke." Sometimes her mother hands her articles and asks, "What does that say?" pointing to the product name. At other times Jill reverses the role and asks her mother what various labels "say."

Jill is growing into reading naturally.

Ryan regularly looks over the backside of the newspaper his dad reads at breakfast. One morning he pauses, his spoon midway between his bowl and his mouth.

"Dad! There's 'frigerator' in the paper!" he exclaims.

"What do you mean, son?" his dad asks in preoccupation.

"It says 'frigerator' just like over there," he says, pointing to the label his mother had attached to the refrigerator door. (A week before, she had stuck several labels on objects around the kitchen. When her husband came home, he looked around and asked with wry good humor, "What's the matter, Mary, can't you remember what they are?")

Ryan is three; he is beginning to exhibit some of the behaviors of a natural reader.

Alison at age four spends several short periods each day in dialogue with her dolls or with herself "reading" books. She often sorts them into piles on the floor, naming each one in turn and placing them in stacks according to some system of categorizing known only to her. After carefully sorting, she then asks her dolls which book they would like to hear.

"Oh, I don't think you want me to read that one," she'll say, if she is in the mood for a longer session. "I know one you want to hear. It's my *best* book. It says, 'Are you my mother?' It has a big 'Snort' in it. See that?" and she holds the book open so the dolls can see the illustrations.

Then she selects one doll, again, according to her own private criteria, places it in her lap, and proceeds to "read" the book, *Are You My Mother?,* page by page. She has heard her parents read the story so often that she has now memorized it completely. Sometimes, she will inadvertently skip a page or two and exclaim, "Oh, we skipped something! I better go back because you want to hear *that* part." If she grows tired, she'll say, "Oh, you don't want to hear about that. This page sounds better."

Occasionally Alison will say to her doll, "I'll bet you don't know what that says," pointing to a picture caption. "That says 'Snort.' But that's not the little bird's mother. It must be somebody else."

Alison is a natural reader.

David, Jill, Ryan, and Alison are among those very young children who are natural readers or are well on their way to becoming so *before* they enter school. Natural readers are those children who learn to read in much the same way and for many of the same reasons that they learned to talk. They have received neither formal instruction nor systematic sequencing of skills. They have grown into reading without having surmounted any major obstacles or without having passed any major milestones. Indeed, the line between when they did not and did read is dim, often obscured. The trip has been made without any undue stress, pain, or strain. They are not all extra bright, nor do they all come from so-called privileged socioeconomic backgrounds. They are a mix in all respects. However, each child does share some environmental features with the other children.

The World of Natural Readers: Factors Associated with Learning to Read Naturally

A substantial amount of information about natural readers has been collected from study and research during the past two decades. Results indicate that several factors are common to the backgrounds of these early readers who learned to read without formal, systematic instruction.

Reading to Children

Children who grew into reading naturally were read to by parents and other persons in the home environment. Dolores Durkin (1966) found that *all* children in her study of early readers in New York were read to by parents. In a similar study of children in California, a large percentage of the children was not only read to by parents, but also by older siblings. Eunice Price notes that of the thirty-seven gifted children reported in her study, thirty-four were read to from birth, "or when they were able to sit up" (1976, 46). G. P. Plessas and C. R. Oakes (1964), M. M. Clark (1976), and K. Gardner (1970) are among others who have found that being read to in the home is a major factor associated with early reading.

Many children were read to just prior to nap time in the afternoon and at bedtime in the evening. These are times when they are likely to be more receptive to listening because they are wound down from the countless explorations that fill the days of young children. (Then, too, the mother is more likely to be able to "catch" them at these times!) They are ready to cuddle in a warm lap and to listen to the familiar sounds of a parent's voice.

In addition to reading stories to children prior to rest times, mothers often engaged in incidental reading to children during other periods of the day as they encountered print in the everyday environment. They pointed out labels around the home used in packaging food: Cheerios, bacon, Oreos, sugar, Cheese Whiz, and Tide. Other examples of print were noted and named. No formal teaching was involved; rather, mothers would make casual comments, for example, when handing a box of cereal to a child, "This says Cheerios."

Availability of Reading Materials in the Environment

A wide variety of materials and examples of print was available in the environment of most natural readers. Storybooks, nursery rhymes, Golden Books, fairy tales, factual picture books on a variety of subjects, and children's classic literature were readily available, and many were read and reread by parents at the request of children. The Dr. Seuss books were often-mentioned favorites for story time listening. Between reading times with parents, the books were usually easily accessible for children to look at, to leaf through, and in some cases to chew on! Where older siblings were present, the books were often used to "play school."

Printed materials in the form of books were only part of these children's reading environment. J. W. Torrey (1969) describes how one child learned to read labels on canned food by watching television commercials. Commercials often present a product by showing its name in print, pronouncing it during the sales pitch, and simultaneously demonstrating what it can do! Many parents can attest to the fact that television is an influence in a child's learning to read; children frequently recite messages along with commercials as well as repeating them over and over at times when the television is turned off.

Parents as Reading Models

Parents in most studies of natural readers not only provided a variety of printed materials for their children and read to them regularly, they were also readers themselves. They regularly read a variety of materials for varied purposes: newspapers, magazines, best-sellers, and the like. By reading in the home, parents demonstrated repeatedly that reading was an important and pleasurable experience. Reading as a valued activity was communicated to children, who, in turn, came to view reading as a source of interest and pleasure for themselves. Concerning this point, William H. Teale in a review of studies of early readers states, "In this way, it seems the parents acted as models for reading behavior, and the children attempted to emulate such a model" (1978, 928).

Ryan, one of the natural readers mentioned earlier, was often observed by one of the authors modeling his father's reading behaviors. He would move his small rocker near the large one where his father sat reading, look to see how his father's legs were crossed, cross his in like fashion, open his book, and proceed to "read."

Bobbie read to Jill from birth. During Jill's infancy they would often lie together on the bed, and Bobbie would read aloud a novel or magazine in which she was currently interested. The needs of both mother and child were served well, although in different ways. Bobbie could enjoy the message of what she was reading; Jill could experience the rhythm, the intonations, and other comforting sounds of her mother's voice.

Availability of Writing Materials

Studies of early readers revealed that a surprising number were also early "scribblers."

> *Mother* (*irately*): Who wrote *D* on the back of the sofa?
>
> *Diana:* In green crayon?
>
> *Mother* (*surprised*): Yes. . . .
>
> *Diana* (*firmly*): Not me!
>
> (Dorothy Butler and Marie Clay 1979, 12)
>
> When Isaac was four years old, he copied the names of six of his favorite superheroes and attached the "signs" to the refrigerator. When one of the signs disappeared, Isaac exclaimed, "Hey, where's my Aquaman sign?" Indeed it was missing (Cohn 1981, 659).

According to Durkin, ten of the forty-nine children in the California study "first learned to print, then to spell, and only then to read." A blackboard was available in all forty-nine homes. "Almost without exception the starting point of curiosity about written language was an interest in scribbling and drawing" (1966, 57, 108). From this early stage, many children moved on to copying objects and letters of the alphabet and to concentrated efforts to learn to copy their names.

Children's interest in writing and the ready access to writing materials in the home can stimulate them to move back and forth, when ready, between the two worlds of communication: reading and writing. *Learning to read is reinforced by writing, and learning to write is reinforced by reading.* In the early stages of writing, what the child scribbles may seem far removed from the symbols of conventional writing. He often invents his own code, but he can "read" it well with the meaning he intends. Anne Haas Dyson provides this example of how the message in early writing efforts is augmented by talk.* Tracy, a kindergartner wrote:

A		
		8
	B	
		5

> The uninformed might read this as 'A, B, 8, 5.' . . . but Tracy read her writing like this:
>
> That's my apartment number [A].
> My next door neighbor's is [B].
> That's how old my brother is [8].
> That's how old I am [5] (1981, 776–77).

*Source: Anne Haas Dyson, ORAL LANGUAGE: THE ROOTING SYSTEM FOR LEARNING TO WRITE, *Language Arts,* 58, No. 7, pp. 776–777, National Council of Teachers of English, Urbana, Illinois, 1981. Used with permission.

Glenda L. Bissex describes the use of invented spelling in her five-year-old son's early writing; like Tracy in the example above, Paul had no trouble reading his code with the message he intended. One day, after trying unsuccessfully to get his mother's attention away from a book she was reading, he used rubber letter stamps to print the following message which *did* get the attention he wanted: "RUDF" (Are you deaf?!) (1980, 3). Another message he delivered was the following one done on a typewriter: "EFUKANOPNKAZIWILGEVUAKANOPENR."

> He read it aloud to me ("If you can open cans, I will give you a can opener"), pointing to the appropriate letters and pausing between words; so I mentioned that many writers put spaces between words. He said something like, "I know, but you didn't tell me before," and typed: EFU WAUTH KLOZ I WEL GEVUA WAUTHEN MATCHEN (If you wash clothes I will give you a washing machine) (1980, 11).

Responsive Persons in the Environment

Young children make endless demands on parents, and they learn quite early how to "work" them to get what they want. Bonnie Lass describes her fifteen-month-old son's technique for getting to hear a story. "He soon learned that the demand 'Read!' made with book in hand was a hard one to deny" (1982, 25).

One of the major findings coming out of Burton White's (1978) Harvard preschool studies is the importance of a child's using adults as resources in interpreting all facets of the environment. This assistance accelerates the child's learning by enabling him to make sense of the world around him more quickly.

Studies of early readers have a very similar corollary in the important role that parents play in responding to children's interests in books and reading—parents of early readers consistently showed a willingness to help. Not only were they willing to help, but the situations to which they responded appeared to be crucial.

> From family interview data it appeared that most of the parental help which lead to the child's early reading ability was given in response to the child's questions and requests for assistance (Durkin 1966, 135).

Parental help, then, was not given in a formal, systematic manner. It was incidental and spontaneous in response to the children's expressed needs at the moment as they sought to find answers to specific questions. Nor were the children given much more than they requested. Seldom did parents take more than a few moments to answer children's myriad questions during the course of the day. "What does that say? Where's my name? How do I print 'Aunt Lucy'? How do you make a *P*?" were usually answered in a few seconds, and then both child and parent continued with the business at hand.

In instances where adults attempted to "teach" in a formal sense, the results were not as effective as those in which information was first requested by children (Durkin 1966). Where a child is not interested, he is extremely adept at "escape." He simply leaves his body and takes his mind elsewhere.

These, then, are the factors most commonly associated with natural readers, those children who learn to read before entering school and without formal instruction. Their world is a reading environment—one filled with much print and many materials for creating one's own print; one populated with caring adults who enjoy reading themselves and are willing to spend time with children in answering their questions, sparking their interests, and reading books to them.

How were these factors instrumental in developing natural readers? What, specifically, were children able to put together that enabled them to learn to read as easily and as naturally as they had learned to talk?

The Payoff from a Reading Environment

Each of the factors associated with early readers, which were discussed above, contributed in specific ways to the children's learning to read. No one factor alone was sufficient to do the job, but rather, the sum total of elements combined to produce a natural growing into reading. We can identify *some* of these elements.

Recognizing Print as Meaningful

Ultimately, children learn to read by reading. Initially, of course, they do not recognize enough print to make sense of it. This gap must be filled for them; someone else has to do their reading for them.

Adults and older children in the environment can provide this service in countless ways during the preschool years. The bits and pieces of print that make up the everyday world of the child—such as labels, traffic signs, comic strips, posters, washroom doors, T-shirts, buttons, storefronts, theatre marquees, and lunch boxes—can be identified in response to children's questions, and/or they can be *pointed out* and named. These kinds of print are very much like everyday spoken language, and the contextual clues to meaning are immediately available in the situation.

Through experiences with environmental print, children begin to realize that print is meaningful, a concept that is basic to learning to read. When children see and are told "stop" and "no parking" on street signs, "sports center" on a storefront, "bubble gum" and "banana nut" on labels in an ice cream store, "chocolate chip" and "peanut butter" labels on cookie packages, "Frosted Flakes" and "Cheerios" on cereal boxes, "men" and "women" on restroom doors, they begin to realize not only that print has meaning but also that difference in printed marks makes a *difference* in meanings.

Distinguishing between Print and Speech

When parents read to children from books or other connected discourse, children are given the opportunity to develop another important concept that aids in learning to read: print and speech are different.

Written language is not talk written down; it is impossible to show in print all the meanings the human voice and body language can convey. For example, the same words can be *spoken* in such a way that a different meaning is conveyed each time.

1. "*You're* not going skating today." (implying that others may go but you cannot)
2. "You're not going *skating* today." (implying that you may do other things today but not skating)
3. "You're not going skating *today*." (implying that you may go tomorrow or some other time but not today)

The previous examples are only the tip of the iceberg as far as the meaning being conveyed in spoken context. Stress on a word alone has been shown to change meaning. However, when coupled with body language, a much richer and more complex meaning could have been conveyed by each of the utterances. In example 1, a mother might be implying much more than "*You're* not going skating today!" She may also be getting across a second message by the way she puts her hands on her hips and looks directly at her child. The body message may be, "I've told you a hundred times to clean up your room; you're not going out of the house until you do!"

Because the context in which language is spoken is known to all participants, much can be abbreviated or left out; many "pieces" of language can be used without distorting the message. In the foregoing "skating" example, the mother does not have to explain why the child cannot go skating today. The preceding week's hassle over a dirty room is a part of the whole context in which one sentence is spoken. She might just add the one liner, "Now hop to it!" and both mother and child would have no trouble getting the full message.

Written language is yet another thing. Absence of voice and body, which carry such a heavy meaning load, means that other communication vehicles must be found for this purpose. Punctuation and other marks used in print are an attempt to make up for the missing voice and body language, but they are poor substitutes at best in replacing the rich oral meaning load.

Another adjustment has to be made for print. The situations around which written language evolves have to be described and expanded upon, or else the context will not be sufficient to convey the meaning to the reader. The writer *must* give more in words to the reader than the speaker must give to the listener if clear communication is to be achieved.

Further, written language has many patterns, many conventions that distinguish it from spoken language. Words have more clearly defined boundaries than those in speaking. "Did you catch any?" in spoken language is likely to resemble something quite foreign looking in print: "Dijakacheny?" "Once upon a time" is a frequent introduction in some types of story print, but it is highly unusual in speech.

Story and poem structures use many devices not found in everyday conversations. "Repetitive sequence" and "cumulative sequence" are often found in literature for young children. In repetitive sequence episodes are used over and over.

One dark and stormy night I came upon a haunted house.
I tiptoed into the yard. No one was there.
I tiptoed onto the porch. No one was there.
I tiptoed into the house. No one was there.
I tiptoed into the living room. No one was there.
I tiptoed into the dining room. No one was there.
I tiptoed into the kitchen. No one was there.
I tiptoed into the cellar. No one was there.
I tiptoed upstairs. No one was there.
I tiptoed into the bedroom. No one was there.
I tiptoed into the TV room. No one was there.
I tiptoed into the bathroom. No one was there.
I tiptoed up to the attic. . . .
I was there.

(Bill Martin, Jr., "The Haunted House," 1980, 14)

An example of cumulative sequence is "This Is the House that Jack Built." "Each new line (episode) adds a new thought before repeating everything that went before" (Martin 1980, 17).

Children gain familiarity with these and many other structures and patterns unique to print by hearing a variety of types of literature read. Unless they become familiar with the nature of written language, they are likely to approach written language with the expectation that it is the same as spoken discourse. When they find it is not, they are apt to have difficulty in anticipating or predicting meaning. Anticipating what comes next in reading is vital to comprehension. It is not unlike going to one's door when expecting a friend only to find a stranger without. Confusion always arises when the expected is replaced by the unexpected.

Developing Reading-Like Behaviors

Children who have spent their preschool years in a reading environment are likely to pass through distinct stages in becoming natural readers. The stages are discernible to parents in the behaviors of their children. Children will begin to request, sometimes almost plead, repeated readings of a favorite story; they will select the same book or books over and over to bring to story time. Adults grow tired and bored with the same old "Green Eggs and Ham" after the umpteenth reading. Not so, the young child. As the story becomes more and more familiar, he will gradually move through a number of stages or reading-like behaviors.

First, there is listening, sometimes a looking at pictures; then the child may mumble along intermittently with the reader. Next comes the "correction" stage when skipped pages bring the admonition, "You *skipped* that part!" The child will pick up the book and "read" to a doll, the cat, or just to himself from time to time as Alison does earlier in this chapter.

Parents assume the child memorizes stories from repeated listenings. Indeed they often do reach the point of reproducing the story almost word for word simply by looking at pictures. Kenneth Hoskisson has this to say:

> What the children have been doing though is paying attention to meaning. They have stored the meaning, not the exact words of the stories. . . .
>
> This memorization aspect of children's knowledge of the written language appears to be a very important component and should receive more attention than it has because all children seem to go through this phase of constructing their knowledge of the written language when learning to read naturally (1979, 492).

Memorizing the story sense is an aid in learning to read in yet another sense. Familiarity with the message enables the child to anticipate or predict what is coming next, a vital strategy as already mentioned earlier. Before long, the child will begin to supply words when a parent pauses during reading. The child is literally *bringing meaning to print;* and in reading what the brain says to the eye matters more than what the eye says to the brain!

Knowing what the story is about, coupled with reading to the child when he can see the print and the pictures on the page, leads the child quite naturally into identifying specific words. He may begin by pointing and asking, "What does that say?" "Show me where it says 'Snort.' " "Is that the puppy's name?" "Where does it say 'two shoes?' " The parent responds by giving the answers. Hoskisson (1979) calls this

Pre-schoolers, ages 4, 3, and 2, exercising reading-like behaviors.

"assisted reading." As parent and child read together, the child assumes a larger and larger role in the reading process. The child repeats phrases and sentences after they are read by the reader. When the child begins to notice that some words are repeated in the print, the reader leaves out some of the words the child might recognize, and he fills them in. Finally, when the child can read most of the words, the adult fills in only the words not recognized by the child (1979, 494–95).

The importance of pictures accompanying printed materials should not be overlooked by adults when reading to children.

> Pictures play an important role in books which are read to young children because they provide contextual situations that bridge the gap between the concrete experiences children have in the real world and the abstract experiences that are presented by authors. Pictures provide the context, the visual images that help children relate what they know to what is being presented in the story. Pictures assume the role of the contextual situations children were in when they learned to speak.
>
> . . . . .
>
> Pictures help put children in the immediate vicinity of the story characters and setting and thus enhance comprehension (Hoskisson 1979, 491–92).

The foregoing paragraphs, which describe the stages through which a child moves toward literacy as a result of being read to, reflect a unique characteristic of children that is seldom recognized and even less frequently appreciated. In the words of David D. Doake:

> We find that preschool children are able to direct, regulate, and monitor their own learning to read strategies just as they do in learning to talk and walk. Given the

opportunity to operate with large chunks of whole, meaningful language, they will begin to manage their own learning in highly sophisticated and creative ways, just as they do in learning to speak their language (1979, 1).

They will learn to teach themselves to read.

In sharing books with parents—reading with or being read to—children acquire other valuable insights and attitudes that are important for developing naturally into fluent readers.

Developing Affect: Feelings, Sensitivities, and Empathy

The following episode occurred between one of the authors and her young nephew: "Aunt Margaret, I can't say the words, but if you'll let me sit in your lap, I'll read you the story."

Being held in the warmth, comfort, and security of an adult's lap while listening to a story and looking at the pages can be an extraordinarily pleasurable and rewarding experience. According to Robert A. and Marlene McCracken, "This is an emotional conditioning to books: children associate books with love and warmth and parents" (1972, 19). Such an atmosphere not only builds stronger emotional bonds between parent and child, but the child also senses that books are a source of enjoyment. This appreciation can help build a lifelong commitment to reading so that many more children who *can* read will continue to do so.

Sharing books with children can result in rich returns in the area of personal affective growth. Margaret Greer writes, "The basic element in affective development is *feeling,* the direct experiencing of any phenomena at a given moment" (1972, 337). Listening to stories provides many opportunities for children to feel with the characters, to identify with them, and in a sense to become them. The ability to empathize, to feel outside one's self is a noble human quality achieved over years of growth. A giant step at "walking in someone else's shoes" can be made early by way of book sharing experiences.

Children often engage in extended practice in responding emotionally to books they have heard read. Listen to a little "night music" coming from four-year-old David's room after he had been watered, dried, and put to bed for the night:

(in cadence—with deep voice): Fee Fi Fo Fum!
I smell blood of Eng-lish-mun!

He practices several times, each time changing pitch and stress to get exactly the sounds and meanings he wants in order to depict the fierce and threatening nature of the giant. When satisfied with the effects, he moves on to *The Three Billy Goats Gruff* to explore more "mean" sounds, this time from a troll instead of a giant.

Trip, Trap, Trip, Trap!
(*lower voice*) Who's that walking on *my* bridge?!

Jill's older brother, Jim, often reads *Hansel and Gretel* aloud to her with full sound effects, including "tears" at appropriate places. The following ensued one day as Jill sat "reading" at the breakfast table after everyone else had gone.

The mean old witch said, "Gretel, stick your head in to see if it's hot!" But Gretel didn't want to. "Please, Witch, I don't want to. I'm afraid!" (*loudly with feeling*): "Boo Hoo, Boo Hoo, Boo Hoo!"

One author's favorite emotional sharing of books as a child was to gather all the younger brothers and sisters together periodically to read page 213 from *Robin Hood.*

> "Hold me up, Little John, so I can shoot the arrow to where I want to be buried," was read in a sorrowful tone. "There," said Robin, in a weak voice as he fell back into the arms of Little John. "Bury me there."

Four-year-old brother Jay's rendition when he was alone with page 213 went something like this:

> (*in quavering voice*) "Here, Little John. Help me hold my bow. It's sooooo heavy. I can't shoot it. You do it for me. Then Robin dropped dead. Robin, don't leave me!" (*sounds of loud crying noises!*).

Affective experiencing at tender ages!

Acquiring Book and Print Awareness

Many printing conventions are so familiar to adult readers that they are surprised to find that children do not know them. Which is top? Which is bottom? Where do you start? All these and many more conventions of print that are taken for granted by experienced readers have to be learned by young children. Julie M. T. Chan observes:

> Children learn some of the mechanics of reading by having stories read to them. They notice that a book has a beginning, middle, and end and that it should be held so that lines of print and the pictures can be seen. They notice that the reader's eyes move back and forth, from one side of the printed page to the other. By observing the reader casually gliding his hand along the lines of print, children learn that reading is an activity done from left to right, from one line to the next, and from page to page until the story ends (1974, 9).

Children exhibit a variety of other "emergent reading behaviors" (Doake, 1979) that reflect a growing awareness of additional features of print. They begin to identify individual words. Ryan's discovery of "frigerator" in the newspaper his father was reading is an example. An often-repeated question after children have listened to and partially memorized a story is "Where does it say . . . ?" Some children learn first the words that are part of picture captions often within conversation "balloons." "That says 'Snort,' " Alison would say each time the word appeared with the steam shovel in an illustration from *Are You My Mother*? Recurring sentences were next identified word for word: "Are you my mother?" and "No, I am not your mother!"

While building a sizeable store of words recognized on sight, children will begin to make finer and finer distinctions about print by using more and more visual cues. They begin to pay attention to individual letters, particularly the first one in words. Often this attention to the smaller "pieces" of print is associated with the first attempts at writing, especially one's name. Children may make such observations as "My name starts just like 'banana!' "

Children will now spend considerable time playing around with the individual sounds of language. For example, Cohn reports the following dinner conversation between her two young children:

> *Anna:* There's an "oo" in Chinese food.
>
> *Isaac:* Chinese food starts with F. F for food.
>
> F, F, F. Then comes D.

Your Turn 1.1 Identifying potential natural readers.

Observe in a preschool and a kindergarten class. The period(s) of observation should be long enough to get a good idea of what the children are doing and saying as they participate in activities.

1. Identify children you consider to be potential natural readers.
2. What reading-like behaviors do you see? Be specific.
3. Which children may already be natural readers, that is, are they already reading?
4. Arrange for the teacher to set up an interview with a parent of a child who is already reading and ask about the child's experiences with books and reading in the home. Which of these experiences is similar to those associated with natural readers in this chapter? (Phone interviews may be quite satisfactory, so long as the teacher has alerted the parent to the event.) Record data and bring it to class for discussion.

Anna: There's an N in Chinese food. Nese. Hey, knees!
(*pointing to her knees*) (1981, p. 554).

Another example from Isaac (same page): "What's a very bad word that we don't use in our house that starts with 'S?' "

These, then, are some of the rewards, the rich dividends that accrue to those children whose parents provide them with many opportunities to experience books and other print in the everyday world. Through the early years, children are exposed to written language in its total context via stories or words and phrases in a meaningful environment. The sense, the whole, comes first; otherwise, there is no basis for meaning. From repeated experiences through listening to and following along in story reading, children gradually move toward the *parts* that make up text—the words and the letters that have little or no meaning outside a total context. They move along the same path and in much the same natural way that they come to know and to speak their language. They learn to read naturally without stress, pain, or anxiety. The absence of such negative emotions not only enables children to learn to read, but it also increases the likelihood that they *will* read because even the learning how has been exciting and pleasurable. Responsive adults, usually parents, are the key to such an extraordinary accomplishment.

Much that has been learned from studies of natural readers and the reading- and writing-like behaviors of preschoolers (Teale and Sulzby 1985) can be combined with what is now known about language—its nature and the way it is learned and used—to form a far-more-productive journey to literacy in the future than that of the past has been for many children. In the process, some rather sweeping changes in attitudes and practices in teaching children to read are indicated.

Summary

Each individual strives for fulfillment—the basic need for adequacy is a fundamental motivation. So it is not necessary to motivate "healthy" people. Everyone wants to be as adequate as possible in any situation.

Children are not motivated the way the teacher wants necessarily, but they are motivated in terms of their own basic needs. So, the teacher's role is *not* one of prescribing, making, molding, or forcing: it is, according to Arthur Combs, the role of facilitator, encourager, helper, assister, colleague and friend (1965, 33). Teachers do not teach children to read. They provide the kinds of experiences that enable children to *learn* to read.

Children bring all their individual differences to the classroom—whether they are four, six, or eight. A few want to do a great deal of reading and writing activity; some want to participate without being consumed by it; and a few will direct their thoughts to activities *not* related to reading and writing.

In chapter 2 we identify and examine practices and attitudes related to reading instruction that hinder rather than aid children's acquisition of literacy. We also propose alternatives to guide teachers in developing natural readers in the classroom setting. As the basis for the practices we advocate, we examine the nature of language, its acquisition and use, and the nature of the child and how learning is achieved. We explore the relationships between these two concepts as they relate to developing literacy and according to their implications for reading instruction.

References

Bissex, Glenda L. *GNYS AT WRK*. Cambridge, Mass.: Harvard University Press, 1980.

Butler, Dorothy, and Clay, Marie. *Reading Begins at Home*. Auckland: Heinemann Educational Books, 1979.

Chan, Julie M. T. *Why Read Aloud to Children?* IRA Micromonograph. Newark: International Reading Association, 1974.

Clark, M. M. *Young Fluent Readers*. London: Heinemann Educational Books, 1976.

Cohn, Margot. "Observations of Learning to Read and Write Naturally." *Language Arts* 58 (May 1981): 549–56.

Combs, Arthur. *Professional Education of Teachers*. Boston: Allyn and Bacon, 1965.

Doake, David B. "Book Experience and Emergent Reading Behaviors." Paper presented at meeting of the International Reading Association, Atlanta, May 1979.

Durkin, Dolores. "Children Who Learn to Read at Home." *Elementary School Journal* 62 (October 1961): 15–18.

———. *Children Who Read Early*. New York: Columbia University Teachers College Press, 1966.

Dyson, Anne Haas. "Oral Language: The Rooting System for Learning to Write." *Language Arts* 58, no. 7 (1981): 776–84.

Eastman, Philip D. *Are You My Mother?* New York: Random House, 1960.

Gardner, K. "Early Reading Skills." In *Reading Skills: Theory and Practice,* 18–23. London: Ward Lock Educational, 1970.

Greer, Margaret. "Affective Growth Through Reading." *The Reading Teacher* 25 (January 1972): 336–41.

Holdaway, Don. *Foundations of Literacy*. Sydney: Ashton Scholastic, 1979.

———. *Stability and Change in Literacy Learning*. Exeter, N.H.: Heinemann Educational Books, 1984.

Hoskisson, Kenneth. "Learning to Read Naturally." *Language Arts* 52 (May 1979): 489–96.
Huey, Edmund Burke. *Psychology and Pedagogy of Reading*. Cambridge, Mass.: M.I.T. Press, 1968. (Reprint from New York: Macmillan, 1908.)
Lass, Bonnie. "Portrait of My Son as an Early Reader." *The Reading Teacher* 36 (October, 1982): 20–28.
Martin, Bill, Jr. *Strategies for Language Learning*. Tulsa, Okla.: Educational Progress Corporation, 1980.
McCracken, Robert A., and McCracken, Marlene. *Reading is Only the Tiger's Tail*. San Rafael, Calif.: Leswing Press, 1972.
McCracken, Marlene, and McCracken, Robert A. *Reading, Writing and Language. A Practical Guide for Primary Teachers*. Winnipeg: Peguis Publishers Limited, 1979.
Plessas, G. P., and Oakes, C. R. "Prereading Experiences of Selected Early Readers." *The Reading Teacher* 17 (1964): 241–45.
Price, Eunice. "How Thirty-Seven Gifted Children Learned to Read." *The Reading Teacher* 30 (October 1976): 44–48.
Taylor, Denny. *Family Literacy*. Exeter, N.H.: Heinemann Educational Books, 1983.
Teale, William H. "Positive Environments for Learning to Read: What Studies of Early Readers Tell Us." *Language Arts* 55 (November/December 1978): 922–32.
Teale, William H., and Sulzby, Elizabeth, eds. *Emergent Literacy: Writing and Reading*. Exeter, N.H.: Heinemann Educational Books, 1985.
Torrey, J. W. "Learning to Read Without a Teacher: A Case Study." *Elementary English* 46 (1969): 550–58.
White, Burton L. *The First Three Years of Life*. New York: Avon Books, 1978.

2

Children and Their Language

Outline

Why Children Learn Language
  Innate Language Capacity
  Curiosity: The Compulsion to Know
  The Need to Communicate
How Children Learn Language
  Stages of Oral Language Development
    Prelinguistic stage
    Holophrastic and telegraphic speech
    Expansion and refinement
  Experimentation/Testing/Feedback
  The Role of Parents in Language Learning
    Designer of the child's environment
    Consultant to the young child
    Giver of information
The Nature of Language
  Language as a System of Rules
  The Components of Language
    Phonological
    Syntactic
    Semantic
  The Cues to Meaning: Signal Systems of Language
    Phonological cues
    Grammatical cues
    Semantic cues
    Redundancy
  Surface Structure and Deep Structure of Language
Language: Spoken, Unspoken, and Written
  Comparison of Oral and Written Language Usage
    The contexts
    The purposes
    The audiences
    The forms
    The demands
  The Nature of Unspoken Language
    Sign language
    Body language
    Voice language
  Learning to Talk and Learning to Read
    Participation in a language-rich environment
    Acquisition of deep structure and surface structure
    Changing pattern of errors
    Top-down progression of language learning
    Comprehension via prediction
    Motivation in language learning
    Pairings of language units with meanings
    Graphic representation of nonverbal cues in print
  Basic Insights about Reading
    Children must be able to distinguish words
    Children must be able to see that word units are composed of smaller units—letters—and that these are related to spoken language
    Children must understand that the printed words in a book are language, that they can be interpreted in terms of a story or useful information
Summary
References

Guide Questions

1. What are three theories that explain *why* children learn language?
2. Why are the processes of experimentation, testing, and feedback crucial to language learning and development?
3. Why is language considered a complex system of signals?
4. How does spoken language differ from written language?
5. What are the basic similarities between learning to talk and learning to read?

Terminology

phonology
phonemes
syntax
grammar
prelinguistic stage
holophrastic speech
telegraphic speech
morphemes
experimentation/testing/feedback
language cues
hypothesis testing
phonological cues
grammatical or syntactic cues
intonation
kernel sentences
transformations
embedding
content words
affix
inflections
redundancy
surface structure
deep structure
situational context
prediction
top-down progression

With few exceptions, children everywhere learn to speak and to use the language of their culture to convey and to receive meanings. This remarkable feat is achieved in a relatively short period of time with what Burton L. White (1978, 91) calls "breath-taking" speed. Given the complexity of language structure, the natural ease with which children develop oral language is truly amazing. Little if any actual teaching takes place, and adults tends to assume that children will learn language as a consequence of *being*—and they do. The help that *is* extended is usually neither systematic nor planned; it develops spontaneously as a natural consequence of interacting with the young child as she explores her everyday world.

The "why" and "how" children learn language is explored here along with an examination of the nature of the language itself. A look at the similarities and differences between oral and written language and the importance of oral language competence—as it relates to learning to read—complete this chapter. Table 2.1 is an overview of these concepts.

Table 2.1 Digest: Children and Their Language

The Child's Language Depends on:	The Steps in Learning Language are:	How Language Works:	How Language Is Used:	Both Learning to Read and Learning to Talk:
1. Capacity to learn 2. Curiosity for learning 3. Need to communicate with others	1. Prelinguistic stage 2. Holophrastic stage 3. Hypothesis-testing and refinement of language 4. Utilizing help from adults and asking questions	1. A system of rules restricts word order. 2. Meaning is aided by phonology, syntax, and semantics. 3. Deep structure carries the meaning.	1. Use of oral and written language depends on (a) contexts, (b) purposes, (c) audiences, (d) forms, and (e) demands. 2. Unspoken language may be (a) sign language, (b) body language, and (c) voice language.	1. Contain patterns of error 2. Use whole-language or a top-down progression 3. Utilize predicting, sampling, confirming, and correcting. 4. Should be intrinsically motivated 5. Are nonsense without *Meaning* 6. Differ in that print requires distinguishing individual words

Why Children Learn Language

There have been no universally accepted answers to why children learn language. (Perhaps if they could know how complicated the structure of language is from the standpoint of linguistic analysis, they would be overwhelmed with the magnitude of the task and decide to remain mute!) In a sense we are left in the position of seeing a miracle without being able to explain it satisfactorily at present. Whenever further study and research provide logical explanations to the question, those explanations will likely identify dual sources that account for language learning: (1) qualities within the individual and (2) factors within the environment. Individuals may be preprogrammed biologically to learn language: they *do* have a built in propulsion to explore—to know all facets of their world. This curiosity can be the trigger that taps into and activates the innate potential for language development. The environment itself is filled with people who constantly communicate and interact through language. So, children must learn language in order to meet their own needs within the social contexts of which they are a part.

The ability to imitate, practice, and store what is heard in the social context of language use is not sufficient to explain how language is acquired.

> All children are able to understand and construct sentences they have never heard but which are nevertheless well formed, well formed in terms of general rules that are implicit in the sentences the child has heard. Somehow, then, every child processes the speech to which he is exposed so as to induce from it a latent structure (the implicit general rules of the language). The discovery of latent structure is the greatest of the processes involved in language learning and the most difficult to understand (Brown and Bellugi 1964, 144).

Innate Language Capacity

One theory about language acquisition is that human beings are biologically equipped to learn language. Dan I. Slobin (1966a, 1966b), David McNeill (1966), and Noam Chomsky (1965, 1968, 1975) are supporters of this theory. According to the theory, humans are innately preprogrammed to acquire the rules that govern the structure and use of language. A child does not simply imitate and reproduce what he hears; rather, he learns categories and rules that are the basis of generating utterances he has never heard before. Paula Menyuk writes that "the child must learn the syntactic, semantic and phonological rules of his language. He must learn these rules so that he can understand and produce an infinite number of possible sentences in his language" (1971, 16). He can and does because he is born with the capacity, the predisposition. Children have the potential to do all of the following that relate to the rules of the structure of language:

1. Recognize and label abstract features. For example, "The boy ran quickly" is a *sentence.*
2. Recognize specific features and their functions that comprise a larger unit. "The boy" is a noun phrase; "ran quickly" is a verb phrase.
3. Test utterances for fit with what comprises a sentence: the utterance contains both a noun phrase and a verb phrase, therefore, it is a sentence (Menyuk 1971, 16).

The foregoing analysis *does not* imply that there is a conscious level recognition of the structure of language as expressed in the terms above. Rather, the child's unique predisposition to learn language provides an intuitive grasp of the rules of the grammar involved.

Curiosity: The Compulsion to Know

Mary Ellen Goodman writes, "It is the nature of children to be intensely curious about the world and eager to play a part in it" (1976, 7).

Curiosity—the need to explore, to come to know, to make sense of the world—is a second uniquely human characteristic that can explain in part why language is acquired. The child is born into spoken language: from birth she is immersed in it during most of her waking hours. Because language occupies such a prominent place in the child's total environment, it is only natural that her curiosity would lead her into exploration and experimentation of the human sounds surrounding her.

Around eight months of age, children acquire the skill of moving around under their own power. Accompanying this new skill is an insatiable curiosity about all the physical aspects of the environment. White (1978, 118) concludes that during "hundreds of hours prelocomotive children spend looking at distant, unreachable objects, they build up quite a head of steam with respect to an interest in exploring the rooms within which they live." Things which adults seldom see become totally absorbing to the crawling child: a speck of dust, a pill bug crawling along the floor, a thread unraveling from a drape, and the dead leaves collecting in a potted plant.

As motor skills improve, the child's world expands and so does the speed at which she is able to explore it. She responds accordingly. (The time may be one of trauma for parents because infants can make no distinction between what is and what is not safe, or between what is valuable and what is inexpensive. Small wonder that the first words of many children are *No! No!*)

As the child continues to grow, she begins to venture more and more into the world beyond home and neighborhood. She is accompanied by the same intense curiosity, the same need to know that was present when she was largely confined to smaller quarters. The four-year-old gathers leaves, puts them into a pail, and then pours them all over her head. She splashes through water and licks droplets off a twig. She empties drawers, cabinets, and boxes. Then she fills them up again. She bangs endlessly on a foil pan with a wooden spoon. She climbs—everything and everywhere. She crawls into, out of, under, over, through, and around. All this compulsion to explore is seen not merely as a means for satisfying curiosity but, according to Robert White (1959, 297–333), it also serves the very basic need to be *competent* in coping with the environment and, thereby, derive satisfaction that comes from competence.

Accompanying much of this experiencing of the world is spoken language from older persons in the environment. The language used by parents is usually not so much that of teaching as it is of sharing, or of helping the child to interpret her world. Rachel Carson captures beautifully this difference between "teaching" and "sharing":

> If a child is to keep alive his inborn sense of wonder without any such gift from the fairies, he needs the companionship of at least one adult who can share it, rediscovering with him the joy, excitement and mystery of the world we live in (1956, 45).
>
> It is possible to compile extensive lists of creatures seen and identified without ever having caught a breathtaking glimpse of the wonder of life. If a child asks me a question that suggested even a faint awareness of the mystery behind the arrival of a migrant sandpiper on the beach of an August morning, I would be far more pleased than by the mere fact that he knew it was a sandpiper and not a plover (1956, 83).

In response to whatever the child's immediate interest is, parents provide a lot of labels, explanations, and admonitions! The child gradually learns to give labels to that which is concrete in her world. The raw material that builds the meanings before she has words is "vacuumed" from the environment in her endless quest to satisfy her curiosity about the environment. Her own language development moves through a series of highly predictable stages that will be discussed in the following section of this chapter.

And so, curiosity is at once the ignition and the fuel for knowing. "It is the motivational force underlying all learning and development and achievement. . . ." (White 1978, 118).

The Need to Communicate

The child is born into, is part of, a social environment; otherwise, she could not survive. Unlike some other species, the human infant cannot care for herself without the help of others for the first few years of life. A major characteristic of being human is the formation of groups of individuals, and a basic necessity for group functioning is to have a communication system. To serve this need, language has been invented many times down through the history of mankind.

> So the child "essentially acquires language because it is there, a part of his environment, and because vocalization is part of his repertoire of behavior. He acquires language because he learns that vocal behavior brings rewards, just as other animals learn that certain behaviors within their repertoire will bring them rewards. The infant produces some vocal behavior which causes a change in the environment which then leads to the reduction of some physiological drive (hunger, thirst, pain, fear). The environmental consequences reward the infant for his vocal behavior (Menyuk 1971, 248).

According to Nancy E. Taylor and Jacquelyn M. Vawter, the many purposes that oral language serves account for the ease with which it is learned by the vast majority of children (1978, 941). Continued experience with language enables the child to acquire the sounds, the meaning units (words), and the rules that govern the way words are arranged to make sense. A knowledge of the rules of language, tacit though it is, in essence provides a child with a master key to generating an infinite number of sentences to communicate her messages.

The child learns about the purposes and all the intricacies of the language system only as she participates in oral communication. She must, therefore, have many opportunities to talk, to interact at the verbal level with others in the environment. As she experiences language in this direct manner, her own competencies and skills draw continually closer to those of mature speakers; and there is a corresponding increase in the effectiveness of her communication.

How Children Learn Language

Just as with the question of *why* children learn language, there is no common agreement among authorities as to *how* language is learned. Until more definitive explanations are gleaned from current and future research, we must proceed on the basis of the most promising theories presently available. Again, theories from the field of psycholinguistics have been chosen for that purpose by the authors.

In the foregoing section, the elements required for language learning were identified: (1) the child is preprogrammed biologically to acquire language; (2) curiosity is the motivation to explore, to know, and to make sense of the environment—a large part of which is language; and (3) the need to communicate is built into the social context. Thus the child has the means, the necessity, and the opportunity to learn language. How she uses these elements in learning to produce and to comprehend spoken language is the subject of this section.

In essence, to produce and to understand oral language require that the child find out the rules that govern the phonology (sounds), the semantics (meanings), and the syntax (grammar) systems of her language. (A detailed description of the nature of language and its systems follows in the next section.) The child must come to know not only the sounds of her language but also the permissible combinations that can be made to produce meaningful symbols; she must learn word symbols and attach the meaning to them that is common to those with whom she communicates; and she must learn the prescribed system for combining words to communicate her message. To accomplish all this, children universally move through the same predictable stages.

Stages of Oral Language Development

Prelinguistic stage. The vocal activity of the first few months of life consists mainly of experimenting, babbling, playing around with sounds, and manipulating the speech organs. Of course, babies do cry in response to physical discomforts, but none of these sounds could be termed language. Somewhere around four months, babies often discover the delights of using their own saliva to produce a variety of sounds. "This involvement with sound is a prelude to the beginnings of true language learning . . ." (White 1978, 80).

The babbling stage is a source of delight to parents as they eavesdrop on these experimental sessions. They may note times when the child startles herself with the sounds she produces much as a puppy startles itself with its first bark! Interestingly enough, studies of this stage of sound production have shown that babies the world over produce the same sounds, and further, they make sounds as infants that they will never again produce. Basically, they are capable of making all the sounds for all the languages known to mankind, but as they absorb more and more of the predominant sounds of the language spoken around them, they retain the ability to produce those sounds but lose the ability to make the others.

Between eight and twelve months of age, infants begin to comprehend numerous words even though they cannot say them. In fact, the ability to understand language far exceeds the ability to produce it throughout life. Marvin L. Klein notes, "Most children enter school with a comprehension vocabulary two or more times the vocabulary they use in oral communication" (1981, 447).

> By three years of age, experts estimate that most children understand most of the language they will use for the rest of their lives in ordinary conversation. Notice I said most children *understand* most of the language they will use in ordinary conversation. There is an important difference between the growth of *understanding* language and the growth of *producing* language.
>
> Children begin to learn to understand language earlier and at a more rapid rate than they learn to use it orally. The first five or six words should be fairly well understood by the time a child is nine or ten months of age. But he may not *say* five or six words until he is two years of age or even older. Nevertheless, in both cases he may be a very normal child (White 1978, 111).

The first words understood are those coming directly out of the child's experience with her environment: "Mommy, Daddy, names of family members, and pets—often known idiosyncratically ("doody" for Judy), bye-bye, baby, shoe, ball, cookie, juice, no-no, wave bye-bye" (White 1978, 84).

Parents are urged to talk to infants throughout the early months of life even though the child will understand little at first. "It is understandable why some people do not speak very much to a baby who is less than a year and a half old. Monologues are not very rewarding" (White 1978, 93). However, the child needs to become familiar with the sounds and patterns of spoken language so that she can learn to make verbal responses of her own.

Holophrastic and telegraphic speech. Between the eleventh and twelfth month of life, infants begin to move out of the playing-around-with-sounds stage into one in which sounds are intentionally produced to express a specific need or desire. E. Brooks Smith, Kenneth S. Goodman, and Robert Meredith write that this phase is sometimes called the "unitary stage" (1976, 18) because the child is actually beginning to produce meaningful units of language.

Holophrastic speech is comprised of one-word utterances that name people, things, and events in the child's immediate environment. Single words are used to express whole sentences; the "sentences" themselves can have a variety of meanings, depending on the need or interest of the child at the moment. Frank Smith writes, "Drink, for example, might mean anything from 'Bring me a drink' to 'look at that drink' to 'I do not want that drink and I have just thrown it all over the floor' " (1972, 39).

Children not only use a single word to express a variety of meanings, but they also use appropriate intonation to get their intended meanings across. Jean Malstrom notes that the word *daddy* can be spoken in such a way as to mean "Where's Daddy?" "Daddy is here!" or "Come here, Daddy" (1977, 7).

Children begin to experiment with stringing collections of sounds together. They may produce long strings of sounds that have all the intonations of adult speech but no word meanings. They begin to experiment with putting words together in ways that clearly reflect simple forms of syntax. The expressions children hear will often be repeated in abbreviated or telegraphic form in which the meaning-loaded words (nouns, verbs, and descriptive adjectives) are retained along with the correct word order, but the function words (prepositions, articles, and conjunctions) are left out. "He's going to drink water" may become "He drink water," or "The milk is all gone" may become "Milk allgone."

Expansion and refinement. Once the child begins to use words and combine them in meaningful sequences, her language development literally explodes. Between eighteen and thirty-six months many children acquire all the basic rules that govern mature speech. They can produce most of the sounds of adult speech along with the appropriate intonations; they can combine words according to the rules of grammar. The number of words in their speaking vocabulary increases rapidly. They acquire the grammatical morphemes, those units of language that are added to basic sentences or words to alter meanings:

1. Present progressive, *ing* (Bobo sleep*ing*)
2. And
3. *In* and *on* (*in* box, *on* table)
4. Plural, *s* (toy*s*)
5. Past irregular (*went, broke*)

6. Possessive, *'s* (Anthony*'s* blanket)
7. Uncontractible linking verb *is* (*Is* the blanket yellow?)
8. Articles, *the, a,* and *and*
9. Past regular, *ed* (play*ed*)
10. Third person regular, *s* (play*s*)
11. Third person irregular, *s* (doe*s*, ha*s*)
12. Uncontractible auxiliary *is* (*Is* Daddy sleeping?)
13. Contractible linking verb, *s* (Daddy*'s* hungry)
14. Contractible auxiliary, *'s* (Blacky*'s* barking)

(Malstrom, 1977, 9, citing Roger Brown, 1973, 281)

Along the way toward achieving adult norms of speech, children continue to experiment, to try out, to refine their language skills.

Ruth Weir recounts the following monologue of two-and-a-half-year-old Anthony after he has been put to bed:

> What color—What color blanket—What color mop—What color glass. . . . Not the yellow blanket—The white . . . It's not black—It's yellow . . . Not yellow—Red . . . Put on a blanket—Yellow light . . . There is the light—Where is the light—Here is the light (1962, 19).

So, children continue to teach themselves language by repeating the "play" they first used with sounds.

Their tendency to overgeneralize some of the rules they are acquiring produces expressions that adults find so amusing. "I wented home," "She falled down," and "She taked my cookie" are examples that the child is indeed acquiring the rules of gramar; the exceptions, the irregular forms, have not yet been deciphered.

Interestingly enough, children can fool adults sometimes with the size of their vocabulary and the sophistication of its use. For example, one of the author's nieces was telling her about a monkey that ran away from its mother. The child was asked how large the monkey was. Pressing her two index fingers together, she began to spread them slowly apart, all the while watching intently the expression on her aunt's face. She stopped when the fingers were about three inches apart. The aunt replied, "Oh, I think monkeys are bigger than that!" Whereupon the young one rapidly spread her fingers as far as her arms could reach in opposite directions. Clearly, the child *had* a word in her speech for which she did not have an accurate meaning.

More often than not, though, the opposite is true. Children *have* more meanings than they can express. An example is provided by Scotty: We had been tracking a jackrabbit in the snow for some distance. Shanna, age four, was cold and not particularly interested in rabbits anyway; so she began to cry and complain. Scotty, age four, also, continued to follow the rabbit trail with much concentration. Finally, he looked up at Shanna in great exasperation and said, "Shanna, *be quiet!* I can't *hear* the rabbit tracks!" Saying what he really meant, "You're making so much noise I can't concentrate on what I'm looking at," was a bit too complicated for his speaking vocabulary.

Below is another example from Scotty, who clearly had a concept but not an understanding of the word to express it: We sat in my Volkswagen Bug on a hot summer's day having a drink at the A & W Root Beer stand. Scotty, then age three, sat in the front seat while his older brother and a friend, both age five, sat in the back seat.

All was going well from those quarters judging from the loud, slurping sounds as the two older boys drank through straws. In the front seat, however, things were not going so well with Scotty. Instead of sucking through the straw, he *blew*. Sprays of root beer went all over both of us. I tried to tell him to suck, not blow. I tried to explain *how* to suck. Still no success. Then, from the back seat came, "Scotty, you know. Do it like your pacifier!" That did it!

By three to four years of age most children have acquired and can apply the basic systems of spoken language sufficiently to generate language that has all the elements of adult speech. This is not to imply that they have completed language learning. They simply have the basic foundations. Language will be expanded and refined throughout life as new experiences produce an ever-growing repertoire of words and ways to put them together to communicate.

Experimentation/Testing/Feedback

Even though not enough is yet known about how children acquire their language, psycholinguistics offers some promising guidelines that may lead to more definitive answers. Children are not seen as passive recipients of language, absorbing it simply by being in its presence. Children are active participants in the language game. Their whole mode of operation is one of continually trying out ways to get their meanings across and then altering their approach when these attempts do not succeed.

Imitation plays a part. Children *do* learn to make sounds that approximate adult speech by repeating what they hear. They do learn to pronounce words, and they practice from adult models the intonation patterns they hear. But if their only source of language learning were what they hear, that learning would be severely limited; the child would be able to produce only those sentences previously heard. The situation would be analogous to needing a separate key for each door in a skyscraper. The fact is that most of the sentences we generate in a lifetime of talk are those we have *not* heard before. There must be a master key that will provide access to any door encountered.

The key to learning language is to become familiar with *how the system of language works*. The child must determine the rules that govern the production and understanding of meaningful utterances. English has a prescribed order for combining words to make meaning. "He went to the store" is an appropriate combination by the rules of syntax. "Store he the went to" is not. When a child knows, albeit implicitly, the way in which words must be combined to convey meaning, she can then generate an infinite number of sentences to express her meanings. There are also rules for combining individual sounds to make sense. *Q* is almost always followed by *u;* therefore, "qail" is probably not a permissible combination. *T* can be followed by all vowels, but not by all consonants. *Tb, tc,* and *td* are not allowed by the rule. Certain affixes can be attached to some words but not to others: "He talk*ed* loudly" is acceptable, but "He went*ed* home" is not.

Discovering what the rules are (how language works) and how to use them is the other side of the language learning coin. Even though the child is totally unconscious of the process, she repeatedly conducts experiments to test hypotheses about the rules of her language against the feedback she gets from the test.

> Children who have just begun to talk frequently make statements that are completely obvious. A child looking out of a window with you will say something like "See big plane" although you may even have pointed the plane out in the first place. Why then should the child bother to make the statement? The answer is because the child is learning, conducting an experiment. In fact, a child could be conducting no fewer than three different experiments at the same time in that one simple situation.
>
> The child could be testing the hypothesis that the object you can both clearly see in the sky *is* a plane, that it is not a bird or cloud or something else as yet unidentified. When you say, "Yes, I see it," you are confirming that the object is a plane; positive feedback. Even silence is interpreted as positive feedback since the child would expect you to make a correction if the hypothesis were in error. The second hypothesis that the child might be testing concerns the sounds of the language, that the name "plane" is the right name for the object, rather than "pwane," "prane," or whatever else the child might say. Once again the child can assume that if you do not take the opportunity to make a correction, then there is nothing to be corrected. A test has been successfully conducted. The third hypothesis that the child may be testing is linguistic, whether "See big plane" is a grammatically acceptable and meaningful sentence in adult language. The feedback comes when the adult says, "Yes, I can see the big plane." The child learns to produce sentences in your language by using tentative sentences for which you both already know the meaning, *in a situation which you both comprehend* (Smith 1978, 90–91).*

Smith further contends that in hypothesis testing

> . . . there must be a chance of being wrong. It is obvious there is nothing to be learned if you know you are right; you know it already. But in addition, being wrong is more informative. . . . When you are wrong you know your hypothesis is inadequate. We learn from our mistakes. (1979, 93)†

In spoken language, the situation in which language is used provides many cues to the meaning of what is heard.

> At the beginning of language learning infants must be able to understand sentences of a language before they can learn a language. I mean that children do not come to understand utterances like: "Would you like a drink of juice?" or even the meaning of the single words like "juice" by figuring out the language or having someone tell them the rules.
>
> Children learn because initially they can hypothesize the meaning of a statement from the situation in which it is uttered—an adult is usually carrying or pointing to a drink of juice when a sentence like "Would you like a drink of juice?" is spoken (1979, 96).‡
>
> . . . . . .
>
> Children do not learn language to make sense of words and sentences; they make sense of words and sentences to learn language (1979, 96).

An added benefit of the situational context of spoken language is that the child is relieved of the need to verbalize excessively. This is particularly important in early language learning when production abilities are limited. Because the situation carries

*From UNDERSTANDING READING 2/e by Frank Smith. Copyright © 1978 by Holt, Rinehart and Winston. Reprinted by permission of CBS College Publishing.

†Reprinted by permission of the publisher from Frank Smith, *Reading Without Nonsense* (New York, Teachers College Press, © 1984 by Teachers College, Columbia University. All rights reserved.) p. 93.

‡Reprinted by permission of the publisher from Frank Smith, *Reading Without Nonsense* (New York, Teachers College Press, © 1984 by Teachers College, Columbia University. All rights reserved.) p. 96.

so much of the message implicitly, the child can respond with limited words and still comprehend and be understood much as occurs in the previously discussed holophrastic phase of language learning. In short, the situation in which language is used enables the child to bring meaning to speech.

The Role of Parents in Language Learning

In studies of the early years of hundreds of children, particular scrutiny was given to the first three years of life. Based on these studies, White and his associates conclude that the period between eight months and two years is a crucial one for establishing behavior systems which will enable the child to reach her fullest potential in language, curiosity, intellectual, and social development. White further concludes that the quality of parenting observed during studies of this period was such that no more than one child in ten achieves anywhere near potential in the above four areas. Parents, especially mothers, who are the ones likely to spend the most time with infants at this age, seem to be the key influence in shaping young children during this time and in setting them on the road to attaining the most of which they are capable. Some parents in the study were simply more gifted than others in two areas that seemed to spell the difference between a child's becoming highly competent in language and social skills, and in curiosity and intelligence. These were in the roles of "designer of the child's environment" and of "consultant to the young child" (White 1978, 137–38).

Designer of the child's environment. The most competent parents provided ready access to the living area. The child could roam and explore to her heart's content. In doing so, her curiosity was broadened and deepened, new interests were developed, and the sensory data for building new meanings and generating new language were greatly expanded (White 1978, 137).

Consultant to the young child. Effective parents in the study starred in the role of consultant. In response to requests or questions from the infant, these mothers were adept not only at answering those questions but also in injecting ideas that could lead the child to *further* questions, additional explorations and new answers.

> Effective mothers pause to see what the child is interested in. They identify the subject, then usually provide what is needed by the child. They also provide a few words related to the topic in question, using language that is at or slightly above the child's apparent ability level; and they express a related idea or two. For example, if the child comes to you with what looks like a little animal figure with unusually large feet, you might suggest that "Those feet are really large. Daddy has big feet, too, doesn't he, and you have small feet" (White 1978, 138–39).

A similar example is cited by one author's recent experience while observing two preschool children playing house. After half an hour of play, the children seemed to have used all their ideas, and they appeared ready to drift off to another activity. The author walked over, knocked on the playhouse "door" and asked if she might use the phone because her car had run out of gas. One child looked at the other as if to ask "Is she nuts?" and then replied, "I'll have to ask the Daddy." After a whispered conversation with "the Daddy," she handed an imaginary telephone to the adult saying, "Here it is. Don't twist the cord!" During the next five to ten minutes, the caller requested a phone book, a drink of water, and started a conversation about how to make brownies. Then she dismissed herself by saying, "Oh, here's the man with my gas. Thank you. Good-bye!" Thirty minutes later the two children were still engaged in animated conversation and activities related to cooking and telephoning.

Giver of information. Parents provide two kinds of information to children—*general* and *specific. General* information is that which comes from hearing an abundance of adult language. *Specific* information is given to a child when she needs it in response to a request or a question—when a child is testing a hypothesis. Feedback from the parent, as already noted, is the means by which the child confirms or corrects predictions about language and its structure. Parents serve this purpose when they engage in expansions of the child's language.

> For example when the child says "want milk," the parent "expands" the statement into "You want some milk, do you?" or "May I have a glass of milk, please." An adult expanding child language is providing a specific adult-language surface structure that the child already has in his mind. It is not a simple matter of "correcting," but of giving information so that the child can verify a rule that he has just applied, at a time when he can relate it to the appropriate deep structure (Smith 1972, 41–42).*

The Nature of Language

The discussion of the nature of language that follows is based on current psycholinguistic theory. Even though, as noted numerous times in preceding sections, much about language learning remains a mystery, some of the tenets from psycholinguistics promise to be our most productive ones to date for understanding the mental processes underlying language learning and use.

Language as a System of Rules

There is an order and system about language that can be considered a microcosm rivaling that of the universe. All the "pieces" and the way in which they fit together to produce human communication are governed by specific rules that language learners must acquire in order to develop proficiency in producing and understanding that language. As already mentioned, children learn the rules of language in a wholly unconscious manner, and in so doing, they acquire a master key to communication that lasts a lifetime. They are able to use these rules to generate and to comprehend an infinite number of sentences as needed.

Sounds in speech (and their symbolic representations in writing) can only be combined in prescribed ways to produce intelligible words. Words cannot be strung together haphazardly without becoming nonsense. Meanings of words are largely determined by rules of placement within sentences, by endings that may be attached, and by the relationship among words which is shown by function words.

*From Frank Smith, "The Learner and His Language," in Richard Hodges and E. Hugh Rudorf, LANGUAGE AND LEARNING TO READ, Boston: Houghton Mifflin Company, 1972, pp. 41–42. Used with permission.

Table 2.2 The Components of Language

Phonology	Syntax	Semantics
Phonology is the study of the distinctive sounds of language. 1. There are forty-four distinctive sounds, called phonemes in the English language. 2. The alphabet is an imperfect representation of these sounds. 3. Phonemes combine into meaningful units of language called morphemes. 4. Stress, pitch, and juncture (called suprasegmentals) are distinctive features of English that *change meaning.* 5. Phoneme-grapheme relationships are often confusing because the same sound can have many variant spellings, and different sounds may have the same spelling.	Syntax, the grammar of the language, is the set of rules governing how morphemes are combined into sentences. 1. Word order is an important distinctive feature of English. *Example* I see a bird. Not: See I bird a. 2. There are only a few basic "kernel" sentence patterns. a. Noun, verb b. Noun, transitive verb, object c. Noun, linking verb, predicate noun or predicate adjective d. Noun, verb, prepositional phrase 3. Transformations: a. Passive voice b. Questions c. Negatives d. Imperatives e. Using *it* and *there*	Semantics is the study of the meanings communicated through language. 1. The listener or the reader must rely on context clues: meanings depend upon context. 2. English language contains many figures of speech, idiomatic expressions, slang expressions, antonyms, homonyms, homographs, and synonyms. 3. English contains many words borrowed from other languages. 4. The suprasegments: pitch, stress, and juncture are phonemic because they change meanings, *but they are also* semantic because they communicate meaning changes.

In operation the rules act as signals or cues to meaning. When both sender and receiver understand the cues, effective communication can take place. All the necessary cues are present only in a total language context, that is, in what Bill Martin (1980, 3) calls "whole chunks of meaning" rather than isolated bits and pieces. See table 2.2 for an overview of the concepts involved.

The Components of Language

Phonological. The sound system of language is comprised of individual sound units, or phonemes. These individual sounds, few in number, are the building blocks for spoken language. Out of no more than a few dozen sounds, all the utterances of English can be generated. Without conscious effort, the child who is immersed in oral language learns not only to make the individual sounds and combine them into meaningful utterances, but she also learns which sounds are important to *her* language. By prescription, according to the rules of sound combinations, the child learns to generate an infinite number of words.

Daniel R. Hittleman notes that the child also learns appropriate intonation from hearing language spoken. Intonation consists of stress, pitch, and juncture. Stress refers to loudness or softness in production of sounds. Pitch is how high or how low the voice is in making sounds. Juncture refers to pauses between units of speech—syllables, words, phrases, and sentences (1983, 32). (The importance of intonation in conveying meaning in spoken language is developed more fully in a later section of this chapter.)

Syntactic. The order in which words are put together is extremely important in producing unambiguous meanings in the English language. "He flew the kite" is in keeping with the rules of word order, but "Kite flew the he" is not. English has the following basic sentence patterns:

1. Noun-verb or subject-verb structures.
   Birds fly.
2. Noun-verb-noun or subject-verb-direct object structures.
   Freddy threw the stick.
   The gerbil ate the sunflower seed quickly.
3. Noun-verb-noun-noun or subject-verb-indirect object-object structures.
   John gave Harry a watch.
   Father gave me a new bat.
4. Noun-linking verb-noun or subject-linking verb-predicate noun. A linking verb is the verb *to be*.
   Walter is a monitor.
5. Noun-linking verb-adjective or subject-linking verb-predicate adjective structures.
   Shelia is pretty.

   (Hittleman 1983, 33)*

An infinite number of sentences can be generated by transforming, or changing, these "kernel sentences" according to prescribed grammatical rules. Five common kinds of transformations include:

1. Passive voice.
   Kernel: John gave Harry a watch.
   Transform: A watch was given to Harry by John.
2. Questions.
   Kernel: Freddy threw the stick.
   Transform: Did Freddy throw the stick?
3. Negative.
   Kernel: Walter is a monitor.
   Transform: Walter is not a monitor.
4. Imperative.
   Kernel: George gives Alice a new book.
   Transform: George, give Alice a new book!

*Source: Daniel R. Hittleman, DEVELOPMENTAL READING, K–8: TEACHING FROM A PSYCHOLINGUISTIC PERSPECTIVE, Second Edition, pp. 33–35. Copyright © 1983 by Houghton Mifflin Company. Used with permission.

5. Beginning with *it* and *there*.
   Kernel: Answering a teacher is wise.
   Transform: It is wise to answer a teacher.
   Kernel: Birds are flying.
   Transform: There are birds flying.

   (Hittleman 1983, 34)*

Still other sentences can be formed by the application of rules for *embedding:* expanding or combining sentences or sentence parts.

1. Compounding. Words, phrases, and independent clauses are combined to form compound subjects, compound predicates, compound objects, and compound sentences.

   Kernel: Carol sat.
   Carol waited.
   Betty sat.
   Betty waited.
   Transform: Carol and Betty sat and waited.

2. Modification. Adjectives, adverbs, qualifiers, adjective and adverbial phrases, and adjective and adverbial clauses are added.

   Kernel: The man gave away chickens.
   Transform: The little man who wore a red hat gave away three chickens.

3. Apposition. Words, phrases, or clauses are used in apposition with nouns.

   Kernel: Gerald Ford was President of the United States.
   Gerald Ford nominated Nelson Rockefeller for Vice-President.
   Transform: Gerald Ford, President of the United States, nominated Nelson Rockefeller for Vice-President.

4. Subordination. Words, phrases, and clauses that are closely associated with the main idea are added.

   Kernel: John bought an ice cream cone.
   John was not really hungry.
   Transform: Although John was not really hungry, he bought an ice cream cone.

5. Parallel structure. A series of ideas in the form of equally important phrases or clauses is added.

   Kernel: The children had to read a story.
   The children had to draw a picture.
   The children had to write three sentences.
   Transform: The children had to read a story, draw a picture, and write three sentences.

   (Hittleman 1983, 34–35)*

*Source: Daniel R. Hittleman, DEVELOPMENTAL READING, K–8: TEACHING FROM A PSYCHOLINGUISTIC PERSPECTIVE, Second Edition, pp. 33–35. Copyright © 1983 by Houghton Mifflin Company. Used with permission.

Semantic. A third component of language is semantics, which deals with meanings, or words "and the relationship of meaning to syntax and phonological structure" (Hittleman 1983, 35).

Words in the English language can be categorized into two basic types: *content words* and *function,* or *structure, words.* Content words carry the meaning load of utterances; they include nouns, verbs, adjectives, and adverbs. In and of themselves, they usually carry meaning having referents in the real world. Function, or structure, words, on the other hand, have no real-world referents and, therefore, have no meaning in isolation. Function words signal the presence of content words and show relationships among words in a sentence. Function words include noun determiners, verb auxiliaries, prepositions, and conjunctions.

Just as word order in sentences can be changed to effect new meanings, word meanings, too, can be altered by the addition or deletion of specific endings called morphemes. A morpheme is the smallest meaning bearing unit in language. There are two types: *free* and *bound.* For example *boy* is a free morpheme; standing alone, it makes sense. *S* added to *boy* to make it plural is a bound morpheme; *s* carries no meaning in isolation. Prefixes and suffixes are morphemes used to change word meanings: *happy* becomes *un*happy and *doubt* becomes doubt*less.* Word meanings can be altered by the use of affixes to indicate tense, number, quality, state or manner, and parts of speech.

The Cues to Meaning: Signal Systems of Language

Language could aptly be described as a complex, interrelated network of signals. Each of the foregoing components supplies certain types of cues that signal specific meanings. It is these signal systems generated by specific rules of language structure that learners of language must acquire; once the acquisition is made, proficiency in communication is possible. Children develop an intuitive grasp, an internalized response to the underlying rules that govern the generation of these cue systems. In addition to the cue systems within language itself, equally important cues to meaning are within the user, whether one functions as a listener, reader, writer, or speaker.

Phonological cues. Phonological cues are signals to meaning that are provided by the sounds, sound patterns, and intonations of spoken language. Through specific things, happenings, and events, and through experimentations with the sounds of language, the child begins to sense the distinctions in sounds by which meanings are signaled. He gradually learns that even minimal differences in sounds signal differences in meaning, as, for example, in *pit* and *bit, pet* and *pat.* He comes to recognize those combinations of sounds that convey meaning and those that do not: *dog, man, hit* against *ghrd, sxfee, klorpe.*

Children learn early the cues to meaning that are carried by *the way words are spoken.* Stress in saying "no" can result in varying degrees of intensity. "No" said to a child about to pull an object off onto her head is stressed differently and results in a stronger meaning of "no" (noness!) than saying to a child, "No, I don't think we'll have time to go to the zoo today, but we will go another time." Children learn that raising pitch of the voice at the end of an utterance signals a question. They learn to detect the meaningful units into which language must be divided, if comprehension is to result. Voice pauses are used to signal the end of phrases and sentences in the flow of discourse.

Grammatical cues. Signals to meaning are made by a number of grammatical or syntactic cues. These include word order, inflections, or word endings, and function words. Two sentences may contain exactly the same words but have entirely different meanings. The order of words determines their function; their purpose, or function, determines their meaning. Constance Weaver explains the relationship thus:

> Snoopy kissed Lucy.
> Lucy kissed Snoopy.
>
> In the first sentence, Snoopy did the kissing and Lucy was the recipient of the kiss; in the second sentence, Lucy did the kissing and Snoopy received the kiss (1980, 18–19).

A second grammatical cue to meaning is supplied by inflections or word meanings, devices that show a relationship among words in a thought unit.

> There are various word endings which may signal a word's grammatical category (noun, verb, or whatever) and hence to some extent determine its meaning. Take for example, the words *chaired, runner, whiten,* and *closely.* The *-ed* on *chaired* suggests that the word denotes an action rather than a place to sit; the *-er* on *runner* suggests that we are talking about a person; the *-en* on *whiten* suggests an action (as in Clorox will whit*en* your clothes); and the *-ly* on *closely* suggests the manner in which some action is carried out (as in She examined it closely) (Weaver 1980, 17).

Function words provide a third kind of grammatical cue to meaning. As already stated, these are words that have no meaning in themselves; their purpose is to signal different word categories and to show how words in a sentence relate one to another. Function words are classified by the role they play in sentences:

1. Noun markers. Included in this category are words such as a, an, the, their, this, my, some. Their purpose is to signal the appearance of a noun or noun phrase.
2. Verb markers. Included in this category are words such as: (a) forms of to be, to have, and to do used as auxiliary verbs; (b) other auxiliaries, such as: will, shall, ought, may, can. They signal the oncoming of a verb or verb phrase.
3. Qualifiers. Included in this category are words such as: very, too, and much. They signal the relative strength of an oncoming adjective or adverb.
4. Prepositions. Included in this category are words such as: up, down, in, out, out of, above, and below. They combine with noun forms to create phrases that modify other parts of speech.
5. Clause markers. Included in this category are words such as: (a) the relative pronouns: whom, whom, which, what, that, and (b) the subordinating conjunctions: if, because, although, even, while, and until. They all signal the onset of a dependent clause.
6. Question markers. Included in this category are such words as: who, why, how, where, when, what, did, are, is, have, do, has. They often begin sentences and signal question transformations.
7. Negatives. Inlcuded in this category are words such as: no, not, never, nor, none (Hittleman 1983, 36–37).*

*Daniel R. Hittleman: DEVELOPMENTAL READING, K–8: TEACHING FROM A PSYCHOLINGUISTIC PERSPECTIVE, Second Edition, pp. 36–37.

Semantic cues. Semantic cues are those which derive from one's experiences in the everyday world. They are the concepts (meanings) one has developed and the labels (word symbols) used to identify the concepts. These are basically the *content* words of language. While content words carry enough meaning in themselves to provide some cues to those meanings, they must be used in whole utterances in which the context gives additional cues before they have unambiguous connotations.

An example of the way in which word order changes word function and, therefore, meaning is shown by the example below where the same word becomes a different part of speech (its function changes), and it simultaneously acquires a different meaning all because of placement in the total context of an utterance.

She had a *run* in her stocking.
I must *run* to the bank.

Run in the first sentence is a direct object and is a noun meaning "a long hole in the stocking." In the second sentence, *run* is part of the predicate and is a verb designating an action engaged in by the subject. Only in the flow of language can one identify the word as noun or verb. Notice this also:

Time *flies* like an arrow.
Fruit *flies* like a banana.

Redundancy. In addition to the previously described ways in which meaning is indicated by language signals, another important feature of the language cue system is redundancy. Redundancy is the occurrence of multiple cues to meaning, that is, a given meaning is signaled in more than one way. In the following sentence are four cues that the subject is plural: *The boys carry their backpacks.* The four cues are (1) the bound morpheme *s* added to *boy* makes it plural; (2) the verb *carry* would be *carries* if the subject were singular; (3) *their* is plural in contrast to either *her* or *his* if the subject were singular; and (4) since *backpacks* is plural, there must be more than one boy.

While redundancy is an important aid in learning oral language, it becomes crucial when the child begins to deal with print. Here, as in oral language, the child is not only aided in deriving meaning because multiple cues are given for the same information, but she receives another benefit that helps enormously in unlocking print.

> . . . redundancy provides a narrowing of elements in the language that can fill certain slots. Only certain sounds can occur after /T/ in *Tom.* Only certain words can occur after *Tom. After Tom saw,* still fewer words are possible. *After Tom saw a,* possible correct words are more restricted. Furthermore, the unknown word *monkey* must fit equally well into a number of such restricted settings.
>
> The process by which the child immediately or eventually knows this word is *monkey* is a kind of tentative "zeroing in." Successive sets of redundancy cues narrow the number of possible words in the language that can fit. As he responds to these redundant cues, the child is guessing, but he is an enlightened guesser. He is using his knowledge of language, his past experience, and his developed concepts. If he makes a mistake, there are almost always abundant additional cues to tell him that he is wrong and to tell him what is right (Smith, Goodman, and Meredith 1976, 276).

Your Turn 2.1 Language as a system of signals.

Select a 3-to-5 page passage from a third grade basal reader.

Identify all the cues to meaning and categorize them according to the. four cue systems in the foregoing section.

Other examples of redundancy are supplied by Richard E. Hodges and Hugh E. Rudorf:

(a) "q" must be followed by "u."
(b) In the sentence "He was watching Mary." *watching* has three cues to its function as a verb: its position in the sentence, the use of *was* with it, and its *ing* ending (1972, 153).

In a sense, then redundancy is like a "fail-safe" component built into language. As one listens to or reads the normal flow of language, she is not required to get every single cue to meaning; when cues are missed, the same information will be repeated. This enables both listener and reader to sample language and arrive at meaning much faster and more efficiently than would be possible if cues were given less frequently or had to be noted more carefully.

Within language, then, are many cues that enable the user to arrive at meanings. The system of signals is derived from the basic rules that prescribe *what* can be communicated and *how* the process is carried out. The beauty of language learning is that what appears to be enormously complicated—when analyzed and described as we have done above—comes naturally and unconsciously to the child as she develops skills in the use of spoken language. A grasp of the language in spoken form provides the basis for bridging into the written form as naturally and as easily as learning to talk. Reading does not require a whole new communication system beyond that already acquired in speaking.

The child can and does bring meaning to spoken and written language. These meanings come from her intuitive grasp and knowledge of the cues within language and from cues within herself.

Surface Structure and Deep Structure of Language

Cues to meaning come from two major sources: within the structure of language and within the user herself. Chomsky, almost two decades ago, introduced two concepts that refer to these sources. Both have become major components of psycholinguistic theory as it relates to spoken and written language skills development.

All language, regardless of its form, has two distinct characteristics, a *surface structure* and a *deep structure*. Surface structure refers to the observable features of language, such as

> . . . the part of language accessible to the brain through the ears and eyes.
>
> Surface structure is the visual information of written language—the source of information that is lost to the reader when the lights go out—but it is also the part of spoken language—the part that is lost when a telephone conversation is broken (Smith 1978, 70–71).*

The previous section contained some examples of the cuing systems in language which deal primarily with surface structure: the grammatical relations signaled by word order and function and word endings.

However, what we see and what we hear in language are not all we get. The signals from surface structure, whether in visual or aural form, are limited in their capacity to supply adequate cues to meaning. An additional source of information is required if misconceptions and ambiguity are to be avoided in all forms of communication. For example, the surface structure can be changed without making a difference in meaning.

Active voice: The man is washing the car.
Passive voice: The car is being washed by the man.

On the other hand, the same surface structure may have more than one possible meaning.

I had Mary for lunch and made sandwiches.
  I am a cannibal.
  I invited Mary to have lunch with me.

Flying planes can be dangerous.
  The plane is dangerous.
  It is a dangerous job for pilots.

Visiting professors may be tedious.
  The professor may be tedious.
  Going visiting may be tedious.

The chickens were too hot to eat.
  The chickens were fresh out of the oven.
  The chickens were highly seasoned.
  The chickens had been out in the hot sun.
  The chickens had been stolen.

From the above examples, it is clear that what one gets from what one sees and hears in communication is not always enough to generate adequate meanings. One must have more than she gets from surface structure alone. Deep structure is required. *Deep structure,* as opposed to surface structure, can be neither seen nor heard: it is invisible, nonobservable. Deep structure is the *meaning* of language. "The term is apt. Meanings do not lie at the surface of language but far more profoundly in the minds of the users of language: in the mind of the speaker or writer and in the mind of the listener or reader" (Smith 1978, 71).

Deep structure or meaning comes from within the users of language; it is brought to the task of communicating by them. The signals or cues to meaning from the user are derived from personal perceptions and interpretations of experience with the world; it is the sum total of one's experience and knowledge. This store of meanings which is brought to bear on the surface of language makes comprehension possible.

The importance of experience and the way it shapes meaning will be further explored in chapter 3, but a personal example will suffice here: One author's concept, or meaning, for *cold* was forever altered by an experience in the dead of winter on the

Your Turn 2.2 The role of deep structure in comprehension.

Using the same story from which you selected the passage for Your Turn 2.1, tell what deep structure (knowledge of concepts in the content) would be required for the reader to comprehend the story.

Yukon River above the Arctic Circle in Alaska. Shortly after arriving for a week's consultant work in the public schools, the temperature began to drop. It finally reached −65° F. (below zero, that is!). The meaning of *cold* at this level was derived from watching the effects on the humans in the environment, including the author herself. Moving about from place to place outside heated buildings was almost prohibitive. Five minutes exposure outside produced a searing pain in the lungs with every inhalation of breath and a frosty rim of ice on the fur around the parka hood with every exhalation. Those who had to go out moved about like large, overstuffed ghosts in an eerie world of frozen fog, where visibility was measured in inches. At last, when a plane could come in to provide escape, there was an agonizing, long wait sitting on the plane while compressed air from a five gallon tank was used to pump air into the plane tires which had deflated on landing. The author wiggled her toes and fingers to keep them from freezing; she lost count somewhere after three hundred "wiggles." Ice formed in thicker and thicker layers on the plane windows as breath moisture condensed and froze. (Even now, my "surface structure," or what I print here, can convey only a minute part of my "deep structure," my meaning for *cold* from an Arctic experience.)

Language: Spoken, Unspoken, and Written

The popular conception of language is that it has two major forms—spoken and written. Actually, however, it has three—spoken, unspoken, and written. In an oral context language has two distinct elements, both of which are crucial in conveying meanings: The verbal message or *what* is said and the nonverbal message or the *way* words are delivered. Of the two elements, the unspoken message is often far more potent as a medium of communication than the actual words spoken. Written language, too, has dual features; however, the nonverbal aspect of written language has neither the strength nor the power to shape meanings as effectively as the nonverbal component of oral language.

In this section the similarities and differences between spoken and written language are described, and the nature of nonverbal communication is analyzed. How children learn to communicate in all three media is examined.

Comparison of Oral and Written Language Usage

"Speech and print are not different languages—they share a common vocabulary and the same grammatical forms—but they are likely to contain different distributions of each" (Smith 1978, 80). Smith contends that spoken and written language differ for a number of reasons: (1) their *purposes* are different, (2) the *contexts* in which each occurs are dissimilar, (3) the *audiences* they serve are not the same, and (4) the *demands* they make on participants are diverse. The *forms* of spoken language are both aural and visual—the visual being observation of voice and body language cues as language is spoken. Print, on the other hand, is largely visual.

The contexts. Spoken language (and its unspoken counterparts, intonation and body language) takes place in a social setting: it is between or among people (unless, of course, one talks to oneself or simply listens to a speaker). But primarily, spoken language occurs when there is at least a two-way exchange. Written language, on the other hand, occurs as an exchange of meanings between a reader, who is present, and a writer, who is absent.

As a consequence of the presence or absence of participants, spoken and written discourse have different ways in which meaning is verified. In a conversational exchange between two people, the speaker constantly monitors the reactions of the listener to be sure that understanding is taking place; if either the verbal or nonverbal signals from the listener indicate comprehension, the speaker continues. If not, then the speaker changes the discourse in an effort to make the meaning clear. The speaker may restate, give examples to illustrate, ask questions of the listener, and/or use a variety of facial expressions or changes in voice. (Children will often admonish the listener to "pay attention"; adults have been conditioned to use other less-direct means, but they may wish they could be as blunt as children in situations where the listener is inattentive.)

But verification or feedback on written discourse is entirely different. To verify or to resolve confusion, readers must reread what is written to check for clarity of ideas in the author's message itself; they must also check their own interpretation of the message as a source of error (Smith 1978, 82).

The contexts differ in another way. Dolores Durkin writes that "the speaker's message is often concerned with concrete, everyday objects, with shared experiences, with the immediate environment, and within a time period that is familiar to both speaker and listener" (1981, 30).

Whereas conversation takes place in a specific environment (situational context), William H. Teale believes that "written language is characterized by *isolation* from a situational context" (1978, 927). The writer must supply as much information as she can to help bridge what may be a gap between the subject about which she is writing and the reader's background information related to the subject. But the writer cannot do it all; unless the reader can bring some knowledge of the topic to the text, no comprehension will be possible.

Mention has already been made of the way in which the situational context of spoken language is of particular importance to the young child learning language. Because the context in spoken language provides so many cues to meaning, learning to converse is a far less difficult task than is dealing with print in which the context may not be familiar to the young reader.

The purposes. The purposes of spoken and written language differ. Speech is the medium of exchange between persons who are physically present or who can hear one another by some electronic device (telephone, television, and so forth). Spoken language has adapted itself to being heard. The sounds of speech run together naturally in ordinary discourse. Consequently, there is often a difference between how we say things and how we write them. Written language is not an exchange between persons physically present: it is designed to be read. It is more precise in the division of discourse into individual meaning units:

Print	*Speech*
Are you catching any:	Cetchanenny?
What are you using?	Wachoozin?

Vocabulary may contain greater variety, and sentence structure will likely be more complex than is that of spoken language.

The syntax of speech is less formal and less complex than that of print, partly because the speaker does not need to supply as much information in speaking: the situational context takes care of a sizeable part of meaning. Then, too, the speaker can use juncture (pauses) to divide the flow of speech into meaningful units—phrases and sentences. The speaker can supply additional information anytime he perceives that his message is not getting across to the listener.

Writers "can and do assist readers with explanations, illustrations, and, in the area of graphic aids, with paragraph indentation and punctuation. Although marks like commas and periods should help with the segmentation that is required for communication, readers are on their own in using them" (Durkin 1981, 31). Because these aids are available does not mean that readers will use them—poor comprehension in beginning readers, as well as those at higher levels, indicates that "failure to organize text into phrasal units is a major and enduring deficiency" (Durkin 1981, 31).

The audiences. Oral language is primarily between two individuals or among several persons in relatively small groups. Quite often individuals are known to each other, or they are from common backgrounds, or they share similar interests and purposes. Because of these bonds of familiarity, people engaging in oral discourse are far from beginning at ground zero in communication. They know what to predict about each other's verbal behavior; this greatly increases the likelihood of comprehension between them. Their conversations may be segmented into bits and pieces covering a variety of different topics. Much can be left out in these exchanges because their shared common background can be used by each to fill in the gaps.

The audiences to whom authors address their messages are different from those involved in oral communication in several ways. Size of the "reading" audience is almost always infinitely larger, even though the subject of a book may be of interest to only a fraction of the population. The prior knowledge and understanding of the topic may vary greatly among the individuals for whom the topic is relevant. The reader needs and expects more detailed development of fewer topics. The reader can pick up, put down, and return to the printed page as she likes. Print has a continuity, a permanence that speech does not have.

The forms. There are no words as such in ordinary speech. Oral language consists of voice sounds that are strung together in a variety of patterns accompanied by varying pitches, stresses, junctures, and body movements. Spoken language is transitory: it is lost as it is spoken, unless, of course, it is electronically recorded. Written language consists of individual symbols (letters) arranged to form meaning units (words) that are separated by blank spaces and organized into groups called sentences. Graphic symbols—periods, commas, and italics—are used to show some of the nonverbal signals present in speech.

The demands. The nature of spoken and written language make different demands on recipients. In speech fewer demands are made on the listener to process a heavy verbal load; the situational context and the nonverbal aspect of spoken language supply many cues to meaning, which do not have to be spelled out in words. But the transient nature of speech places a great demand on the short term memory of the listener; one must "grab" as much as possible as words are spoken because they are not ordinarily repeated.

Written language, by contrast, makes a different demand on the reader. Because of the absence of situational context and many nonverbal cues, these must be supplied by the writer. The verbal load to be processed and retained by the reader is thus increased. And where the message is still not clear, the reader's only recourse is to return to the print. The reader is bound to the print and what she can remember of it. This places a heavy demand on long-term memory (Smith 1978, 80–82).

The Nature of Unspoken Language

Spoken language is a dual system in which two kinds of messages are communicated simultaneously. One message is carried by the words said; the other reflects the feelings, attitudes, and values *about* what is said. The verbal component is a message; the nonverbal element is a message about a message. Each of the two systems has its own unique structure, its own code to express meaning. Of the two, unspoken language is where the true meaning of an exchange usually lies. Mere words can convey many different messages: the particular meaning they have in a specific instance depends on what the sender *intends* them to mean. The intended meaning is conveyed by the way words are spoken—the intonations of the voice and the "language" of body movements.

If clear meanings are to be exchanged, the sender and the receiver must be tuned in to these same dual wave lengths of oral communication. The receiver must interpret not only what is spoken but also that which is unspoken. Misinterpretation of either causes a breakdown in communication—meaning is lost.

The beauty, or the magic, of "silent" language lies in the way it loosens the bonds, the restrictions of mere words so that we can experience far more than we can ever *know*; we can *feel* far more than we can ever *say*. It is this component of communication, more than any other, that enables us to relate effectively one to another. Imagine our inadequacies, for example, when trying to comfort bereaved ones with words only. A touch or other nonverbal behavior comes much closer to conveying what we actually feel.

There are three ways in which meanings beyond words are signaled: by sign, by body, and by voice.

Sign language. "Sign languages which consist of one form of nonverbal communication consist of pictures. These may be stylized representations of actual things, places, or events, or they may be symbols of these situations. (For example, the international motoring pictures and symbols are examples of pictorial language" (Hittleman 1978, 27).*

Body language. The body is used in a variety of ways to express meanings without words. Gestures, facial expressions, the way one moves the body in general, and where the body is positioned in space relative to other persons are all signals of meanings. Raising the hand implies not only a verbal message, "I want to speak," but there is also a second message implying a feeling or value about consideration of others—taking turns.

The raising of eyebrows usually signals a feeling of surprise or question about something seen or heard. Rapid speech can indicate excited anticipation of a welcomed meeting (or escape from an unwelcomed one). Where people stand or sit in relation to one another in conversing carries a message about feelings they have for one another. Loved ones are separated by the least distance; friends occupy the next space out; acquaintances are farther removed; strangers are beyond.

Voice language. Finally, the voice is a strong vehicle for nonverbal messages. Intonation is the "tune to which language is sung" (Smith, Goodman, and Meredith 1976, 274). Intonation is a composite of *stress, pitch,* and *juncture,* all of which combine to signal meanings in speech.

Stress is the emphasis given by the voice to different sounds in the stream of speech. Changing stress from one word to another can completely alter the meaning of what is spoken. This has already been demonstrated in chapter 1: "*You're* not going swimming today" (meaning others may, but *you* are not) or "You're not going *swimming* today" (implying that you may do other things today, but swimming will not be one of them). A change in syllable stress within a word can change the part of speech and, therefore, the function of a word: "He made a rec'ord"; "I will re cord' the song."

Pitch consists of the rises, falls, and steadiness with which sounds in speech are produced. Questions in English are signaled by a rise in the voice at the end of sentences. "By varying the pitch pattern of the single word *what,* we can make it mean, 'Go ahead, I'm listening,' 'I don't hear you,' or 'I didn't understand you,' 'You're kidding,' 'I can't believe what you just said,' and many other things" (Smith, Goodman, and Meredith 1976, 274).

Juncture is the way the voice is used to make pauses that divide utterances into segments of meaning: words, phrases, and sentences. The division of the stream of speech into meaningful units is crucial to comprehension. The same is true with print in reading: unless the reader is able to perceive words in phrases, comprehension is likely to be severely distorted. In the sentence "He went into the house," the phrase "into the house" is signaled by a pause (imperceptible though it may be) between *went* and *into.* If the juncture point comes within the phrase, there is an unexpected break in the flow of speech that results in confusion. Children exhibit this lack of phrasing when they read word by word as if they are reading a list. They are calling words and little comprehension may result.

***Daniel Hittleman, DEVELOPMENTAL READING: A PSYCHOLINGUISTIC PERSPECTIVE, Chicago: Rand McNally, 1978, p. 27. Used with permission of Houghton Mifflin Company.**

Your Turn 2.3 Communication of meaning in speech.

Observe two people in conversation.

1. What body language is each using to convey meaning?
2. How does the situational context (the environment and their knowledge of the topic of discussion) influence the oral language being used?

Learning to Talk and Learning to Read

There are many similarities in acquiring initial competencies in spoken and written language. Even where differences do occur, both processes contain mutually dependent and highly interrelated elements. Both are best learned naturally, that is, without formal instruction in an environment that is rich in talk and print and that provides for the direct involvement of children in speaking and reading.

Participation in a language-rich environment. Neither talking nor reading can actually be taught. The "rules" by which oral and written language are constructed often defy definition; even if they did not, how could they possibly be explained sufficiently to be intelligible to a child learning language? Consider, for example, "the rule for pronouncing the past tense of regular verbs (as in *laughed, loved,* and *waited*)" (Weaver 1980, 147). Or take the more complicated irregular forms. What is the rule for and how would one explain *go, went,* and *gone*? There is no way to teach these basics of language; children must learn them by their own efforts as they strive to make sense of the language they hear in the everday world. They must try out, test, correct, and test again the language that surrounds them.

Children not only learn speech or verbal competencies by using them in a language-rich environment, but they also acquire the nonverbal code in the same way. In other words, they learn what to say and how to say it. Paul and Happie Byers describe the nonverbal behaviors of a twenty-month-old child who wanted a drink of water from an adult. The child had obviously acquired a lot more nonverbal than verbal skills!

> To get me into communication with him the child stood in front of me, looked at my face, and vocalized loudly. All three elements were required. If he had not stood in front of me I wouldn't have noticed that he was confronting me, searching my face, and "talking" to me. If he had not looked continuously at my face I would not have known that his "talking" was directed at me. If he had not vocalized loudly, I might have assumed that he was merely staring at a visitor. He had learned, then, to combine three nonlanguage elements: (1) a body orientation in relation to me that was close enough for him to touch me and facing me with his body; (2) a search of my face so that he could "catch my eye"; and (3) vocalization, which was loud before we made eye contact and which dropped the moment we made eye contact (1972, 15).

Participation in a variety of contexts provides children with the opportunity to acquire knowledge of which behaviors are appropriate in certain contexts and which are not allowed. Where they have not yet learned the relation of message to context, amusing and sometimes embarrassing incidents (for adults) can occur:

> A group of children were playing near some adults. There was much whispering and giggling; they were telling each other "dirty" words and knew that such words had to be whispered if adults were near. But among them was a younger child, who learned

> one of the new "dirty" words and went to his parents and whispered the word to them. The older children had learned that dirty words had to be whispered *in the presence of adults,* i.e., in a certain context. But the younger child had not yet learned that the whispering was related to the context, and assumed that certain words were simply "whisper words" (Byers and Byers 1972, 18).

Children learn both verbal and nonverbal aspects of communication according to the social context of which they are a part. Communication is clear so long as the verbal message and the nonverbal message are understood by both speaker and listener. But nonverbal behaviors can differ from group to group. When they do, as in the following example, and when participants use similar oral language but operate from different nonverbal codes, communication is not effective. The scene involves a white teacher working with a white child and a black child in the classroom. There is a marked pattern of contrasts in the behaviors between white teacher/white child and white teacher/black child.

The white child comes from a background similar to that of the teacher; consequently, both share a common code of nonverbal behaviors which signal meaning. They know what to expect from each other, and communication is enhanced. The white child waits for pauses to initiate conversation with the teacher; she "catches the eye" of the teacher to get attention; there is little "search" or trial-and-error behavior. Physical contact from the teacher is readily and comfortably accepted.

The behaviors exhibited by the black child and white teacher are in sharp contrast to the smooth, easygoing, predictable exchanges just described; they resemble more a kind of approach-avoidance dance between the two. Both move toward physical contact numerous times but achieve it only fleetingly in the form of a light touch from the teacher followed by withdrawal by the black child. The child glances repeatedly at the teacher in a kind of searching behavior but never catches the appropriate pauses in which conversation could be initiated; when she does catch the eye of the teacher, she characteristically diverts her gaze. Neither teacher nor child quite seems to know how to get things going; neither knows quite what to expect of the other; communication is unsatisfactory (Byers and Byers 1972, 23–25).

Just as children learn verbal and nonverbal communication skills by being immersed in oral language, they learn to read by being immersed in speech and print and by having the opportunity to *use* both. This point has already been made in chapter 1. Suffice it to say here that children should be encouraged to read the signs, labels, and other forms of print that surround them in the everyday environment, and they should be read to and with—from an early age.

Acquisition of deep structure and surface structure. In speech deep structure, or meaning, precedes surface structure or actual production of sufficient words to express the meaning intended. In other words, children have a lot more meanings in their cognitive stores than they have words for expressing those meanings. They resort to pointing, voice emphasis, and other nonverbal behaviors to fill in what they cannot verbalize.

> So it is with the natural acquisition of reading. When they first depart from familiar, memorized texts, children are better able to get the meaning than to reproduce the author's exact words. Just as children's utterances become increasingly closer to adult models, their rendition of a written text will become increasingly closer to the surface structure of the text . . . (Weaver, 1980, p. 149).

Changing pattern of errors. In learning to talk, children's errors can indicate progress. The tendency of children to overgeneralize rules in oral language is well known. They often use *-ed* endings to form past tense for both regular and irregular verbs. The result is expressions like "wented," "tooked," and "breaked." Such overextensions are a clear indication that they are indeed learning the rule for forming regular forms of past tense.

When learning to read, children exhibit a similar pattern of errors. At first they reproduce the sense of the story without a close correspondence to what is actually printed: they reproduce the deep structure, not necessarily the surface structure. In repeated readings, they produce successively more accurate renditions of the print or surface structure.

Top-down progression of language learning. Learning spoken language and reading proceed from wholes to parts rather than from parts to wholes. Children do not first learn to speak isolated sounds, then blend them into words, and finally combine words to form sentences. As has already been presented earlier, children acquire whole words or several words that they use to stand for complete messages. (See holophrastic speech, p. 25.) They *begin* with meaning. They do the same in learning to read naturally. They begin with meaning that is found only in the whole of language, and then they move to parts. In studies of miscues, Yetta and Kenneth Goodman concluded that "a story is easier to read than a page, a page easier than a paragraph, a paragraph easier than a sentence, a sentence easier than a word, a word easier than a letter" (1981, 438).

Comprehension via prediction (Smith 1978). Prediction is the key to comprehension of both spoken and written language. When we speak or read, we bring all that we know, all the meanings we have derived from past experiences, to bear on the task. The more familiar we are with a given situation or a given text, the more likely we are to anticipate or predict correctly what will transpire. Children who learn to read their own utterances or who have learned the story sense from repeated hearings of a given story are able to get the meaning (comprehend) far more quickly and easily because they know what is coming, or what to expect.

In oral exchanges, the situation is similar. The child must anticipate or predict on the basis of the immediate situation around her. If she asks for a drink when someone turns on a hydrant, she expects to get water. She would be surprised to get orange juice because her prediction or expectation is for something else! Likewise, children who are familiar with a story will anticipate word for word what its reading will produce. They are quick to correct when the reader changes a word or skips a page. So, in speaking and in reading, children predict on the basis of what they already know. If predictions are accurate, uncertainty has been resolved—and understanding has been achieved.

Motivation in language learning. Frank Smith writes that "children do not learn to read in order to make sense of print. They strive to make sense of print and as a consequence learn to read."

> This order of events is identical with the way in which spoken language is learned. Children do not learn to talk in order to "communicate" and to make sense of the

> language they hear. As they try to make sense of the language they hear spoken around them, they learn to understand speech and to use it for communication (1979, 132–33).*

We have described at length some basic parallels between learning to talk and learning to read. There *are* some differences in the nature of the two forms. These differences necessitate adaptations for learning to read more effectively.

Pairings of language units with meanings. In discussing the differences between learning to talk and learning to read, Courtney Cazden observes the following:

> In oral language the child has to learn relationships between meanings and sounds. The raw material for the child's learning processes consists of a rich set of pairings of meanings and sound—for that is what language in the context of ongoing experience is. In reading the child must learn relationships between oral language—which he now knows—and letters of the alphabet. But a rich set of pairings of oral and written language is much less available. It is available when the child is read to while sitting on an adult's lap (not when read to as part of a group in school); it is available when the bouncing ball accompanies TV commercials; it is available whenever the child points to any writing and asks "What's that say?" and it is available whenever the child himself tries to write. Provision of a rich set of sound-word pairings can be built into deliberately planned environments—in the classroom or on TV. But the necessary pairings don't just happen for written language at school as they do for oral language at home (1972, 140–41).

Graphic representation of nonverbal cues in print. The importance of body language and intonation in conveying meaning beyond that carried by words has already been described. Written language does not have the advantage of a nonverbal element for conveying meaning. Instead, the reader must rely on graphic representations for these nonverbal features: punctuation, paragraph indentation, italics, and underlining. These aids help, but they are poor substitutes, at best, when compared with the richness of meaning carried in the nonverbal context of spoken language.

This difference between spoken and written language strongly indicates that children need to be made aware of these graphic devices and the way in which they affect meaning in print. A considerable amount of this awareness can be developed by listening to stories when the voice reflects, among other things, the pauses for commas and lowering of pitch for periods (Durkin 1981, 31).

Basic Insights about Reading

Three basic insights must be built as the child deals with print.

Children must be able to distinguish words (Smith 1979, 129). They must recognize the differences in patterns of print by which words are formed, and they must realize that these differences are significant to meaning. Words, letters, and sentences do not exist in spoken language: they are features of *written* language. As such, they will be new ideas to children who have not learned them in the everyday environment through exposure to print and responses from parents that point out "That word says 'refrigerator.' "

*Reprinted by permission of the publisher from Frank Smith, *Reading Without Nonsense* (New York, Teachers College Press, © 1984 by Teachers College, Columbia University. All rights reserved.) pp. 132–133.

Children must be able to see that word units are composed of smaller units—letters—and that these are related to spoken language (Smith 1979, 130). Letters exist only in print, but the child must learn to recognize that these elements have a direct correspondence (imperfect though it is in English) to a feature in spoken language—phonemes, or sounds. Words can be *said:* "horse" not only *means* "horse"—it also has a spoken counterpart "horse."

Children must understand "that the printed words in a book are language, that they can be interpreted in terms of a story or useful information" (Smith 1979, 131). When a child hears an adult read a book, the child does not necessarily make the connection that the reader is getting the words from the print on the page. Teale (1978, 927) cites a reference from Jean-Paul Sartre's *Words,* in which Sartre describes his puzzlement as his mother first read a story rather than telling it as she always had before.

> I grew bewildered; who was talking? about what? to whom? My mother had disappeared: not a smile or trace of complicity. I was in exile. And then I did not recognize the language. Where did she get her confidence? After a moment, I realized: it was the book that was talking (1964, 33).

Summary

There are similarities and differences between oral and written language and the way in which each is learned. Both are parts of a larger picture—human communication.

Reading can be a natural extension of oral language because the child comes to print knowing much about his language, which has been derived from a spoken context. Learning to read becomes a tapping into, a building on, those skills and competencies. In this way, the child can and does become literate as naturally as she has become proficient in speech.

References

Brown, Roger. *A First Language: The Early Stages.* Cambridge, Mass.: Harvard University Press, 1973.

Brown, Roger, and Bellugi, Ursula. "Three Processes in the Child's Acquisition of Syntax." *Harvard Educational Review* 34 (1964).

Byers, Paul, and Byers, Happie. "Nonverbal Communication and the Education of Children." In *Functions of Language in the Classroom,* edited by Courtney B. Cazden, Vera P. John, and Dell Hymes. New York: Columbia University, Teachers College Press, 1972.

Carson, Rachel. *The Sense of Wonder.* New York: Harper and Row, 1956.

Cazden, Courtney. *Child Language and Education.* New York: Holt, Rinehart and Winston, 1972.

Chomsky, Noam. *Aspects of the Theory of Syntax.* Cambridge, Mass.: The MIT Press, 1965.

———. *Language and Mind.* New York: Harcourt Brace Jovanovich, 1968.

———. *Reflections in Language.* New York: Random House, 1975.

Durkin, Dolores. "What Is the Value of the New Interest in Reading Comprehension?" *Language Arts* 58 (January 1981): 23–43.

Goodman, Mary Ellen. *The Culture of Childhood: Child's Eye Views of Society and Culture.* New York: Columbia University, Teachers College Press, 1976.

Goodman, Yetta, and Goodman, Kenneth. "Twenty Questions About Teaching Language." *Educational Leadership* Vol. 38 (March 1981): 437–42.

Hittleman, Daniel R. *Developmental Reading, K–8 Teaching from a Psycholinguistic Perspective.* 2d ed. Boston: Houghton Mifflin, 1983.

Hodges, Richard E., and Rudorf, E. Hugh. *Language and Learning to Read, What Teachers Should Know about Language.* Boston: Houghton Mifflin, 1972.

Klein, Marvin L. "Key Generalizations About Language and Children." *Educational Leadership* Vol. 38 (March 1981): 446–48.

Malstrom, Jean. *Understanding Language: A Primer for Language Arts Teachers.* New York: St. Martin's Press, 1977.

Martin, Bill, Jr. *Strategies for Language Learning.* Tulsa, Okla.: Educational Progress, 1980.

McNeill, David. "Developmental Psycholinguistics." In *The Genesis of Language,* edited Frank Smith and George A. Miller. Cambridge: The MIT Press, 1966.

Menyuk, Paula. *The Acquisition and Development of Language.* Englewood Cliffs, N.J.: Prentice Hall, 1971.

Miller, George A. "Some Preliminaries to Psycholinguistics." *American Psychologist* 20 (1965): 15–20.

Satre, Jean-Paul. *Words.* London: Hamish Hamilton, 1964.

Slobin, Dan I. "Grammatical Transformations and Sentence Comprehension in Childhood and Adulthood." *Journal of Verbal Learning and Verbal Behavior* 5 (1966a): 219–27.

———. "Comments on Developmental Psycholinguistics." In *The Genesis of Language,* edited by Frank Smith and George A. Miller. Cambridge: The MIT Press, 1966b.

Smith, E. Brooks; Goodman, Kenneth S.; and Meredith, Robert. *Language and Thinking in School.* 2d ed. New York: Holt, Rinehart and Winston, 1976.

Smith, Frank. "The Learner and His Language." In *Language and Learning to Read,* edited by Richard Hodges and Hugh E. Rudorf. Boston: Houghton Mifflin, 1972.

———. *Understanding Reading: A Psycholinguistic Analysis of Reading.* 2d ed. New York: Holt, Rinehart and Winston, 1978.

———. *Reading Without Nonsense.* New York: Columbia University, Teachers College Press, 1979.

Taylor, Nancy E., and Vawter, Jacquelyn M. "Helping Children Discover the Functions of Written Language." *Language Arts* 55 (November/December 1978): 941–45.

Teale, William H. "Positive Environments for Learning to Read: What Studies of Early Readers Tell Us." *Language Arts* 55 (November/December 1978): 922–32.

Weaver, Constance. *Psycholinguistics and Reading from Process to Practice.* Cambridge, Mass.: Winthrop Publishers, 1980.

Weir, Ruth. *Language in the Crib.* The Hague: Mouton, 1962.

White, Burton L. *The First Three Years of Life.* New York: Avon Books, 1978.

White, Robert. "Motivation Reconsidered: The Concept of Competence." *Psychological Review* Vol. 66 (1959): 297–333.

3

The Nature of Children

Outline

Guide Questions

1. Can you explain the phrase "knowing before language"?
2. Can you describe Piaget's model of learning as it relates to the young child?
3. Can you explain how cognitive categories, or stores of personal meanings, are formed and why they are considered hierarchical in nature?
4. Can you compare the sensory-motor stage of intellectual development with that of the preoperational stage?
5. How does the young child's concept of self change over time and what are the factors associated with this change?
6. In what way are the Little Prince's drawings and the Chocolate Child in this chapter examples of egocentrism?

Terminology

curiosity	categories
cognitive development	concepts
cognitive structures	distinctive features
sensory motor	perception
sensory-motor schemata	affective development
object permanence	preoperational stage
"theory of the world"	reverse thinking
adaptation	spatial egocentrism
assimilation	egocentrism
accommodation	concrete operations
	formal operations

Scotty, age three-and-one-half years, lay on his stomach in the grass, his chin resting on his hands. His eyes were almost level with the sidewalk, which ran the length of the front lawn. He was intently watching the progress of an inchworm (also called a measuring worm) as it made its way along the cement. Occasionally, Scotty lifted himself on all fours and scooted down the lawn to keep the worm in view. Once, he placed a finger in the path of the worm and watched as it continued up, across, and down the "obstacle" to resume its journey on the other side. After the passage, he examined his finger minutely on all sides. Another time, he broke a blade of grass and placed it in the path of the traveler. When the worm had both ends on the grass, Scotty carefully lifted it about two inches off the ground and watched closely as the worm "measured" around on the leaf to find a way to resume his trip. After a few moments, he returned the leaf to the sidewalk, and the inchworm continued on its way. The whole worm-watching episode took the better part of an hour! Then Scotty went to report to his mother.

He described with great animation and many gestures how the worm "mashed hisself together" and then "stretched out a long way like this," and he demonstrated by spreading his arms as far apart as he could reach. "He didn't have any feet to walk, and I gave him a bridge," he continued, demonstrating with his finger, "and he walked right there! But he was afraid to jump out of the 'chute, so I put him back down!" he finished with delight.

Bobbie was four when she first tried to help a bug. She and her brother, Jay, who was five, spent a lot of time playing "cars" in a sandy lane in front of the house. One day as they played, a large green bug came pushing a marble-sized ball of damp manure along with its back feet. But the terrain was pretty rough with "mountains" and "ditches," which had been constructed as an obstacle course for cars. The bug had a difficult time trying to negotiate the first "mountain." Each time the bug almost got the ball to the top, it would lose control and down the ball would roll to the bottom.

After watching the bug make several unsuccessful attempts to get the ball up and over, Bobbie gently said to the bug, "Here, that's too heavy for you. I'll help you," and she carefully took the ball from the bug and placed it on top of the sand cone. The bug immediately began a frantic search for the missing ball, running about in first one direction and then another. "Here it is right here," Bobbie said, pointing to the ball. But the bug continued to run about. After a few moments, she commented to the bug, "Bug, you are dumb for not letting me help you!" Then she put the ball back beside the bug and removed the "mountain" with her foot. The bug retrieved the manure ball and rolled it into the leaves beside the lane.

These episodes are excellent illustrations of a quality that best describes the nature of young children—*curiosity.* This chapter describes the role that curiosity plays in a child's coming to know and to feel about his world and himself in it. Mary Ellen Goodman writes,

> It is the nature of children to be intensely curious about the world and eager to play a part in it. . . . Curiosity and an appreciation of novelty are powerful factors in connection with attention and learning, and they are in the nature of man from birth (1976, 7, 9).*

Similarly, Burton L. White writes,

> "Nothing is more fundamental to solid educational development than a well-developed sense of curiosity" (1978, 222).

White also felt that

> [curiosity] is the motivational force underlying all learning and development and achievement. . . . [and that] the major requirement is to support and broaden his curiosity. Implicitly, such behavior on your part makes it clear to the child that to be curious, to be learning, to be exploring, is something that you strongly approve of (White, 1978, 118, 177).

Rachel Carson's phrase "the sense of wonder" is also a definition of curiosity with associated overtones of feeling and knowing (1956, 45). Curiosity, then, is an inborn drive, a compulsion to know, to make sense of the world. It is the ignition system for the major activity of the young—exploration. Exploration involves direct experiencing, acting upon the environment. Curiosity raises questions to be answered; exploration and search are the means for finding those answers; learning is the resolution of questions asked, a comprehension of the unknown.

Curiosity has its own dynamics, its own self-contained and internally consistent system for perpetuation and renewal. Initially, the world of the child is all unknowns; therefore, all questions. The questions are not necessarily at a conscious level. For example, in a previous illustration, Scotty did not ask himself, "I wonder what the worm will do if I put my finger in the way." He acted without verbalizing, but the underlying purpose was the same as though he had asked. As the child explores, acts upon, and experiments with the environment, some questions are answered while simultaneously others are raised. Scotty might try a bigger "bridge" next time—a piece of wood instead of a finger. Bobbie might give the manure ball back to the bug and wait longer to see if it would find a way to surmount the sand mountain obstacle. The need to know, to find answers, initiates the whole cycle once again. So long as curiosity flourishes, learning thrives.

But curiosity can be a fragile quality. Even though it is born with the child, White asserts that "it is not at all inevitable that he will have his curiosity deepened and broadened anywhere near as well as he might" (1978, 113). The preservation and development of this most previous gift depend on fertile soil and a favorable climate: adults and others who support, share, and encourage the child's explorations; freedom

*Reprinted by permission of the publisher from Mary Ellen Goodman, *The Culture of Childhood: Child's Eye View of Culture and Society* (New York, Teachers College Press, © 1976 by Teachers College, Columbia University. All rights reserved.) pp. 7, 9.

to make mistakes; tasks that are within the capability of the child; introduction of the novel, or the new, different territory when the old becomes familiar; and contexts made of sense, not nonsense. Under these conditions, curiosity as an innate drive triggers a lifelong pursuit of knowing—making sense of the world.

The remainder of this section is an elaboration on various aspects of cognitive learning: how a child learns, how he structures, organizes, stores, retrieves, and expands his ever-increasing store of knowledge and skills.

Cognitive Development: In Pursuit of Knowing and Making Sense of the World

Frank Smith writes, "It is in the nature of childhood to strive to make sense of the world. . . . Making sense of the world . . . [is a] continual process of relating the unfamiliar to what is already known . . ." (1975, 131, 1). But how does the whole process begin when the infant possesses no "knowns"?

Infancy: Knowing before Language

Learning occurs when new information (unknowns) is assimilated or accommodated into existing cognitive schemata (knowns). Newborns have no store of meanings and no language. They possess neither sensory nor motor skills. In the beginning they cannot focus the eyes on specific objects, and movements are random and uncontrolled. What babies *do* have at birth, however, is an extraordinary potential, an innate capacity for achieving all of the above skills plus innumerable others throughout a lifetime. In this first stage of development, which Jean Piaget has called "sensory-motor" (birth to two years), children build the foundations on which all future intellectual development rests.

Coming to know and knowing in the sensory-motor stage are quite different from later stages when children have developed a cognitive store and can mentally manipulate that store through language. In the beginning, infants learn by acting on the environment. According to Hans G. Furth, they "think" by acting. "The external act does not *represent* knowing but *is* knowing" (1970, 28). "Bottle" and "drinking" are one and the same.

Infants first learn to see or focus on specific objects. They are attracted to the movement of objects rather than the objects themselves. They also learn to direct and control movements: they touch and grasp. They learn to coordinate the sensory (seeing) with the motor (touching or grasping) activities.

Objects do not exist apart from the infant's acting upon them. Most infants less than a year old will not look for an object when they see it put out of sight; out of sight is indeed out of mind. What they cannot see does not exist in the mind of others either. Barbara P. Geismer and Antoinette Suter (1972) believe the poem "Hiding" illustrates this ostrichlike perception.

HIDING

I'm hiding, I'm hiding,
And no one knows where;
For all they can see is my
toes and my hair.

And I just heard my father
Say to my mother—
"But, darling, he must be
Somewhere or other;

Have you looked in the inkwell?"
And mother said, "Where?"
"In the Inkwell?" said father. But
I was not there.

Then "Wait!" cried my mother—
"I think that I see
Him under the carpet." But
it was not me.

"Inside the mirror's
A pretty good place,"
Said father and looked but saw
Only his face.

"We've hunted," sighed mother,
"As hard as we could
and I AM SO AFRAID that we've
Lost him for good."
Then I laughed out aloud
And I wiggled my toes
And father said,—"Look, dear,
I wonder if those

Toes could be Benny's?
There are ten of them, see?"
And they were *so* surprised to find
Out it was me!

—Dorothy Aldis*

At this stage in which attention to things is action bound, infants are highly distractible. They will go through all the bodily motions of getting ready to move toward an object and may even begin the move, but if a ball rolls into view, they immediately turn their attention to the rolling ball and forget about the original object of interest.

Through these early actions, children develop sensory-motor intelligence, a kind of action-knowing that is not to be confused with the intelligence involving thinking and logic, which comes later when children can think about and know without acting out.

The products of action-oriented behaviors are, to use Piaget's phrase, "sensory-motor schemata." They are, in fact, the actions themselves: focusing, reaching, touching, and grasping. These schemata combine to form a more advanced schema, eye-hand coordination, when the infant focuses on and directs his hand toward an object. He

*"Hiding" by Dorothy Aldis reprinted by permission of G. P. Putnam's Sons from ALL TOGETHER by Dorothy Aldis, copyright 1952 by Dorothy Aldis, copyright renewed 1980 by Roy E. Porter.

develops an even higher level schema when he discovers quite by accident in touching that he can *make* something move. He has now derived a means-end schema, which is often repeated.

Children build rapidly on these first sensory-motor schemata to produce increasingly more complex ones. For example, unlike the infant of the first year, eighteen months to two-year olds will search for a toy that is hidden. This signals the development of a schema of *object permanence.* The searching behavior is an indication that children are becoming detached from a dependence on acting in order to know. It marks a transition from knowing-by-acting-upon to knowing-by-thinking-about. Knowing can be represented symbolically. For example, "sensory-motor knowing of sleep . . . is *actual* sleep." But when the child pretends or plays the role of going to sleep, his knowing is beyond the sensory-motor stage—"it is no longer tied to the external action. The child can represent his knowing in symbolic sleep" (Furth 1970, 28).

Children's fascination with movement during the sensory-motor stage provides the roots for development of one schema that is important to all future learning in general and to learning to read in particular. On the basis of movement of objects in the environment, young children begin to form the schema for anticipating or predicting happenings and states in their world. That they are developing this schema is evident in many of their actions. For example, in the act of kicking a piece of paper with a foot, the child simultaneously anticipates movement of the paper. Or in a laboratory situation children's predictive behavior is sometimes shown in terms of anticipated and unanticipated outcomes. An infant is repeatedly shown a small car moving down an incline until it collides with a post and stops abruptly. With each repetition the baby focuses intently on the moving car and laughs aloud each time it bumps into the post. Then the experimenter changes the pattern; the post is removed and the car is allowed to roll to the end of the plane and fall off the table. The unexpected event completely surprises the child; he interrupts a chuckle, wrinkles his brow, and stares with wide eyes.

A few years later when children begin to learn to read, the ability to predict on the basis of past experiences and knowledge of language structure enables the child to make meaning of print.

The intellectual accomplishments of children in the first two years of life are truly monumental, and nearly all are achieved before the emergence of language or receiving formal instruction. Natural learning indeed! Knowing is at first action driven; it is synonymous with doing. Actions themselves are the first schemata on which all other schemata will be fashioned. Gradually, action-knowing gives way to mental operations, thinking about rather than acting out. Children's mode of knowing changes, but their fascination with and curiosity about the new, the unknowns, will, under favorable conditions, continue to spark their continuing drive to make sense of their world.

The model of learning that follows and the description of the way in which it works are largely a composite of concepts from three eminent scholars in the field of child development and cognitive psychology: Frank Smith, Jean Piaget, and Asahel Woodruff. Many of their concepts have great similarity; they are basically distinguished by differences in terminology. Except for Piaget, who was a pioneering giant in child study, these authors have drawn on the ideas and research of theorists dating back to the early part of the present century.

We continue our description of the individual's journey to literacy with the qualifications made earlier in this text: the theory and analysis of what learning is and how it takes place are tentative; we operate from the best information we have at present; we have only begun to learn about learning. As new understandings are gained from continued research, we will alter theory and analysis accordingly.

A Model of Learning and How It Operates

From the rudimentary beginnings of the first year of life just described, children move through successive stages in which the products of learning—the meanings derived from experience with the environment—accumulate in an ever larger and increasingly more-complex store of knowledge and skills. Smith calls this composite of meanings "a theory of the world in the head" (1975, 1978, 1979). The theory, or the child's idea of what the world means, becomes the basis for what he perceives and how he interprets or makes sense of all incoming information from each encounter with his environment. He continually strives to relate new experience to what he knows already. When a child relates what is new to what he already knows, he comprehends or understands. He has made "sense of the world." When he has comprehended, he has learned. "Anything they cannot relate to what they know already will not make sense. . . ." (Smith 1975, 10).

Two examples of the process of making sense of incoming information by relating it to meanings already held are analyzed below. The episode of Scotty's trying to come to terms with a drinking straw and a mug of root beer (chapter 2) illustrates the confusion that exists until a connection is made with something already meaningful. Scotty needed to connect the label *suck* with a meaning he already had in order to use the straw effectively. But the adult was not able to help him make a connection because Scotty understood neither her demonstration nor the instructions given for sucking the beverage through the straw. Scotty's brother understood the problem intuitively, and he supplied the connection when he made the analogy, "Scotty, you know. Do it like your pacifier!"

A second example is from one author's first experiences with linguistics in a graduate course. She had labored long to make sense of the major concepts without success; then one day while sitting on a stone wall (literally!) during a coffee break, the whole puzzle was solved in a flash. By analogy, she connected the unknown to the known. "Oh, Wow! It's just like the body and its systems, each of which serves a special function, is composed of interrelated subparts, and is interrelated to form a complete whole. Linguistics, too, is composed of the systems of phonology, morphology, syntax, and semantics—each of which can be broken into smaller, interrelated subunits. Each system performs a particular function, and all are interrelated to form the whole—linguistics. It fits! It makes sense!"

Analogy can be an excellent route from the familiar to the unfamiliar, whether it is formed by the striving learner or by one who is attempting to aid him. Much of what teaching is involves supplying analogies to enable the child to bridge from the known to the unknown. Children are often better at "teaching" in this sense than are adults.

Assimilation and accommodation. The terms *assimilation* and *accommodation* are used by Piaget to describe the process by which new information is linked with that which is already known. Dorothy G. Singer and Tracy A. Revenson write:

> According to Piaget, *adaptation* is the most important principle of human functioning. Adaptation is the continuous process of using the environment to learn and learning to adjust to changes in the environment. It is a process of adjustment consisting of two complementary processes, *assimilation* and *accommodation.* Assimilation is the process of taking in new information and fitting it into a preconceived notion about objects or the world (1979, 13).

Assimilation is the means by which the child first tries to understand new experiences, and he tries to fit them into old solutions. Singer and Revenson give a number of examples to illustrate the assimilation process:

1. The child has the "notion of grasping or sucking the breast or bottle; he will do the same with any other object placed before him, such as a rattle or puppet."
2. He has learned that small things can be bent, and he tries to bend cookies and crackers (1979, 15).

When new data do not fit into existing meanings, the old schema (interpretation of experience) must be changed, altered in some way in order for the new information to make sense. This is the process of *accommodation.* "The infant who tries to drink milk from his rattle (assimilation) soon learns that rattles only make noise. The rattle is no longer a substitute for feeding (accommodation)" (Singer and Revenson 1979, 15). By experimenting with crackers, the child discovers that, unlike some other small objects, they do not bend. He must amend his old way of thinking to accommodate the fact that crackers *do not* bend: they break.

Encounters with the world constantly produce new data that must be either assimilated into existing mental structures, or the structures themselves must be changed to accommodate the new information. Assimilation into what is already present necessitates no real adaptation; the absence of a need to adapt leaves the learner in a state of equilibrium. But each time new information does not fit into existing meanings, a state of disequilibrium ensues. The learner strives for resolution of the problem of "nonfit," that is, he strives to restore equilibrium, or compatibility. Thus all learning, by Piaget's definition, can be seen as a process of adaptation.

Features and functions of cognitive structures. The accumulation of meanings that are derived by each individual from direct interaction with the environment and the way these meanings are organized in the mind have been given various labels by writers. Smith (1975) uses *cognitive structure,* and Piaget (1963, 1965, and 1969) uses *schema* (plural is *schemata*) to describe not only the mental store of what is known but also the organization of that content in the mind of the learner. Charles Hacker (1980), Michael Strange (1980), and Dolores Durkin (1981) have reviewed a number of schema models for the purpose of relating schema theory to reading comprehension. (The major findings of these analyses and their implications for learning to read are discussed in chapter 4.) Asahel Woodruff (1961) uses *concepts* to describe the accumulated store of meanings and feelings related to various objects, events, and circumstances encountered in the environment.

To avoid confusion here, concepts are distinguished from categories. Concepts have all the properties of categories *plus* language symbols, or word referents. Categories can exist before a name is attached to them. "Infants distinguish classes of objects from each other long before they have names for them; in fact it is generally necessary to have a cognitive category before a name can be learned" (Smith 1975, 15). This is another way of saying that meaning comes first, or before the label or word is attached. The child first develops a meaning for "snow" *before* the word "snow" is used.

Regardless of the terminology—cognitive structure, schemata, or concepts—all have a number of common features:

1. Categories and/or concepts have a strong influence on the way new experiences are perceived and acted on.
2. Information is systematically organized in the mind; there is no hodge podge of unrelated bits and pieces. The system is composed of categories or groupings of related meanings.
3. There is a system of rules that define criteria or "distinctive features" (Smith 1975, 14) for placing objects, events, and circumstances into given categories.
4. Categories and/or concepts are interrelated in an increasingly complex network as the individual continues to add new data. This network is arranged in a hierarchy of categories or concepts at different levels.
5. All concepts have two highly interrelated components *meaning* and *feeling*.
6. Categories and concepts and the interrelated network of which they are composed are continually changing by the processes of *assimilation* and *accommodation* as additional experiences produce new information.
7. Finally, categories come to have symbolic representations in the form of language. Words come to stand for the accumulated store of meanings and feelings related to given objects, events, and situations in the world. The "category" now becomes a "concept."

An analysis of how these various features of "knowing" function in learning and storing information about the world follows.

Through direct experience with the environment, the child continually receives stimuli through the senses. Smith writes, "The brain takes these raw neural signals, decides how to interpret them and transforms them into sights and sounds and all the other fabric of our conscious experience." This is basically the process of perceiving: "The brain decides what is 'out there' in the world on the basis of the incoming information and prior expectations. . . . [and] our perceptions are colored by what we know, by what we expect to see, or by what we would like to see" (1975, 26, 27, 28). The old story of three different people looking at the same barn, yet each perceiving it differently according to his own background or experience is an illustration: The child thinks, "What a great place to play!" The artist responds, "What a picture its weather-beaten timbers would make! The farmer muses, "It would store a lot of hay for winter feeding!" Figure 3.1 gives a graphic illustration of this point.

Perception requires a category system. "There is no possibility of identifying or categorizing an object unless there is a category to put it in" (Smith 1975, 27). Furthermore, there is no way to determine category placement unless there are criteria or

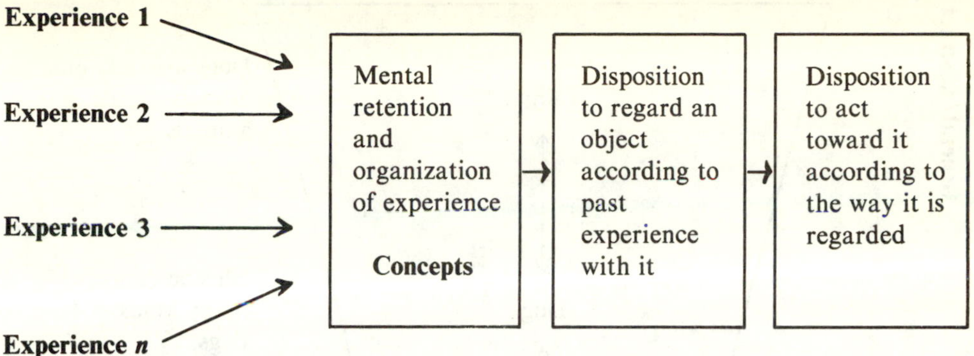

Figure 3.1. How concepts form from experience to become predispositions for future behavior. From BASIC CONCEPTS OF TEACHING by Asahel D. Woodruff. Copyright © 1961 by Harper & Row, Publishers, Inc. Reprinted by permission of Harper & Row, Publishers, Inc. p. 70.

"distinctive features" for allocating the object to a given category. "In order to identify any object, something about it that is distinctive must be discriminated to permit its allocation to a particular category" (Smith 1975, 15) When a child is told the name of an object, *dog,* for example, he is being given the category. Smith sees this as presenting the child with a problem, that of his having to discover the criteria that distinguish the object from all others. Until he does, he will classify all four-legged creatures as *dogs.* We seldom ever try to provide the criteria (explain the difference, for example, between dog and cat) by which objects are differentiated. It is far too difficult, and, as Smith contends, it is totally unnecessary because the child is quite capable of making his own distinctions through repeated attempts at classifying and getting appropriate feedback from others on whether or not he is correct.

But categorizing becomes even more complex from the standpoint of its analysis. (In terms of *learning* to categorize, the child is not aware that the process is difficult. He learns to identify and classify all manner of phenomena with ease in a very natural way from the first few weeks of life.) The same object can be placed into several categories, all of which have their own set of distinctive features.

An important feature characterizes the interrelated meanings in a hierarchical system. The lower the category in the system, the higher the personal meaning associated with it. The converse is, of course, also true: the higher the category, the lower the level of personal meaning attached. The explanation is that only the lowest level concept or meaning is experienced directly. Thus at each higher level, meanings become increasingly more general, more inclusive, and, therefore, more abstract as they become farther and farther removed from one's own direct involvement and personal experiencing. The process is shown in figure 3.2. I can associate Sheeba with a German Shepherd, dog, and animal, but only at the level of "Sheeba" does she have rich personal meaning.

The interrelationships among categories also function to combine lower-level meanings to form broader categories at higher levels. Figures 3.3, 3.4, and 3.5 illustrate this process of combining categories into a hierarchy of meanings.

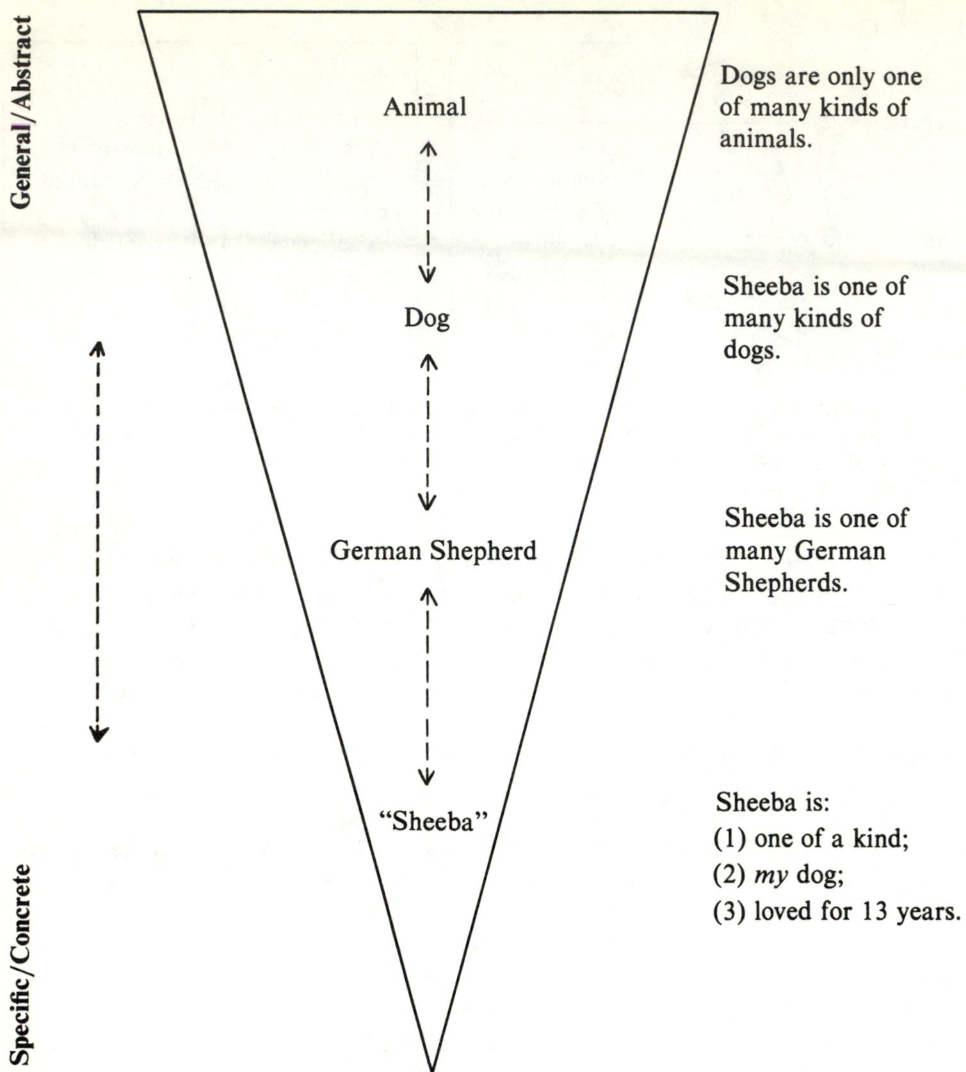
General/Abstract
Animal
Dog
German Shepherd
"Sheeba"
Specific/Concrete
Dogs are only one of many kinds of animals.
Sheeba is one of many kinds of dogs.
Sheeba is one of many German Shepherds.
Sheeba is:
(1) one of a kind;
(2) *my* dog;
(3) loved for 13 years.

Figure 3.2. Levels of personal meaning in a hierarchical system.

Miles V. Zintz and Zelda R. Maggart write,

> Elementary concepts have a three-part structure: differentiation, abstraction, and ordering. Differentiating involves distinguishing apples from oranges, bananas, chicken, rocks, or water, for instance. Abstracting from such elements a concept that some are food and some are not food would be another mental operation. Ordering things that are conceptualized as food into different categories of food, such as fruits, vegetables, and meat, is yet another mental operation. Whether these three operations follow a fixed sequence is not clear, although they are often diagrammed in a hierarchy as here (1984, 311) (see fig. 3.5).

Learning from Experience

The Conceptual Learning
The Symbolic Learning
"That's Rain, Billy."
"It's snowing, son."
"Now the sun is shining, Buster."
"All this is weather my boy."
"It's cold and icy, now."
A Specific Concept of **rain** +
A Specific Concept of **snow** +
A Specific Concept of **sunshine** and **heat** +
A Specific Concept of **ice** and **cold** =
A General Concept of **weather**

Figure 3.3. Specific concepts accumulate to form general concepts. From BASIC CONCEPTS OF TEACHING by Asahel D. Woodruff. Copyright © 1961 by Harper & Row, Publishers, Inc. Reprinted by permission of Harper & Row, Publishers, Inc. p. 73.

Every concept has two basic elements: *meaning* or intellectual core and *feeling* generated by values. Figure 3.6 depicts these two components and their interrelationship. Woodruff expands on this theme as follows:

> Man is a rational being, but he is also an emotional being. He not only thinks, he also feels. . . . Neither feeling nor thinking exists independently of the other. Every experience with the world generates both information and feeling because the individual "judges" everything in terms of what it seems to be doing to his self" (1961, 75, 76).

The type of experience one has with elements in the environment produces certain emotional reactions: if the experience is perceived as "good," the individual has a positive feeling and develops a preference or value for that object, event, or circumstance. The reverse is also true: a "bad" experience produces negative feelings and a negative value or nonpreference. These feelings combine with what one knows to determine to a large extent how one will react or behave in future encounters with similar phenomena. In many cases the emotional or feeling component is a stronger determinant

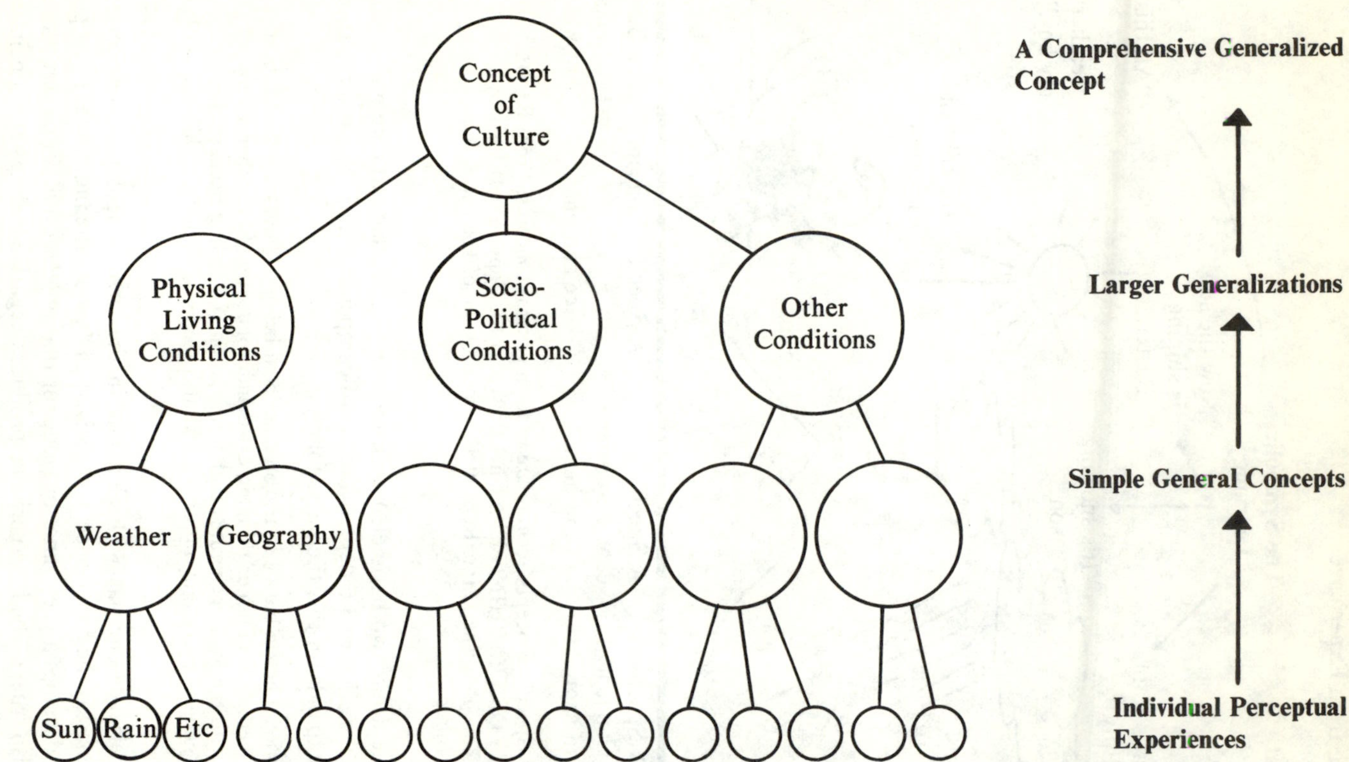

Figure 3.4. How concepts accumulate into wide and deep comprehension. From BASIC CONCEPTS OF TEACHING by Asahel D. Woodruff. Copyright © 1961 by Harper & Row, Publishers, Inc. Reprinted by permission of Harper & Row, Publishers, Inc. p. 74.

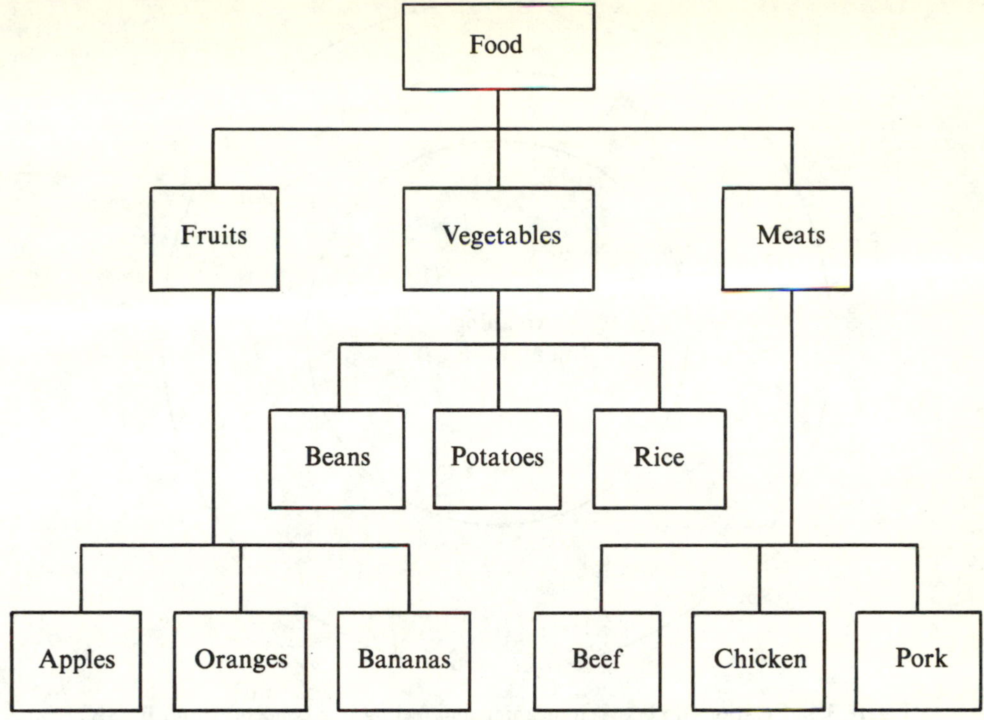

Figure 3.5. Combination of concepts to form increasingly broader categories. Source: Margaret Greer, "The Effects of Studying the Structure of Concepts and Cognitive-Emphasis Social Studies Units on Selected Cognitive Processes of Fifth-Grade Children," Unpublished doctoral dissertation, Graduate School, University of New Mexico, Albuquerque, New Mexico, 1969, p. 70. Copyright 1969 by Margaret Greer.

of behaviors than the rational. Intellectually, a man may know that smoking is detrimental to health, but emotionally, he can manipulate and distort the fact to fit his feelings—his strong desire, his preference for continuing the habit. (The interdependence between knowing and feeling is shown in figure 3.7.)

One's cognitive structure, his mental store of knowledge and feelings about the world is constantly changing. "Minds are not comfortable with passivity; the absence of uncertainty, which demands action, is boring and aversive" (Smith 1975, 37). Because of the innate quality of curiosity, the human has a built-in drive to explore, to come to know the unknown. He is an active seeker of the new, of whatever he does not know. In short, he is a perpetual learner. This is his natural state. This learning leads to an ever-changing, ever-expanding cognitive store. As new experiences bring new information, the new data must be linked with old cognitive structures through the processes of assimilation and accommodation already described. Sometimes new concepts are added. Examples are all the new concepts coming out of modern computer technology: Fortran, Apple II, word processor. Sometimes old categories are expanded

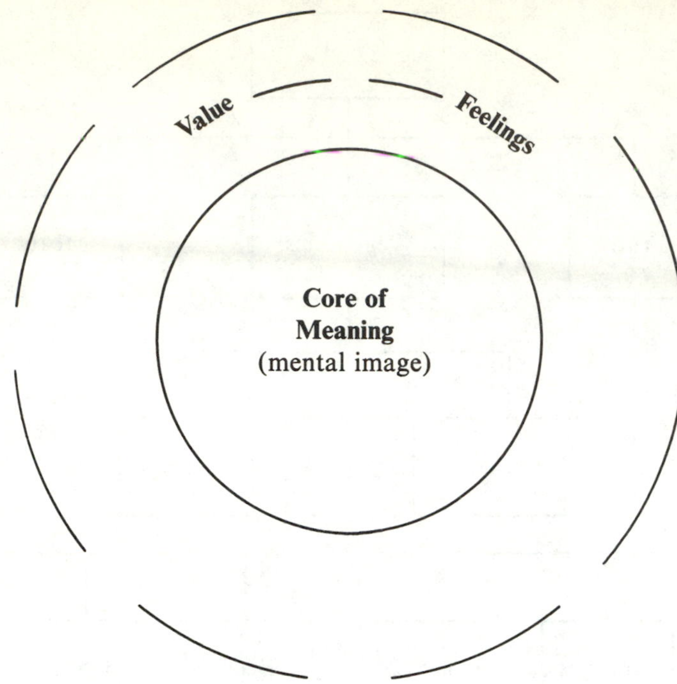

Figure 3.6. Relationship between meaning and feeling in a concept. From BASIC CONCEPTS OF TEACHING by Asahel D. Woodruff. Copyright © 1961 by Harper & Row, Publishers, Inc. Reprinted by permission of Harper & Row, Publishers, Inc. p. 77.

to assimilate new information. Scotty and the drinking straw have already been described. Still at other times, new experiences bring information that require the alteration of the whole network of category interrelationships.

Ryan was faced with this necessity one day as he listened to his mother and an aunt talk about relatives in Texas who were part of the whole extended Smith family. In part of the discussion the two adults made reference to the cousins and their various parents. After awhile, Ryan suddenly asked, "Is Daddy a daddy in Texas?" The question indicated that he needed additional criteria for categorizing kinship relationships and also for relating the various categories that form a kinship network. He was not able to see his father serving in the same role in different places!

A first visit to an urban center in Alaska is often a confrontation with a whole system of stereotyped *mis*conceptions that form the cognitive structure of some individuals. Instead of finding dog teams, igloos, icy trails, and blubber, one, in fact, finds automobiles, paved streets with abundant lighting, homes, and multi-storied office buildings that are carbon copies of those found elsewhere in the United States. Supermarkets carry a full line of nationally distributed products, and a tradition of art and cultural activities—including movies, a symphony orchestra, and nationally recognized repertory theatre and opera—are available.

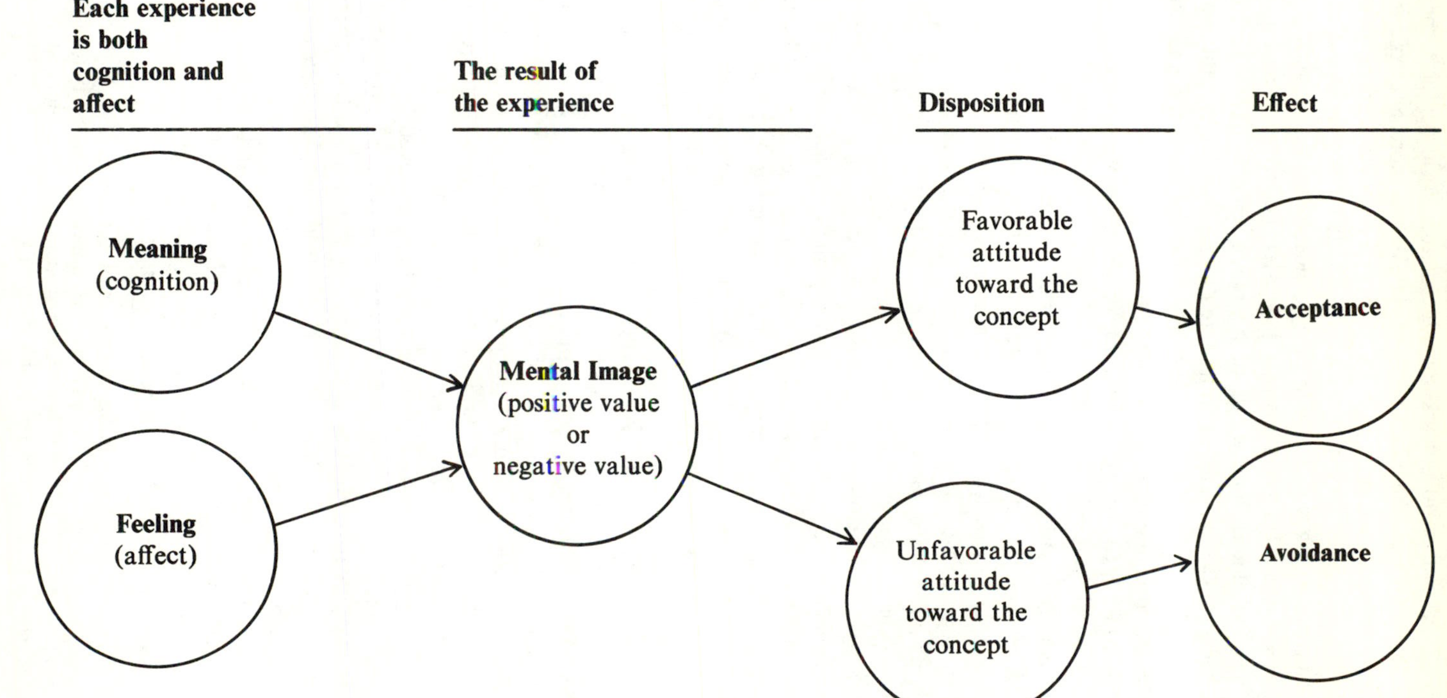

Figure 3.7. Every experience affects attitudes and feelings and predetermines cognitive success. From BASIC CONCEPTS OF TEACHING by Asahel D. Woodruff. Copyright © 1961 by Harper & Row, Publishers, Inc. Reprinted by permission of Harper & Row, Publishers, Inc. p. 79.

Finally, much of the content of one's knowledge of the world comes to be represented in symbolic form through the labels of language. Words represent experiences with the world. This is a momentous development in several respects. It eliminates the necessity to "reinvent the wheel." One can use *rain* without having to repeat all the experiences by which its meaning was derived. Many concepts can be related through language labels: *Weather* stands for a composite of lower-level concepts including rain, snow, wind, sunshine, and clouds. The words of language operate like a shorthand system. They can be held in the mind and manipulated mentally. One can think about the meanings without having to act them out, and one can weigh, balance, and predict consequences before action is taken. Through words one can communicate with oneself. Through a common system of word symbols, one can communicate, or share meanings and feelings, with others.

Language and cognitive structures have a number of similarities. Both are systems of interrelated hierarchical meanings. Language units are interrelated by a system of rules, while cognitive structures are formed when units of experience are organized into a hierarchy of categories. A child who calls all four-legged animals *dog* or all men *daddy* has correctly associated a name with a category (in his own mind), but he has not fully differentiated the category.

Interestingly, a paradox always exists between the rich store of meanings built in the process of experiencing the world and the verbal skill of expressing it. The store always exceeds that which can be expressed in words. No matter how well one describes a sunset, there remains forever a large residue of meaning that is inaccessible for sharing except with oneself. Of course, the more articulate one is, the closer the verbal message resembles the private store of meanings. Yet, the result remains the same as when one attempts to exhale the last breath of air from the lungs. It cannot be done: something remains. This residue represents the feeling side of being and will be described more fully in the second major section of this chapter.

There is a special benefit in having both a public store (language) and a private store (feeling) of meanings. With the former one can communicate with others. With the latter, the private store of feelings, one cannot only communicate with himself in a far richer way than he can with others, but he can safeguard his own uniqueness as an individual. One can operate in a very free and creative way when unencumbered by the necessity to find words. Einstein is said to have been annoyed by constant requests to explain (verbalize) his thinking. His contention was that he operated best and gave birth to his most creative ideas by first operating in his subverbal sphere, his *preconscious domain* as Lawrence S. Kubie (1961) phrased it in *The Neurotic Distortion of the Creative Process.*

Verbal skills should never be taken as the full measure of understanding. Children in the age group (birth through eight years) about which we write are a particular case in point. They do differ from adults in their thinking and in their use of language. This produces what Goodman calls the *underestimation fallacy.*

> The problem is the inability of many adults to appreciate the extent of a child's perceptions, his ability to understand interpersonal relations, and his ability to cope with frustrations, tensions, and troubles. It is true that his perceptions, understandings, and his abilitiy to handle his emotions and problems are likely to differ both

Your Turn 3.1 Schemata as categories of interrelated meanings.

Select a word (person, place, thing, or quality).

1. Jot down rapidly all the words you associate with the word you selected.
2. Compare your list with someone else's in the class. Why do the lists differ?
3. Arrange your list in a category system of simple-to-more-abstract items. Draw lines to show relationships among the parts.

> qualitatively and quantitively from those of the adult. The child's lesser ability to verbalize will of itself reduce the fullness and clarity of his communications, if not of his conceptualizations. But the differences are of degree, not kind (1976, 3).*

One of Smith's major points in three books (1975, 1978, 1979) reflects another kind of "underestimation fallacy" that concerns the ability of children to handle most of their own learning. "Only a small part of what we know is actually *taught* to us. Teachers and adults are given all together too much credit for what we learn as children" (1978, 86). Children must handle most of their own learning because it is *not possible* to teach them much of what they must learn. Smith graphically illustrates this point in his discussion about how a child goes about learning to distinguish between objects in the environment, in this case, *cats* and *dogs*.

> Consider for example what it is that we know that enables us to tell the difference between cats and dogs. What were we taught that has given us this skill? It is impossible to say. Just try to write a description of cats and dogs that would enable a being from outer space—or even a child who has never seen cats and dogs before—to tell the difference. Anything you might want to say about some dogs, that they have long tails or pointed ears or furry coats, will apply to some cats and not to other dogs. The fact is that the difference between cats and dogs is implicit in our heads, knowledge that cannot be put into words. Nor can we communicate this knowledge by pointing to a particular part of cats and dogs and saying, "That is where the difference lies."
>
> Differences obviously exist between cats and dogs, but you cannot find and do not need language to distinguish them. Children without language can tell the difference between cats and dogs. Cats and dogs can tell the difference between cats and dogs. But if we cannot say what this difference is, how can we teach it to children? What we do, of course, is point out to children examples of the two kinds of animal. We say, "That is a cat" or "There goes a dog." But pointing out examples does not teach children anything; it merely confronts them with the problem. In effect, we say "There is something I call a cat. Now you find out why." The teacher poses the problem and leaves the child to discover the solution (1978, 86–87).†

Stages in the Intellectual Development of the Child

Antoine de Saint-Exupery ponders about some questions in his classic, *The Little Prince.*

> And after some work with a colored pencil I succeeded in making my first drawing. My Drawing Number One. It looked like this:
>
> 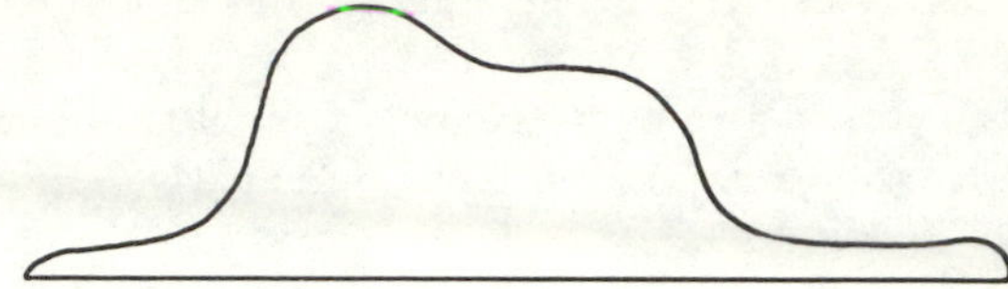
>
> I showed my masterpiece to the grown-ups, and asked them whether the drawing frightened them.
>
> But they answered: "Frighten? Why should any one be frightened by a hat?"
>
> My drawing was not a picture of a hat. It was a picture of a boa constrictor digesting an elephant. But since the grown-ups were not able to understand it, I made another drawing: I drew the inside of the boa constrictor, so that the grown-ups could see it clearly. They always need to have things explained. My Drawing Number Two looked like this:
>
> 
>
> The grown-ups' response, this time, was to advise me to lay aside my drawings of boa constrictors, whether from the inside or the outside, and devote myself instead to geography, history, arithmetic and grammar. That is why, at the age of six, I gave up what might have been a magnificent career as a painter. I had been disheartened by the failure of my Drawing Number One and my Drawing Number Two. Grown-ups never understand anything by themselves, and it is tiresome for children to be always and forever explaining things to them (1971, 3–4).*

Children differ from adults in the way they "make sense of the world"—how they perceive and think about it. The late Swiss psychologist Jean Piaget studied the intellectual development of children for many years. His findings have been the best single source for gaining invaluable insights into the development and workings of a child's mind. He analyzed children's reasoning as a key to how they learn. His conclusions were that all children pass through four distinct stages of intellectual growth. The first two stages are relevant to children in the birth-through-eight-years range, which this text encompasses. Some of the major characteristics of children's perceptions and mental operations during these two stages are described below. (Much of how an infant perceives and acts on the world has been described in an earlier section of this chapter. Only a brief overview of the sensory-motor stage is given here.)

Sensory-motor development. In the first two years of life infants are primarily physical beings, acting rather than thinking. Their movements are random—without deliberate intent. They kick and flail legs and arms and grasp in reflexive action. Infants at first are not aware that hands are an extension of themselves. Gradually, during this period, they gain control over movements and can then direct them intentionally toward some end. They can reach for objects. They can begin to form mental images of objects because they come to have permanence; even when the object cannot be seen, it still exists for the child. There is increased exploratory-experimental behavior: babies find they can drop things and will practice the behavior until there is nothing more to drop. Near the end of the sensory-motor stage, children develop a considerable mental store of meanings from physically acting on the world; this mental store becomes the basis for transition to thought. They begin to think before acting, although they may still act out thinking before trying a solution to a problem. Piaget's observations of his young daughter illustrate this transition behavior.

> When Piaget gave Lucienne a box with a chain tucked inside it, she attempted to retrieve it but was not successful because the opening was too small for her hand to fit inside. Lucienne opened and closed her mouth in an attempt to signify that the box needed a wider opening. Piaget calls this opening of the mouth a motor indicator or symbol that stands for the box and its opening. This imitation of the box by Lucienne helped her to formulate a plan. Indeed, she then put her finger in the box, enlarged the slit and retrieved the chain. Imitation in the form of a motor signifier marks the way for the beginnings of thought, and the movement into the next main developmental stage (Singer and Revenson 1978, 32).

Preoperational development. The skills and abilities and the mental images developed during the first stage are all a prelude to what Piaget phrases the *preoperational stage.* It should be kept in mind, however, that individuals do not totally leave behind all the characteristics of one stage simply because agewise they have advanced to the next. For example, the close relation between physical or motor operations and thought carry through into adulthood for many persons. One of the authors thinks maps are made only for traveling north! In that direction "things" like mountains and valleys are on the "correct" side of the road. They are on the "wrong" side when she travels south. To get landmarks in their proper perspective, she has to turn body and map around to face north.

While most adults may not require this physical aspect of map reading, the residual, the acting-out element from the sensory-motor stage can be seen in the way many adults give directions. Instead of simply saying, "Go straight two blocks, turn right; go one block and take a left," they will turn to face the route being described and act out the directions with hands and body.

Much of the delight (and also the consternation) that adults experience with the *preoperational-stage* child (ages two through seven-to-eight years) results from the sizeable differences in the way each thinks. The drawings of the Little Prince that introduced this subsection are an excellent example. The adult's thinking is logical because he has vast cognitive structure or schemata out of which to make sense. The preoperational child, however, has no such store because his experience is limited; by adult standards his thinking is prelogical. His reasoning is inconsistent: he generalizes without an accurate, underlying, common denominator. One four-legged animal is a *dog* therefore, all four-legged animals are *dogs.*

The following quote is an excellent synopsis of the major characteristics of the preoperational child:

> The preoperational child is completely egocentric. Although he is beginning to take a greater interest in the objects and people around him, he sees them from only one point of view: his own. This stage is the "age of curiosity." Preschoolers are always questioning and investigating new things. Since they know the world only from their limited experience, they make up explanations when they don't have one. Children's beliefs that natural phenomena are man-made and that everything has life are ways in which they create explanations for confusing experiences (Singer and Revenson 1979, 19–20).

It is during the preoperational stage that children's thought differs most from that of adults. The Little Prince explains:

> If I have told you these details about the asteroid and made a note of its number for you, it is on account of grown-ups and their ways. Grown-ups love figures. When you tell them that you have made a new friend, they never ask you any questions about essential matters. They never say to you, "What does his voice sound like? What game does he love best? Does he collect butterflies?" Instead, they demand: "How old is he? How many brothers has he? How much does he weigh? How much money does his father make?" Only from these figures do they think they have learned anything about him (de Saint-Exupery 1943, 16).

The thinking of the child at this stage produces "wrong" answers by adult standards; actually, they are more incomplete than "incorrect." To approach adult answers, the child must learn to make finer distinctions among objects in groups.

Initially the child groups on the basis of broad general criteria before he moves to finer distinctions that are part of the basis of adult logic. This kind of mental economy enables the child to handle a vast array of sensory data without becoming confused. *He makes sense to himself,* if not to adults.

The "incompleteness" of children's thinking results from (1) extreme egocentrism, seeing the world only from his point of view and his inability to understand that anyone else could see it any other way, and (2) his perceptions, which are also quite limited: he is rooted to what he can see in the here and now. He centers or focuses on only one feature or attribute of an object at a time, and he categorizes on this basis. A small child in the neighborhood used to regularly visit one author and ask if her "Daddy" could come out and play. She was focusing on only one characteristic for defining *daddy:* he, like her own father, was the biggest male in the household. So, the author's husband was termed *daddy*!

The above example also illustrates the limitations of preschoolers to understand relationships *among* objects; some objects can belong to more than one category at the same time. A *daddy* can be not only a *husband,* but a *brother,* an *uncle,* and a *cousin!* And a *daddy* can be a *daddy* in more than one place, like Texas and Alaska!

Another example of the distortion that centering produces in part-whole relationships is the following from Piaget:

> He presented children with a box containing twenty wooden beads, most of the beads painted brown and only two beads painted white. When Piaget asked the children if there were more wooden beads or brown beads, the three-to-five-year-olds would always answer that there were more brown ones. They seemed to understand that *all* the beads were wooden, and that *some* were brown and others white, but they still insisted that

> there were more brown beads. They *saw* some brown ones, and didn't consider the fact that a bead could be brown and wooden at the same time. They could not think simultaneously of the whole and its parts, that the class "wooden beads" contained both subclasses "white beads" and "brown beads" (Singer and Revenson 1979, 83).

The preoperational child cannot yet *conserve,* which, according to Piaget, means understanding that objects, states, and quantities remain the same even if there is a change in appearances. In a classic experiment, Piaget shows children two identical glasses of liquid, then he pours the liquid from one glass into a tall, thin one and asks which has more. Preoperational children always replied, "The tall one." The criterion for "more" was "tall." Children also focused on a single feature when identical balls of clay were changed; one was elongated before their eyes, and for the children, it became the bigger. The single distinct feature of "bigger" was "longer."

These examples also demonstrate that preoperational children cannot *reverse* their thinking processes, which is one of the major prerequisites for logical thinking. Had they been able to envision the pouring of the water from the tall glass back into the original glass or the rolling of the elongated ball back into its original shape, they would have been able to see that quantity had not changed; they would have been conserving.

When Ryan asked if his daddy was a "Daddy in Texas," he was exhibiting what Piaget calls *spatial egocentrism.* He could see that his dad was a dad in Alaska; but how could he be the same elsewhere, that is, from another perspective. "Spatial egocentrism is the tendency to view an object from only one perspective—one's own. A child may see his bedroom as neat and clean and cannot understand why his mother has declared it a disaster area" (Singer and Revenson 1979, 87). The same writers describe how Piaget discovered this characteristic of children's thinking when he took his young son for a ride one day. The child was not able to identify a mountain that he knew quite well from his own garden window.

Much has already been written in this text about language. A brief summary of Piaget's ideas on the subject will suffice here. Children's first speech is entirely egocentric, that is, the child communicates with himself, often in language which is unintelligible to others. He first babbles for the sheer satisfaction of hearing sounds. He begins to engage in a lot of monologues. "Whether a child is alone or in the middle of a group of children, he talks to himself, about himself, for himself. He is oblivious to any listeners" (Singer and Revenson 1979, 60).

Toward the end of the preoperational stage, children begin to move into what Piaget calls *socialized speech.* They begin to listen and to respond to others. "The functions of language shift from being a way of giving oneself pleasure to being a way of exchanging ideas or opinions" (Singer and Revenson 1979, 63). The exchanges often take the form of criticism, commands, requests, threats, questions, and answers (1979, 65–66). Thus the child moves from egocentric to socialized speech over a period of years; he moves from thoughts based on self and the concrete to others and the more abstract.

The egocentric nature of children's thought, writes Barry J. Wadsworth, "is gradually broken down during the preoperational period primarily by interaction with peers and other children" (1978, 107).

This is a very cursory description of Piaget's ideas about children's perceptions and thinking during the first seven-to-eight years of life. It should be clear that their

Your Turn 3.2 Reading instruction and the preoperational child.

Given the characteristics of the preoperational child, do the following:

1. List three reading-related activities that would be compatible with these characteristics and three which would not be compatible.
2. Explain your reasoning.

thinking differs widely from that of adults for a number of reasons, most of which are related to their (1) extremely egocentric nature during this period, (2) limited background of experience, and (3) insufficient language facility. In this state their thinking is not so much inaccurate as it is inadequate and incomplete. Accurate thinking and meanings require a larger look, a bigger picture, than that provided by a strictly egocentric orientation. Over time through continued acting upon the environment and by the dual process of assimilation and accommodation, children will indeed develop those abilities and perspectives that will expand their world view. They will learn in the third stage, *concrete operations,* (ages seven-through-eleven years), to conserve, to reverse, and to deal with multiple attributes associated with one object or state. They will be released from dependence on most of the physical aspects of thought—the acting out of ideas. They will still be tied to the concrete, the tangible, however. In the fourth stage, *formal operations* (between ages eleven and sixteen), most children will be released from the concrete. They will be able to think abstractly, to play through the mind the various aspects of a problem, and to hypothesize possible solutions. Language will become an invaluable vehicle in this process. Thinking, therefore, will become more reasoned, more systematic; in short, it will come ever closer to approximating adult standards of logic.

Feeling: The Affective Dimension in Learning

Rachel Carson wrote,

> "I sincerely believe that for the child, and for the parent seeking to guide him, it is not half so important to *know* as to *feel.*"

She continued:

> If facts are the seeds that later produce knowledge and wisdom, then the emotions and the impressions of the senses are the fertile soil in which the seeds must grow. The years of early childhood are the time to prepare the soil. Once the emotions have been aroused—a sense of the beautiful, the excitement of the new and the unknown, a feeling of sympathy, pity, admiration or love—then we wish for knowledge about the object of our emotional response (1956, 45).

We identified curiosity as the major characteristic initiating all learning for the young child, both cognitive and affective. We discussed the nature of cognitive learning in terms of how a child comes to make sense of and to know his world. The affective counterpart of all learning is now developed as a dimension equal in importance to cognitive development. Actually, the two domains are totally inseparable: they occur simultaneously in concert with all experiences, but the magnitude of each is best seen by examining each separately.

The same curiosity that ignites the quest for finding answers about the world produces simultaneously feelings about the experiences of which meanings are made: one both thinks and feels in each encounter with the environment. Consequently, all concepts have both a meaning component and a feeling component.

Egocentrism and the Young Child

Names (title)

Adult (passing a four-year-old in aisle of a supermarket):

"Hi! What's your name?

Child (*with a giggle*): "Don't *you know* my name?!"

Lost

Kindergartner (*on first day at school while standing in doorway of a sixth-grade classroom*): "Hey, teacher! Where do I go now?"

During the first two years of life, the child's total dependence makes him the center of the family universe; otherwise, he would not survive. Much of the activity in the home revolves around satisfying his needs. It is natural as he enters the second stage of development, the preoperational period, that all his perceptions and feelings about his world would be egocentric. The term has already been discussed in the previous section of this chapter. The child perceives and interprets everything in terms of how it appears to him; as far as he is concerned, he continues to be the center of the universe: all events are viewed in terms of how they affect him. As in the case of the chocolate child (Fig. 3.8), the child does appear dirty and messed up to the adult, but the child himself is delighted because he is now all covered with chocolate—something which gives him pleasure. "The subject of all feelings is the self. It is the centerpoint, the determining point in feelings" (Woodruff 1961, 75). Figure 3.8 and the two episodes, "Names" and "Lost," are examples of the foregoing concept.

The feeling process produces not only values and attitudes about things external to the child, but it also generates within him certain values and attitudes about himself. How a child comes to view himself is perhaps the most crucial determinant of what he will become in terms of his own unique potential. We turn now to a review of the developing affective dimension of the young child.

The Developing Affective Dimension of the Young Child

The self. During the first few weeks of life, the infant exhibits few emotions except those connected with physical needs. He cries when he is hungry, wet, or otherwise uncomfortable but his predominant state is sleep. He gets a great deal of satisfaction from rocking or sucking. During the period from six weeks to three months, "The first signs of positive emotional expressions are found with the onset of social smiling." It is possible at this stage that the source of feeling producing the smile may be related more to a state of comfort than to a specific individual. Rage, too, appears not to be directed toward others but to a feeling of physical discomfort (White 1978, 44, 45).

By the fourth or fifth month, the infant becomes a full-blown "smiler." He also begins to laugh. "Along with the emergence of laughter is another particularly interesting social and emotional phenomenon, the tickle response" (White 1978, 65). According to White, this may be a function of the infant's growing social awareness. The

Figure 3.8. Test case: The chocolate child. Source: Burton L. White, *The First Three Years of Life* (New York: Avon Books, 1978), p. 207. Used with permission.

awareness of others in the environment and interactions with them increase at an ever-accelerating rate, not only through the sensory-motor period but also throughout the preoperational phase from two through seven-to-eight years.

It is in the early months of life that groundwork is laid for much of the future affective growth and development of the young child. Responding promptly to a baby's cries leads to a feeling of being loved and cared for. Feeling loved and cared for generates trust and a sense of security. Security is a state of feeling that allows one to risk dealing with the unknowns of the world, that is, to risk *learning*. The young child who feels loved and cared for will be more willing to follow the urgings of his curiosity into unexplored territory. When his ventures succeed, he feels good and will continue to search out and make new meanings for himself. However, if he should fail and encouragement, support, and positive feedback from others in his environment are not forthcoming, he may eventually shy away from venturing forth for fear of failure. In a sense, then, he becomes learning disabled.

The preoperational child continues to be egocentric to a large degree—he continues to interpret events from his point of view and how he judges their effects on him. But at the same time during this period, strong counterforces are at work that slowly erode his egocentric cast, gradually making it possible for him to learn to consider the ideas and feelings of others. He learns to be part of something more encompassing than himself. He becomes part of an ever-larger and larger group of other individuals. Rather than a strictly self-centered being, he develops into a social being.

The self and others. The self and others are inseparable from the beginning of life. Self is largely defined by relations with others. What children come to feel about themselves is largely a product of what they sense others to feel about them. "Against the yardsticks—the standards—provided by others the child learns to measure himself. . . . The people around a child, as they react to him, in effect hold up before him a mirror in which he sees himself" (Goodman 1976, 46).*

The family is a crucial factor in the affective development of the young child. The child's initial encounter with "others" is ordinarily within some type of family unit. At least the mother is usually part of the child's world from birth. The unit often includes the father and other siblings. Even more members are included in units that may consist of part of an extended family. The family, whatever its composition, also tends to have some kind of stability and continuity, at least for the first few years of most children's early childhood. (The rapid rise in the divorce rate over the past decade may imply some qualification of the previous statement, however.)

It is not essential for the child to have affluent surroundings (although severe poverty can be destructive to the full development of much of the child's potential), or an extraordinary amount of parental and/or sibling attention, or highly educated parents, or even a conflict-free environment. Rather, the *quality* of relationships among the family members and the way they respond to the child are the most decisive factors in setting him on the path to a rewarding and satisfying emotional life.

The family is also important because it is part of the child's world during the crucial early years of life when so much of the potential for future development is established. Teachers and parents need to understand the great importance of the first three years of life. The older one gets, the less the flexibility necessary for major changes to occur in any facet of one's personality.

> What it all boils down to is that there *is* capacity for change, including dramatic improvement after the child is three years of age. However, it is often very difficult to bring about desired changes, and more often than not, remediation will not be achieved. We must therefore pay much greater attention to the prevention of difficulties, to the prevention of loss of capacity and potential from birth, rather than continue the way we have been going (White 1978, 258).

As the preoperational child grows, his sense of self and his identification and differentiation of others continues to be shaped by an ever-larger social environment outside the immediate family.

> The culture of early childhood incorporates a system of social categories into which the little child places the others he knows and hears about. It also provides ready-made concepts and attitudes concerning persons who fall into categories such as class, race, sex, kin, and nonkin, occupations, even individual qualities (Goodman 1976, 41).†

*Reprinted by permission of the publisher from Mary Ellen Goodman, *The Culture of Childhood: Child's Eye View of Culture and Society* (New York, Teachers College Press, © 1976 by Teachers College, Columbia University. All rights reserved.) p. 46.

†Reprinted by permission of the publisher from Mary Ellen Goodman, *The Culture of Childhood: Child's Eye View of Culture and Society* (New York, Teachers College Press, © 1976 by Teachers College, Columbia University. All rights reserved.) p. 41.

This sorting and labeling process continues throughout life, but the basic categories and the feelings and attitudes associated with them remain pretty constant for most individuals.

The quality of young children's interpersonal experiences is a powerful determinant of how they come to view themselves and others. Where their record of successes is high, they acquire confidence in their ability to satisfactorily achieve specific ends. Ruth Strickland writes, "Confidence is a memory of past successes" (1951, 441), and Marie Hughes later added, "The confident child can enter all learning activities with eagerness and abandon" (1970, 6). Seeing oneself as competent increases the likelihood of success. Each success leads to a further strengthening of one's concept of self as worthy. The satisfaction generated by success produces a multitude of feelings, all of which enhance the concept of self: pride, delight, worthiness, well-being, security, and belongingness are but a few.

Where children's record of successes has been few, and where they have not been given positive support for their efforts, the opposite can be true. Some will have little confidence in their ability to achieve: their self-image will be negative, and they will see themselves as incompetent, inconsequential, and ineffective. Feelings of fear, apprehension, longing, despair, and, sometimes, rage may develop. Their existence can become a vicious circle in which lack of belief in their own competence is reflected in vain attempts to relate to others, to belong, to be recognized, and to be accepted. The harder they try, the more bizarre behaviors may become; the more bizarre the behaviors, the greater the degree of rejection. In the extreme, they become isolates, forever circling the social melieu in the attempt to find an opening.

Theirs is "a slow dance on the killing ground." They may continue to try to fit in, eventually achieving some degree of success, or they may cease efforts and withdraw altogether. In either case their birthright of having the opportunity to become a fully functioning individual has been subverted.

In her studies of cross-cultural patterns of childhood, Mary Ellen Goodman (1976) found only two "universals" of childhood—*affection* and *guidance*. The importance of affection in shaping the self-image and the nature of interrelations with people in the environment has been noted. The need for *guidance* is a universal need equal to that of affection. Because of the strong egocentric nature of young children, they must gradually learn that each is one of many and that others have feelings and needs just as they do. They must develop an awareness of the feelings of others and be able to empathize or feel with them. All this is accomplished best with parental guidance that is provided consistently and opportunely along the way. Failure to receive this assistance can lead to inhibited social growth and development, which increases the likelihood of poor interpersonal relations.

> Disorder and callous indifference to the rights and feelings of others become inevitable when little children are held to be incapable of "understanding" the needs of other people and of respecting those needs. If they are not held accountable from infancy, for the effects of their acts on others, then willful and egocentric children will become lawless and callous adults (Goodman 1976, 160).*

*Reprinted by permission of the publisher from Mary Ellen Goodman, *The Culture of Childhood: Child's Eye View of Culture and Society* (New York, Teachers College Press, © 1976 by Teachers College, Columbia University. All rights reserved.) p. 160.

The expanding world of the child leads to an ever increasing awareness of others.

Confusion of affection with guidance can distract parents from fulfilling their guidance responsibilities. Some parents consider guidance to be the antithesis of affection. But the two are not opposite; indeed, guidancc is a higher state of affection because its application is more difficult when a child is testing boundaries than is affection expressed spontaneously when a child is complying with acceptable behavior. There is a fear that setting limits and establishing clear expectations about their child's behavior will lead to rejection by the child. The setting of boundaries does often lead to the child's testing of those boundaries, but it does not lead to a rejection of those who set them. The task of parents is to provide feedback to the child on the "tests" he conducts. He will probe until such is forthcoming; if no feedback results, he will likely feel uncertain and confused. Confusion accumulated over time can lead to undesirable behavior patterns, sometimes extreme examples. A tyrant is no less intolerable because he comes clothed in rompers cuddling a teddy bear! The preoperational child is by no means "home free" in becoming a sensitive, caring member of society, but with appropriate guidance couched in affection, he can make long strides toward becoming more without making others less.

And so, from birth through seven-to-eight years is a crucial period in the affective development of young children. They begin the journey to full selfhood with a narrow, egocentric orientation within the family nucleus. From there they move into an ever-larger world of many "others." They begin to define themselves in terms of their relations with others, first within the family and then within the larger social context. They come to feel not only about themselves but, with increasing sensitivity, about others, also. Parental affection and guidance provide indispensable assistance along the way.

Summary

Innately endowed with curiosity, young children are natural learners. Questioning and exploring form their most characteristic state. Out of their endless quest, they come to know and to feel about every facet of their world. In this chapter we have examined all three dimensions of young children's learning: curiosity, cognition (knowing), and affect (feeling). In the remaining chapters of this text, we will show how these dimensions relate directly to learning to make sense of the world of print.

References

Carson, Rachel. *The Sense of Wonder.* New York: Harper and Row, Publishers, 1956.

de Saint-Exupery, Antoine. *The Little Prince.* New York: Harcourt Brace Jovanovich, 1971.

DeStefano, Johanna S. "Research Update: Demonstrations, Engagement and Sensitivity: A Revised Approach to Language Learning—Frank Smith." *Language Arts* 58 (January 1981): 103–12.

Durkin, Dolores. "What Is the Value of the New Interest in Reading Comprehension?" *Language Arts* 58 (January 1981): 23–43.

Furth, Hans G. *Piaget for Teachers.* Englewood Cliffs, N.J.: Prentice-Hall, 1970.

Geismer, Barbara P., and Suter, Antoinette. *Very Young Verses.* Boston: Houghton Mifflin, 1972.

Goodman, Mary Ellen. *The Culture of Childhood: Child's Eye Views of Society and Culture.* New York: Columbia University, Teachers College Press, 1976.

Greer, Margaret. "The Effects of Studying the Structure of Concepts and Cognitive Emphasis Social Studies Units on Selected Cognitive Processes of Fifth-Grade Children." Ed.D. dissertation in Miles V. Zintz and Zelda R. Maggart, *The Reading Process,* 4th ed. Dubuque, Iowa: William C. Brown Company Publishers, 1984.

Hacker, Charles. "From Schema Theory to Classroom Practice." *Language Arts* 57 (November/December 1980): 866–71.

Hughes, Marie M. "Language—Function of Total Life Situation." Mimeographed paper, 1970. Seminar at the University of New Mexico.

Kubie, Lawrence S. *Neurotic Distortion of the Creative Process.* New York: Noonday Press, 1961.

Piaget, Jean. *The Origins of Intelligence in Children.* New York: W. W. Norton and Company, 1963.

———. *The Child's Conception of the World.* Totowa, N.J.: Littlefield, Adams and Company, 1965.

Piaget, Jean, and Inhelder, Barbel. *The Psychology of the Child.* New York: Basic Books, 1969.

Singer, Dorothy G., and Revenson, Tracey A. *A Piaget Primer: How a Child Thinks.* New York: International Universities Press, 1979.

Smith, Frank. *Comprehension and Learning.* New York: Holt, Rinehart and Winston, 1975.

———. *Understanding Reading a Psycholinguistic Analysis of Reading and Learning to Read.* 2d ed. New York: Holt, Rinehart and Winston, 1978.

———. *Reading Without Nonsense.* New York: Columbia University, Teachers College Press, 1979.

Strange, Michael. "Instructional Implications of a Conceptual Theory of Reading Comprehension." *The Reading Teacher* 33 (January 1980): 391–97.

Strickland, Ruth. *The Language Arts in the Elementary School.* Boston: D. C. Heath and Company, 1951.

Wadsworth, Barry J. *Piaget for the Classroom Teacher.* New York: Longman, 1978.

White, Burton L. *The First Three Years of Life.* New York: Avon Books, 1978.

Woodruff, Asahel D. *Basic Concepts of Teaching.* concise ed. San Francisco: Chandler Publishing Company, 1961.

Zintz, Miles V., Maggart, Zelda R. *The Reading Process.* 4th ed. Dubuque, Iowa: William C. Brown Company Publishers 1984.

Part Two

New Directions

Chapter 4, "The Case for Change," identifies specific problem areas in reading instruction and suggests procedures to implement change that will strengthen school reading programs. From previous overemphasis on teaching skills and phonics, we urge more emphasis on setting the purposes for reading and on insuring comprehension of the material read. From previous teacher-controlled skills lessons, we urge a change to arranging an environment in which children will work hard to satisfy their needs to learn to read and to solve problems—with the teacher serving as a facilitator and questioner to keep the process working effectively. From a traditional stance of teachers "making children learn to read," we urge an acceptance of differences and of the realistic need to offer beginning reading opportunities to children who want to read whether they are now four years old, or six, or eight. Finally, we have made a strong case for putting reading in proper perspective as *one of many* important facets in children's overall growth, development, and learning.

In chapter 5, "The Psycholinguistic Bridge to Reading," we suggest a means for extending oral language to written language, the evolving of literacy in the individual, risk taking as psycholinguistic guessing, and keeping reading a pleasurable experience. Further, the roles of guiding learning, building on children's strengths, and "following the child's lead" are explored.

4

The Case for Change

Outline

The Past Record in Reading: How Successful Have We Been?
- Adult Reading
- Reading Problems
- Corrective and Remedial Programs

Problem Areas and Corrective Measures in the Beginning Reading Program
- Imbalances in the Program
  - Overemphasis on skills and subskills
  - Underemphasis on comprehension
  - Additional components: either missing or underemphasized
- Failure to Begin with Strengths of Young Children and to Build on the Naturalness of Their Learning
- Failure to Delineate the Roles of Teacher and Learner
- Insufficient Schemata and the Use of Basal Readers
  - Insufficient schemata
  - Basal readers
- Worship of the Reading God

Summary

References

Guide Questions

1. Criticisms of past reading instruction are cited throughout this chapter. With which ones have you had personal experience?
2. What were the effects on your learning to read?
3. Why is "prediction" viewed as a major factor in reading comprehension?
4. What is the meaning of Frank Smith's cardinal rule for reading instruction, "Make learning to read easy"? How can this be accomplished?
5. How are schemata related to David P. Pearson and Dale D. Johnson's statement, "Comprehension is building bridges between the new and the known?"
6. According to your own experiences, how do you agree or disagree with the criticisms about basal readers in this chapter?

Terminology

systems approach
phonics
learning disabled
decoding
skills and subskills
comprehension
accountability
strategies
predicting
sampling
confirming
integrating
experience curriculum
schemata
language competence
predictable books
language experience
narrative language
book or story language
expository language
basal readers

No area of the school curriculum from kindergarten through grade twelve receives as much attention as does reading. For generations the public, parents, and educators alike have been concerned with finding ways to help more children become better readers. Enormous sums of money, time, and energy have gone into this enterprise for years. Volumes are written each year reporting the analysis, dissection, and scrutiny of every facet of the subject. Every few years, a new approach, a new program, a new bandwagon is heralded as "The Answer"—finally.

In terms of attention given the subject, we care a great deal about reading. In terms of results—the questions we have asked, and the course we have pursued—we have not cared enough. We have looked for a panacea that would in one stroke solve all our problems; this myopic course has blinded us to the fact that the basic solution lies not in a method, a program, or a gimmick, but rather in *an understanding of the nature of language, the nature of learning and the reading process itself.* In the past few years, a number of educators have made consistent efforts to probe these areas. As a result, what is now known about children and how they learn and expand their language skills, if effectively used, should enable almost all children to achieve literacy.

Kenneth S. Goodman observes:

> Comprehension of connected discourse has finally become the focal concern of those interested in the study of language and thinking. The lonely few who argued so long that reading, language, and cognition must be studied in the context of real people using real language in real situations have been joined by a growing interdisciplinary army. Language and cognition are being put back into the social-cultural context from which they were abstracted (1978a, 919).*

Meanwhile, many of the things we do in the classroom say we do not care. We continue to violate both what we *say* we believe and what we *know.* After many years of observation of elementary schools in action, we can only conclude that the professional educators in decision-making roles are not very serious about any need to teach communication skills to boys and girls.

We continue to operate from "tunnel vision," being more committed to first-grade *material* than to first-grade *children.* Many teachers appear in classrooms with an inflexible mental outline (or one is handed to them in the form of a scope-and-sequence chart) of precisely what should be done to teach reading at each grade level.

Though we espouse "beginning where the child is," in practice we often ignore individual differences. Children from different ethnic backgrounds are given materials

*Source: Kenneth S. Goodman, BREAKTHROUGHS AND LOCK-OUTS, *Language Arts,* 55 (November/December, 1978), p. 919, National Council of Teachers of English, Urbana, Illinois. Used with permission.

to read whose content is totally foreign to anything they know. Children who are already reading are taken through a readiness program, or they are required to complete worksheets on skills that they obviously do not need to be taught because they are already reading with understanding. Reading progress is measured primarily in terms of skills performance rather than in terms of comprehension. The major focus of beginning reading instruction continues to be on the "nonsense" of language—the sounds and letters that in isolation, have no sense. This focus on "pieces" has resulted in making reading difficult; in so doing, it has increased the probability of failure. Many children may have been turned off to reading. (Specific problem areas and some proposed corrective measures will be developed in detail in the third major section of this chapter.)

The Past Record in Reading: How Successful Have We Been?

Adult Reading

The quantity and quality of adult reading can be taken as one measure of the success of past reading instruction. How well do adults read? How much? For what purposes? Virginia Matthews has the following to say:

> It appears that about 25 percent of the adults cannot read at all, or read with barely enough skill (functional literates) to allow them to survive on a painfully deciphered diet of forms to be filled out, street signs, instructions and the like; while another 25 percent of any given population constitutes the core of reasonably regular and "serious" or "quality" readers. This leaves a full 50 percent consigned to an uncertain gray area of occasional, usually job-related readers—those who read when they are required to, and rarely by choice or with any degree of pleasure (1973, 159).

Reading Problems

Reading problems have neither diminished nor have they gone away. They continue to be the subject of heated discussion, both locally and nationally, among parents, political leaders, educational researchers, and grandparents, as well as teachers, principals, and reading specialists. Obviously much dissatisfaction continues to exist about the product. During the late 1960s and the 1970s, we sought answers in more instruction time, more teachers, more teaching materials, more specialists, more methods courses for teachers after school. Publishers have inundated the market with workbooks, programmed lessons, management systems, and expensive gadgetry. But it is clear in 1985 that, up to now, we have not successfully changed the unsuccessful achievement of the "masses" in reading performance.

Corrective and Remedial Programs

Both corrective and remedial programs have continued to proliferate. With a major thrust begun in the 1960s federal funding of numerous "compensatory education" programs was started. Most of these were either directly or indirectly concerned with the development of literacy. They were established and administered by a vast bureaucratic organization of titles and agencies: Title I; Chapter I; Headstart; Follow Through; Public Law 95–142 to name a few. Remedial reading courses became a required part of teacher education programs in universities all over the country. Remedial reading teachers and reading specialists began to appear on the staffs of public schools in increasing numbers. The foregoing picture continues to prevail. Obviously, all is not well in "River City"—at least not in reading.

Problem Areas and Corrective Measures in the Beginning Reading Program

In past and present instructional programs, many factors have blocked children's learning to read naturally and proficiently. When these blocks to successful beginning reading are examined individually, they tend to cluster about a few large categories. These categories and the specific elements of which each is composed are discussed in this section.

Imbalances in the Program

Overemphasis on skills and subskills. Beginning reading is too often taught with a heavy emphasis on teaching *about* reading as the initial step. Whether the term used is *phonics, word recognition,* or *decoding,* the focus is on the "pieces" of language: the emphasis is on visual recognition of individual symbols (letters) or combinations of symbols (parts of words and words). Learning activities are often carried out in isolation from meaningful context. This practice means that comprehension will generally be secondary.

Craig Pearson writes that over the past four decades "reading has been effectively redefined as its components, rather than as the sum of its components" (1980, 26). It has become a "systems approach" in which skills have been segmented, divided, and subdivided into smaller and smaller units. Teaching children has become an oversystematized process of *pretest, teach skills, and retest* on each of the hundreds of skills comprising so-called management systems. This is a long, laborious process that may cause many teachers to have little time in their schedules for anything else. Some children may be left in a position similar to the blind men with the elephant. The parts supply so little information that the whole is never recognized; the whole turns out not to be the sum of its parts but a collection of poorly related or completely unrelated appendages.

Once the systems approach was firmly in place, publishers and some commercially oriented educators saw a golden opportunity to develop a lucrative market; the move was to supply as rapidly as possible all manner of materials for the new technology. Phonics and word-analysis skills fit beautifully into the "programmed" skills development format. Phonemes, syllables, and isolated words can be easily and quickly entered into programmed frames. A massive output of phonics materials has flooded the marketplace. We have phonics materials in the form of kits, packets, learning packages, programs, systems, pictures, filmstrips, games, charts, tapes, and many others.

Rather than making use of all these commercial materials, teachers would do well to consider Dolores Durkin's *Strategies for Identifying Words* (2d ed., 1980) as a source that supplies the information needed to guide children's learning in this area. It is a well written monograph for the classroom teacher to use in developing a balanced word recognition program through use of context, structural analysis, and phonics.

Many authorities in the field of education have pointed out some of the consequences of an overemphasis on skills in reading instruction:

1. Carol Chomsky (1976), Kenneth Goodman (1978b), and Sam Sebesta agree that too many children are excellent "decoders" but do not know what they have decoded. They can call words, but they cannot read.

2. "National Assessment of Educational Progress in reading shows shortcomings in certain aspects of comprehension, not in 'sounding out' " (Sebesta 1981, 547).

3. Subskill mastery has been equated with literacy; it is not (Goodman 1978). The measure of success has become the scores made on skills tests. An illustration of this point is given by A. Sterl Artley:

> Sara, a first grader, brought home a note from her teacher asking the mother to give her daughter assistance with long and short vowel sounds, saying that her daughter's advance to the next level would be postponed until she could pass the skill test on vowel sounds. The surprising thing was that Sara was already reading fluently at home from materials of third grade level. Regardless of this fact, the teacher still insisted that Sara had to "pass the test" (1980, 546).

4. The inability of many children to come to grips with the excessive emphasis on skills and the resulting poor performance on skills tests tends to inflate the number who are labeled "learning disabled." In many schools we see primary children labeled as having various perceptual and other reading problems whose number far exceeds what would be expected in a normal population sample. Rather than a learning problem, the problem for most may be that of not having learned what could come very naturally under a more meaning-oriented system.

5. Where perceptual problems do exist and, therefore, require early and special intervention, the identification and help may not be forthcoming. Under a "pieces" emphasis approach, it is too difficult to determine whether a real learning problem exists or whether it has been created by the instructional system. The two examples below illustrate this point. First (figure 4.1) is the case of Aaron, age six years.

Janet Black writes that this message shows that Aaron has made a beginning toward appropriate writing. She says:

1. He has the idea that letters can be put together to express his thoughts.
2. He can write his thoughts.
3. He has a general idea about the directionality of print.
4. He does not know and/or finds it difficult to demonstrate that there are spaces between words.
5. His spelling consists primarily of inventions (mi-my: snac-snake) with some transitions (si-is) and sight words (he), (and).
6. He has little knowledge of punctuation (1980, 512).

In Aaron's case, it would be quite premature to label him "learning disabled." He likely needs a lot of reading and writing experience whereby he can move toward accepted standards of written language production. He needs time to practice and to develop naturally what he has already begun.

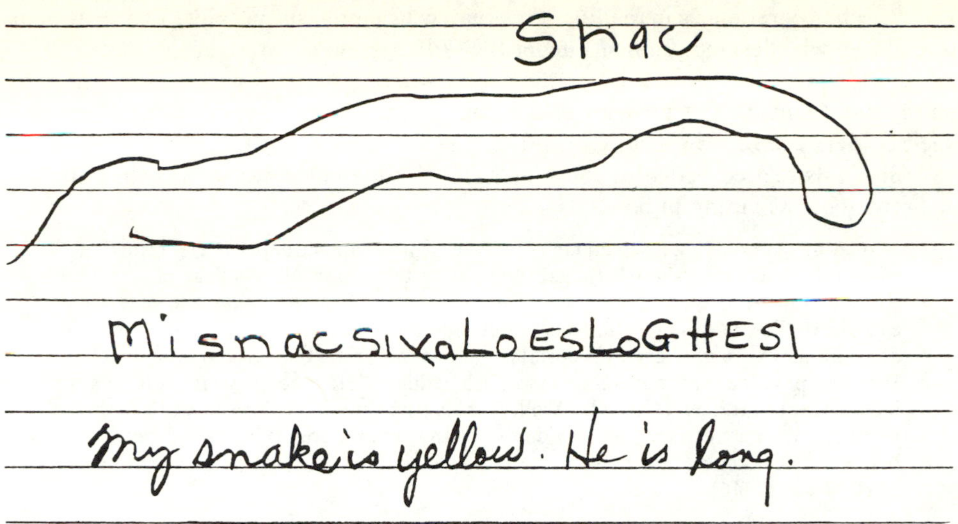

Snac
MisnacSIxaLoESLoGHESI
My snake is yellow. He is long.

Figure 4.1. Aaron's invented spelling. Source: Janet K. Black, THOSE MISTAKES' TELL US A LOT, *Language Arts,* 57 (May 1980) p. 512, National Council of Teachers of English, Urbana, Illinois. Used with permission.

The second example is Freddie, a second grader, who may indeed have a perceptual problem. He made six reversals in second-grade spelling. He wrote:

sgg *for* eggs
dig *for* pig
doy *for* boy
bet *for* pet
nude *for* under
mat *for* am

The teacher wrote on his paper, "You made *too* many mistakes."

Freddie brought the teacher a problem. Not such a big problem if the teacher had been prepared to deal with it. As it turned out, the teacher failed to identify the problem, and Freddie had trouble for a long, long time.

6. Children can develop a distorted idea of what reading actually is in a program where skills are highly overemphasized. Reading comes to mean decoding instead of comprehending. The following example from Artley illustrates this point:

> I asked Jerry, a third grade friend of mine how he liked reading.
>
> "Do you mean school reading or home reading? he replied.
>
> "What is the difference?" I queried.
>
> "School reading—yuk, but the books I read at home are cool. They are about sports and camping and things I like."
>
> But his response about school reading interested me and I probed further.
>
> "Well, you see," Jerry said, "Reading is like math. It's drill and rules and words, and 'purple monsters.' "
>
> "What do you mean—purple monsters?"
>
> "You know, those purple ditto sheets that the teacher hands out each day. School reading just isn't any fun" (1980, 546).

7. The poorer one is in reading, the greater the emphasis on skills. The treatment for children who develop problems under the skills system is "more of the same." Darrell R. Morris writes, "Remedial reading is not seen as an extension or elaboration of the regular language arts program, but rather a type of 'emergency room' where disabled readers can receive a daily injection of skills" (1979, 500).

8. Skills related activities consume so much time in the school day that little, if any, remains for reading in books.

> A reading supervisor expressed concern that, as a group, students in the remedial program appeared to show little gain in reading test scores after a year of intensive training. On being questioned concerning the nature of the program, the supervisor explained. "We use diagnostic tests to determine the skills in which each student is deficient and then we have appropriate practice materials to overcome the deficiencies. We have practice materials of all kinds," she added. "How about your materials for independent reading?" I asked. "Well, frankly, the time is so short to work with each pupil on skill mastery that we just don't get any free reading done. We depend on that being done at home or in the subject areas—social studies, science, and the like" (Artley 1980, 546).

Thus children are deprived of the best means not only for acquiring the skills but also for the opportunity to reinforce them through *practice.* Morris (1979) contends that this system works so that the rich get richer while the poor get poorer. The better the reader, the less time spent in skills work, with a corresponding increase in the time freed for independent reading in books; the poorer the reader, the more time spent in skills activities, which results correspondingly in less time for reading.

9. Children rarely are helped to see why the skills are useful in learning to read. A few years ago, Dolores Durkin visited a number of primary classrooms and then made some value judgments about the phonics instruction she saw. She said there was lots of phonics being taught everywhere she went but that she felt much of it was poorly presented. Then she went on to describe some features of the phonics instruction she had seen. This is what she wrote:

> One flaw becomes apparent just as soon as instruction gets underway . . . only rarely are beginners in phonics given the opportunity to understand *why* it is useful to know the sounds that letters stand for in words. Instead teachers have them puffing and blowing and snorting long before the reason for such behavior ever comes clear to the children, if it ever does. Unfortunately, this failure to demonstrate the usefulness of phonics often persists into advanced instruction where a surprisingly common practice is to have children apply phonic learnings to words they are already able to read (1974, 152).

10. Frank Smith cautions against creating dependency on a system that is not entirely reliable.

> I think it would be difficult to exaggerate the complexity and unreliability of phonics. To take just one very simple example, how are the letters *ho* pronounced? Not in a trick situation, as in the middle of a word like *shop,* but when *ho* are the first two letters of a word? Here are eleven common words in each of which the initial *ho* has a different pronunciation—*hot, hope, hook, hoot, house, hoist, horse, horizon, honey, hour, honest.* Can anyone really believe that a child could learn to identify any of these words by sounding out the letters (1979, 56–57)?*

*Reprinted by permission of the publisher from Frank Smith, *Reading Without Nonsense* (New York, Teachers College Press, © 1984 by Teachers College, Columbia University. All rights reserved.) pp. 56–57.

11. Another facet of this overemphasis is the way oral reading is used in the classroom. The function of oral reading is, in fact, to share the feelings and ideas of an author with oneself and other listeners. But as Barbara Taubenheim and Judith Christensen point out, "round robin" reading, which is characteristic of some reading circles in the classroom,

> is for diagnosis of a child's word recognition skills; however, diagnosis of oral reading errors is better accomplished in a one-to-one situation and not in a group. Diagnosis is not an activity which should be open to public scrutiny. The teacher is probably not tapping the child's maximum level of achievement in word recognition, since the child has an audience which distracts him/her for one or more reasons. In addition to the factor of group distractions, the audience may influence the reader to concentrate only on accurate pronunciation to the exclusion of comprehension. Accurate pronunciation is spotlighted. Since pronunciation is the key to success, children begin to develop an incorrect concept of reading—that reading is just decoding.
>
> A more efficient way for children to practice word recognition skills is to read materials silently at their independent level, that is, the level at which they can read with ease and with no help. First, a child can read much faster silently than orally; therefore, the child who reads silently is much more productive in terms of words read. Second, teachers supply books for instruction which are at a higher achievement level than the books a child reads for enjoyment. As a result, the child is not practicing word recognition but receiving instruction in these skills (1978, p. 975).

12. An enormous amount of money is spent on reading materials, a large percentage of which is skills related. Malcolm C. Douglas (1973) observes that the money spent on skills materials (workbooks, kits, packets, and programmed lessons) decreases the amount spent on reading materials (books, newspapers, and magazines). Pearson also notes the highly commercialized vested interests that promote and perpetuate the system. One is the publisher of materials who is in business first, last, and foremost to make a profit.

> So long as there is general public trust that a phonics worksheet on the initial *sh* blend is a significant educational tool, and so long as enough children circle worksheet examples correctly, then all else falls into place and the system stands firm (1980, 28).

With the release of each new national assessment of reading proficiency scores, pressures are exerted to intensify the whole spiral of spending. Public pressure increases on the schools to raise test scores; teachers are caught in the accountability squeeze to show improved skills test scores; local, state, and federal governments are pressured to provide more funds to meet the skills tests objectives. Publishing houses and vendors of all kinds of educational "software" and "hardware" rush to compete in the lucrative market.

Underemphasis on comprehension. A number of factors have obscured comprehension as a priority in the learning-to-read process.

1. Instructional factors limit comprehension focus. The stress on skills development, primarily that related to decoding print, has been discussed in the previous section. Skills taught in isolation from meaningful print have made learning to read more difficult for many young children. The real purpose of reading is to understand, to comprehend, the intended message of the author. Anything that does not contribute

to this end is secondary in the instructional program. We cannot "give" children comprehension any more than we can "give" them reading; we can do much to help them to understand print by developing a number of strategies to arrive at meaning. Decoding strategies are *one* portion of the journey to literacy.

Durkin (1978–1979) found almost no instruction in comprehension during her study and observation of reading classes in grades 3–5. But if comprehension is the sole purpose of reading, it follows logically that it should be the central focus of instruction from the beginning. It certainly is for children who learn to read naturally outside the confines of formal instruction. These children read to get a message. They deal with whole, meaningful text that *has* a message. They acquire the skills of attending to specific features of print *as they read,* not as *preparation for* reading.

A third factor that has kept comprehension out of central focus has to do with the way in which it has been traditionally defined and used in reading instruction. Comprehension has been regarded as a set of discrete skills and subskills, just as have word recognition skills. We have literal, interpretive, critical, and creative categories, according to many reading authorities. Each of these can be broken down into numerous subskills.

But some researchers question the definition of comprehension as a hierarchy of skills. Comprehending the message of print is a *thinking* process, which involves the simultaneous processing of many facets of written language. All are so interrelated that any attempt to isolate any one of them presents the probability of distorting it. An *inference,* for example, cannot be made without the *literal,* the factual, connotations of the printed message.

Smith believes that comprehension is the *basis* of all skills and *not* a special kind of skill.

> We should be careful not to take one step forward by making comprehension a main concern and two steps back by expecting that it can be fitted into an operationalized straight-jacket, taught (and measured) in small packages. Rather comprehension should be regarded as a condition always to be fostered, both by ensuring that activities and materials always make sense to children and by helping children to develop conceptual frameworks and strategies of inquiry relevant to the skills we expect them to master (1977, 866).*

In discussing the Pennsylvania Comprehensive Reading/Communication Arts Plan (PCRP), a program designed to put comprehension at the center of language learning (both spoken and written forms), Pearson says, "PCRP's research-based contention is that reading comprehension can be reliably tested as one skill only; the testing of smaller elements is not only counterproductive but generally unreliable" (1980, 30).

John Downing contends that the "so-called 'reading skills' are largely mythical"; they have no identifiable basis in the analysis of actual reading behaviors. Rather, comprehending print is *a* skill in which the key process is the *integration* of a "complex set of behaviors that make the total pattern" (1980, 535, 536). Young children learn to integrate all the cue systems of written language by developing and using specific *strategies* for responding to those cues in a total language context.

*Source: Frank Smith, COMPREHENSION, *Language Arts,* 54 (November/December, 1977), p. 866. National Council of Teachers of English, Urbana, Illinois. Used with permission.

2. The strategies used in the process of comprehending, as contrasted to the skills just discussed, have only recently become a major focus. The strategies or operations that the young reader must learn to use in order to achieve understanding include *predicting, sampling, confirming* (or *correcting*) and *integrating*. Predicting is the ability to anticipate upcoming meaning in a line of print; sampling is focusing on the most relevant cues in the print; confirming is verifying the prediction after reading or correcting where prediction was erroneous; integrating is the simultaneous processing of all cues to arrive at meaning.

Prediction is the major strategy in processing print. It is based on the reader's cognitive store of meanings and language proficiency (knowledge of syntactic, semantic, and graphophonic cues).

Figure 4.2 illustrates how prediction strategies function in the overall process of proficient silent reading.

Confirming strategies involve the testing of predictions to see if the print makes sense to us. If sense is made, our predictions have been confirmed, but if predictions are disconfirmed, that is, they do not produce meaning, then one regresses to pick up additional cues or continues reading to build additional context to arrive at comprehension. When the reader needs to reread or reject the sentence because of semantic or syntactic unacceptability, she is using the process in figure 4.2 to confirm or disconfirm.

> Beginning readers also test their predictions while they read. The more cues they have available to them as they interact with print, the more appropriate their predictions and confirmations will be. For example, illustrations accompanying stories are important sources of information that beginning readers utilize in order to test their hypotheses about story content. It is these interactions that are involved as readers *predict* and *confirm* as they read (Goodman and Burke 1980, 7).

Integrating strategies involve deciding what information we wish to remember. We decide on the basis of our purposes for reading and on how the content relates to our view of the world (our existing schemata). When the reader successfully integrates meaning gained with her past experience (world view), she uses figure 4.2 as an integration process.

3. What then are the implications for beginning reading instruction where comprehension is the central purpose of teaching activities?

First, if young readers-to-be are to learn to make sense of print, then they must begin with print that makes sense in the first place—not the "pieces." They will begin with whole language in books and other forms of connected discourse. They will be helped in their efforts to develop individual strategies for making meaning as the need arises out of their own reading. Activities for developing these strategies will make sense to them because they recognize the purpose they serve.

Second, the greater portion of the school day will be spent in reading context so that children are given the necessary reading time in meaningful content to practice and reinforce the skills they are developing.

Third, learning to read takes years; proficiency develops over a lifetime. Children differ in the rates at which they achieve literacy: they cannot be pressured into the accomplishment of the task on a predetermined time schedule. Goethe once said, "The

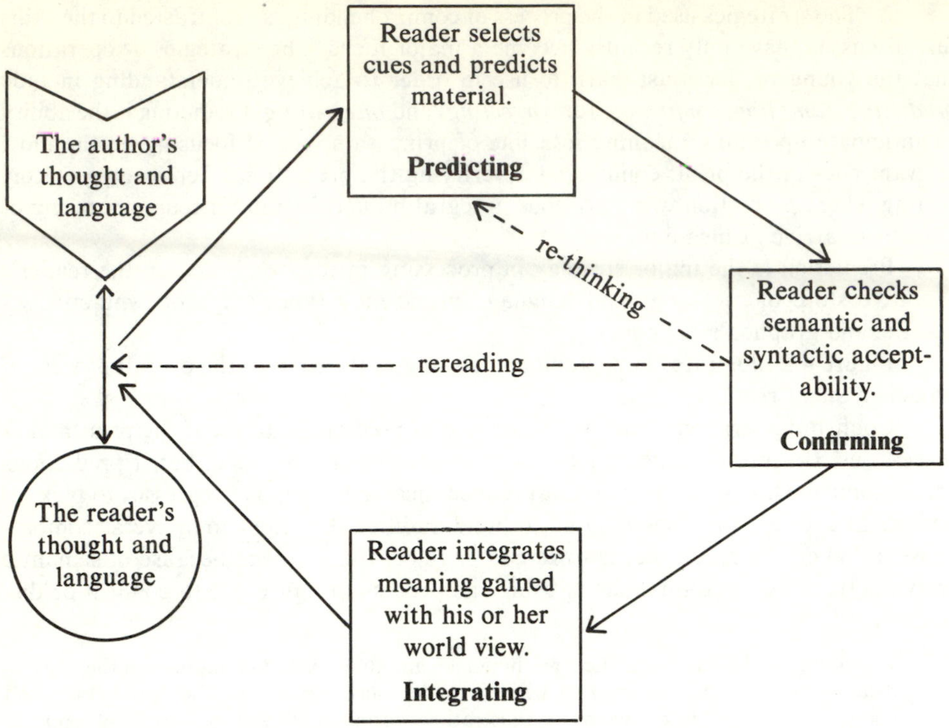

Figure 4.2. Model of proficient silent reading (focus on predicting). Source: Yetta Goodman and Carolyn Burke, READING STRATEGIES: FOCUS ON COMPREHENSION, Richard C. Owen Publishers, Inc., New York, New York, 1980, p. 5. Used with permission of publishers.

dear people do not know how long it takes to learn to read. I have been at it all my life and I cannot say that I have yet reached my goal." Nowhere in the "universe" of reading is it more important to keep this idea in mind than with beginning readers.

No one sets time limits and exerts pressures on children's learning to use oral language, to walk, to ride a bicycle, or to play the piano. All these competencies are developed and refined in stages. In the initial phase there is an unconscious preoccupation with learning the ways and means to achieve the task, but the end result, the goal, is never obscured by the child. Command of the "how to's" increases in proportion to the time spent using them in practice. And so it is with reading.

Learning to read can come a long way in the few short years at primary level, given favorable conditions. The child learns to command most of the mechanics of print and many of the strategies for comprehending will emerge and be developed. However, the level of sophistication and maturity in comprehension in no way approaches that of older children and adults who have arrived at levels of abstract thinking. To hold otherwise is to have unreasonable expectations that exceed the intellectual competence and experience background of the preoperational child. What we do and what we expect in comprehension development, particularly, must be tempered by this reality.

Additional components: either missing or underemphasized. In beginning reading programs that overemphasize phonics and other word recognition skills, insufficient attention is too often given to the development of strategies for comprehending. Other elements of an effective program may be given relatively little attention, or they may be neglected entirely. The following components are crucial to the design and implementation of an effective beginning-to-read program, and they must be included.

1. Sufficient time must be provided for reading. This includes time spent *listening* to stories as well as *reading* itself. If children are going to learn to read by reading, they must read. They not only develop emergent reading behaviors through book experience, they also reinforce the skills and strategies through much practice.
2. A sufficient quantity and variety of materials must be readily available in the classroom. The range of competencies and interests in reading vary widely among a group of children; provision for these individual differences must be made so that all children use the materials which best suit them individually.
3. Abundant opportunities to participate in concept and language-building experiences must be provided. Young children bring many strengths to the classroom, but a large part of their school day should be spent in extending and expanding their cognitive and affective stores and language usage. There is much more to know, to feel, and to say. The more meanings the child has to bring to reading, the greater her chances of success and the more naturally she will learn to associate meaning with print.
4. Sufficient opportunities must be provided for children to participate in experiences that integrate all the skills of communication: listening, speaking, reading, and writing. Effective communication is a total system, not an isolation of its parts. We can analyze the parts separately, but in actual use all are interrelated and operate simultaneously to produce a meaningful exchange of ideas.

Failure to Begin with Strengths of Young Children and to Build on the Naturalness of Their Learning

As described in the first chapter, most children bring to school many strengths upon which literacy acquisition can be built. These strengths are (1) curiosity, or the drive to know; (2) the meanings and feelings about the world that have been derived from experiences, and (3) oral language competence. These are the "knowns" by which the child makes sense of all future encounters with the unfamiliar, the "unknowns" of his environment. David B. Doake further explains:

> Young children can assimilate and accommodate new learning if it makes sense in accordance with what they already know. If what they are being directed to learn does not have any meaning in itself and cannot be fitted into their existing schemata, the task becomes an impossible one (1979, 5).

Building on the strengths of children and creating an environment for natural learning dictate that early school experiences will *not* be focused primarily on formal reading instruction and a highly academic emphasis in reading readiness. There will be no mad rush into books. This in no way implies that children will not have experiences with books and learning to read; it simply means that such will not be the *central* focus of instruction for children as they begin schooling. They will have far *more* than book-related experiences.

The major emphasis will be to provide many and varied concrete, firsthand opportunities for the continued exploration of and acting upon the environment already begun by the child long before he comes to school. The child has had several years of experience in learning in this natural way. He has learned to make meanings by solving the problems of the unknowns he has met. He has already built a large repertoire of meanings and feelings stored as schemata in his mind as a result of these experiences. He is on secure ground.

There are many ways to "know" a frog, or anything else for that matter. One can look at pictures or see a film; one can hear a description read from a book or told in an explanation. But the best of all possible ways to know a frog is to hold it in one's hands and feel its moist bumpiness as it wriggles around; to watch its throat expand and hear the muffled croak; to see the color, the raised set of eyes, and the webbing between the toes; to smell the warm earthiness of the creature; to watch the smooth motion of its body as it swims in a tub of water.

Children learn best by experiencing the world directly and then reconstructing, reconstituting, or re-presenting it in ways that are appropriate to their interests and abilities. By reconstituting experience, recasting it in their personal molds, the children integrate new learning about the world into their own personal conceptual systems. The primary purpose of education is to give children many opportunities to experience interaction with the environment and then to reconstruct or re-present that experience through their own thought systems or conceptualizations.

There are many reasons, then, for a primary focus on an experience curriculum during the early years of schooling. First, it encompasses learning skills and concepts the child already has. Second, it provides for the practice and further development of the learning skills she brings: the inquiring into, the questioning, and exploration by which problem solving is achieved. Third, the child's store of meanings (her schemata) is increased and expanded. And finally her language competence is increased.

Where print is a familiar part of this world of concrete experiencing, the child will begin to explore it as she does all other unknowns. Learning to read will be another problem to solve; she will have the necessary problem-solving ability and the conceptual store for bringing meaning to print. Emergent reading behaviors will begin to appear. She can and will learn to read—naturally.

The following generalizations are a summary of many ideas that the authors have explored, and these ideas are widely accepted principles about young children and reading.

1. Learning to read is an extension of the two communication skills children already have. They have been listening and speaking for several years. They already know and use the grammar of their language.
2. Children can grow into reading rather painlessly, if we follow their interests, needs, and motivations. Follow *their* lead. Tell *them* what *they* want to know.
3. The job of reading requires deliberate word identification in the beginning. The more foreign the sentence to the child, the more slowly and deliberately she must study and "decode" each word. That is why she will have least difficulty with her own sentences.

This little girl makes her own creative arrangement.

4. Children arrive individually and at their own good time at a level of optimum readiness to move from oral language to "written down" language. If we are wise, we would be observing for that point in each child's language maturity.
5. Expanding and enriching competent oral language performance is the greatest need most children have for establishing a curiosity about "what do words say?"
6. Little children learn (understand) phonics through reading (and having need for it); they do not learn to read through phonics, which cannot help them if they do not know they need it (Smith 1983, 5, 12, 31).
7. Getting from the beginning stage to the mature stage requires: (a) automatic understanding of the deep structure of the language—not the prònunciation of the words in the sentences; and (b) years of practice under the most encouraging, positive, rewarding circumstances.
8. Each child *must* start reading in the language she knows best, whether it is English, Spanish, black English, or any other nonstandard dialect. This view is shared by James Cummins 1978; Bruce A. Gaarder 1972; Fred Genesee, G. R. Tucker, and Wallace E. Lambert 1978; Lester Golub 1978; Nancy Modiano 1966.

Failure to Delineate the Roles of Teacher and Learner

So long as teachers fail to distinguish between teaching and learning, they will continue to undertake to do *for children* that which only children can do *for themselves*. Teaching children to read is not passing reading on to them. It is certainly not endless hours spent in activities *about* reading. Douglas (1973) contends that "reading cannot be taught directly and schools should stop trying to do the impossible."

Teaching and learning are two entirely different processes. They differ in kind and function. The function of teaching is to create the conditions and the climate that will make it possible for children to devise the most efficient system for teaching themselves to read. Teaching is also a public activity: it can be seen and observed.

Learning to read involves all that each individual does to make sense of the world of printed language. Almost all of it is private, for learning is an occupation of the mind, and that process is not open to public scrutiny.

If teacher and learner roles are not interchangeable, what then can be done through teaching that will aid the child in the quest for literacy? Smith has one cardinal rule and guideline for all reading instruction. "*Make learning to read easy*—which means making reading a meaningful, enjoyable and frequent experience for children" (1979, 143). Making learning to read easy would include the following:

1. *Read to children that which they cannot read for themselves,* just as the parents of natural readers do for their young children in the preschool years. Have older children from the upper grades come in on a regular basis to read to children individually or in small groups. Have parents or other adults do the same.
2. *Read from a variety of materials with a high interest level*—stories, poems, riddles, jokes—all of which are fun for the beginning reader. Later, add material that provides information about topics you have observed the children to be interested in.
3. *Provide a reading environment* by having an abundance of reading materials readily available in the classroom—comics, wordless picture books, predictable books, Mother Goose and other storybooks, riddle and joke cards, newspapers, magazines, and informational books on a variety of topics.
4. *Have older proficient readers tape stories* and store the cassettes for children to use in a listening center.
5. *Provide flannel boards with appropriate cut outs for children to tell stories* to themselves or to others (the teacher should also tell stories).
6. *Have writing materials readily available:* pencils, crayons, and paper.
7. *Have a scrap or "attic box" filled with a collection of odds and ends* for children to sort through, touch, and talk about in whatever way they choose.
8. *Provide time* to engage in all of the above activities: it will be available when the use of drill or ditto sheets and workbook pages are kept within reason.
9. Above all, *provide a multitude of hands-on experiences,* as described in the previous section, for children *to do* and *to talk about.*
10. With the emergence of reading behaviors, *provide information and help as the child requests* them. The information should be given on an informal basis, but direct instruction should be provided, also. Whenever several children are asking the same kinds of questions, the teacher can form a small group to demonstrate and explain the puzzling concept. Then time for trying out the new concept is provided.
11. *Begin to prepare language experience stories* by recording the child's talk about an experience in the classroom. Make "booklets" that can be displayed about the room. Provide materials for children to make their own books. Have children tape a story of their own to be transcribed later by older children.
12. As children develop additional competencies and interests in reading, *provide more time in frequently spaced periods for them to read.* Reading ability grows with *practice.*

13. *Continue to share books with the whole group by reading daily.* Your own attitude and commitment to reading is a model which demonstrates that reading is an enjoyable, worthwhile activity.

These are only a few of the ideas that can be used to help children grow naturally into reading. Many more will be suggested in the chapters to follow.

When the roles of teacher and learner are seen for what they are, and when both teacher and learner fulfill them appropriately, then much of the pressure and frustration for both is eliminated. Learning to read *is* made easier when teachers create an environment where children are given the opportunity to solve the problem of learning to read by reading.

Insufficient Schemata and the Use of Basal Readers

The source of major deficiencies in many current instructional programs in beginning reading result from (1) plunging children into structured reading activities without their having adequate schemata, or knowledge store, to make sense of those activities, and (2) the nature of basal reader materials, which most children are expected to use in learning to read, and the way these materials are used in reading instruction.

Insufficient schemata. "Comprehension is building bridges between the new and the known" (Pearson and Johnson 1978, 24). The point has already been made several times, but, again, the more meanings ("knowns") a child brings *to* reading, the more she gets *from* it. These meanings, or schemata, are the child's cognitive store of concepts derived from experience with her environment.

Schemata are of two types where reading is concerned. The first are those concepts that are derived from the child's day-to-day interaction with her environment. These schemata are a composite of the cognitive and affective meanings the child has formed about the physical environment and the people and things in it. Depending on experiences, these schemata will include an array of concepts and subconcepts: *mother, father, cat, house, toy, food, store,* and *shirt* are but a few. These are the child's meanings with which a match is made with those in the context of printed material.

Much that is done in many beginning reading programs requires children to deal with content for which they have little, if any, schemata for building meaning. An example of an extreme version of this practice is giving Navajo or Eskimo children stories in which the content is totally outside their field of experience. When they have no meanings to relate to the content, what they read is nonsense. Stories that depict Sally and John saying good-bye to father who wears a suit and carries a briefcase as he leaves for his office in a twenty-story building just do not mesh with the experience of children whose fathers go out in a kayak to spear seals or plant corn in the desert.

The second category of schemata which is required for comprehension in reading is that related specifically to print. John Downing wrote that these include (1) understanding the communicative functions of print and its relation to spoken language (specific meanings can be associated with printed symbols), and (2) understanding the reading task: its purposes and its technical characteristics (1979, 36).

Teaching practices should not be built on the assumption that children already know what print and reading are all about—many do not. Teacher talk about "words"

Learning is culturally related. The girls are using their feet as anchors while braiding drawstrings for their parkas in the old way. The foot was used because traditional Inuit homes, skin tents and snow houses, afforded no firm anchor for this activity. Inuujuag School, Arctic Bay, Northwest Territory, Canada.

and "sounds" and "letters" may be a foreign language to many children: they have no schema for such. If they were not confused by the unfamiliar content of the text, they will surely be by the terminology used in instruction.

Effective beginning reading instruction, then, builds on the schemata that children have in order to make it possible to bridge to the schemata they do not yet possess. The materials they read and the instruction they are given begin with that which is already familiar.

The language-experience method is an excellent way to begin (Roach Van and Claryce Allen 1970; Sylvia Ashton-Warner 1971; John Downing 1979; Charles J. Hacker 1980; Mary Anne Hall 1978, 1981; Doris Lee and Roach Van Allen 1963; Bill Martin, Jr., 1980; Robert and Marlene McCracken 1972, 1979; Russell G. Stauffer 1970; Jeannette Veatch, et al. 1973). Language experience uses the language of children to make the text for reading. It, therefore, begins with the schemata children have already built from their own experiences. The language-experience approach becomes the means for building schemata about the functions of reading and the nature of the reading task itself.

> As children see their spoken thoughts put into written form, they can grasp the concept that communication is the purpose of reading. Communication is stressed as children speak, see the speech represented by printed symbols, and then read the written representation of their speech. The association of meaning with the print is built into the reading of the personally created materials of the language experience approach. As the child sees his speech encoded into the printed symbols, he is aware of communicating through writing. As he reads or listens to the written representation of his thoughts, he is communicating through reading (Mary Anne Hall, 1981, p. 2).

Children should be given many opportunities to *hear* the language of books before they are asked to read. Book language is not the same as that of everyday speech.

It is more formal and more impersonal. Most of the materials used in beginning reading are in narrative style, or "story" language. Children would more likely be familiar with this form (if they have been read to in the early years) than they would be with expository language. Expository writing differs from that of narration. It is the language used to convey information; the content is largely factual. Expository language requires different strategies for making sense than does narration. These are the strategies for learning how to learn: picking out important points, remembering them, and using them for particular purposes.

Language experience is an excellent way to build schemata for making sense of narrative and expository styles. Material in expository form can be generated by concrete experiences. Children take a trip to the railroad station, return to school, and discuss what an engine looked like. The teacher writes down these descriptions for use in reading. Recipes for making all kinds of food can be read to children and then followed with the help of the teacher in actually making a product. After the project, discussion is held about the ingredients, quantities, measuring, and the sequence of preparation. Again, the content of discussion is written by the teacher and is used as an expository type reading text. Following this same procedure, narrative text can be generated when the teacher records stories told by children.

Finally, though it is perhaps inconceivable in a literate society, some children may have had little experience with what Kenneth Goodman calls "environmental reading." They, therefore, have no schemata for it. Goodman wrote, "Environmental reading is the reading one must do in the course of interacting with a literate environment. The toothpaste tube, the cereal box, the milk carton, street signs, billboards, bus markings and door markings . . ." (1980, 846).*

The easiest way to expand children's familiarity with "environmental print" is to bring products into the class for discussion and to go out into the community to explore the abundant examples of environmental print found there. Items already in the environment may be given appropriate labels—potatoes, chair, table—and left for children to explore on an incidental basis.

Additional ways to help children acquire the necessary schemata for learning to read various styles of writing will be given throughout this text.

Basal readers. In most primary classrooms, basal readers are the predominant material used to teach children to read. Basal readers are books published in a series for grades kindergarten through six and above. Vocabulary is controlled and skills are sequentially and systematically developed grade by grade. A wide variety of supplemental materials is available for skills development, including workbooks and ditto masters. Despite its prevalence, the basal system is flawed.

1. The basal system (the materials and their use) comes equipped with its own built in "blocks," that is, it sometimes introduces unnatural language. Bruno Bettelheim and Karen Zelan observed the following:

    > The texts of preprimers and primers consist of words that can be readily sounded out. But these words are often combined in sentences that no one would ever say. Such a text is actually harder for the beginner to read. For example, because the child usually learns early to recognize the words "store" and "man," one widely used basal text

*Source: Kenneth S. Goodman, VIEWPOINTS: FROM A RESEARCHER, *Language Arts,* 57 (November/December, 1980), p. 846, National Council of Teachers of English, Urbana, Illinois. Used with permission.

(*People Read*, one of the Bank Street readers) tells about a "store man" when referring to a salesman. Out of a wish to make learning to read easy, children who know the word that the text of this story means to convey are asked to recognize and use in their reading a phrase that rarely comes up in writing or speech. To compound the irony, the phrase appears in a book whose title by implication promises to tell how everybody reads and what they read. The result is that children may be provoked to errors by the discrepancy between ordinary language and the uncommon language of the book (1981, 29).

2. By their very nature, basals are counterproductive to reading for enjoyment.

Shelton Root, in a paper presented at the International Reading Association National Conference in New Orleans, detailed features of the basal reader system that hinder rather than aid the acquisition of literacy: "It quite honestly is not the purpose of basals to help children learn to enjoy reading. Candidly, it isn't even a minor purpose. The *purpose* of the basal is to *teach* kids the *mechanics* of reading" (1981, 13).

3. Basal reading programs provide such detailed guidelines for what to do in the teacher's guide that teacher innovation may be stifled.

Root also contends that the preparation and follow-up activities prescribed for teaching the mechanics can require far more time than the actual reading itself. Root notes, "Reading systems invert the entire teacher-teaching tool relationship, in that it is the system which now uses the teacher, not the teacher who uses the system. The teacher is now under control of the tool" (1981, 9).

4. Basal readers often create teacher dependence. Once teachers begin to use basals, they may easily become a "security blanket" for their reading instruction.

Before reading in basals, children should first be given many opportunities to read written language for which they already have the appropriate schema—their own language-experience stories and favorite stories that they have heard many times and have "read" along with a proficient reader. (See "Shared-Book Experience" in chapter 7 that develops this concept more fully.) After extensive exposure to these two types of materials, children may have acquired sufficient knowledge about print to make profitable use of some basal materials. The teacher may acquaint children with basal style language by reading stories from them. The stories should be selected for interest and appeal to children. Old basals can be torn apart to form individual "books" of each story. Young children are more often "turned on" to soft covers—small booklets—than they are to hard covers with many stories inside, the format characteristic of most basals beyond preprimer and primer levels.

These "adapted" basal materials should not be used with all the suggestions in the teacher's edition. They should be read as any other story material without large doses of "preparation" and "follow-up." Help should be provided when it is requested, or when it is obvious that there is a need—and it should be provided within the context of what is being read.

Basal readers, when selectively used, can be *one of many* excellent sources provided in beginning reading instruction. Materials should be chosen to meet specific needs and interests of individual children, not as a common prescription for all children. (In chapters 7 and 8 we have described a variety of ways in which basal readers and basal materials can be effectively used to teach children to read naturally.)

Worship of the Reading God

For a very long time, the ability to read has been the measure of all things. Our value and thinking of reading has congealed into a regimented and constrictive pressure system that dominates much of what we say and do. This mentality may indeed be the greatest of all blocks to reading success. Children must not only learn to read, but they must also do it in a hurry—at least by the end of first grade. In recent years, pressures have pushed that timetable downward into kindergarten in many schools. If children can be expected to read in first grade, then *why not* in kindergarten? When this thinking becomes sufficiently entrenched, there is no reason to believe that it will not be extended even to lower levels.

Of course, as indicated in chapter 1, there are some four-year-olds interested in mastering print—and they *do* read. More five-year-olds do, too. Traditionally we have "pushed" reading for six-year-olds, and many have, indeed, learned to read. But there are likely as many seven-year-olds who need to grow into reading more slowly as there are five-year-olds who read early. And a few may not be curious about print until age eight. The school must provide for *all* children across this range of readiness for reading.

The pressure to read (and the earlier the better) is not lost on children. A young brother of one of the authors came home from his first day in first grade, tossed his preprimer into the wastebasket, and announced that he was not going to school anymore! When his mother asked why he was so upset, he replied that he had not learned to read—all day!

Children who do not meet the timetables set by the expectations of adults for acquiring literacy have new pressures imposed. They are likely to be labeled deficient by whatever the term, and they are placed in "remediation" where "catch-up" pressure is applied.

Both parents and children often find their own self-worth being defined in terms of success in reading. There is no greater satisfaction and pride than that shown by parents as they sit down with a child who can read. But where a child is slower to meet the learning-to-read deadline—for whatever the reasons—the affective climate may be completely changed. What the child cannnot do is seen as a personal reflection on the parents, and their disappointment is not lost on the child. Both can feel less worthy.

Failure to measure up is also reflected in the attitudes of children toward each other in school. They know quickly who can and who cannot read. While it is not usually a William Golding's *Lord of the Flies* (1954) operation, the effects can be devastating to the feelings of self-worth of those who have not achieved this "Greatest of All Accomplishments."

Finally, the teacher can also be part of the cycle of put-down, even though there is no conscious recognition of the process. Regardless of what is said, actions carry the intended message to the child. When the unspoken message is that one has not measured up, additional weight is added to an already overburdening load.

Making reading the "Number One End" in all education has some other debilitating effects in addition to those already mentioned. They are similar to those that

Your Turn 4.1 Reading instruction in the classroom.

Arrange to observe two-to-four full sessions of reading instruction in a primary classroom.

1. Record the following
   a. Materials being used.
   b. Types of activities children are engaged in.
   c. What the teacher does.
2. Analyze what you saw in terms of some of the major criticisms in this chapter.
3. Does what you observed support or refute the criticisms? Explain.

result when reading is postponed until children first learn about the mechanics of reading. The same kind of moratorium can be placed on participation in activities by which children develop a variety of other interests, talents, and abilities. First, they must concentrate their energies and time in learning to read. Individual children may have a special interest in and aptitude for planning and carrying out special projects, such as making collections of all kinds. They may just enjoy playing with items in a scrap collection or looking at things under a microscope. They may be adept at leadership in groups of children, or they may be interested in making elaborate and involved structures whose purpose and meaning are known only to themselves. All of these ways by which a child comes to explore and know her world by pursuing her interests and developing new ones can be severely limited, if children are forever being required to read first.

Among other important things that children must learn is to be able to relate to, to get along with, members of a group. These skills can only be learned as children interact with each other. Someone has said, "Perhaps we can learn to live with poor readers, but how do we cope with a bigot?" But an even more-important question is, "Must we make such a choice?" When learning to read is put in proper perspective, it will not be allowed to overshadow all the other kinds of learning that are necessary for becoming a well-developed and fully functioning human being.

Children can and should learn to read; they must also be given the opportunity to learn other skills and to develop new concepts and interests that are equally important. Neither has to be sacrificed to the other where individual differences are respected and provided for in the total curriculum of the young child. Any practice that ignores and runs roughshod over the individual differences among us is intolerable. Reading is not a god; respect and provision for individual differences is the supreme guideline for teaching children anything—particularly reading. Reading is *only one* of many things to know.

Summary

Many knowledgeable, caring, conscientious, and hardworking teachers populate thousands of classrooms across the country. However, too many still follow practices which violate the best that is known about the most effective ways to develop literacy. These practices act as blocks in one way or another by interfering with the natural way in which children can learn to read. We have identified a number of these blocks and have proposed specific ways to remove them so that children have the opportunity to grow into reading as naturally as they learn to achieve so many other competencies.

References

Allen, Roach Van, and Allen, Claryce. *An Introduction to a Language-Experience Program.* levels 1–3. Chicago: Encyclopaedia Britannica, 1970.

Artley, A. Sterl. "Reading: Skills or Competencies?" *Language Arts* 57 (May 1980): 546–49.

Ashton-Warner, Sylvia. *Teacher.* New York: Simon and Schuster, 1971.

Bettelheim, Bruno, and Zelan, Karen. "Why Children Don't Like to Read." *The Atlantic Monthly* (November 1981): 25–31.

Black, Janet K. "Those 'Mistakes' Tell us a Lot." *Language Arts* 57 (May 1980): 512.

Chomsky, Carol. "After Decoding: What?" *Language Arts* 53 (March 1976): 288–96, 314.

Cummins, James. "Educational Implications of Mother Tongue Maintenance in Minority Language Groups." *Canadian Modern Language Review* 34 (February 1978): 395–416.

Dechant, Emerald, and Smith, Henry. *Psychology in Teaching Reading.* 2d ed. Englewood Cliffs, N.J.: Prentice-Hall, 1977.

Doake, David B. "Book Experience and Emergent Reading Behavior." Paper presented at meeting of the International Reading Association, Atlanta, May 1979.

Douglas, Malcolm C. "Stop Trying to Teach Reading." *Los Angeles Times* 25 February 1973.

Downing, John. *Reading and Reasoning.* New York: Springer-Verlag, New York, 1979.

———. "Reading—Skill or Skills?" *The Reading Teacher* 35 (February 1982): 534–37.

Durkin, Dolores. "Phonics: Instruction That Needs to Be Improved." *The Reading Teacher* 28 (November 1974): 152–56.

———. "What Classroom Observations Reveal about Reading Comprehension Instruction." *Reading Research Quarterly* 14 (1978–1979): 481–533.

———. *Strategies for Identifying Words.* 2d ed. New York: Allyn and Bacon, 1980.

Elkind, David. "The Curriculum Disabled Child." Paper presented at the University of Florida, Gainesville, 15 May 1978.

Gaarder, A. Bruce. "Bilingualism and Education." In *The Language Education of Minority Children, Selected Readings,* edited by Bernard Spolsky. Rowley, Mass.: Newbury House Publishers, 1972.

Genesee, Fred; Tucker, G. R.; and Lambert, Wallace E. "An Experiment in Trilingual Education." *Canadian Modern Language Review* 34 (1978): 621–43.

Golding, William. *Lord of the Flies.* New York: G. P. Putnam's Sons, 1954.

Golub, Lester. "Evaluation Design and Implementation of a Bilingual Education Program, Grades 1–12, Spanish/English." *Education and Urban Society* 10 (1978): 363–84.

Goodman, Kenneth S. "Breakthroughs and Lock-outs." *Language Arts* 55 (November/December 1978a): 919–20.

———. "Acquiring Literacy is Natural: Who Skilled Cock Robin?" *Theory into Practice* 16 (1978b): 309–14.

———. "Viewpoints: From a Researcher." *Language Arts* 57 (November/December 1980): 846–47.

Goodman, Yetta, and Burke, Carolyn. *Reading Strategies: Focus on Comprehension.* New York: Richard C. Owen Publishers, Inc., 1980.

Goodman, Yetta, and Goodman, Kenneth. "Twenty Questions about Teaching Language." *Educational Leadership* (March 1981): 437–42.

Hacker, Charles J. "From Schema Theory to Classroom Practice." *Language Arts* 57 (November/December 1980): 866–71.

Hall, Mary Anne. *The Language Experience Approach for Teaching Reading.* 2d ed. Newark, N.J.: International Reading Association, 1978.

———. *Teaching Reading as a Language Experience.* 3rd ed. Columbus: Charles E. Merrill, 1981.

Hoffman, Stevie, and Fillmer, H. Thompson. "Thought, Language and Reading Readiness." *The Reading Teacher* 33 (December 1979): 290–94.

Huey, Edmund Burke. *The Psychology and Pedagogy of Reading.* New York: The Macmillan Company, 1908. Reprint. Cambridge: The MIT Press, 1968.

Lambert, Wallace E., "Cognitive and Sociocultural Consequences of Bilingualism." *Canadian Modern Language Review* 34 (1978): 537–47.

Lamme, Linda L., et al. *Raising Readers, A Guide to Sharing Literature with Young Children.* New York: Walker and Company, 1980.

Lee, Dorris, and Allen, Roach Van. *Learning to Read Through Experience.* New York: Appleton-Century-Crofts, 1963.

Martin, Bill, Jr. *Strategies for Language Learning.* Tulsa, Okla.: Educational Progress Corporation, 1980.

Matthews, Virginia H. "Adult Reading Studies: Their Implications for Private, Professional and Public Policy." *Library Trends* 22 (October 1973): 159.

McCracken, Robert A., and McCracken, Marlene. *Reading is Only the Tiger's Tail.* San Rafael, Calif. Leswing Press, 1972.

McCracken, Marlene, and McCracken, Robert. *Reading, Writing and Language. A Practical Guide for Primary Teachers.* Winnipeg: Peguis Publishers Limited, 1979.

Modiano, Nancy. "A Comparative Study of Two Approaches to the Teaching of Reading in the National Language." New York: New York University School of Education, 1966.

Morris, R. Darrell. "Some Aspects of the Instructional Environment and Learning to Read." *Language Arts* 56 (May 1979): 497–502.

Page, William D., and Pinnell, Gay Su. *Teaching Reading Comprehension.* Urbana, Ill.: National Council of Teachers of English, 1979.

Pearson, Craig. "The Main Event: Reading vs. Reading Skills." *Learning* 9 (November 1980): 26–30.

Pearson, P. David, and Johnson, Dale D. *Teaching Reading Comprehension.* New York: Holt, Rinehart and Winston, 1978.

Root, Shelton. "What Place Pleasure in the Reading System?" Paper presented at the International Reading Association Conference, New Orleans, 1981.

Sebesta, Sam. "Why Rudolph Can't Read." *Language Arts* 58 (May 1981): 545–48.

Smith, Frank. "Comprehension." *Language Arts* 54 (November/December 1977): 866.

———. *Reading Without Nonsense.* New York: Columbia University, Teachers College Press, 1979.

———. *Essays into Literacy.* Exeter, N.H.: Heinemann Educational Books, 1983.

Stauffer, Russell G. *The Language Experience Approach to the Teaching of Reading.* New York: Harper and Row, Publishers, 1970.

Taubenheim, Barbara, and Christensen, Judith. "Let's Shoot 'Cock Robin'! Alternatives to 'Round Robin' Reading." *Language Arts* 55 (November/December 1978) 975–77.

Veatch, Jeannette, et al. *Key Words to Reading: The Language Experience Approach Begins.* Columbus: Charles E. Merrill, 1973.

5

A Psycholinguistic Bridge to Reading

Outline

Psycholinguistic Principles and Learning to Read Naturally
- A Psycholinguistic Definition of Reading
- Acquisition of Literacy as a Natural Extension of Oral Language Learning and Use
- Understanding of and Having a Need for the Functions of Print in the Development of Literacy
- Reading as Bringing Meaning *to* Print Rather Than Getting Meaning *from* Print
  - Visual and nonvisual information
  - Acquiring and using visual and nonvisual information
- Risk Taking as a Vital Element in Learning to Read
- Learning to Read as a Pleasurable Experience

New Perspectives in Reading Instruction
- Teaching Reading: A Redefinition
  - Greater emphasis on actual reading activities with proportionately less time spent on activities *about* reading
  - Clarification of the roles of teacher and learner in the acquisition of reading
  - Methodology in teaching reading based on knowledge and understanding of the nature of language and its use, the nature of cognitive and affective development, and the nature of the reading process
  - Instruction beginning with the strengths of the young child, followed by focus on extension and refinement of developing competencies of the young reader
- Building on the Strengths that Children Bring to Reading
  - Rationale for building on strengths
  - The strengths that children bring to reading
  - The strengths that children *may* bring to reading
- Extending and Expanding Insights, Knowledge, and Competencies in Reading

Summary

References

Guide Questions

1. What does "a psycholinguistic bridge to reading" mean?
2. How is reading seen as the process of "bringing meaning to print" rather than "getting meaning from print"?
3. How can you contrast a psycholinguistic definition of reading with more traditional definitions?
4. How can you describe the succession of "emergent reading behaviors" through which children move in developing as natural readers?
5. What is meant by the following statement? "The greater the store of nonvisual information, the less the need to attend to visual information."

Terminology

psycholinguistics	cognitive store
alphabetic system	risk taking
encode	whole language
recode	successive approximations
decode	functions of print
reading strategies	metalanguage
learning-to-read continuum	cognitive clarity
deficit model	visual information
strengths model	nonvisual information
concepts about print	

Much of the writing about psycholinguistics and reading focuses on descriptions of the fluent reader. Our concerns here are how *fluent* readers become that way; we have, therefore, worked backward from the goal of fluency to focus on the *process,* that is, the means used to achieve the end—literacy. In focusing on the process, we have described how children grow into reading naturally without formal instruction prior to entering school. We believe there is a strong link between psycholinguistics and learning to read naturally. The premises of psycholinguistics are concerned with the nature of language and how children learn to use it as naturally as they learn many other competencies during the early years. These premises provide an excellent rationale and specific guidelines for parents and teachers who would help children in the process of achieving literacy.

We further believe that a strong theoretical base which explains why we do what we do to create an environment for developing literacy is absolutely essential. Too often in the past, educational practices were based in the conventional wisdom born of tradition rather than in logical reasons and clear-cut understandings. Too many practices have been continued without practitioners knowing why they do what they do in teaching reading. Unless we know *why* we do what we do, we have little, if any, basis to justify our actions, and we have no logical recourse for evaluating and improving our efforts. Learning to function effectively in a literate world is too important a task to be left either to chance or to tradition.

Children bring many strengths on which to build literacy, even though there is a wide range of differences among them on a learning-to-read continuum. Some are already readers, others know relatively little about print, but most fall somewhere between these two extremes. By identifying and building on what children already know, reading teachers are providing all the maximum opportunity to become fluent readers.

This chapter will examine ways in which certain psycholinguistic principles can be used to develop an instructional program that builds on the strengths of children and thus provides a bridge to natural reading.

Psycholinguistic Principles and Learning to Read Naturally

A Psycholinguistic Definition of Reading

Kenneth S. Goodman (1967, 1970) described reading as a psycholinguistic "guessing game" involving an interaction between thought and language by which the reader attempts to *reconstruct* the author's meaning. Beginning readers bring to the task a store of meanings and attitudes derived from experience, and they also have a repertoire of basic knowledge of and skills in oral language. With this background, they are able to anticipate what the written message is likely to be. Reading then, according to Yetta Goodman and Dorothy J. Watson, becomes "an active process in which readers use the strategies of sampling, predicting, confirming or correcting, and integrating information in order to derive meaning from the graphic, syntactic and semantic cues provided by the author" (1977, 869). All these basic cue systems are present only in the wholeness of language in print, not in isolated words and phrases. In reading all are processed simultaneously as the reader attempts to reconstruct the writer's message. Only the graphic system may be unfamiliar to beginning readers.

An explanation of how a young child uses knowledge of oral language and background experience to make sense of print by sampling, predicting, and testing for meaning is given in the following example from Moira McKenzie:

> He is in the early stage of reading (tackling print) but his attempts at integrating his cueing systems, his sources of information are apparent as he works on the text.
>
> *Text:* I like fish and chips for my tea.
>
> *Child:* I like fish and chips for my dinner tea.
>
> Alek uses his implicit knowledge of language, and his experiences—he knows *fish and chips* go together. He reads the last word incorrectly but he knows it is a noun, and a meal time—. His life experience eliminates breakfast time. He tries *dinner* because of the initial sound, so he corrects—"it must be tea." He re-reads the page correctly, satisfied now that the message is correct. He demonstrates how he checks his language cues against his visual information, using his growing phonic knowledge. He shows how, even at this early stage of tackling print, he predicts and checks his predictions against other information (1977, 321).

Acquisition of Literacy as a Natural Extension of Oral Language Learning and Use

Many elements are common to the acquisition of speaking and reading competencies. Speech is composed of individual sounds (phonemes), which are clustered together to form meaningful units. The listener learns which sounds are significant to meaning and which are not. For example, there are many variations in the way different speakers pronounce the same phoneme in English. "Just as we call many different colors and shades of color red, we hear many different sounds as /t/" (Goodman 1970, 13). All these variations are ignored; they are treated as though they are the same because they make no difference in meaning. But where differences in sounds are significant to meaning, the listener "tunes in" as in *bit* and *pit*.

> *Perception in language is and must be both selective and anticipatory.* To be aware of what is significant in language one must ignore what is not. Perception to be functional in listening must be augmented by anticipation. The sounds are so fleeting and follow each other so rapidly that time does not allow for each to be fully perceived and identified. Mastery of the phonological system, however, and of the grammatical system as well, enables the listener to use partial perceptions and sample the input. Under some circumstances, of course, the partial perceptions may be too fragmentary or distorted and the listener may have to ask for repetition. But, to be quite blunt, what we think we hear is as much what we expect to hear as it is what we do hear (Goodman 1970, 13–14).*

In both components of oral language—listening and speaking—children learn not only to distinguish between sounds and to treat them differently, according to whether or not they are significant to meaning, they also acquire the implicit rules for combining sounds into meaningful units (words) and for stringing these units together into meaningful discourse (phrases and sentences). They develop a large oral vocabulary, the symbolic representations of meanings derived from experiences in the world. In listening to speech, children learn to predict or anticipate meaning and to sample the stream of oral language to confirm their predictions.

Children who learn to read naturally—as described in chapter 1—use all the above pre-existing oral language skills and background experience to deal with the printed form of language. Written English is an alphabetic system, where graphic symbols (letters) are used to represent oral language. Individual letters are combined into larger units of print (words) according to the same rules used in combining oral sound sequences. Words in print are combined in certain ways to form sentences according to the rules of syntax, which govern both oral and written forms of language. The same processes of predicting, sampling, and confirming or correcting that the child has already learned to use in making sense of oral language are used to make meanings from print. Young readers-to-be do not, indeed, have to start from scratch!

Print does have some visual aspects which, of course, are not part of speech: letters, spacing between words, arrangement of words in a horizontal sequence from left to right across a page, the progression of lines of print from the top of a page to the bottom, the development of text from front to back, and the use of graphic devices in the form of punctuation marks for representing meaning available only in the intonations of spoken language.

When children are born into an environment that is rich in the use of oral and written language, they are equipped with the necessary ingredients for developing competencies which can be applied to make meaning from print. Hearing and seeing stories read over and over first supplies a meaning base from which the child can begin to make finer and finer distinctions about print. Knowing the meaning of a passage enables the child to predict what comes next in the oral version. Examples were cited earlier in which young children will "correct" adult readers when anticipated words are omitted.

In a series of what Marie Clay (1972), David B. Doake (1979), and William H. Teale and Elizabeth Sulzby (1984) have called "emergent reading behaviors," the child moves quite naturally into dealing with print. First, the child will begin to retell the memorized story by looking at the pages and by perceiving picture clues. Awareness of the link between speech and print comes with attention to individual words; the child begins to ask questions such as, "What does that say?" or "Where does it say that?" Other associations between spoken and printed forms are also occurring simultaneously in everday experiences with nontext language: labels, television, signs, and so forth. Repeated exposures to print in the above contexts and the monitoring of responses by adults lead to an ever-larger store of words recognized on sight. Smith calls this "reading without phonics," and he describes the process that children use to recognize individual words without sounding them out:

> Nor is there any fundamental difference between the way we learn to recognize objects and the way we learn to recognize written words.
>
> . . . .
>
> The answer is that we recognize words in the same way that we recognize all other familiar objects in our visual world—trees and animals, cars and houses, cutlery, crockery, furniture and faces: "on sight." We can recognize the thousands of words with which we are familiar for the same reason that we recognize all the thousands of other things, because we have learned what they look like (1979, 58).*

Smith further contends that we recognize not only words and objects in the same way, but the similarities also apply to letters (1979, 110–11). His analysis parallels that of Goodman referred to earlier in discussing the distinctive and nondistinctive features of spoken language. The visual forms of print for the same letter can vary in the way they are written—*K* and *k,* for example. Though they look different, both are treated the same by the reader because they make no difference in meaning. But the differences between *k* and *h* are significant to meaning. So, we learn to recognize words and letters on the basis of visual features that make a difference in meaning, and we ignore those which do not.

Along with growing attention to and recognition of individual words by sight in the context of reading itself, children begin to pay attention to the significant features of letters that make a difference in meaning. This is often observed as children say, "That starts just like my name." or "Show me how to make a *p*." The focusing on individual letters can also be observed in the self-corrections that beginning readers make when they realize that a word they have pronounced does not make sense in the printed context. The following is an example:

> *Text:* The boy put his *lunch* on the table.
> *Child:* The boy put his *bunch* on the table.

Amy looked at the sentence again asking, "What's a bunch?" in obvious puzzlement. Then she looked closely at *lunch* a moment and said "lunch." "That sounds better!"

It is very important that children be permitted to self-correct, to demand meaning of the sentence. If an adult quickly corrects or says, "How does the word begin?" or "Does it start with *b*?" children move on a precarious treadmill that teaches "all I have to do is pronounce it right."

In addition to beginning to associate many aspects of oral language in their attempts to make sense of print, children come to be aware of certain conventions about books and print. As they watch when parents reread a story, they are shown and/or see that one starts at the top left of the page and moves to the right along a line of print, sweeps back to the left and repeats the operation, moving to the bottom of the page. One also holds a book so that it is right side up. The first clue to this aspect of books is likely from illustrations: children will begin to turn the book so that trees and boys are not standing on their tops. Some children begin to notice the spaces used to

*Reprinted by permission of the publisher from Frank Smith, *Reading Without Nonsense* (New York, Teachers College Press, © 1984 by Teachers College, Columbia University. All rights reserved.) p. 58.

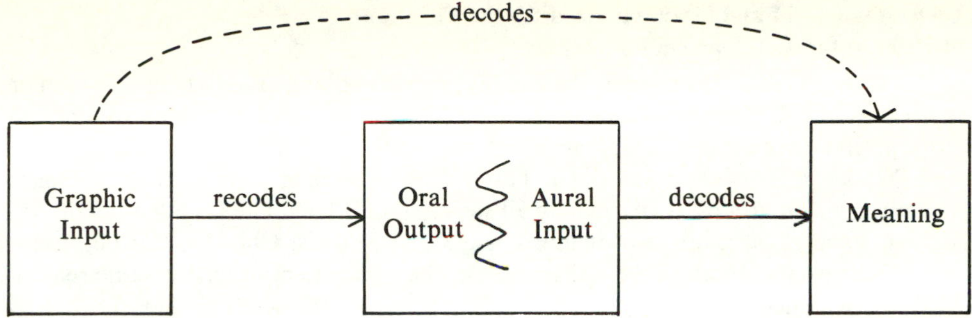

Figure 5.1. Early reading. Source: Kenneth S. Goodman, READING: PROCESS AND PROGRAM, National Council of Teachers of English, Champaign, Illinois, 1970, p. 17.

separate words and to understand their purpose, but many children may not know what a word or a letter is, even though they know words and letters. This poses no particular problem until the teacher begins to use the terms in talking *about reading*.

So, children who learn to read pretty much on their own by using what they know about oral language and experiencing the world begin first with *meaning* as it exists in the whole of language. With meaning as a guide, they then move gradually to the "parts," the *words* and then the *letters* that constitute print. They begin to associate symbols they see with the sounds they already have in spoken language. These phonic skills thus develop naturally out of the process of reading, not in isolated study *about* reading as occurs when these "pieces" are first taught outside meaningful context. Figure 5.1 is a concise summary of how the beginning reader uses oral language competencies to develop skills with print.

> The child here recodes graphic input as speech (either outloud or internally) and then utilizing his own speech as aural input, decodes as he does in listening. Notice the model assumes some direct decoding from print to meaning, even at early stages.
>
> In this diagram, *recode is used to mean going from code to code (aural to graphic)*; decode is reserved for processes that go from code (in either form) to meaning. In this sense, comprehension and decoding are virtual synonyms while *word-calling and sounding-out are recoding processes*. A third term, encode, is used to mean going from meaning to code (again either written or oral) (Goodman 1970, 17).*

As children increase and expand their skills and sight word store through continued experiences in reading, the need to process visual information in detail (focus on individual letters) decreases; they can move more and more directly from print to meaning without having to pronounce individual letters and words. Each moves toward becoming a fluent, silent reader.

*Source: Kenneth S. Goodman, READING: PROCESS AND PROGRAM, National Council of Teachers of English, Champaign, Illinois, 1970, p. 17. Used with permission.

Understanding of and Having a Need for the Functions of Print in the Development of Literacy

Roger Brown (1958, 7) says that the central function of language (whether spoken or written) is its use to make reference. Children first learn those words, both spoken and written, that have concrete referents in the real world.

We learn that which serves our purposes. The need to communicate, to share meanings within groups, is common to all societies; oral language functions as the vehicle for face-to-face, in-the-present exchange of meanings. Children learn oral language because its functions serve their needs. They learn to read for the same reason: needs are satisfied by the purposes that print can serve. In societies where print does not exist, there is an absence of the need to deal with it, and children do not learn to read.

Children living in a society where they are inundated by print develop a need to make sense of that medium.

> They will be most aware of the print that has functions which overlap those of oral language such as that which names and identifies—logos and brand names of cards, cereal boxes, peanut butter jars, or their own names—that which controls—signs for stop, exit, no parking. If they have a lot of experiences with books and newspapers, they may become aware of the more abstract functions of providing information or entertainment through literature (Goodman 1977, 311).*

In his writings about reading, John Downing (1979), too, emphasizes the importance of a child's understanding the functions of print as a necessary element in the learning-to-read process. He cites examples of recent research in which progress in reading was highly correlated with children's understanding of the functions of literacy. He goes even further to make understanding the functions of print the first of two major aspects that are required for developing an understanding of the reading task itself. The second is understanding the technical features of language. Technical features, for example, include the metalanguage, the terms used to talk about print—*word, letter,* and *sound.* Most children cited in research studies had developed little, if any, understanding of the terms, though teachers used them frequently in reading instruction.

Downing combines these two aspects of understanding the reading task into what he terms the "cognitive clarity theory" of learning to read. The theory is summarized below in eight cognitive clarity postulates:

1. Writing or print in any language is a visible code for those aspects of speech that were accessible to the linguistic awareness of the creators of that code or writing system;
2. this linguistic awareness of the creators of a writing system included simultaneous awareness of the communicative function of language and certain features of spoken language that are accessible to the speaker-hearer for logical analysis;
3. the learning-to-read process consists in the rediscovery of (a) the functions and (b) the coding rules of the writing system;

*Source: Kenneth S. Goodman, ACQUIRING LITERACY IS NATURAL: WHO SKILLED COCK ROBIN? in *Theory into Practice* 1977, 16:311, College of Education, Ohio State University, Columbus, Ohio. Used with permission of publisher and author.

4. their rediscovery depends on the learner's linguistic awareness of the same features of communication and language as were accessible to the creators of the writing system;
5. children approach the tasks of reading instruction in a normal state of cognitive confusion about the purposes and technical features of language;
6. under reasonably good conditions, children work themselves out of the initial state of cognitive confusion into increasing cognitive clarity about the functions and features of language;
7. although the initial stage of literacy acquisition is the most vital one, cognitive confusion continues to arise, and then, in turn, to give way to cognitive clarity throughout the later stages of education as new sub-skills are added to the student's repertory;
8. the cognitive clarity theory applies to all languages and writing systems (1979, 37).

Many young children live in a stimulating environment in which they learn naturally to make the necessary distinctions about the technical features of printed language, and they come to understand at least some of its functions. But not all young ones will have had a preschool reading environment that fosters sufficient growth in understanding the functions and features of print. The problem for the teacher becomes that of determining what understandings the child does have and then using these understandings to expand and extend reading competencies. This is the second major topic of the present chapter.

Reading as Bringing Meaning *to* Print Rather Than Getting Meaning *from* Print

Visual and nonvisual information. We have already stated that there are two kinds of information necessary for learning to read: visual and nonvisual. *Visual information* is that which the eye sees, the print on the page. *Nonvisual information* is that which already exists in the head. Of the two types, nonvisual information is the more important when reading is viewed as a thinking process.

It is possible to pronounce any number of words without being able to understand what they mean. Children who have had an overdose of attending to the visual aspects of print can become excellent word callers, but they are not readers unless they understand that which they pronounce. Adults can identify with this dilemma of being able to deal with visual information without being able to make sense of it. The examples below illustrate this point.

> What *Is* in a Name?
>
> A second-grader labors long over a new word he has encountered in his reader. He finally sounds it out but he never realizes that it is his *own name*—Miguel! (An anecdote from Kenneth Goodman in Jerome C. Harste and Carolyn L. Burke, 1978, 55).
>
> Damas or Caballeros?
>
> Mary and Audrey, age seven, went with their parents to a Spanish restaurant for dinner. In the course of the dinner, they obtained permission from their mother to go to the restroom.

> Now I must explain that the words on the doors for the restrooms were *damas* and *caballeros* instead of ladies and gentlemen. Mary and Audrey had heard enough Spanish language and they knew enough phonics that they had no trouble with the pronounciation.
>
> After they had been gone only a couple of minutes, they came running back to their parent's table and chorused, "Are we *damas* or *caballeros?*"

There is also a trade-off between visual and nonvisual information:

> The more nonvisual information you have when you read, the less visual information you need.
>
> The less nonvisual information you have when you read, the more visual information you need (Smith 1979, 14).*

The more one knows about how reading works and the larger the store of concepts in the content of print, the less one must rely on visual information on the printed page, and, the more fluent reading is.

Nonvisual information is more important than visual information because "there is a severe limit to how much visual information the brain can handle" (Smith 1979, 15). The brain processes much greater quantities of print in the same amount of time where the content is already familiar. For example, when one looks at a line of random letters, the most that the brain can process is four-to-five letters.

J L H Y L P A J M P W K H M Y O E Z S X P E S L N

But as individual symbols are arranged in increasingly familiar contexts (for example, words), the quantity of symbols processed in a single glance increases proportionately.

SNEEZE FURY HORSES WHEN AGAIN

Most readers identify at least two words or the equivalent of ten-to-twelve letters (Smith 1979, 18–23).† We make the same amount of visual information go twice as far in the second example by making use of nonvisual information already stored in the brain: we already know how letters go together in English to form words. This eliminates the necessity of paying attention to each letter because it reduces the number of possible alternatives with which we must deal. The letters in the first example are not arranged by any "rule" known to us; and there are far more possibilities as to what they may be.

*Reprinted by permission of the publisher from Frank Smith, *Reading Without Nonsense* (New York, Teachers College Press, © 1984 by Teachers College, Columbia University. All rights reserved.) p. 14.

†Reprinted by permission of the publisher from Frank Smith, *Reading Without Nonsense* (New York, Teachers College Press, © 1984 by Teachers College, Columbia University. All rights reserved.) pp. 15, 18–23.

The opposite is true in the second example, where symbols are arranged according to "rules," thus reducing the number of possibilities for what each letter might be by the rules for their grouping. One who knows the rules can predict very rapidly on the basis of this nonvisual information what the whole is without having to deal with each part separately.

The preceding explanation—of what fluent readers are able to do and how they do it—does not explain how they got to be that way. How young children figure out the system and use it can be determined by a brief review of how natural readers develop.

Acquiring and using visual and nonvisual information. As children experience and interact with their everyday world, they accumulate a vast amount of information. This information is stored in their minds in a very systematic way: related meanings are grouped together into a system of interrelated categories at a variety of levels as was described in chapter 3. This organization of knowledge represents one's schema, script, or cognitive structure. It becomes the "known" by which all new information is comprehended. This knowledge base is brought to the reading task. The larger the base, the more the reader has to draw upon in dealing with the concepts in the text, and the greater the probability that he will understand the message of the author. Where no knowledge of a concept is present in one's cognitive store, there is nothing to which the meanings of the author can be related, and therefore, they will not be understood.

In learning to read, the cognitive store—the nonvisual information—must include knowledge about many aspects of print. Knowledge of the types of printed discourse must be developed. The child becomes familiar with and develops a "story schema" by hearing stories read. Knowing how story language sounds makes it possible for him to anticipate meanings when he begins to read stories himself. Or, a schema the child already has developed from experience may be used to generate text, which the child can then learn to read. One might use a "bus ride" schema, as suggested by Pearson and Johnson 1978, p. 45, and talk about riding a bus. The teacher writes down the ideas, and they are then used as reading material.

Our Bus Ride

The bus is big.
It is yellow.
It came to get us.
We all climbed on.
We went to the zoo.
The bus driver was a woman.
The bus can go fast.
We stopped at stop lights.
We rode a long time.
We got to the zoo

Carol Chomsky described a group of third graders who had two full years of phonics behind them; they had indeed developed many phonics skills, but they made little sense of what they were able to decode. She wrote, "The attempt to (read) was almost painful, a word-by-word struggle, long silences, eyes eventually drifting around the room in an attempt to escape the humiliation and frustration of the all too familiar, hated situation (1976, 288).

As a first order of business, teachers must provide beginning readers with text that makes sense and is, therefore, most predictable. Reading stories repeatedly to children until they have all but memorized the text is an effective first step toward helping children to begin to figure out some of the unique characteristics (McKenzie 1977). Meaning is first, then, a focus on individual words and letters follow.

As children begin to understand how print works, this information then becomes part of their nonvisual store of information. It becomes their schema for reading; and this schema is then used to make sense of print. For example, the discovery that an unknown word begins with the same letter as a known word provides the child with important information which can then be used to identify many new words. It is the knowledge—the schema—that first letters provide an important clue to identification that enables the child to look in the most productive place. This schema becomes a mind-set that can be used in all future encounters with unfamiliar words in print.

When children have heard a story so often that its meaning has been memorized, they have the foundation for identifying words by using the total context to predict what they are. Discovery that context can be used to identify words adds another schema, or knowledge base, in the child's growing repertoire about the features of print and how he can use them to arrive at meaning. Continuation of experiences with reading thus builds an ever-larger nonvisual base for dealing with the visual aspects of print.

Risk Taking as a Vital Element in Learning to Read

Learning implies dealing with the unknown; the unknown always has a degree of uncertainty and, therefore, is an element of risk. O'Henry's "The Lady or the Tiger" is a classic example of risk taking. When the door is opened, which will come out—the lady or the tiger? The answer is unknown until the story character is willing to resolve the uncertainty by risking a turn of the knob. And so it is with learning to read. The reading process for the young child is indeed a whole series of risks because reading is a complex of many competencies, all of which are unknowns to the beginner.

But children coming to the reading task are no strangers to risk taking, for it has been a basic element in all learning from birth. All explorations of the environment by which the child accumulates meanings about the world are by their very nature ventures into the unknown and so couched in uncertainty. The outcomes may be either positive or negative—either way they are bases for learning. Learning to walk involves the risk of falling down, perhaps many times. Touching objects can result in either pleasant or unpleasant sensations: a stove can be too hot, but a "security blanket" can be warm and soft and satisfying. Learning to stack blocks is to risk their tumbling down. Learning to ride a bicycle is to risk skinned knees and sore hands. Taking a toy away from another child may result in being banged over the head with it in return.

Learning to speak the language of the child's world involves risk taking by experimenting with sounds and words to determine their effects on the listener. The results are unpredictable until the child is able to approximate the forms that the listener knows. When, for example, the young child says "more cun" and the adult does not supply more "cun," the child's intended result has been denied: his risk has not paid off. He must attack the unknown in another way. He may then point to bacon on a plate and repeat "more cun." Failure to communicate his meaning the first time led to the provision of an additional cue—pointing. Where "more bacon" is forthcoming along with, "Oh, you want more bacon." The child's uncertainty about how to get his meaning across has been reduced. What was unknown now becomes a "known" and can be used in the future to communicate more effectively.

Propelled by curiosity, young children are natural risk takers. They do not ordinarily back away from attempting to overcome uncertainties because of negative results: they simply search for and try out ways that *will* work. Negative results often produce far more learning because the child has learned what does not work, and he must still come up with alternatives that will produce the desired effects. Each attempt is a lesson in problem solving. A child falls down and pulls himself up by a chair. In falling, he learns that a chair can help him to stand, so he practices holding on to the chair and walking around it. He finds that the mother does not know what "cun" is, so he points.

Backing away from risk taking because of negative results has to be learned: it is not a natural inclination of the young child. Fear of risk taking comes about when there is lack of encouraging, supportive responses from those persons who are part of the child's world.

The strong support base given by parents of natural readers and the role it plays in a child's learning to read was described in chapter 1. This support provides the basis for exploring and experimenting with print by filling the child's world with print and opportunities to scribble. In response to children's specific questions,"What does that say?" or "How do you make an *M*?" parents provide answers. When a child says, "That's a cat." when a dog passes by, the parent replies, "No, that's a dog." and leaves the child to work out the criteria for distinguishing between the two. These criteria are worked out by the child by conducting further tests and receiving additional feedback from parents.

As was stated earlier, learning to read is a process that requires much risk taking. There is much to be known, the many uncertainties about how the system works. Children cannot be supplied with the answers, but they can be supported in their efforts to find their own way through the maize. They must engage in a variety of activities, all of which are forms of risking: predicting, sampling, and confirming or correcting. They have already engaged in the same activities in learning oral language. Supportive adults provide the bridge by which they now learn to read by applying these same strategies to make sense of print. Children predict meaning and sample print on the basis of feedback from themselves or from adults according to whether or not sense is made. Below is a good summation of the importance of support for risk taking in learning to read:

> Might children have tunnel vision because they are afraid of making a mistake? Neither comprehension nor learning can take place in an atmosphere of anxiety. Prediction, like learning, is a risky business and a child must feel that the risks are worth taking. Children who are afraid to make a mistake will not learn, and they will not even demonstrate the reading ability that they might have acquired (Smith 1979, 35).*

*Reprinted by permission of the publisher from Frank Smith, *Reading Without Nonsense* (New York, Teachers College Press, © 1984 by Teachers College, Columbia University. All rights reserved.) p. 35.

Your Turn 5.1 Risking in reading.

Risk taking has been described here as a vital element in learning to read. After parental responses to a child's efforts at home, the teacher is probably the most-important influence in determining a child's willingness to take risks.

1. Can you remember an incident(s) when you were willing to learn by revealing your own ignorance? What happened? Did the result encourage or discourage you from further risk taking? Explain.
2. On the basis of your experiences, what would you, as a teacher, do to create a climate that would be conducive to risk taking in learning to read?
   (Be prepared to share your thoughts with others.)

Learning to Read as a Pleasurable Experience

Both *process* and *content* in reading are potential sources of enjoyment. Katherine K. Newman writes, "One of the functions of reading content is to evoke emotions" (1978, 978). We described in chapter 1 how sharing books with young children can build an "emotional conditioning" to books which can lead to the attitude that reading and books are a source of pleasure. We described the way in which children practice responding emotionally to the content by repeating well-known passages with full sound effects. Sylvia Ashton-Warner (1971) used content that had high emotional overtones for children. Each child supplied words out of his own experiences—words that had intense personal meaning. These words were then used to make the text from which each child learned to read. (Using content that is derived from the child's personal experiences to compile text for beginning readers will be more thoroughly developed under the language experience approach in chapter 7.)

Margaret Greer describes the way in which sharing content by reading aloud to children is an excellent way to promote affective development in general and feeling toward reading in particular:

> Perhaps no experience provides greater possibilities for nurturing affective growth through involvement in the feeling process than does listening to the teacher read a story or book. Oral reading makes possible the setting of an affective tone not available in silent reading. Through pitch, stress, rhythm, and intonation, the reader can "play" the content much as a fine pianist interprets a musical score.
>
> As the child listens, the feeling process is activated. Descriptions of places, events in the story, and the emotions associated with them come to represent similar situations from his own experience. He feels with the characters being portrayed, relives story experiences being described. Once he has identified with the emotional theme of the story he is capable of participation in a broader dimension of the affective process—empathy.
>
> Now he can share with other listeners what he feels about the story situation. Whereas sensitivity and identification are personal matters between himself and the story content, empathy is a group sharing of that which each has derived on his own through the former two. The process of sharing establishes a different atmosphere for feeling, a new direction for relating one to another (1972, 340).

In chapter 3 we described the way in which the quality of children's experiencing the environment directly affects how they come to view themselves and others. The more successful they are in their undertakings, the more self-confidence they have and the greater the possibilities for learning. Jerome Bruner writes that

> success does three important things: first, it makes you feel that you can succeed again; it decreases the feeling of helplessness. Second, it gives you a confirming instance of a good solution which you can use in similar problem solving situations in the future. And third, success encourages people to vary their behavior, to be a little more daring (1982, 60).

The child's experience in the process of learning to read must be successful. Bruno Bettelheim and Karen Zelan write that "his experiences in learning to read may decide how he will feel about learning in general, and even about himself as a person" (1982, 5).

Where most of a child's learning experiences have been successful and, therefore, enjoyable, he approaches learning to read much as he does other unknowns in his world—with, writes Johanna DeStefano, an "absence of the expectation that learning will not take place" (1981, 111). The classroom teacher can do much to increase the probability that children will succeed in learning to read. We have already cited many possibilities; we shall repeat below only those that deserve emphasis here.

1. *Begin with whole-language text, the meaning of which is already familiar to the child.* To be successful, the child needs all the cues to meaning he can get; whole language provides most of the cues. Familiarity with the content increases the likelihood that the child will be able to reproduce the meaning whether or not it exactly matches the print. In the early stages reproducing meaning is satisfying enough to bring pleasure.

Another important reason for using whole language is that many concepts about reading, which the child must develop to become a successful reader, can only be learned by directly interacting with whole language. Gloria M. McDonell and Bess E. Osburn (1978) make the following relevant points in discussing Marie Clay's longitudinal study of how groups of New Zealand children learned to read.

> Her research found that children move through stages of readiness as they learn about two distinct sets of concepts about print. The sets of concepts Clay identified have to do with: 1) the visual aspects of print and 2) the language concepts about print.
>
> The language concepts identified by Clay which are required for success are: 1) an understanding that print can be turned into speech to provide a message; 2) a knowledge that pictures can be used as a guide to that message; and 3) a realization that print must be as sensible as spoken language.
>
> The visual concepts are among those which many children come to school failing to understand: 1) the directional constraints of print, that print moves from left to right; 2) that a word is surrounded by spaces; and 3) that the concept of word and letter are not the same. Imagine the confusion that would exist in these children's minds when teachers use terms that are so vague to them.
>
> Finally, the New Zealand researcher found that successful readers were those who were able to integrate their knowledge of language and their understanding of the conventions of print. In her study, children demonstrated this in several ways. They used their finger to point to the words as they were reading. Dr. Clay calls this voice-print match. Another and more advanced indication of this integration was the ability

> of the successful reader to self-correct. Without prompting from the teacher, these readers were able to use their knowledge of the cues available to them to predict what a word might be. When this prediction seemed incorrect, either visually or because it did not make sense, they automatically reread to correct their error. These children had acquired a self-regulating ability indicating they had learned that print carries a particular message which must be reconstructed from both visual and language cues.
>
> Perhaps the most critical finding of the Clay research is the fact that none of these concepts or readiness skills can be learned unless the child interacts with books and print. To attempt to isolate these skills for mastery apparently only slows or interferes with the rate at which they are acquired. Teachers of successful readers provide many opportunities for children to discover the relationships between print and language by giving them books to read, and then reinforcing their understanding of these relationships through writing activities (1978, 26–27).*

2. *Begin reading instruction with materials in which children have exhibited an interest.* To develop these interests in the first place, provide an abundance of written materials that children are free to explore and that you or an aide can read *to* them.

3. *Help children to develop an accurate conception of what reading is by keeping skills in proper perspective during instruction.* Children should come to see skills for what they are—a means to achieve their goals

> From the very beginning, the child must be convinced that skills are only a means to achieve a goal, and the only goal of importance is that he become literate—that is, come to enjoy literature and benefit from what it has to offer (Bettelheim and Zelan 1982, 6).

It is not difficult to get an idea of what a child thinks reading is. Parents often ask their children what they did in school; the dialogue below gives two different responses to the same question. The first response reveals a gross misconception about what reading is all about; the second indicates that the child has an accurate understanding of what reading is.

Response 1

Parent (to first-grader): What did you do in school today?

Child: We read.

Parent: What did you read?

Child: A, Apple, /ă/.

Response 2

Parent: What did you do in school toay?

Child: We read.

Parent: What did you read?

Child: The Town Mouse and The Country Mouse.

4. *Provide opportunities for children to produce closer approximations of actual text with successive readings, and give them time to self-correct miscues as they are able.*

*Source: Gloria M. McDonell and Bess E. Osburn, NEW THOUGHTS ABOUT READING READINESS, *Language Arts,* 55 (January, 1978), pp. 26–27, National Council of Teachers of English, Urbana, Illinois. Used with permission.

Study and observation of natural readers provide some excellent guidelines to help young children acquire literacy when they come to school. Constance Weaver wrote, "Contrary to what one might think, it is possible to preserve most if not all of these features of natural reading acquisition in the classroom" (1980, 150). Most children could learn to read as easily and as naturally as they learn to talk; both competencies develop best outside the confines of formal instruction as it was practiced in the past. As stated at the end of chapter 1, and as has been implied many times throughout this text, some radical changes are indicated in the way we define and conduct teaching.

Teaching Reading: A Redefinition

If the goal of producing greater numbers of natural readers is to become a reality, then teaching must be seen in a different light than has been the case to date. Redefinition will include shifting the emphasis from "piece" studies to actual reading activities, clarifying teacher/learner roles, restructuring the methodology, and utilizing the strengths of children in the teaching/learning process.

Greater emphasis on actual reading activities with proportionately less time spent on activities about *reading.* Young children tend to emphasize meaning from the beginning of the learning-to-read process. As they read in whole written language, they acquire many skills of reading pretty much on their own. But their focus is always on the end—meaning—not on the means, or the process by which meaning is achieved. Seldom is the end obscured by the means.

Many adults, on the other hand, particularly some teachers of beginning reading, tend to fix on the *process* of acquiring literacy rather than the goal to be achieved as a result of the process. Too few activities are provided to help the child derive skills from dealing with meaningful context. As children are given more opportunities to interact with whole written language, skills development becomes a product of the process rather than a prerequisite to the process. The major role of instruction shifts to helping children develop strategies to achieve skills.

Skills are a product of a strategy (process). When children are asked to identify certain consonant blends in words, for example, the identification is a skill. If they can do it correctly, they already have the skill; hence, there is no reason to teach them what they already know. But if they cannot do it, then they should be helped to develop the strategies that will enable them to achieve the skill. The major strategies required for learning to read are the same as those developed by children in learning to talk: predicting, sampling, and confirming or correcting. Figure 5.2 and the discussion from Weaver explain the differences between skills and strategies and the place each occupies in reading.

> Most approaches to reading emphasize the development of reading *skills.* Though some of these are "comprehension skills," a great deal of attention is paid to skills for pronouncing and/or identifying words. In contrast, most psycholinguists emphasize the development of *strategies* for getting meaning from connected text. Figure 5.2 illustrates this difference. In the word-centered skills approaches, children are taught to use their stock of sight words, their phonics and structural analysis skills, and (often last) their understanding of context in order to identify words. Concern with comprehension typically comes later, after the selection has been read. But in a

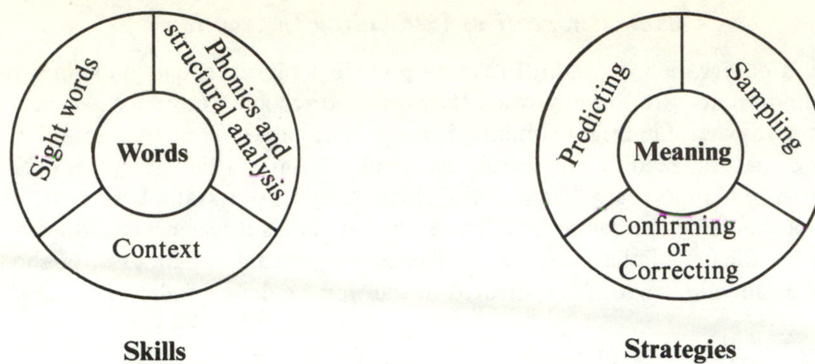

Figure 5.2. Skills versus strategies. Source: Constance Weaver, PSYCHOLINGUISTICS AND READING: FROM PROCESS TO PRACTICE, Little, Brown and Company, 1980, p. 144. Used with permission of author.

> meaning-centered strategies approach, children are actually taught to use their comprehension of a text to help them identify the words. They are taught to use context of all sorts to *predict* what will come next; to *sample* the visual display, using a minimum of grapho-phonic cues to confirm or modify their prediction and to tentatively interpret a word; and to use following context to *confirm* or *correct* this tentative interpretation (1980, 144–45).

Clarification of the roles of teacher and learner in the acquisition of reading. Effective teaching is based on *following the lead of the child.* It is not difficult to tell where children are in oral language and reading development, because they tell in countless ways where they are in figuring out both systems. Teachers and parents look to the child for cues; these cues then become the basis for assisting the child in building an efficient system to process oral and written language. The example below, provided by Miles V. Zintz, illustrates how one mother followed her child's lead as the child grew into reading.

> Debbie was a very bright little girl who talked fluently in sentences when she was one year old. She listened for long periods of time to Mother Goose when she was 18 months old. She could study magazine pictures and "tell" four- and five-sentence stories about them when she was two. One day when she was three years old, she was sitting in the car downtown with her mother. Without warning, she spelled the name of the department store across the street, "B-A-R-N-E-Y-S," and asked, "What does that spell, Mother?" When Debbie was three and one-half years old, she began studying the comic strips in the newspaper and spelling out words for her mother to pronounce for her. When she had spelled out a series of words and waited each time for the pronunciation, she could, all by herself, keep in mind what the words were telling her, and at the end of the short sentence, repeat the complete sentence (1981, 11).

Teaching children to read (or anything else for that matter) means providing appropriate stimulation, guidance, and opportunities to solve their own problem of acquiring literacy by building an efficient system for mastering print. Then just as parents assume their children will learn to talk, "we can do children the credit of assuming that they can learn to read" (Weaver 1980, 151) because they do.

Your Turn 5.2 Skills and strategies in the reading process.

Have a second- or third-grade child read to you a basal reader story. The text should be at the level the teacher has assigned to the child. Use a tape recorder to record reading. Analyze the child's reading according to the following:

1. What difficulties does the child have?
2. How are these difficulties handled—what strategies are used?
3. How well do the strategies work in solving problems?
4. What skills has the child already developed? List skills specifically.

If the above makes teaching appear too simple, it is because the magnitude of what *stimulation* and *guidance* involve is not clearly understood. Both require that the teacher provide opportunities that make learning to read easy for the child. ("Easy" in this sense is in no way synonymous with an absence of energy or effort.) It means that the activities in which the children participate must have purpose and meaning for them.

In earlier discussion of Burton White's studies of the first three years of life, it appears that mothers of competent children seemed to have a special aptitude, an intuitive gift for designing the child's environment and consulting with him. In response to children's questions or requests for help, these mothers were adept at identifying the problem and in providing what was needed. No systematic teaching was involved; consultation was more often given "on the fly" in only a few moments. In a similar fashion the parents of natural readers engaged in little, if any, formal instruction; instead, they identified and responded to the needs of children on request. The most successful teachers of reading also seem to have a special insight into—perhaps an intuitive grasp of—what children are trying to do and of responding appropriately to those attempts.

Methodology in teaching reading based on knowledge and understanding of the nature of language and its use, the nature of cognitive and affective development, and the nature of the reading process. Since this point is developed as a continuing thread throughout the text, further elaboration is not considered necessary. Chapters 6–8 deal with specifics of methodology in terms of program components, activities, and materials that reflect a strong commitment to concepts which have been derived from research in language and cognitive development over the past fifteen-to-twenty years.

Instruction beginning with the strengths of the young child, followed by focus on extension and refinement of developing competencies of the young reader. These two instructional components are fully developed in the following section and in chapters 7–9.

Building on the Strengths that Children Bring to Reading

As we have already stated, young children enter kindergarten or first grade at a variety of levels on the learning-to-read continuum. Some natural readers have acquired the basic knowledge, strategies, and skills for fluent reading. Others may have insufficient depth in these basic areas, but they are well on their way to fluency. The majority of children do not enter school as natural readers, that is, as having already developed some minimum level of fluency. Some may have had little, if any, exposure to print in books and other connected discourse, but most will have encountered a considerable quantity of print in the everyday world, such as labels and signs. Limited exposure to connected discourse has not provided the necessary opportunities to learn about the conventions of print: the "rules" governing the organization of print, the relation of print to speech, the distinctive features by which words are identified, and the language unique to different types of printed text. But regardless of their position relative to printed language, all children bring a number of strengths on which acquisition of literacy can begin.

Rationale for building on strengths. Most teachers support the long revered admonition that we must begin where each child is, that each is unique in his own right, and that these individual differences must not be ignored. Hence, Goodman developed his rationale for building on strengths.

> *Too much time has been spent trying to find weaknesses and deficiencies in children which might explain their lack of success in learning to read.* A flexible, relevant reading curriculum would capitalize on the strengths of children of both sexes and of all shapes, sizes, colors, ethnic and cultural backgrounds, dispositions, energy levels, and physical attributes. Every objective in reading must be relevant to the pupils we are teaching (1970, 28). (Italics added)*

However, too often in actual practice what we *do* belies what we *say*. In practice we operate more often than not from a "deficit model" (Zintz 1975, 6), rather than from one of individual uniqueness and the strengths inherent therein.

The Deficit Model

A deficit model of teaching is the opposite of a "strength" model. Deficit focuses on what a child *does not* know. Educational practices are replete with specific examples of this mentality in operation. Preset standards at each grade level are defined for what a child should do in reading. The results are that children who are "behind" are pushed to "catch up," while those who are ahead are given a handicap so that they do not have an "unfair" advantage. In any classroom situation where individuals of varying competencies are involved and are allowed to develop without restrictions, we expect to find a wide spread in achievement levels. Individuals who were more competent at the beginning should remain so at the finish, and those who were less competent may still be behind the leaders.

Children who enter school already fluent readers are sometimes given the "handicap" of having to go through "readiness" for reading. What a waste! Children who are "behind" according to readiness test scores are given special attention to make up for the deficiency. After a year in school, children are "measured" again; those who have not attained the standard for at least a minimum level of performance are then labeled. Whatever the term, be it "remedial," "modified primary," or "immature," the meaning is the same—deficient.

*Source: Kenneth S. Goodman, READING: PROCESS AND PROGRAM, National Council of Teachers of English, Champaign, Illinois, 1970, p. 28. Used with permission.

In intraclass groupings for reading, the same "deficit" mentality operates. A standard is set, children's performance is measured against that standard, and then children are sorted according to how well they measure up. Groups are again labeled accordingly.

As has been implied above, tests are too often used to focus on weaknesses rather than on strengths. Test results are examined to determine the areas in which children are "behind" so that a major "push" can be made in those areas. Even in day-to-day evaluation, we seldom say by our checking system and comments, "Wow, you got two *correct* out of ten!" Instead, we check what is *wrong* and implicitly say, "You *missed eight*." Children do not fail to get the drift. After a year or more of negative feedback, they may start to share the teacher's emphasis on deficits and begin to feel that school is a game in which a "strike out" takes precedence over "homerun," at least where reading is concerned.

The labels used to identify the "deficient" can have some extremely detrimental consequences on how children feel about themselves and their ability to learn to read. No matter what reading groups are called—be it Redbirds, Bluebirds, and Robins or Hares, Tortoises, and Tigers—children get the message. They know who the Buzzards are and why. Those who figure out the system first are sure to share their findings with those who might take a bit longer to arrive at the same conclusion: "You're in the Hare Group; that means you can read fast." or "You're in the Redbird Group; that means you are really a Buzzard because you don't read good."

Unfortunately, the above is not the only negative consequence of labeling by deficiency. Labels, once fixed, tend to endure; once a Buzzard, always a Buzzard. Young readers find themselves in a double bind. Having started behind (deficient), they are likely to stay behind because catching up means that regardless of the progress they make from where they began, they can only catch up if they leap farther in the same amount of time than their "nondeficient" peers do. Children who do not catch up after expending considerable energy and effort may feel that they cannot succeed, so why try. Thus a vicious circle is set in motion.

Focus on weaknesses is also destructive because strengths, if not ignored all together, tend to be obscured. An example is a child who reads well with understanding but does poorly on phonics worksheets. The report home says "Troy needs to work on phonics." A second example comes from a college student of one of the authors. Margie recounted the following about her own learning-to-read experience:

> When I was in school it was not until the second grade that I realized I really could read. When I started first grade, I *thought* I could read because I was already reading. The teacher had us read so she could put us into the proper reading groups. Well, she must have thought I could read, too, because I was put into the Bluebird Group, the really Top Group. Before long, though, I began to have trouble in the reading circle. I would always read ahead to myself while the others took turns reading aloud. When it came my time to read, I never knew the place. After awhile, the teacher put me in The Next Lowest Group; I've forgotten what it was called. The same thing happened; I couldn't read when it was my time because I still didn't know the place. Finally, I was put in the Low Group—along with four boys who had started there. I thought I must have gotten worse in reading, that I really didn't know how after all.
>
> Well, the next year I was put into the Low Group to start with because that's where I was last year. (I remember wondering how the second grade teacher knew where I was supposed to be!) Anyway, I thought I'd better "keep up" if I was ever going to learn to

> read. So, I did, but sometimes it was hard and it made me sleepy, too. When it came my time, I knew the place and I read like the Wind. The teacher was amazed. "How did you get put into this group?" she said. I guess she forgot, so I had to tell her that she did it. I went to the Top Group and was there until I got to junior high where there weren't any more groups in reading.

By any measure, a deficit model has strong negative connotations in the many facets that comprise teaching and learning.

The Strengths Model

Where the strengths model is the focus, the whole picture of teaching and learning is cast in a different light: the positive is accentuated, and the results will most likely be radically different from those discussed under the "deficit model."

First, success becomes the focus; present strengths have been derived from past successes. No child is considered inadequate because each brings strengths to the reading task, regardless of whether he reads or not. As we discussed earlier, success determines how one feels about himself; a positive self-concept generates confidence in self. If one sees himself as competent and capable, he will engage willingly in the risk taking that learning to read requires. He begins with a solid, sure footing on the journey to reading proficiency.

There is a double payoff for children when the bridge to reading is built on the strengths they bring. First, they can operate with confidence because they begin with that which is already familiar, and, second, they have the basis for assimilating or accommodating the new information with that which is already known.

When strengths are identified and built on, individual differences are considered and respected. Success is measured not in terms of how far one has to go to meet a preconceived standard set for all children in a particular group, but according to how far they have come from where they began. Children's progress is measured in terms of their own unique abilities and worth, not by comparison with others whose strengths may differ from their own.

The concept of deficient will be unnecessary. What the child does not know will simply be considered a fertile area to be explored and developed just as any other unknown. The learner will be "moving toward" rather than "catching up."

The labels that have been used to denote deficiencies with the resulting negative messages will no longer be used. Where the strengths of each child are the focus of instruction, labels are difficult to fix, because the comparative basis from which they are derived has been eliminated. The caste system that results from comparative labeling based on what children do not know will never have to be broken because it will not have formed in the first place.

Finally, if all the foregoing sounds like an impossible, utopian dream, a naive disregard for reality, then it may be that we have too long looked backward to the negative rather than forward to the positive in reading instruction. We must no longer ignore all that has been learned about the power of positive reinforcement and self-fulfilling prophecies. We must recognize that the biggest block to children's learning to read has been interference with the natural way they have learned everything else. We must accept the responsibility for having turned reading into an unnatural, more-complex task than it actually is.

The strengths that children bring to reading. With few exceptions, all children come to reading with abundant strengths in two major areas: *life experience* and *language competence.* Propelled by curiosity, the need to know and make sense of their world, young children have acquired an extraordinary number of strengths in both areas. These strengths are the basic foundations on which literacy is then built. In a very real sense they form a bridge to literacy.

Life Experience

Children's major activity in the preschool years is exploring the world. Regardless of the type of environment in which children live, they acquire a rich store of meanings. The way in which meanings are derived from experience and the way these meanings influence all future learning have already been described in detail. A brief summary of the major points should suffice here. Children are constantly taking in information and impressions about this world. These become the raw materials out of which they make meanings. Through the processes of assimilation and accommodation, they sort the new data according to their relationship to what is already known. A category system of related meanings is formed on the basis of distinguishing criteria, which each child defines. The system constantly expands as new information is encountered. This becomes the cognitive and affective stores, the schemata for operating on the world and making sense of it. Labels are attached to meanings and language emerges.

Preoperational children's thinking differs markedly from that of adults, but this fact in no way diminishes their ability to draw on the nonvisual store of meanings when they encounter print. They learn to predict quite naturally the meanings from print by drawing from what is already known. Goodman described the interrelationship between strengths, experiences, and learning to read in the following way: (a) "Readers brings prior experiences into play in response to the graphic input," (b) "Readers organize the meanings they are constructing according to existing concepts and reorganize experience as they read," and (c) "Vocabulary is largely a term for the ability of children to sort out their experiences and concepts in relation to words and phrases in the context of what they are reading" (1970, 16).*

Language Competence

Children have a truly remarkable capacity to learn and use language. Formal instruction is seldom, if ever, provided. They learn to reproduce the sounds of their language. Each learns the rules by which sounds are combined to form meaningful units and by which these units are combined to form phrases and sentences. They learn the rules by which words can be changed to convey different meanings. They learn to use all the subtleties of unspoken language to convey meaning. Each acquires the capacity to note features that make a difference in meaning and to ignore those which do not. In listening they process what is heard by predicting, sampling, and confirming or correcting in order to arrive at meaning from spoken discourse. They discover the functions of oral language that fit their needs and use them accordingly. They will have a speaking vocabulary of several thousand words by the time they enter kindergarten.

*Source: Kenneth S. Goodman, READING: PROCESS AND PROGRAM, National Council of Teachers of English, Champaign, Illinois, 1970, p. 16.

In summary, each has acquired the basic structure of the language and is quite skilled in its use. Children bring a host of language strengths to deal with language in print.

The strengths that children may *bring to reading.* What children know about reading and, therefore, the strengths they possess depend on the quantity and quality of their experience with print prior to the time they enter the world of formal education. Some children, as in the case of natural readers, will have acquired most, if not all, of the competencies, knowledge, and insights enumerated below. The teacher will find it necessary to observe closely each child to determine the strengths each brings. Children who possess the strengths cited here have already reached a high level of fluency. Most children who begin kindergarten or first grade will have some, but not all, of these strengths.

The strengths related to printed language are organized below according to major categories and subcategories.

1. Understanding of the relations between written and spoken language.
   a) Written language can be converted to speech; speech can be written down.
   b) Meaning underlies both forms.
   c) Both have a common system and structure.
2. Understanding of visual concepts about print.
   a) In English print is processed from left to right horizontally and from top to bottom vertically.
   b) Words are composed of letters, and sentences are composed of words; the meanings of "letter," "word," and "sentence" differ.
   c) Words are surrounded by space.
   d) Print is divided into units of meaning—phrases and sentences—by punctuation; different marks are used to show different meanings—pauses, questions, and exclamations.
3. Understanding of a variety of functions and styles of written language.
   a) Story language.
   b) Expository language (information books and textbooks).
   c) Conversational language.
4. Performance competencies.
   a) Recognizes many words on sight.
   b) Uses graphic, syntactic, and semantic cues to predict meaning.
   c) Monitors reading through oral language; self-corrects when miscues interfere with meaning.
   d) Attends to critical features to identify words: letters, word shapes, spelling patterns (Kavale and Schreiner 1978, 35).
   e) Reflects in oral reading the language of print; talking like a book (Clay 1972, in McKenzie 1977, 320).
   f) Uses phrasing when reading text.
   g) Uses strategies of prediction, sampling, and confirming or correcting to process print.

Extending and Expanding Insights, Knowledge, and Competencies in Reading

What children know about language and reading constitutes the strengths that form the foundations to help them become successful readers. What children do not know becomes the basis for extending and refining those elements to produce fluent reading. Teaching is primarily a matter of determining what is known and not known by the children and then providing opportunities for bridging from the knowns, or strengths, to the unknowns. This process is the subject of chapters 6–8.

Summary

We have described a new basis for reading instruction that builds directly on a number of principles drawn from research and study of language, thought and reading. An understanding of these principles calls into question many past practices and points to a new direction for helping children to acquire literacy. When knowledge of language and how it is acquired and used are the foundation for instructional practices, learning to read becomes a natural extension of oral language development, and children can grow into reading as naturally as they have learned to communicate in speech.

The next three chapters identify and describe in detail the components of an instructional program that is designed to enable children to learn to read naturally.

References

Ashton-Warner, Sylvia. *Teacher.* New York: Simon and Schuster, 1971.

Bettelheim, Bruno, and Zelan, Karen. "Why Children Don't Like to Read." *The Atlantic Monthly* 248 (November 1981): 25–31.

———. *On Learning to Read, The Child's Fascination with Meaning.* New York: Random House, Vintage Books, 1982.

Brown, Roger. *Words and Things.* New York: Free Press, 1958.

Bruner, Jerome. "Schooling Children in a Nasty Climate." *Psychology Today* (January 1982): 57–63.

Butler, Dorothy, and Clay, Marie. *Reading Begins at Home.* Auckland: Heinemann Educational Books, 1979.

Chomsky, Carol. "After Decoding: What?" *Language Arts* 53 (March 1976): 288–96.

Clay, Marie. *Diagnostic Survey.* London: Heinemann Educational Books, 1972. Includes full details for the administration of the "Concepts about Print Test," entitled *Sand.*

DeStefano, Johanna S. "Research Update: Demonstrations, Engagement and Sensitivity. A Revised Approach to Language Learning—Frank Smith." *Language Arts* 58 (January 1981): 103–12.

Doake, David B. "Book Experience and Emergent Reading Behavior." Paper presented at meeting of the International Reading Association, Atlanta, May 1979.

Downing, John. *Reading and Reasoning.* New York: Springer-Verlag, New York, 1979.

Goodman, Kenneth S. "Reading: A Psycholinguistic Guessing Game." *Journal of Reading* 6 (1967): 126–35.

———. *Reading: Process and Program.* Champaign, Ill.: National Council of Teachers of English, 1970.

———. "Acquiring Literacy is Natural: Who Skilled Cock Robin?" *Theory Into Practice* 16 (1978): 309–14.

Goodman, Yetta, and Watson, Dorothy J. "A Reading Program to Live With: Focus on Comprehension." *Language Arts* 54 (November/December 1977): 868–79.

Greer, Margaret. "Affective Growth Through Reading." *The Reading Teacher* 25 (January 1972): 336–41.

Harste, Jerome C., and Burke, Carolyn L. "Toward a Socio-Psycholinguistic Model of Reading Comprehension." *Viewpoints in Teaching and Learning* 54 (July 1978): 9–34.

Kavale, Kenneth, and Schreiner, Robert. "Psycholinguistic Implications for Beginning Reading Instruction." *Language Arts* 55 (January 1978): 34–40.

McDonell, Gloria M., and Osburn, E. Bess. "New Thoughts About Reading Readiness." *Language Arts* 55 (January 1978): 26–29.

McKenzie, Moira. "The Beginnings of Literacy." *Theory Into Practice* 16 (1977): 315–24.

Newman, Katherine K. "Do You Eat Potato Chips When You Read?" *Language Arts* 55 (November/December 1978): 977–79.

Pearson, David P., and Johnson, Dale D. *Teaching Reading Comprehension.* New York: Holt, Rinehart and Winston, 1978.

Smith, Frank. *Psycholinguistics and Reading.* New York: Holt, Rinehart and Winston, 1973.

———. *Reading Without Nonsense.* New York: Columbia University, Teachers College Press, 1979.

Teale, William H., and Sulzby, Elizabeth, eds. *Emergent Literacy: Writing and Reading.* Exeter, N.H.: Heinemann Educational Books, 1984.

Weaver, Constance. *Psycholinguistics and Reading: From Process to Practice.* Cambridge, Mass.: Winthrop Publishers, 1980.

Zintz, Miles V. "Are You Attending to the Affective Domain in Your Classroom Reading Program?" Presentation at the Nineteenth Annual Reading Conference, the McLean County ISU Reading Council, University Union Illinois State University, Normal, Illinois, September 1975.

———. *Corrective Reading.* 4th ed. Dubuque, Iowa: William C. Brown Company Publishers, 1981.

Part Three

An Instructional Program for the Development of Natural Readers

Chapters 6–8 present an instructional program for the development of natural readers. Chapter 6 focuses on two major components of the program: (1) the assessment of strengths that children bring to the classroom, and (2) the elements of an experience curriculum designed to enrich and expand children's concepts and oral language competencies. Both areas are seen as crucial bases for building an effective program for learning to read and write naturally.

Chapter 7 discusses the three developmental phases through which young children grow into reading. These phases include (1) building a support system for reading, (2) focusing on print, and (3) functioning as a reader. We have also delineated suggestions for specific activities, arranging a learning environment, and management techniques that enable the child to grow through these three stages.

Planning the reading program for young children requires skilled organization and management. Chapter 8 contains a description of five aspects of this task: (1) arranging a learning environment that is strongly motivating and that operates efficiently; (2) selecting activities and materials that will constitute an effective program; (3) grouping—knowing when to work with individuals, small groups, or the whole group; (4) managing time in the classroom; (5) involving parents in their child's development of literacy.

Chapter 9 is a summary statement of the major premises of this text.

6

Informal Assessment and the Development of Concepts and Oral Language Competencies

Outline

Informal Assessment of Strengths
- Interests in Books
- Understanding of Functions and Features of Print
- Strategies for Attending to Specific Features of Print
- Understanding the Metalanguage of Print
- Level of Oral Language Competence
- Understanding the Conventions of Writing

Expanding and Extending Concepts and Oral Language Competencies
- Sensory Experiences
  - Sight
  - Sound
  - Taste and smell
  - Touch
- Science Experiences
  - Plants and food
  - Animals
  - Earth
- Making Materials and Equipment
  - Recipes
  - Basic equipment
- Concepts and Field Trips
  - Building concepts
  - Field trips
- Construction Projects
  - Painting with string, spool, or sponge
  - Making a mural
  - Making a shoe-box train
- Cooking Recipes
- Rhythm Experiences
- Creative Experiences
  - Make-believe animals
  - Flannel board stories
  - Finger plays
  - A funny kind of world
  - How would you feel?
- Dramatic Play Experiences
- Problem-Solving Experiences
  - Listening to solve riddles
  - Seeing relationships and making inferences
  - Balancing objects
  - Collecting junk

Summary

References

Guide Questions

1. Why should informal assessment and the development of concepts and oral language competencies be the initial major focus in a primary reading program?
2. Can you explain the spread of differences in general competence at each grade level shown in figure 6.1?
3. What implications do these differences have for reading instruction at a given grade level?
4. Can you describe the general areas of informal assessment to be used early in the year in the primary reading program?
5. Why may "invented spelling" and variations from printed text in early reading and writing be considered normal behavior for beginners?

Terminology

informal assessment
features of print
conventions of writing
invented spelling

Reading instruction in the first-four grades of formal schooling (K–3), which promotes the natural acquisition of literacy, is designed to enable children *to teach themselves to read.* Teaching is a matter of assessing the strengths of children and then providing appropriate activities, materials, evaluation, and organization that will make possible a natural growing into literacy. Effective instructional decision making is based on a teacher's knowledge and understanding of the major areas we have developed in this text: (1) the nature of language and how it is acquired and used, (2) the child's nature and how she learns, and (3) the nature of the reading process itself. This chapter and chapters 7 and 8 describe such a program.

Children appear to move quite naturally through a series of clearly discernible stages in learning to communicate effectively. (We described the stages of oral language development in chapter 2.) Moira McKenzie describes the stages of growing into reading and writing:

1. *Emergent reading.* A term used by Clay (1972) to encompass the period from the child's first encounters with books and printed materials and during which early concepts about literacy are developed.
2. *Tackling the written language system.* In this period the learner pays more attention to the visual aspects of the written language system itself. He begins to make generalizations and to develop word recognition skills. Gradually he internalizes the rules.
3. *Reading.* The learner has integrated various aspects of reading: the characteristics of stories, the elements of the various language systems, and the visual aspects of print. The reader can now read simple stories with confidence through which he develops his reading power. He continues to refine the more complex reading skills as he reads and writes in a variety of meaningful contexts (1977, 317).*

Any group entering kindergarten is composed of children who individually will be found at different stages. Some will be functioning well as readers already, as in the case of the natural readers described in chapter 1, but others will have had little exposure to written language other than the environmental print of their everyday world.

*Source: Moira McKenzie, THE BEGINNINGS OF LITERACY, *Theory into Practice*, 1977, 16:317, College of Education, Ohio State University, Columbus, Ohio. Used with permission of publisher and author.

These children may exhibit no emergent reading behaviors. Still others will be found somewhere within the middle stage: they are beginning to be aware of the actual visual aspects of print.

Figure 6.1 shows the range of general achievement to expect among children in K–3.

Because of this range of differences among the individuals in a group, we have deliberately not divided the primary reading program into specific grade levels. Children do not learn to read and write according to a lockstep, graded sequence. They never have. In natural learning, any sequential ordering of a reading program must be based on experiences that are compatible with children's strengths when they come to school, not on a preconceived mold of skills to be acquired within a prescribed time frame.

Providing for individual differences certainly does compound the challenges of teaching; it would be much easier to have children enter at the same stage and remain together as they move upward! A well-balanced program, then, must reflect instruction at a variety of levels simultaneously. This does not mean teaching each child individually (such an approach is neither necessary nor possible), but it does require recognizing an optimum time for learning. Some experiences meet the needs of all children, regardless of where they are on the reading continuum. Reading to children is one example. Other experiences will be provided to meet the specific needs of individual children. A small group composing a story with words from their word bank is an example. The language-experience method is composed of a number of activities, some of which are appropriate for the entire class: (1) making a batch of "metric munchies" by mixing chocolate and butterscotch chips in an electric skillet with a can of Chinese noodles; (2) participating in the oral discussion of the activity and watching as the teacher records children's dialogue. Some children who are already dealing more directly with the visual aspects of print may subsequently learn to read the story and begin to use the content to focus on the specific features of print—for example, beginning consonants. Other children who have had relatively little exposure to connected discourse will not be required to learn to read the experience story. Instead, they will turn to other activities, such as listening to story records or tapes and "reading" wordless picture books.

In this chapter we describe two major components of the program for developing natural readers: (1) assessment and use of the strengths of the child in order to design a program for meeting individual differences, and (2) ways and means to develop a rich store of concepts and oral language skills as a prelude to developing literacy.

Chapter 7 describes the major phases through which children move as they grow into literacy. Each is similar to the stages described by McKenzie, but our emphasis is on the *instructional practices* that promote the literacy skills which are characteristic of each stage.

Chapter 8 presents the components necessary to plan and manage an effective primary reading program.

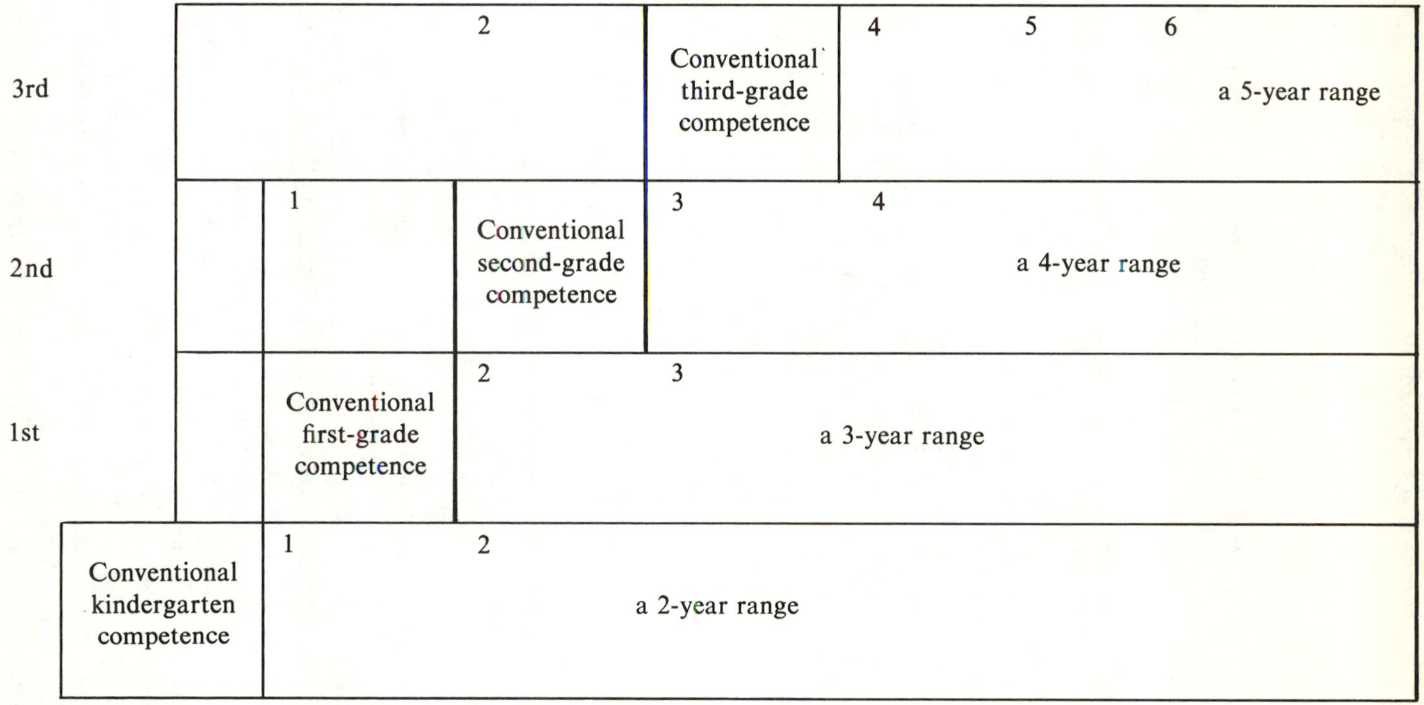

3rd
2
Conventional third-grade competence
4 5 6
a 5-year range

2nd
1
Conventional second-grade competence
3 4
a 4-year range

1st
Conventional first-grade competence
2 3
a 3-year range

Conventional kindergarten competence
1 2
a 2-year range

Figure 6.1. Conventionally defined grade-level competence. Adapted from Zintz, Miles V. THE READING PROCESS: THE TEACHER AND THE LEARNER 3rd ed. Adapted by permission.

Informal Assessment of Strengths

The teacher first determines where each child is on the literacy continuum in order to determine how to proceed with the design of a productive program. However, *assessment* in preparation for structuring a program in which children will learn to read naturally differs considerably from the usual connotations of the term in many current programs. Instead of administering a battery of readiness tests, which focus primarily on the perceptual aspects of reading, the teacher observes the children as they interact with print and with each other in the classroom environment. *Assessment by observation* encompasses a much-broader spectrum of behaviors than those related to a limited range of visual and auditory skills. The teacher observes behaviors to determine children's (1) interests in books, (2) understanding of the functions and features of print, (3) strategies for attending to specific features of print, (4) understanding of the metalanguage (the terms used to talk about print), (5) level of oral language competency, and (6) understanding of the conventions of writing.

The teacher then uses the observed strengths to plan and implement a reading program to build on those strengths. What children do not know is inconsequential when compared with the competencies most bring and on which they must build to make meanings of the unknowns encountered in reading.

Assessment by observation is a more-informal diagnostic procedure than that in which standardized readiness tests are administered to a whole group, and the analysis of which depends mainly on the judgment of the teacher. Teachers continually monitor children's behaviors in the classroom, and if the teachers' knowledge and understanding of children and of the processes they use to learn to communicate are adequate, they possess the requisite qualifications necessary to judge where children are and to plan experiences accordingly. It is important that they do not abdicate this responsibility and relegate assessment to the narrow confines of formal tests. Research results have shown that standardized tests are considerably less reliable and less valid in predicting reading success than the judgment of a competent teacher. Less-experienced teachers may need both formal tests and informal observations.

Informal checklists of behaviors for assessing strengths through observation can be compiled by the teacher for all of the foregoing areas, or the teacher may use or adapt lists that are available from a number of sources. Several examples of checklists and possible items to be included are given below.

A word of caution is in order about the whole area of evaluation. Regardless of the terms used—testing, diagnosis, assessment, diagnostic survey, or others—the whole procedure must be kept simple and within reasonable time constraints. Teachers can spend so much time in testing and related record keeping that little time is left for instruction. Assessing the strengths of children is a crucial element in an effective instructional program, but it should not be allowed to become so unwieldly that it is an end in itself rather than *a means* to better instruction.

Observation by competent teachers during the first few weeks of a school year can provide a wealth of information for decision making about the year's program for instruction. But this initial appraisal is only the beginning. Teachers continue to monitor children's behaviors throughout the term so that the progress noted (or lack thereof) can be used to continue, change, or adapt instruction as needed for individual children.

Teachers should not worry so much about making some errors from time to time in judging what course a child should be helped to pursue at any given period. Where strengths have been misperceived, the behavior of children will certainly signal the need for change. For example, if a child is given material to read because her oral vocabulary and past reading performance indicate that she can handle it, but her actual reading performance is difficult and labored, then material that the child can read without stress is substituted. Meanwhile, the teacher will continue assessment to determine the probable source of the difficulty. In cases similar to the one above, the child may not have adequate understanding of the concepts involved, or she may be unfamiliar with the style of writing. The teacher then knows that she has built on a weakness rather than a strength, and she adjusts instruction accordingly. Suppose further observation strongly indicates lack of familiarity with a given style of writing, exposition, for example. Then the teacher provides opportunities for the child to hear numerous examples of the expository form before again giving it to her to read.

Learning is a dynamic, ever-changing process, and the teaching that guides it must be also. Teaching that does not remain compatible with this dynamism can seriously impede, if not actually block, learning. Taking cues from children's behaviors is the first step in initiating the predominant element in teaching—adapting instruction to match what a child can do at any given stage of development.

Examples of behaviors to be observed in assessing each child's strengths in the general areas related to reading and writing are given below. These may be used to compile a simple checklist for use during the first weeks of school and in subsequent observations throughout the school term.

Interest in Books

Does the child show a general interest in stories and in learning to read print? Does she

1. voluntarily spend time in looking at books or other reading materials?
2. attempt to tell a story while looking at pictures and turning pages?
3. request having the story read aloud?
4. listen attentively when stories are read?

Understanding of Functions and Features of Print

Does the child seem to understand the functions and features of print? Does she

1. " . . . know that a book starts at the front and proceeds, page by page, to the back? (Have . . . [her] show you the 'front' and the 'back'.)
2. " . . . know that the spoken words, as the story is read to . . . [her], arise from the black marks, the print on the page?
3. " . . . know that the print must be 'read' from left to right across the page?
4. " . . . know that, if there is more than *one* line of print, we read the top one first, then the next down, and so on" (Dorothy Butler and Marie Clay 1979,23).

These two boys, age 4, use their "self-selection" time to "reread" a book.

Strategies for Attending to Specific Features of Print

Does the child exhibit any strategies for attending to specific features of print? Does she

1. recognize some words on sight?
2. search for specific visual cues: word beginning, context, and syntax to figure out unknown words?
3. recognize when miscues distort meaning and attempt to make corrections?
4. produce closer approximations of the actual text with successive oral readings of the same selection?
5. "talk like a book" when reading orally?

Understanding the Metalanguage of Print

Does the child seem to understand the metalanguage of print? Does she

1. point out individual "words" in print?
2. locate individual "letters" within words?
3. show you a "sentence" in printed context?

Level of Oral Language Competence

Has the child achieved an acceptable level of oral language competence? Does she

1. possess sufficient vocabulary to communicate without excessive pointing or other body language?
2. use a variety of sentence structures with an increasing number of descriptive terms?
3. tell a story or describe an event that includes the major points?
4. enter easily into oral communication with others in the day-to-day activities of the classroom?

5. raise questions that grow out of classroom experiences?
6. listen attentively to simple directions and explanations?
7. use the basic syntactic structures required to convey unambiguous meanings?

Understanding the Conventions of Writing

How much understanding does the child seem to have about the conventions of writing? Does she

1. voluntarily use paper and pencil (or crayons) to experiment with marking or drawing on paper?
2. experiment with letter forms?
3. reflect awareness of the proper direction for print?
4. attempt to copy words and letters?
5. "read" what she has written?
6. produce strings of symbols in wordlike form?
7. show an interest in seeing her own name (or other words) in print and in attempting to copy them?

Three additional sources of information for compiling an inventory checklist of children's reading- and writing-like behaviors may be found in Marie Clay's "Concepts about Print Test" in *The Early Detection of Reading Difficulties: A Diagnostic Survey with Recovery Procedures* (2nd ed.), Auckland: Heinemann Educational Books, 1979, or the third edition to be published in the fall of 1985; in "A Rating Technique for Observing Early Progress" and in "An Inventory of Writing Vocabulary for Rating Progress." The latter two instruments are found in Clay's *What Did I Write?*, Auckland: Heinemann Educational Books, 1975.

(Note: The "Concepts about Print Test" makes use of a booklet called *Sand:* Figure 6.2 shows sample pages from this booklet. Any number of test items may be selected and adapted for use with other reading materials, however.)

Evaluation of the results from observing a child's classroom behaviors must be guided by the following considerations. The products of children's learning in this first phase reflect their *own versions* of reading and writing. They do not fit automatically into a preconceived adult mold. Clay (1973, 149) in discussing natural language text states that what a child does is reflective of "the order in which children gain command over the structures of English, rather than a simplified adult version of English." Initial behaviors with print reflect a focus on meaning: children "read" by reproducing the sense of what they have heard, not an exact replication of the words as printed. With successive "readings" they move closer and closer to producing the text as it is written. Interestingly enough, their responses during these experiences will often reflect inventions for text they do not recognize. An illustration from McKenzie follows:

> *Text:* Once upon a time there was a poor boy.
> *Child (first reading):* Once upon a time there lived. . . . Once a pon a time lived a boy and he had no mummies and no Daddy and no clothes (1977, 318).

On the third reading several days later, the child reproduced an accurate reading of the sentence without "inventions." She is beginning to focus more on the specific visual aspects of print.

The waves splashed
into my hole in the sand.

Figure 6.2. Sample pages from *Sand*. Source: Marie Clay, SAND (the Concepts About Print Test), (Exeter, New Hampshire: Heinemann Educational Books, 1972), pp. 8–9. Used with permission.

Children appear to learn to write in a similar fashion. They do a lot of experimenting and playing around with symbols before and during the time they are learning the conventions of writing. When a child makes letters backward (Ɔ rather than *C*), it does not necessarily mean that there is a perceptual problem. Children will often play around to see how many ways symbols can be made. Even after they have learned to make many letters correctly, they may sometimes forget how specific ones look. When this occurs, they may supply their own inventions as substitutes, or they may draw pictures like those in figures 6.3 and 6.4.

Research notes on sample:

Shows active use of letter/sound information discovered prior to formal language instruction. Examples: *wus* for once, *a-pon* for upon, *tim* for time, etc.

Shows understanding 'book talk' or how discourse is organized in fairy tales. Examples: Once upon a time . . . and, they lived happily ever after.

Shows active cognitive processing and contextualization of stimulus story in terms of child's own cognitive structure and lexical preferences. Examples: Father Bear, Mother Bear, and Baby Bear (text version) to Father Bear, Mom, and Baby (student version).

Shows growing control of English language conventions. Examples: wordness is handled with dashes rather than linearly down page, left to right and top to bottom orientation.

Indicates control of conventions is not a prerequisite to reading and writing but an outgrowth of the child's meaningful involvement with print.

. . . .

a Byron, grade one, *wrote* the following:

b Byron *read* the following:

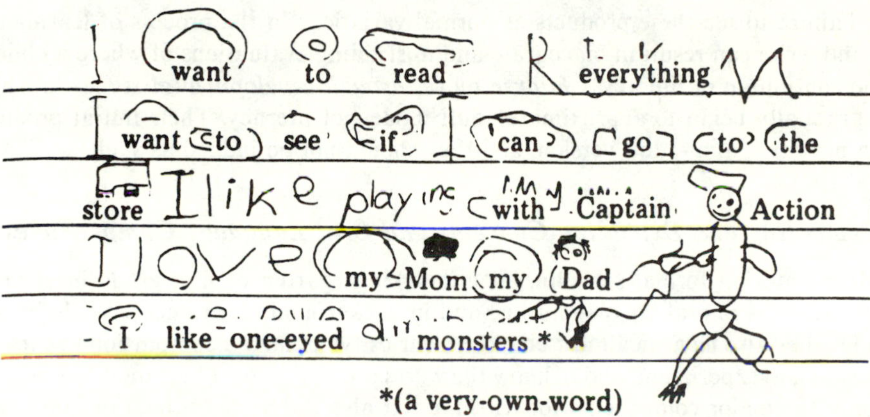

***(a very-own-word)**

Figure 6.3. Invented spellings. Source: Robert A. McCracken and Marlene J. McCracken, READING IS ONLY THE TIGER'S TAIL, Leswing Press, San Rafael, California, 1972, pp. 94–95. Used with permission of the authors.

Matt is a beginning first grader. This sample demonstrates Matt's command of how language functions and his growing control of the conventions of language through a process of involvement. Matt's story is a rendition of the recognizable "The Three Bears" yet personalized in terms of his language and his world. In Matt's writing one sees the importance of process, the interaction of author and reader, a meaningful personalized response to reading, and the centrality of context and meaning; in short, the best a socio-psycholinguistic model of reading comprehension has to offer (Harste and Burke 1978, 57).*

*Source: Jerome C. Harste and Carolyn L. Burke, TOWARD A SOCIO-PSYCHOLINGUISTIC MODEL OF READING COMPREHENSION, *Viewpoints in Teaching and Learning* 54 (July 1978): 57. Bloomington, Indiana: Indiana University School of Education, 1978.

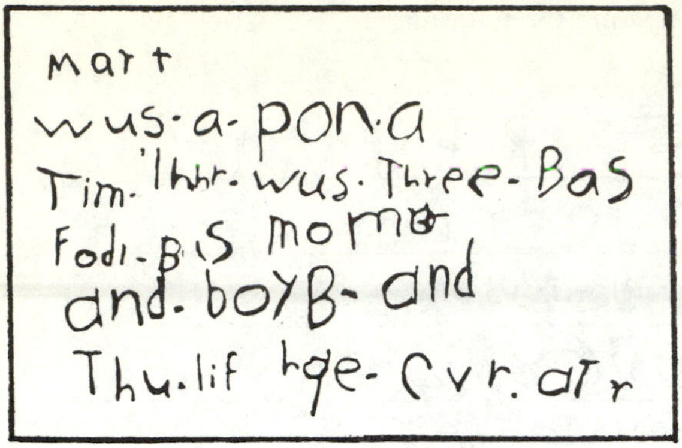

Mart
wus-a-pon-a
Tim-'thr-wus-Three-Bas
Fodi-B-is mom
and-boyB-and
Thu-lif hge-Cvr-aTr

Transcription of story as read by student.

Once upon a
time there was three bears.
Father Bear, Mom,
and Baby, and
they lived happily ever after.

Figure 6.4. Invented spelling. Source: Jerome C. Harste and Carolyn L. Burke, TOWARD A SOCIO-PSYCHOLINGUISTIC MODEL OF READING COMPREHENSION, *Viewpoints in Teaching and Learning,* 54 (July 1978): 57. Bloomington, Indiana: Indiana University School of Education. Used with permission.

Failure to see these products as normal variations in the process of learning to read and write can result in inaccurate and misleading evaluations of where a child is on the continuum of literacy. *Children move through developmental stages* in which they gradually begin to approximate adult models of literacy. Their initial products are in no way a mini-adult version, and they should not be judged as such.

Expanding and Extending Concepts and Oral Language Competencies

Children entering formal schooling at either kingergarten or first-grade level bring many strengths in oral language usage and in background experiences. With few exceptions they also have an almost boundless curiosity: an innate compulsion to explore, to question, to experiment, and to know the world around them. These qualities become not only the major components for learning but also the basic foundations on which to base productive teaching.

In the first year—either kindergarten or grade one—you should focus on providing the children many activities, experiences, and materials to involve them directly in concrete, hands-on exploration of their environment, both within the school and outside its walls. No matter how rich individual children's conceptual store or how competent they already are in oral language, *all* children should continue to build and expand far beyond their entry level in both areas. Literacy is not the direct goal of instruction during the kindergarten/first-grade period, although this may be a major outcome. The dominant goal is to enrich and expand children's knowledge and understanding of their world and to enable them to articulate more effectively those meanings through increased language skills. The richer children's conceptual store and language competence, the more meanings they bring to the world of print and the more naturally literacy can be achieved. The first-year classroom is filled with children who are *doing* things and *talking* a lot about them. At many periods during each day, the classroom will resemble the proverbial beehive; its activity is guided by the same productive organization and purposeful goals.

Your Turn 6.1 Assessing concepts about print.

Locate a copy of Marie Clay's *The Early Detection of Reading Difficulties: A Diagnostic Survey with Recovery Procedures* (2nd ed.), Auckland: Heinemann Educational Books, 1979, or the 1985 third edition. Using the "Concepts about Print Test" in the volume as a model, select items related to the various concepts about print and compile a test to try out with one first-grade and one second-grade child. Select a story from a text at the preprimer level of the basal series for the children to read. Adapt the wording of the test questions to fit the basal reader context. Administer the test to each child; mark and score according to the directions in the test.

1. Compare the score for both children with the figure showing "age expectations for items" at the end of the test. How do your children's scores compare with those of average European children?
2. Were the results what you might have expected? Why? Why not?
3. How did the scores of the two children compare with each other? Were your expectations met or not? Explain.
4. Discuss your data with other class members. (Save your material for an upcoming *Your Turn* in the next chapter.)

Learning to read and write grows directly out of the above experience context. Children will extract whatever is useful to them according to their individual levels of readiness to move toward literacy. The same activities will, therefore, provide different outcomes for different children. For some, the activity may be used to generate written language, which then becomes the content for reading. During the process of reading about their activities, some children will be helped to concentrate increasingly on the visual aspects of print in an effort to figure out how the system of written language works. Still other children will not move directly into the world of print; instead, they may participate in other activities whose major purposes are to expand concepts and enrich oral language usage. Some will play around with writing by scribbling and experimenting and inventing marks on paper; others will function at a more-advanced level by composing their own stories. Donald H. Graves (1983), Charles H. Temple, Ruth Nathan, and Nancy Burris (1982) and others feel that regardless of individual levels of competence, an experience-rich program enables each child to enter and participate according to individual capabilities; and simultaneously, opportunities are ever present for each to move forward when ready.

The activities and materials that follow have been selected primarily as vehicles to extend and expand children's concepts and oral language; they are *to do* and *to talk* about. Even though all may be used to accomplish other purposes, language experiences, for example, we are strongly concerned that children do not begin formal reading instruction as we have described here until they have adequate concept and language backgrounds on which to build toward natural reading.

The activities are enjoyable, involving, and motivating, and they work for the child. They represent only a sampling of the many possibilities for enhancing children's cognitive, affective, and verbal stores. They are arranged in categories according to the type of experiences involved. (See the appendixes for additional sources of information and ideas for building concepts and oral language.)

Sensory Experiences

The following activities, materials, and equipment may be used in a variety of ways in the classroom. Each can become a *center* for specific instruction or for special interests. Most of the materials collected are from the everyday environment and do not require a substantial investment. Children can participate in the collection.

Sight—visual activities, materials, and equipment.

Peep Boxes

Boxes of various sizes are suitable—matchboxes, shoe boxes, and cardboard boxes. Scenes may be made inside and are viewed through an opening in the sides. A second opening in the top lets in light. Scenes may be of desert, arctic, home, or animal environments; seasons; story scenes; and so on.

Magnifying Glasses

Small, inexpensive glasses are available and may be placed with collections of items for examination and exploration by children.

Games

Teacher displays a tray with a few familiar objects (chalk, pencil, book, and so forth), then covers the tray, and asks children to tell what was there. Gradually increase objects. The exercise makes a good small group or partner activity.

Display three items; cover and remove one. Ask children to decide what is missing.

Sound activities, materials, and equipment.

Tin Can Telephones

Punch holes in the bottom of two cans. Connect the cans by using twine or string attached to the bottom of each. Thread the string through the hole in the can and tie around a match or nail so the string will not slip out of the can. Stretch the string between cans and talk and listen alternately through cans.

Sound Games

Have children close eyes, make a familiar sound, then call for identification.

Have one child leave room; others decide on a sound. Child returns, and with closed eyes, attempts to identify the sound when it is made. Children may play this game with partners or in small groups. Suggested sounds: walking, running, pouring water and pebbles in a pan, and so forth.

Taste and smell activities, materials, and equipment.

- Place small amounts of common liquids that have odors in containers and let the children smell them (extracts, perfume, vinegar, household commodities, and others).
- Show children pictures of things and ask them to describe what they think they would smell like.

- In small bowls, place staples that look alike but have different tastes (white sugar, salt, flour, powdered sugar, soap flakes, tapioca, coconut, and others).
- In small bowls, place staples that bear the same name but have different characteristics (white sugar, brown sugar, raw sugar, powdered sugar, sugar cubes, and others) (Barbara J. Taylor 1975, 65).*
- Compare the taste and smell of various forms of the same food: an orange, orange jello, and orange juice.
- Soup: Vegetables may be explored, examined, and prepared for cooking. Prepare and eat soup. Many concepts are derived from the discussions during the preparation and eating: color, texture, taste differences between raw and cooked vegetables, and names of different vegetables.
- The menu for each day may be posted along with picture cutouts from magazines to illustrate the food being served. Make a pocket chart for more convenient change of pictures needed for each day's menu.

Touch activities, materials, and equipment.

Feel Box

Assemble a collection of textures (sandpaper, fur, cellophane, glazed paper, styrofoam, knitted material, flannel, velvet, leather, vinyl, felt, burlap, satin, absorbent cotton, feather, cork, soap, sponge, pebbles, bark, and others). Examine these with children by passing each around and encouraging comments on how each item feels. Leave collection out where it may be examined when children are interested.

The collection of items may be varied from time to time. For example, categories of items can be mixed: nuts, fruits, cloth, rocks, or a single category can be assembled—like different kinds of beans, nuts, and so on.

Children may play a guessing game by selecting items from the box and naming them without looking. They may also describe how each feels.

Guessing Socks

Collect six to eight knee length stretch socks. Place a cup or pint-sized food carton (cottage cheese, butter, and so forth) in the toe of each. Put three objects in each carton (pencil, rubber band, and paperclip). One child puts hand in sock to identify objects by touch. She describes the feel of objects according to shape, texture, and other touch characteristics so that other children can guess what each object is. Objects are then removed from sock to confirm or correct guesses.

Science Experiences

Plant and food activities, materials, and equipment.

- Plant a garden. Provide a special area for each child.
- Go on a nature walk. Gather leaves, cones, and other things.
- Sprout seeds in your kitchen (use screen or plastic tray or flower pots).

*Source: Barbara J. Taylor, A CHILD GOES FORTH, Brigham Young University Press, Provo, Utah, 1975, pp. 65, 120. Used with permission of Burgess Publishing Company.

- Grow some vegetables in water (carrot or turnip tops, sweet potato, and others).
- Grow some fruit or vegetables in soil (pineapple top, avocado pit, and others).
- Plant seeds indoors in empty milk carton (cut lengthwise), muffin tin, egg shells, egg cartons, ice cube trays.
- Let the child water house plants.
- Put strawberry plants in wooden or clay barrel.
- Put a stalk of celery in water containing food coloring. Observe how the color is carried to the leaves.
- Visit a seed store, plant nursery, local orchard, commercial garden, berry patch, or greenhouse.
- Purchase (or grow) squash or pumpkin. Eat the produce but save the seeds. Dry them and roast them for eating, or plant them for growing.
- Visit a local cannery or other food-processing facilities.
- Show the child how you prepare food for storage (refrigerator, pantry, canning, bottling, freezing, and drying).
- Make a drying frame and dry some fruit (make fruit leather).

(Taylor 1975, 120)*

Animal activities, materials, and equipment.

Plaster Prints

Use plaster mixed in baggies to make prints of animals in sand, prints of shells, and handprints. Use Vaseline to grease objects to be imprinted so that plaster will not stick.

Take along supplies on a field trip and make imprints of animal tracks by mixing water and plaster in baggies and pouring directly into the impressions in dirt or sand.

Screen Wire Cages (Insects)

Cut screen wire in rectangular shape and roll into cylinder to fit into a jar lid. A second jar lid the same size forms the top that can be removed when needed. The bottom lid should be attached with glue. Wire can be stapled at the top, or it may be sewn with pieces of thin wire. Insects, cocoons, and similar "creatures" can be kept for long periods of time along with grass and leaves for food.

Insect Collections

Used pill bottles are ideal for preserving small insects. Alcohol can be added or the specimens can be allowed to dry inside the containers. The clear plastic provides easy viewing from all sides.

*Source: Barbara J. Taylor, A CHILD GOES FORTH, Brigham Young University Press, Provo, Utah, 1975, pp. 65, 120. Used with permission of Burgess Publishing Company.

Pets

Pets in the classroom provide many opportunities for concept and oral language development. Guinea pigs are especially suitable; they are large enough to be handled easily and are not particularly difficult to keep clean. They reproduce regularly, and children can observe the entire reproductive cycle.

Pets should be bought from pet stores to be sure they are free from disease.

Some animals can be a permanent part of the classroom environment; others may be brought in from time to time for short visits.

Terrariums

There are three basic types of terrariums: woodland, desert, and bog. Each is distinguished by the amount of moisture and vegetation characteristic of that particular type of terrain. A woodland terrarium can be made in the following way: use a gallon glass jar with a wide-mouth opening. Place on side in holder made by nailing four small pieces of wood to form a rectangle. Place pieces of gravel and charcoal in bottom and add a layer of garden soil (about 1½″ to 2″).

Plants dug from the environment may be grown inside (very small house plants can be substituted). Branches with cocoons, fungi, or molds add special interest for children. Animals such as frogs, salamanders, toads, snails, grasshoppers, and earthworms can be grown successfully. When animals are part of the terrarium, sink a small, shallow, plastic dish or sea shell to serve as a miniature lake. Close jar. If too much moisture forms, leave lid off for awhile, then reseal. Desert terrariums can be made by using sand, small desert plants, and animals.

Earth activities, materials, and equipment.

Bubbles

Inexpensive bubble blowing sets are available at stores, or drinking straws and liquid soap may be used. The following observations can be made: the rainbow colors in bubbles, the effects of air pressure as bubbles burst, and air currents produced by blowing on released bubbles.

Rock Collections

Field trips provide an opportunity for collecting rocks of different colors, textures, weights, and shapes. Children may bring in special rocks that they find from time to time. Displays may be arranged so that children have the opportunity to handle and examine with and without a magnifying glass.

Floating and Sinking Objects

Collections of items—some that float and some that sink—can be collected and children may experiment to find which remain on top of water and which do not.

Fill jar with water, sand, gravel, leaves; shake and let children observe and discuss how *layers* of different materials are formed.

Making Materials and Equipment

"Recipes" for art-related materials.

Textured Paint

Add sand or coffee grounds, plus a little glue, to tempera paint to make a textured paint—especially good for work with hands and fingers.

Finger Paint (Thick)

Mix the following to the desired consistency: water and wheat paste. Add water color or tempera. Soap flakes give additional smoothness.

Finger Paint

Add tempera paint to prepared starch. For this mixture, it is not necessary to wet finger painting paper.

Finger Paint

1 cup laundry starch (dry)	2 quarts boiling water
2 tbl. talcum powder	½ cup soap flakes

(Add a few drops of oil-of-cloves, if desired—smell is improved!)

Mix starch with enough cold water to make a creamy mixture. Add the boiling water and cook until clear, stirring all the while. Remove from heat and add soap flakes and talcum powder; cool. Add dry or liquid tempera paint.

Suggestions: finger-paint paper should be glossy and nonabsorbent, in pieces approximately 11″ × 16″; fold edges of paper to make a crease to prevent curling. Old shirts make good aprons for children during this type of activity.

Play Dough

3 cups flour	1 cup salt	1 cup water

Add dry tempera paint or food coloring to the water to make bright colors. Add water slowly. If mixture is too dry, add more water; if it is too wet, add flour. A bit of alum will help keep dough fresh longer. Store dough in baggies or coffee cans with airtight tops. Keeping the dough in refrigerator lengthens its life.

For dough play, provide tongue depressors, cookie cutters, and rolling pins.

Other basic classroom equipment.

Felt Board and Felt Pieces

Felt shapes of various colors can be provided for use with flannel or felt board. This is good activity for comparing sizes and shapes and seeing similarity or differences in shape, size, or color. Cut several of each of the following in different colors: circle, square, triangle, and rectangle.

Cut pictures from magazines and paste them on felt-backed paper for use in storytelling.

Pegboards

Pegboards may be made in various sizes—large ones for special displays, and small ones for use by individual children. The small boards can be made 1′ square for easy handling. Colored pegs may be bought for filling the holes (beans may be substituted).

Boards may be raised for working on flat surfaces that will not permit items to drop through. Nail strips of molding along two-to-four sides of the backside.

Beads

Colored beads for stringing may be bought (macaroni with large holes can be substituted). Provide a supply of shoestrings with a spool attached at one end to prevent string from passing all the way through.

(Adapted from Joanne Wylie 1969, 167–74)*

Concepts and Field Trips

Building concepts. All activities can become concept building experiences. Ways in which children can learn to put together "pieces" of information gathered from experiences and thus form new meanings are given below.

Classifying Experiences

Assemble a collection of objects for classifying on the basis of a given characteristic: for example, hard, soft, color, size, or shape.

In putting away materials in various centers in the room, have children put them away according to some characteristic. For example, in the dress-up area, sort items by men's clothing, women's clothing, and children's clothing. In block work area, put blocks away according to size.

Opposites

Use balance for developing *up-down* concept. Use box for *in-out*. Use paper towel roll and toy car for same concepts.

Use picture collection to show *short-tall, man-woman, boy-girl.* Roll objects for *fast-slow* concept.

Use shelves to show *top-bottom-middle.*

Field trips. Trips outside the classroom provide excellent opportunities to study the environment and observe it firsthand. Preplanning and follow-up activities provide the opportunity to talk about and to learn many new concepts.

- Set purposes for the trip with children—what to look for and collect.
- Take empty boxes, jars, and bags for collecting. Magnifying glasses are an added attraction.
- Prepare children when possible for the topic of the trip by using pictures, audiovisual materials, and books before the trip.
- Discuss observations along the way.

*Adapted with permission of Macmillan Publishing Company from A CREATIVE GUIDE FOR PRESCHOOL TEACHERS by Joanne Wylie. Copyright © 1969 by Macmillan Publishing Company.

- On returning to the classroom, carry through planned activities, for example, displaying, discussing, and questioning.

Construction Projects

Painting with string, spool, or sponge.

- The teacher pours easel paint into low containers, such as jar tops or muffin tins, and places large pieces of newsprint, 18″ × 24″, on the table or floor. The painting tools are 4″-square pieces of sponge, spools of various sizes, (the larger the better), and 6″-to–8″ pieces of string. (A 12″ piece, knotted in the center and doubled, makes an interesting pattern, as do several pieces tied together.)
- Each of these tools represents a separate art experience and should be introduced separately. There should be a generous number of containers, papers, and tools for the painters to use.
- The children dip the tools in the paint and daub the paint on the paper. They will be delighted with the designs that emerge. It should be remembered that the experience of using these materials and the pleasure of putting paint on paper are most important. The teacher should not expect or direct a child to make a picture—the value is in the doing.

  (Wylie 1969, 92)*

Making a mural. Making a mural is an excellent group activity. Total length should be between 8′ and 10′; a longer sheet becomes difficult to handle. A roll of paper or newsprint will serve.

- The sheet is laid on the floor, and a group of children gather around it. Paint should be in plastic lids or other flat containers, and several paintbrushes should be provided for each color. Before beginning, the children should take time to discuss their ideas, with the teacher remaining in the background so that the ideas and the painting are the group's. When the mural is finished and hung up, the children will enjoy looking at it and admiring their work.
- Another project that is fun is making a two- or three-room house (or other structure) out of large cardboard boxes obtained from a local store. The children color the boxes, draw windows, and paste and decorate the sides (or paint them, if they prefer). The teacher fastens the rooms together with wide paper tape. It is amazing how many different things these boxes can become: boat, store, train, Indian tepee, camp. In the process of creating, the children learn to share their ideas and their tools.

  (Wylie 1969, 98)*

Making a shoe-box train.

- A usable train with short-term durability can be made from combining two parts of several shoe boxes in various ways, painting them, and tying them together with nylon twine, plastic clothesline, or thin rope. With the lid left on, it is a box car; the cover

*Adapted with permission of Macmillan Publishing Company from A CREATIVE GUIDE FOR PRESCHOOL TEACHERS by Joanne Wylie. Copyright © 1969 by Macmillan Publishing Company.

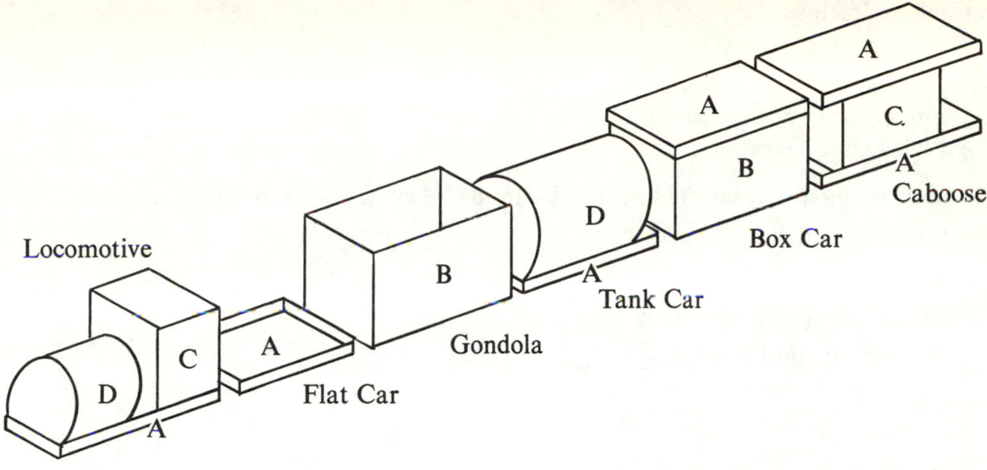

A = lid from adult-size shoe box
B = adult-size shoe box
C = child-size shoe box
D = oatmeal carton

Figure 6.5. Shoe-box train. From RESOURCES FOR CREATIVE TEACHING IN EARLY CHILDHOOD EDUCATION by Bonnie Mack Flemming and Darlene Softley Hamilton, copyright © 1977 by Harcourt Brace Jovanovich, Inc. Reprinted by permission of the publisher.

alone is a flat car; the box alone is a gondola car; an oatmeal or cornmeal carton glued to a box top makes a tank car; a long lid with a small box glued on it and another longer lid on top of the small box makes a recognizable caboose; a long lid with an oatmeal box glued on and with a small square box glued to the end of the oatmeal carton for the cab makes a locomotive (see figure 6.5). Have parents save the necessary boxes for you or ask the assistance of a local Girl Scout, Boy Scout, or Camp Fire Girl group to make one for you. If you make your own, let each child who wishes paint one of the cars.

- Children could help make a picture book of trains. Those with cutting ability may cut the pictures out of magazines or model catalogs. Others can choose precut pictures they wish to paste onto construction paper and put in a colorful plastic three-ring notebook.

(Bonnie M. Flemming and Darlene S. Hamilton, 1977, 479)*

*From RESOURCES FOR CREATIVE TEACHING IN EARLY CHILDHOOD EDUCATION by Bonnie Mack Flemming and Darlene Softley Hamilton, copyright © 1977 by Harcourt Brace Jovanovich, Inc. Reprinted by permission of the publisher.

Cooking Recipes

Butterscotch brownies.
1 package butterscotch bits
¼ cup crunchy peanut butter
3½ cups corn flakes

- Melt butterscotch bits and peanut butter over low heat in a heavy sauce pan.
- Stir in corn flakes.
- Mix well.
- Drop from spoon onto waxed paper.

(Flemming and Hamilton, 1977, 3)

Popcorn.
1 cup popcorn
1/2 cup oil

- Pour popcorn and oil into popcorn popper.
- Listen to the popping sound.
- Watch the popping corn.
- Give each child a single kernel of popcorn to examine.
- Pour popped corn into paper cups. Add salt.
- Count how many cups have been made.

(Flemming and Hamilton 1977, 27)

Tossed vegetable salad.
lettuce
2 carrots
4 c. cabbage
1 cucumber
2 tomatoes
2 small white onions
alfalfa sprouts

- Wash and drain all vegetables.
- Tear lettuce.
- Scrub carrots.
- Cut carrots, cucumber, tomatoes, and part of red cabbage into small pieces.
- Remove skin and cut onions.
- Combine all vegetables into a large salad bowl.
- Toss the vegetables to mix.
- Serve with different kinds of salad dressings and whole wheat crackers.

(Flemming and Hamilton 1977, 107–8)

Stone soup.

1 large, very clean stone
4 cups water
3 large carrots
3 potatoes
2 onions
1 can tomatoes
1 can corn
1 can peas
4 teaspoons beef bouillon
dash of salt

- Heat water in a large pot.
- Add the stone.
- Peel and cut up carrots, potatoes, onions, and celery.
- Boil these ingredients until soft.
- Add tomatoes, corn, peas, and bouillon.
- Add salt and boil 10 minutes.
- Remove the stone.
- Serve with crackers.

(Flemming and Hamilton 1977, 143–44)*

Peanut butter.

1 bag of unshelled peanuts
peanut oil
salt

- Shell the peanuts.
- Remove the red skins.
- Put peanuts into a blender.
- Blend until smooth. Add a few teaspoons peanut oil if needed.
- Serve on crackers.

(Nellie Edge 1975, 154)†

For other sources of recipes that young children can handle easily, see:

Glovach, Linda. *The Little Witch's Black Magic Cookbook.* Englewood Cliffs, N.J.: Prentice Hall, 1972.

Paul, Aileen. *Kids Cooking Without a Stove: A Cookbook for Young Children.* Garden City, N.Y.: The Seabury Press, 1973.

Zweifel, Frances. *Pickle in the Middle and Other Easy Snacks.* Scranton, Pa.: Harper and Row, Publishers, 1979.

Cauley, Lorinda Bryan. *Pease-Porridge Hot: A Mother Goose Cookbook.* Lindhurst, N.J.: G. P. Putman's Sons, 1977.

Rhythm Experiences

Commercial rhythm band uniforms with accompanying music books are available in music stores, or they can be ordered from school equipment distributors. With reasonable care, the uniforms and music books will remain in excellent condition a long time.

If the preschool budget is limited, the teacher may choose to make instruments. Drums can be made from tin coffee cans, wooden mixing bowls, oatmeal boxes, cans, or even coconut shells. The head of the drum, a plastic cover, several thicknesses of heavy paper, or a strong cloth, which can be shellacked, will make resonant tones. The drum head, which is laced over the body of the drum, is fastened in place with thumbtacks or large-headed nails. Drumsticks may be dowels covered with cork or just smooth sticks.

Percussion instruments (bangers) include rattles made by partly filling boxes, cans, or gourds with seeds, shells, pebbles, or nails. Tambourines can be made from sewing hoops or the round tops of cereal boxes, with bells, bottle caps, or any small bits of metal attached to the edge.

Pan lids or large tin can tops if properly smoothed become cymbals when cord handles are attached.

All instruments, commercial or homemade, should be sturdy with no sharp edges or corners. Percussion instruments should be resonant, but not too loud (Wylie 1969, 126).*

Creative Experiences

Make-believe animals.

Purpose: To build vocabulary; encourage creative expression.

Materials: Wall paper, construction paper, scissors, paste, metallic paper, string, and yarn.

Method: Cut a variety of shapes, such as squares, ovals, etc., from wallpaper. Put these, along with metallic paper, string, and other materials into a box labeled "Construct a make-believe animal." The forms are assembled into a make-believe animal and mounted on colored construction paper with wallpaper designs in the background. A sample animal can be made with the materials to give the general idea of how to put one together. Stimulate children to express their own ideas. When the animals are put on display, the teacher can stimulate creative storytelling or writing by questions such as, "Where do you think the make-believe animal lives?" "What can he do?" "Why?" "Does he have a name?" "Let's make up a story about him."

Suggestion: Encourage the use of different materials, for example, construction paper "springs" for legs, yarn for hair, metallic paper for eyes, and so forth.

Adaptations: Adapt geographically and seasonally. Construct make-believe toys, people, flowers, and houses. Creative rhythms might develop from the construction of these make-believe animals using questions such as, "How does he get from one place to

*Adapted with permission of Macmillan Publishing Company from A CREATIVE GUIDE FOR PRESCHOOL TEACHERS by Joanne Wylie. Copyright © 1969 by Macmillan Publishing Company.

another?" Dramatizations of make-believe stunts, using make-believe sign language, and solving make-believe problems might bring insight as well as provide outlets for creative expression (Elinore Milstein 1959, 9).*

Flannel board stories.

Purpose: To develop sequence; to stimulate imagination; to promote group relationships; to provide visual presentation; to promote listening; to develop oral expression.

Materials: Flannel board (or a piece of flannelette covering a chart), construction paper, felt or flannel, sandpaper, stapler, and rubber cement.

Method: Children enjoy making the characters and scenery of a story that they like. These can be used later in retelling the story. The construction can utilize heavy paper or flannel. Sandpaper or bits of flannel should be fastened on the back of paper figures so they cling to the flannel board. Then the child can create a story with words and pictures at the same time.

Suggestions: Provide opportunities for the children to practice with a small group before telling the story to the whole group.

Evaluate in terms of what children liked about each story presentation. No two will be alike, and, therefore, each experience will have is own value.

Adaptations: The teacher may prepare flannel board stories to tell to the group and then let the children use the figures that she made to either retell her stories or create new experiences for the play figures. Inexpensive paper books with large colorful illustrations may be taken apart, and the pictures backed by flannel. A collection of flannel board materials can thus be built up and used as a good language arts independent activity.

Small flannel boards to be used at individual tables are another adaptation. Individuals or small groups can prepare a flannel board story as an independent activity and then share it with the class (Milstein 1959, 21).*

Finger plays. "This Is the Circle That Is My Head" is one of many finger plays. Show this one to the class and then let small groups make up and present their own finger plays.

> This is the circle that is my head.
> *(Raise your arms above your head to make a big circle for the sun.)*
>
> This is my mouth with which words are said
> *(Point to your mouth.)*
>
> These are my eyes with which I see.
> *(Point to your eyes.)*
>
> This is the hair that grows on my head.
> *(Point to your hair.)*
>
> This is my hat all pretty and red.
> *(Put your hands on your head and make a pointed hat.)*

*Source: Elinore Milstein *Language Arts Can Be Creative:* (Washington, D.C., National Education Association, 1959), pp. 9, 21. Used with permission.

This is the feather so bright and gay.
(Use your pointing finger to make a feather.)
Now I'm all ready for school today.
(Adelaide Holl 1970, 22)*

A funny kind of world. This activity has great entertainment and creative possibilities. Show the samples below and in figures 6.6 and 6.7 and ask the children to make up their own "funny kind of world" demonstrations.

How would you feel?
if the color of your hair changed to blue every time you were sad?
if your pencil made music whenever you write with it?
(Meyers and Torrance 1966, 25)†

Dramatic Play Experiences

Concept: Develop the skill to act out a specific characterization.

Main Idea: Students will characterize a well-defined personality. The character should be far removed from the child in age, appearance, and behavior.

Learning Experiences: Most characters are recognized by specific traits or props. The following is a list of possible situations/characterizations and their accompanying props.

1. *Supermarket*—cash register, play money, paper pads, pencils, crayons, punchers, paper sacks, empty food containers, wax food, grocery boxes, and cans with smooth edges.
2. *Beauty parlor*—plastic brushes, combs, makeup and makeup containers, cotton balls, scarves, hair rollers, colored water in nail polish bottles, empty hair spray cans, wigs, and wig stands.
3. *Cooking*—pots, pans, egg beater, spoons, pitchers, salt and pepper shakers, canisters, small bottles with colored water, table cloth, aprons, dish towels, pot holders, play dough, cookie cutters, and rolling pins.
4. *Post office*—index card file, stamp pads, stamps, crayons, pencils, Christmas seals, old envelopes, and stampers.
5. *Doctor and nurse*—tongue depressors, stethoscope, satchel, Band-Aids, cotton balls, uniforms, and caps.
6. *Postman*—hat, badge, envelopes, mail satchel, and mailboxes (milk cartons or cans strapped together and labeled with names of children).
7. *Fireman*—hats, raincoat, boots, and short length of garden hose.
8. *Farmer*—shovel, rake, hoe, seeds, and toy riding tractor.
9. *Plumber*—wrench, plastic pipes, and tool kit.
10. *Gas station attendant*—shirt, hat, and tire pump.
11. *House Painter*—paintbrushes, buckets, cloths, coveralls, and caps.
12. *Policeman*—hat, badge, and whistle.

*Adapted with permission of Macmillan Publishing Company from ADVENTURES IN DISCOVERY, TEACHER'S GUIDE, by Adelaide Holl. Copyright © 1970 by Macmillan Publishing Company.

†Source: R. E. Myers and E. Paul Torrance, FOR THOSE WHO WONDER, Boston: Ginn and Company, 1966, pp. 1, 25. Used with permission of authors.

if it *always* rained on Saturday?

Figure 6.6. What could happen? Source: R. E. Myers and E. Paul Torrance, FOR THOSE WHO WONDER, Boston: Ginn and Company, 1966, pp. 1, 25. Used with permission of authors.

if it were against the law to sing?

Figure 6.7. What could happen? Source: R. E. Myers and E. Paul Torrance, FOR THOSE WHO WONDER, Boston: Ginn and Company, 1966, pp. 1, 25. Used with permission of authors.

13. *Milkman*—plastic bottles and cartons, wagon, basket, white hat, and coat.
14. *Librarian*—books, stamp pad, stampers, cards in books, and shelves.
15. *King and Queen*—crowns, robes, and scepters.
16. *Clown*—baggy clothes, big shoes, rubber nose, makeup, and pointed hat.

(Judy Ireton, et al., 1976, 39)

Problem-Solving Experiences

Listening to solve riddles. Now we are going to find out if you can guess riddles. Listen carefully to what I read. We have been studying circus animals. Can you name the one I am describing? When you know the answer, do not put up your hand, but when I am finished, write (or draw if the children cannot yet write) the name of the animal I have described. *Read:* This animal lives along the river and uses the river for his swimming pool. He is short but very fat and heavy and keeps cool by spending much of his time in the river. His face looks something like a pig's and so does his tail. He has small, popping eyes and small ears and a huge mouth with great teeth. You feel like laughing when you see this animal. He looks as if he needs a girdle on. What animal am I describing? (hippopotamus)

(Applegate 1960, 127).

Seeing relationships and making inferences. For this activity you will need chart paper and picture-word cards appropriate to these pages.

In matching each baby picture with the picture of an adult, encourage the use of complete sentences: "The caterpillar will grow up to be a butterfly." "The tadpole will grow up to be a frog." "The chick will be a rooster when it is grown."

Have the children interpret the picture clues in a picture and tell the story in their own words. The teacher can act as scribe and record the story on a chart for reading and rereading. By now many children in the group may be acquiring a basic sight vocabulary and may be able to point out simple words in the story that they know: cat, dog, boy, tree, and so forth (Holl 1970, 111).

Balancing objects.
balance scale
marbles
macaroni
various sizes and shapes of wooden blocks
metal plates

Wood

First explain how the balance scale weighs objects, indicating which of two compared objects is heavier and which is lighter.

Place a piece of wood on one side of the scale and a lighter piece of wood on the opposite side. Then pass the two pieces of wood to the children so they may compare the difference in weight indicated by the unbalanced scale.

Marbles

Now place two small containers of uneven numbers of marbles on the scale, causing it to be unbalanced. Ask a child to explain what is needed for the two sides to balance and then proceed to balance the two sides. Explain that by adding or taking away marbles from either side of the scale, the position of the balance scale is changed. Let each child participate in at least two manipulations. Help them cause the one side of the balance to be heavier, lighter, or balanced by the addition (Owen W. Cahoon 1975, 42).

Collecting junk. The task of gathering junk is shared by the teacher and the students. Decide together what is needed and how it can be collected. The junk should include both surplus and discarded objects. Commercial, neighborhood, and home sources should be explored. Soliciting and collecting junk are means of rallying community interest and involvement in the school. The teacher can structure junk gathering as a learning experience. Skills such as matching, classifying, and counting can be reinforced as students collect junk. The students will also be practicing writing and speaking skills as they interact with people.

A beginning junk collection might include the following:

wood scraps
plastics
carpet scraps and samples
paper—wallpaper samples, sandpaper scraps, and others
aluminum—foil, cans, and containers
wire, nails, bolts, washers, screws, and nuts
sticks—ice cream and tongue depressors
boxes
old clothes
appliances
fabric scraps
burlap
foam rubber
packing stuff
records
coat hangers
sponges
cardboard fabric bolts
ribbon spools
bones
inexpensive edibles—sugar cubes, licorice, crackers, and candy game parts and old toys
flooring and roofing samples
cartons—egg, fruit, butter, juice, milk, and ice cream

(Sandra Kaplan, et al., 1975, 26).

Your Turn 6.2 Developing concepts and oral language competencies.

Select an experience from any one of the categories listed under the second major topic, "Expanding and Extending Concepts and Oral Language Competencies." Arrange to conduct the activity with a small group (3 or 4 children) in a kindergarten or first-grade class. Prepare the necessary materials, and complete the activity with the children. Tape record the session. Analyze the children's dialogue on the tape.

1. What concepts are involved?
2. Are there any new concepts that might have emerged during the course of the activity? List these.
3. As a teacher, what could you provide in a follow-up session(s) to develop these budding concepts more fully?
4. Listen again to the language of the children on the tape. Analyze this language according to the items listed under the following section heading, "Level of Oral Language Competence."

Summary

Young children begin their formal school experience with a wide range of differences among them in knowledge about written language. In order to design a program that provides for these individual differences, teachers observe children to determine existing strengths in literacy-related areas. The results are then used to make appropriate instructional decisions about each child.

Success in beginning reading depends to a large extent on a rich store of concepts derived from direct experiences and on oral language facility. A major focus at the primary level, then, is to provide an environment in which children participate in many and varied activities accompanied by much talking.

References

Applegate, Mauree. *Easy in English.* New York: Harper and Row Publishers, 1960.

Butler, Dorothy, and Clay, Marie. *Reading Begins at Home.* Auckland: Heinemann Educational Books, 1979.

Cahoon, Owen W. *Cognitive Tasks for Preschool.* Teachers' Guide. Provo, Utah: Brigham Young University Press: 1975.

Cauley, Lorinda Bryan. *Pease-Porridge Hot: A Mother Goose Cookbook.* Lindhurst, N.J.: G. P. Putman's Sons, 1977.

Clay, Marie M. *A Diagnostic Survey: The Early Detection of Reading Difficulties.* Auckland: Heinemann Educational Books, 1972.

———. *Reading: The Patterning of Complex Behavior.* London: Heinemann Educational Books, 1973.

———. *What Did I Write?* Auckland: Heinemann Educational Books, 1975.

Edge, Nellie, comp. *Kindergarten Cooks.* Port Angeles, Wash.: Peninsula Publishing, 1975.

Flemming, Bonnie Mack, and Hamilton, Darlene Softley. *Resources for Creative Teaching in Early Childhood Education.* New York: Harcourt Brace Jovanovich, 1977.

Glovach, Linda. *The Little Witches Black Magic Cookbook.* Englewood Cliffs, N.J.: Prentice Hall, 1972.

Graves, Donald H. *Writing: Teachers and Children at Work.* Portsmouth, N.H.: Heinemann Educational Books, 1983.

Harste, Jerome C., and Burke, Carolyn L. "Toward a Socio-Psycholinguistic Model of Reading Comprehension." *Viewpoints in Teaching and Learning* 54 (July 1978): 9–34.

Holdaway, Don. *The Foundations of Literacy.* Sydney: Ashton Scholastics, 1979.

———. *Stability and Change in Literacy Learning.* Exeter, N.H.: Heinemann Educational Books, 1984.

Holl, Adelaide. *Adventures in Discovery.* (teachers guide). New York: Western Publishing Company, 1970.

Ireton, Judy; Meinema, Jay; Miller, Shirla; Morse, Luella; Peck, Sandra; Thomas, Mary Joe; and Wilson, Diane. *Kindergarten Activities Resource Book.* Anchorage: Anchorage School District, 1976.

Kaplan, Sandra; Kaplan, Jo Ann Butom; Madsen, Sheila Kunishima; and Gould, Bette Taylor. *A Young Child Experiences.* Pacific Palisades, Calif.: Goodyear Publishing Company, 1975.

McCracken, Robert A., and McCracken, Marlene J. *Reading is Only the Tiger's Tail.* San Rafael: Leswing Press, 1972.

McCracken, Marlene, and McCracken, Robert H. *Reading, Writing and Language: A Practical Guide for Primary Teachers.* Winnipeg: Peguis Publishers Limited, 1979.

McKenzie, Moira. "The Beginnings of Literacy." *Theory into Practice* 16 (1977): 315–24.

Milstein, Elinore. *Language Arts Can Be Creative.* Washington, D.C.: National Education Association, 1959.

Myers, R. E., and Torrance, E. Paul. *For Those Who Wonder.* Boston: Ginn and Company, 1966.

Paul, Aileen. *Kids Cooking Without a Stove.* Garden City. N.Y.: The Seabury Press, 1973.

Taylor, Barbara J. *A Child Goes Forth.* Provo, Utah: Brigham Young University Press, 1975.

Teale, William H., and Sulzby, Elizabeth, eds. *Emergent Literacy: Writing and Reading.* Exeter, N.H.: Heinemann Educational Books, 1985.

Temple, Charles A.; Nathan, Ruth G.; and Burris, Nancy A. *The Beginnings of Writing.* Boston: Allyn and Bacon, 1982.

Wylie, Joanne, coord. ed. *A Creative Guide for Preschool Teachers.* New York: Western Publishing Company, 1969.

Zintz, Miles V. *The Reading Process.* 3rd ed. Dubuque, Iowa: William C Brown Company Publishers, 1980.

Zweifel, Frances. *Pickle in the Middle and Other Easy Snacks.* Scranton, Pa.: Harper and Row, Publishers, 1979.

7

Three Phases of Growing into Reading

Outline

Phase One: Building a Support System for Reading
- Reading to Children
  - Whole-class listening
  - Repeated readings
- A Reading Environment
  - Environmental print
  - Connected discourse
  - Classroom centers
  - Sustained silent reading
- A Writing Environment
  - Group writing experiences
  - Individually initiated writing experiences

Phase Two: Focusing on Print
- Using Language Experience
  - Advantages of language experience
  - Components of the language experience process
  - Ideas for developing language experiences
- Using Assisted Reading
  - Assisted reading
  - Echo reading
  - Shared-book experience
- Using Basal Reader Materials
  - Past criticisms and present materials
  - Appropriate use and placement of basal materials
- Components of a Balanced Program for the Development of Natural Readers
- Focusing on the Features of Written Language
  - Developing strategies for using the cue systems of language
  - Integrating the cue systems of written language

Phase Three: Functioning as a Reader

Summary

References

Guide Questions

1. How can you describe the three phases of growing into reading?
2. What types of instruction are compatible with each phase?
3. What are the characteristics of the language-experience approach to instruction that make it compatible with the major psycholinguistic premises of this text?
4. How do basal reading materials fit into a program for the development of natural readers?

Terminology

repeated readings
cross-age helpers
read-along tapes
reading environment
environmental print
connected discourse
wordless picture books
picture storybooks
illustrated books
predictable books
classroom centers
sustained silent reading (SSR)
writing environment
"very own words"
phases of literacy development
language-experience approach
assisted reading
echo reading
shared-book experience
"Big Books"
basal reader series
readiness books
guided reading
graphophonic cues
visual discrimination
structural analysis
visual memory
directionality
cloze activities
prediction strategies
sample strategies
confirmation/correction strategies

Nearly all children entering school for the first time will have had some experiences with print, at least that which is part of the everyday environment—signs, labels on boxes, and others. But not all will have had adequate exposure to connected discourse, which is characteristic of books, magazines, and similar sources. The teacher's task, then, becomes one of building a support system for reading. This consists of selecting activities and materials that will benefit all children, regardless of their previous experience.

Phase One: Building a Support System for Reading

The activities presented in this chapter will provide a support system for reading. They will provide for a wide range of differences. For children who exhibit no emergent reading behaviors, the major purpose of activities will be to acquaint them with various types of written materials and the particular functions and features of this written language. Children who have begun to figure out the system of print, and those who are already reading with a degree of fluency, will have opportunities to broaden these developing competencies.

Reading to Children

The value of reading aloud to children has been well documented in professional literature over the past two decades by authors like Margery A. Galbraith (1983); Richard Johnson and John Adams (1983); Linda Lamme, Vivian Cox, Jane Matanzo, and Miken Olson (1980); Agnes D. Stahlschmidt and Carole S. Johnson, (1984); and Jim Trelease (1982). Dolores Durkin's early studies of natural readers, which were cited in chapter 1 of this text, repeatedly point to the positive influence of parents reading to children from an early age. The benefits to children have already been stated and will not be recounted here, but reading to children must become a standard part of the primary reading program.

The quality of the oral reading is important, especially if listening to stories is to fulfill its potential in aiding children to move naturally into reading. Lamme (1976) used a Reading Aloud to Children Scale (RACS) to determine which factors contributed most to a high-quality oral-reading performance. Her findings are presented below in descending order of importance:

1. child involvement—pausing for listeners to respond by predicting what might happen next, repeat refrains, or fill in words
2. amount of eye contact—glancing up often from text to look at listeners

3. expression in reading—stressing appropriate words
4. voice quality—using variety in volume and pitch
5. word and picture citation—frequently showing words and pictures to listeners during reading of text
6. provisions to see and hear—grouping children where each can see illustrations and hear story
7. highlighting story language and words—attending to and making special features standout: rhyme, repetition, and unusual words.

(Lamme 1976, 886–888)

(A revised RACS for self-analysis of oral reading performance is available in the following volume: Lamme, Linda L., ed. *Learning to Love Literature, Preschool through Grade 3*. Urbana, Ill.: National Council of Teachers of English, 1981. In the same book see Joan I. Glazer's chapter 4, "Reading Aloud with Young Children," pp. 44–45.)

Whole-class listening. All children profit from hearing a variety of materials read, even those who are already readers. For those who are not readers, listening to stories being read provides a natural entry into the world of learning to read. So, from the beginning, children listen regularly to written language being read. A time is set aside everyday for this activity when children can sit in a comfortable arrangement that promotes good listening. Our own experience has been that sitting on the floor around the teacher has a very special appeal to children. The teacher should be positioned so that illustrations in the book can be shown from time to time during the reading. The length of time spent in each session will depend on the children's behaviors; the teacher can gauge this length of time by their attentiveness as a group. The time will be adjusted accordingly. A few children may have much shorter attention spans than the majority of the group; they should be allowed to leave the group to engage quietly in other activities.

During the first year, children should be introduced to all of the following: wordless picture books, predictable books, nursery rhymes, fables, riddles, poems, storybooks, and items of expository writing. (Several appendixes contain bibliographies of materials in the above categories.)

Repeated readings. Along with reading to the whole class, the teacher provides opportunities for individual children to hear the same story, nursery rhyme, or other types of content read repeatedly. Children may become interested in something the teacher has read to the whole class; some may select another source and request hearing it read. By observation the teacher can be guided by the individual child's interest. Not all children will exhibit interest in a particular book at the beginning, but over time and in a good reading environment, the majority will request being read to; this is the time to provide individual listening sessions.

From time to time, the teacher will invite a child who has not requested listening experiences to sit in a quiet corner and listen to her read a story which she believes the child will enjoy. When the session is finished, the teacher will suggest that they may read together again the following day. Quite often this procedure is very effective in stimulating a child's interest in books. Having the teacher all to oneself, even for brief periods is a highly motivating experience for most children—regardless of the activity.

Cross-Age Helpers

The number of children in most beginning classrooms makes it impossible for a teacher to provide time to read repeatedly to each child. Once an interest is stimulated in reading, other means must be found to provide sufficient repetitions for each child. There are a number of alternatives. One of the best and easiest sources of aid is *cross-age helpers*—good readers from the grades above who can come in on a regular basis to read to individual children. Both the younger child and the older one receive benefits. Younger children enjoy the attention of older children; they are made to feel special by it. Older children feel important in their role as teacher and usually find the helping relationship very satisfying. Oftentimes, children can communicate and relate more easily to each other than to the teacher in a learning situation.

In cross-age helping, it is important that the teacher closely monitor the helping relationship. Sometimes personalities may not be compatible; when they are not, the teacher must make another match. Helpers should be carefully selected and prepared for work with younger children prior to beginning the reading sessions. Teachers who send helpers can suggest children whom they consider to be the best candidates. It is important that helpers be mature enough to keep the younger child on task and to relate to him in such a way that the younger child does not feel inferior and inadequate. The difference in ages and the older child's level of reading fluency are not so important so long as the older child can read well the material that the younger child will hear. Agewise, the authors have found that some of the most successful pairings were those in which intermediate-grade children who read poorly at their own grade level were paired with younger nonreaders. The older children who had never been successful in reading before were suddenly stimulated by finding a task in which they could succeed, and they began to work diligently on preparing readings for the helping sessions. (No sixth-grader wants to reveal to a primary child that he cannot read well.)

One of the authors remembers the following revealing episode between two sixth-grade boys in the class. Leon, read at a second-grade level, and the teacher had scrounged up all the "high interest, low vocabulary" materials available and Leon had already read most of them. Now he was practicing with great concentration the reading of "Little Red Riding Hood" when Ben walked by. "Wow!" Ben said, "Is *that* all you can read?" "No, stupid," replied Leon. "I have to get ready to go teach this to the little kids!" Leon's own reading improved markedly over the year he was a helper in a first-grade classroom.

One combination to avoid is pairing a very bright, precocious helper with a younger, slow learner. Too many possibilities exist for the younger child to be intimidated and made to feel inadequate and insecure by the helper's superior performance and condescending attitude. Prevention is far easier than trying to repair the damage once it is done.

Once the helping children have been selected, it is crucial that they know what they are expected to do and how the helping sessions are to be conducted. The primary teacher sits with the helpers as a group to discuss plans. She identifies the children with whom each will work, the material to be used, and the schedule of sessions. Each helper is assigned a spot in the room for work sessions. Each pair should be separated about the room so that nobody is disturbed by the oral reading. The helpers are told that they will read daily to the younger ones for short periods of time. Helpers may spend time discussing the material read at the end of each session, if the younger child appears interested. When the younger child shows an interest in "reading along" with the story, he may do so but at no time does the older child attempt to have the younger child memorize words or focus on the parts of words. It is not unusual for helpers to revert to "teaching" reading as they were taught by hammering away at the "pieces." This is the role model that must be broken if the younger children are to become natural readers. The helper's job is to read to his partner, period! Helpers can easily see how the process works as the younger child begins to follow along and "reads" the story with more and more accurate renditions of the actual text.

The teacher will request that the helpers provide frequent feedback on how things are progressing. She will also meet periodically with all the helpers as a group so that each can share what is occurring in his sessions and suggest directions to take in subsequent helping sessions. Meanwhile, the teacher will monitor the progress of the younger children by reading to, or with, each at least once a week. (Additional information about cross-age helpers can be found in the following sources: Vernon L. Allen [1976]; R. O. Cloward [1967]; DiAnn W. Ellis and Fannie W. Preston [1984]; Stewart Ehly and Stephen C. Larsen [1980]; Fran Lehr [1984]; Peggy Lippitt [1965]; and Charles Nevi [1983].)

Parents and Grandparents

A second source of help in providing repeated readings is to seek *parent* or *other adult help*. Senior citizens are often a very willing and capable source of assistance in the classroom. In some situations, too few adults are available for helping on a regular basis. A workable solution is to combine those who are available with student helpers. In any case, adults should be given the same preparation and follow-up as student helpers.

Read-Along Tapes

A third way to provide for story listening is to prepare read-along tapes, which individual children may use in listening centers on a regular basis. The teacher, another adult, or a student helper can tape the required materials. Young children are quite capable of operating cassette recorders for listening sessions. They use the book from which the tape was made to follow along as they can in each repeated reading. Taping is an invaluable aid even where sufficient outside help is readily available; children have increased opportunity to hear and practice reading selections on a much more flexible basis when they do not have to wait for assistance.

Commercial read-along tapes are also available in many places ranging from supermarkets to school supply houses, and the teacher may want to make some available in the class. (See appendix 12 for a list of read-along records and books.) However, the quality of the tape reproduction and the format of the text should be carefully checked before purchase. The sound on some tapes may not be sufficiently clear, and/or the quality of the tape itself may not be durable enough to justify the expense. Some print is too small and too closely spaced between words and lines for easy beginning reading. The quality of the material and the binding itself may not withstand wear and tear over time. The choice of using either commercial or homemade materials or a combination of the two is up to the teacher. However, our experience has been that

Effective use of a "grandfather" in the classroom. This senior citizen is helping a committee think through their problems in classroom government.

children more often than not prefer the homemade variety, particularly when the tape is made by their own teacher, teacher aide, or student helper. (Additional sources of information about read-along materials may be found in M. R. Sine [1982] and G. Gamby [1983].)

A Reading Environment

Along with reading to children in whole-class and individual sessions, the teacher provides a classroom environment rich in many types of print and opportunities to explore them.

There are two basic categories of print to be made available: (1) environmental print and (2) connected discourse. Children learn from both types.

Environmental print. Environmental print is print that is used in the everyday world to label, direct, and identify. Examples are almost unlimited in our literate culture: street signs, candy bar wrappers, cereal packages, buttons with symbols and slogans, T-shirts, cars and trucks, store front signs, lunch boxes, TV guides, catalogs, stamps, and bottle caps. Environmental print differs from the language of books. Single words and phrases predominate, and because the format is designed to be eye-catching, the print may be anything but standard. Color is dominant; words are used with logos that often overshadow the print. An example of the foregoing is McDonald's restaurant advertising.

The following types of environmental print should be made available in the classroom:

- boxes, cans, and labels from a variety of products, particularly foods
- bottle caps and slogan buttons

- catalogs (mail order, such as Sears; seed and flower and specialty house publications, such as those for toys and sports equipment)
- menus
- stamps and used envelopes
- maps (road and city)
- telephone directories

Connected discourse. Connected discourse is not "packaged" in the same way as most environmental print, because it serves a different purpose. Both types convey messages, but the payoff differs. Connected discourse is in the form of sentences, paragraphs, and chapters or verses. It conveys a number of interrelated meanings gleaned from extended exposure. Environmental print, on the other hand relies on getting a message across in the fastest, most economical way possible, because viewers are not expected to spend much time with it. The format usually consists of a minimum of words augmented by a variety of visual effects—color, logos, and distinctive print. The purpose is to promote a product or a service.

All of the following kinds of connected print should be available in the classroom:

- *Picture books* are those without words in which the story plot is carried by pictures alone. Picture books are also called wordless picture books.
- *Picture storybooks* are those "in which the illustrations play an integral part in the story—the words need the picture to help tell the story." Examples include single fairy tales and illustrated versions of Mother Goose verse.
- *Illustrated books* are those "in which the text is enhanced by the pictures which break up long expanses of words." The pictures are not necessary to story comprehension. (Susan M. Glazer and Carol S. Brown 1980, 28)
- *Predictable books* are written in such a way that children can anticipate quite accurately what the author is going to say.
- *Fiction books* appear in either illustrated or picture-story format.
- *Nonfiction books* supply information to develop specific concepts. *The National Geographic Society* markets an excellent series, "Books for Young Explorers." One title is *Creepy Crawly Things.* It explores reptiles and amphibians. Nonfiction material appears in either of the first-three picture formats above.
- Poetry.
- Jingles, rhymes, jokes, riddles, puzzles, and alphabet books.
- Basal reader materials consist of readiness books, preprimers, primers, first readers, and second readers.
- Children's magazines include *Sesame Street, ZooNoos, National Geographic World, Your Own Backyard,* and *Highlights.*
- Newspapers.
- Magazines, particularly those with many pictures, include *Life* and *National Geographic.*

(See appendixes for other suggested material in the foregoing categories.)

Once a variety of materials from both environmental print and connected discourse have been collected, the teacher provides time each day for children to explore and use the materials as they wish. The purpose is not so much that children will work on reading them as it is to help them become aware of the different types of print and the topics with which they deal. Awareness can arouse interests, which, in turn, can stimulate the child to become involved with print.

Classroom centers. Materials should be easily available and readily accessible for children to explore individually as they wish during the day or with the teacher during periods of direct instruction. This is best accomplished by having a number of centers in the classroom. A general reading center can be located in a corner of the room where low bookcases visually screen off the area. Old beanbags, floor pillows, or carpet squares provide comfortable seating arrangements. One of the authors saw an old bathtub, lined with stick-on carpet squares, used to great advantage in a primary classroom. A variety of other "scrounged" items may be used so long as plenty of space is reserved for several children at a time. Old lamps are a particular favorite. Reading materials in this center should be varied and selected from both environmental and connected types of print. Children use the center individually or in small groups throughout the day to look at and/or read what they can manage.

Other centers can be set up and organized around specific topics or items of interest. A listening center can be set up on a table in another corner with appropriate records, read-along tapes and books, and headsets with either single or multiple outlet recorders for listening. A center for exploring textures in the everyday world can occupy another table. Several magnifying glasses and a collection of cloth scraps, sand, rocks, shells, yarn, and other similar materials are available for examination. Books and pictures relevant to topics should also be included.

Many primary teachers have discovered the effectiveness of materials and activities organized in the centers format. The centers concept is developed more fully in chapter 8. For those who would like additional information and ideas for preparing and using centers, many sources are currently on the market. Most of the appendixes in this text contain a comprehensive listing. Three that the authors have found particularly useful are:

Kaplan, Sandra, et al. *A Young Child Experiences.* Pacific Palisades, Calif.: Goodyear Publishing Company, 1975.

Kaplan, Sandra, et al. *Change for Children.* Pacific Palisades, Calif.: Goodyear Publishing Company, 1973.

Loughlin, Catherine E., and Suina, Joseph H. *The Learning Environment, An Instructional Strategy.* New York: Columbia University, Teachers College Press, 1982.

At times the teacher will work with children in helping them to develop and explore specific topics and materials in a center. For example, she might decide to focus on the theme, "Foods We Eat" with the entire class. The idea would be discussed with children according to how and what they might collect to bring to class for the center. If *eating* foods is not to be part of the project, then children can be asked to bring a variety of empty cartons, cans, and other containers in which foods are packaged. These are arranged in a display where children can explore the various items individually or in small groups, with or without the teacher. The teacher may decide to supply labels reflecting not only the theme of the center but categories of the various types of food represented: meats, vegetables, fruits, and dairy products. Children can spend time sorting and stacking the containers accordingly.

The teacher may spend time with individuals and small groups in exploring different types of materials in the reading center. Wordless picture books can be an excellent entry into reading for some children. She sits with one or more children to look at and reconstruct the story portrayed by the illustrations. Additional time for other sessions will then be provided for the children to "read" the books individually or with an older helper. The next step would be to introduce these children to picture storybooks in the same way. This will lead to reading predictable books.

Sustained silent reading (SSR). The teacher should also provide a time for all children to "read" on their own. According to Marlene I. and Robert A. McCracken (1979), sustained silent reading provides the practice required for learning to read. In the first phase of getting into reading, SSR also provides time for children to explore and become familiar with a variety of print and to stimulate interest in spending time with reading materials. Children can operate at their own levels. For those who are already reading, SSR provides the practice for extending and refining skills, adds to the growing list of words recognized on sight, and develops interests in new topics and types of written language. Children, who can identify few, if any, words, may spend time getting the message by "reading" wordless picture books. Regardless of their individual levels, all children are involved with reading materials during this period of SSR.

The following six rules are guidelines for successful sustained silent reading:

1. Begin with the whole class.
2. Each child selects one book.
3. Each child must read silently.
4. The teacher reads silently.
5. A timer is used.
6. There are absolutely no reports or records of any kind

(McCracken and McCracken 1979, 35).

In initiating SSR with beginners in school, the rules are explained and no deviations are allowed. The teacher will decide how long the first reading periods should be. Young children may be able to sustain interest for no more than a few minutes, but a routine is established: each child selects a book, finds a comfortable place, and reads until the teacher's timer sounds. It is better to have two short periods a day than a longer one in which children become restless. By experimenting, the teacher can determine the appropriate length of time for sessions. As children become accustomed to SSR time, the sessions may be lengthened accordingly. At the end of each session, the teacher and individual children may wish to share something of special interest from their reading, but the sharing is brief and spontaneous, and it contains no instructional overtones.

A Writing Environment

Along with the components of a reading environment, teachers also provide abundant materials and opportunities to encourage writing. As is true with the reading continuum, individual children will be at many different places with respect to interests, perseverance, and skills in writing.

Learning to write complements learning to read. In Durkin's studies of early readers, a considerable number of children first approached reading through experiences with writing, and almost all of the children who were early readers were also early scribblers.

Through observation and research, Marie M. Clay derived some revealing information about the relationships between reading and writing and the stages through which children pass in achieving writing proficiency. "Learning to express ideas in print certainly draws the child's attention to letters and words" (1979, 7). Clay describes the process by which the child learns "to organize his own behavior into an appropriate sequence of actions" (1975, 70):*

> If he was copying he had to co-ordinate the movements of his eyes, as he visually scanned the word, with movement patterns of his hand in reproducing it. And if he was writing the word from memory he had to mentally scan his memories of that word and translate these *in sequence* into movement patterns for writing it. In both activities he was directing his own behavior to analyze words in detail and in sequence. He was calling upon those areas of the brain which are responsible for synthesising collections of information. He had learned how to visually analyze words, and what to study in a word so as to be able to reproduce it, and how to organize his own actions to achieve this writing goal.
>
> . . . .
>
> If a child knows how to scan, how to study a word in order to reproduce it, and how to organize his writing of that word he has the skills to deal with the detail of print. It is probable that early writing serves to organize the visual analysis of print. In addition the child's work provides us with objective evidence of what he has learned.
>
> We can observe the organized behavior in wordwriting.
>
> We can assume functional organization in the brain from observing the correct copying of a word carried out in an appropriate sequence.
>
> We can assume the capacity to synthesise information from several sources as we see a child write a new word without a copy.
>
> My aim in early writing instruction would be to provide many interesting activities to establish and stabilize these strategies for analysing words. I would assume that they would then remain in the child's behaviour repertoire if called into action from time to time. In other words practice in writing would be critical at an early learning stage and of much less value for reading progress once the basic visual scanning and memory strategies were established (1975, 71).*

Children at any early age are intrigued by making marks on paper or elsewhere—oftentimes to the consternation of their parents! Their fascination is perhaps generated by seeing the immediate, tangible evidence of their actions. Further, they are in control; *they* can guide and direct their actions at will to produce different effects. (Marcia Baghban 1984 and Denny Taylor 1983).

*Source: Marie M. Clay, WHAT DID I WRITE? Heinemann Educational Books, Auckland, 1975, pp. 48–49, 70–71.

There are a number of parallels between learning to read and learning to write naturally. Children appear to teach themselves to write in much the same way they teach themselves to read. Without formal instruction, they experiment, try out, and explore the various facets of the writing process. They decorate letters, they invent their own symbols—sometimes reverting to their own "inventions" after they are well into distinguishing and reproducing different letters—and they expect others to know what they have written, regardless of their coding system.

Clay has described a series of concepts and principles that children acquire as they move through very predictable stages in learning to produce writing in conventional form. They appear to teach themselves to write in much the same way they go about teaching themselves to read: from gross approximations, they make finer and finer distinctions in moving toward conventional reproductions of written language.

> Somewhere between three and five years most children become aware that people make marks on paper purposefully, and in imitation they, the children, may produce:

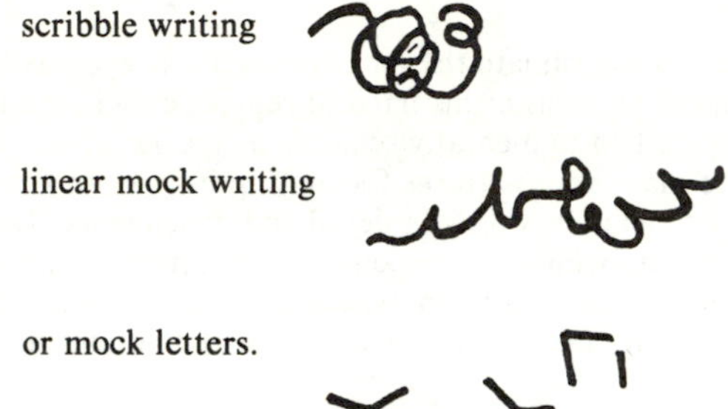

> The linear scribble that fills the lines of a writing pad has, for the child, all the mystery of an unfamiliar code. It stands for a myriad of possible things but does not convey a particular message. The child seems to say "I hope I've said something important. You must be able to understand what I've said. What did I write?"
>
> At the age of 5:5 Sherryl Lyn regarded "S" as her sign and she sat down to write a letter to her grandmother which was virtually variations of an "S" theme. At this stage children's comments seem to indicate that they have faith in the adult's capacity to read what they have written and Sherryl probably expected her grandmother to know what the writing said. She completed the activity with an envelope addressed in linear mock writing, imitating the spatial arrangement of the address to the extent of making three horizontal lines.

aged 5:5

Source: Marie M. Clay, WHAT DID I WRITE? Heinemann Educational Books, Auckland, 1975, pp. 48–49, 70–71.

From her observation of young children and their abilities to write, Clay has described several principles in the process. She encourages others who work with young children to verify these principles through their study of children's work. She has provided a "Rating Technique" for observing the child's performance during the first-six months of instruction, and a "Writing Vocabulary" inventory for the purpose of rating the child's first year of progress. Both instruments and the relevant principles are found in Clay's *What Did I Write?*, Heinemann Educational Books, Auckland, 1975.

Children learn to write by writing; therefore, they will be given many opportunities to write each day when they come to school. Lucy M. Calkins (1983) and Donald H. Graves (1983) write that in the presence of a writing environment, children will begin to exhibit "emergent" writing behaviors just as they will begin to show emergent reading behaviors in the presence of a reading environment.

A variety of writing materials are easily accessible in the classroom: paper of varying sizes and qualities, large pencils, many hues of color markers (washable fluid), and large color pencils and crayons. Paintbrushes with a supply of washable paints and finger paints should also be provided. Many children first approach writing through art. They paint pictures and then move gradually into experimenting with shapes and other marks of their own inventions.

Group writing experiences. The day should be so arranged and organized that two types of activities are provided. One is a time for all children to work with writing materials at the same time. These experiences may grow out of other activities, or a specific focus may be provided by the teacher. For example, if the children have observed a construction crew at work in the morning, after a discussion of what they saw, each child can respond by producing his own version of the event. It is important that the teacher responds by writing a comment or a label appropriate to the children's meanings for those who cannot write. The child's name should be written on all work. For some children, these are the beginnings of seeing the relationship between the printed code and the meanings for which they stand.

Some children will be sufficiently proficient to write in a word or two or a short sentence their versions of what their drawings represent. It is not particularly significant that anyone but the child be able to read what has been written. A few children will be capable of writing a short description in several sentences to accompany their drawings. They will have the system so well developed that the teacher can read what has been written without interpretation from them.

In *Reading is Only the Tiger's Tail* (1972) the McCrackens have collected some delightful examples of these types of children's art/writing efforts. After hearing the teacher read Ruth Krauss's *A Hole is to Dig* and discussing various kinds of holes, the following were produced by first-graders:

A hole is for a
ded dog that got
ran over.

A hole is to get away
from chuck.
Colleen

Source: Robert A. McCracken and Marlene J. McCracken, READING IS ONLY THE TIGER'S TAIL, Leswing Press, San Rafael, California, 1972, pp. 76–78. Used with permission of the authors.

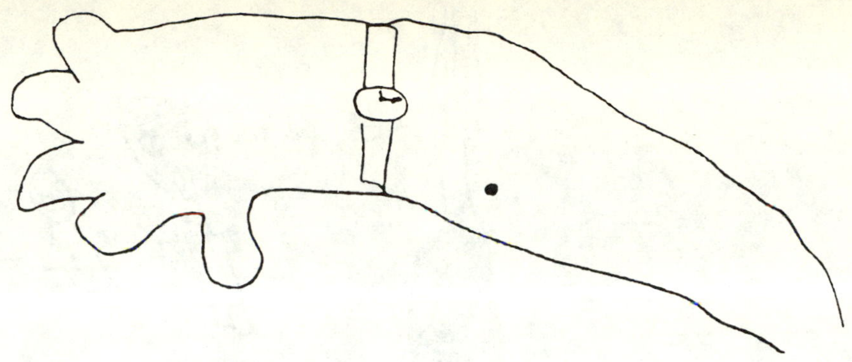

A hole is a shot.
Norma

A hole is in or brechs.
Jody

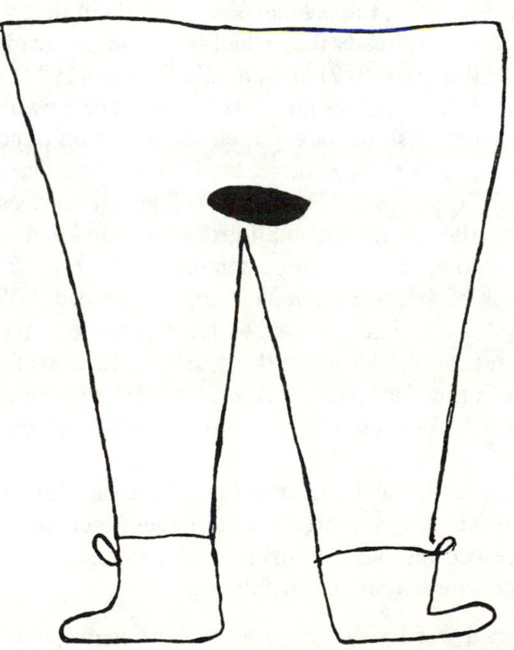

Source: Robert A. McCracken and Marlene J. McCracken, READING IS ONLY THE TIGER'S TAIL, Leswing Press, San Rafael, California, 1972, pp. 76–78. Used with permission of the authors.

A hole is to put a fence post
in. Linda

Source: Robert A. McCracken and Marlene J. McCracken, READING IS ONLY THE TIGER'S TAIL, Leswing Press, San Rafael, California, 1972, pp. 76–78. Used with permission.

In helping children to learn to write, the teacher writes for them that which they cannot write for themselves, just as she reads that which they cannot read. Leonard and Nancy Sealey and Marcia Millmore (1979) and Donald Graves (1983) write that through additional experiences, children will begin to write with their own system of marks and spellings with which they wish to convey their meanings on paper.

Another method of providing for writing experiences for the whole class is "Very-own-words," suggested by the McCracken's (1972, 106–19). The teacher does not work with the entire class at the same time; rather, a small group or individual children in the class discuss ideas that are important to them personally.

Very-own-words is a version of Sylvia Ashton-Warner's "key words." Words that have a strong personal meaning for the child are used to develop the first materials for both writing and reading. The teacher asks each child to select one word for his very own special word. She then writes the word on a 3″ × 8″ card. In subsequent sessions other words are written on cards. A collection of very-own-words is gradually accumulated for each child.

Very-own-words then become the basic material for a number of activities. One suggestion is to make booklets by stapling several sheets of paper together so that each child can use a page a day to record responses to his special collection.

A typical sequence of recordings would be as follows:

1. The child records his very-own-word with a picture and caption only, and discusses his thoughts with teacher and classmates.

2. The child records pictorially, and dictates his thoughts to a teacher or aide who writes them down. The child "reads" his thoughts to the teacher and then "reads" them to a partner or classmates.
3. The child records pictorially and dictates as in Step 2. The teacher encourages the child to spell orally as much of the word as he can, while she writes it for him.
4. The child records pictorially and the teacher sits with him as he writes, helping him with the spelling.
5. The child is independent except for concept development in choosing words. Many second graders and above need only Step 5. (McCracken and McCracken 1972, 108).

The foregoing writing activities and the atmosphere in which they are conducted develop an awareness of and an interest in recording on paper one's meanings by whatever means. Children who originally have little interest beyond marking and drawing in random fashion are motivated to move toward more-conventional writing by watching what the teacher and other children do in writing situations. They will begin to exhibit such emergent writing behaviors as: requests for their names (Show me how to do my name), specific letters (How do you make a *D*?), and copying teacher-written captions and sentences for pictures they have drawn. When work is collected over a period of time, the gradual progress toward more-conventional writing can easily be traced. (An excellent recent book on developing writing skill with third-grade children is Lucy McCormick Calkins's *Lessons from a Child: On the Teaching and Learning of Writing* [Exeter, N.H.: Heinemann Educational Books, 1983].)

What we have described is basically a language-experience approach to developing literacy. It is an excellent bridge to the more formal aspects of dealing with written language. These elements and a more-comprehensive description of language experiences will be given in the following major section of the chapter.

Individually initiated writing experiences. Opportunities and materials should also be provided for children to explore writing on their own as they wish during the day. A convenient way to set up these activities is to prepare a writing center in the classroom with a variety of writing materials along with objects, pictures, and "starter ideas" to write about. Use of the center is explained, and individuals or small groups may go to the center at various times during the day when they want to work with these materials. Activities are neither teacher directed nor teacher initiated. Just as in sustained silent reading, children are given the opportunity to explore the world of writing according to their own interests and capabilities.

Phase Two: Focusing on Print

As we have stated before, there is no magical moment and no clear-cut Rubicon where children cross from not reading to reading. The process is much like that which occurs with physical development; changes come so subtly and in such small increments over a period of time that we are not aware of what is happening along the way. One day, as in a popular song title, we wonder "Where is the little girl I carried?" We can only gain perspective on change and grasp its full impact by looking back to what was in order to gain perspective on what is. Only then is change discernible.

In acquiring literacy, children progress in much the same way. They do not suddenly move from one phase to another. Rather, there is a smooth transition in which they linger in one stage in some respects while gradually beginning to function more and more in the next. Most people cannot remember when or how they learned to read, for the process has been obscured by the end result—reading.

The challenge, the art of teaching is not to assume that learning and change occur in discrete, discernible, lockstep phases and instruct on this basis. Rather, it is to *follow the child's lead* and to provide an environment in which individual children can participate according to wherever their individual levels dictate. Over time individual behaviors combine to form distinct patterns that can be used to make appropriate instructional decisions along the way for each child. Through participation in the rich environment just described, children will exhibit an increasing number of reading and writing behaviors. These emerge and combine into an overall pattern that signals to the teacher which children can profit from help with focusing on specific aspects of written language. The most-pronounced pattern that emerges from children during the early experiences with written language are behaviors which show an increasing attention to and concentration on the visual features of print. They can now profit from direct instruction, which will help them to "know how to look and what to look for," writes Moira McKenzie (1978, 320), as they continue to figure out how the written language system works. Here, an understanding of the "parts" becomes important because the child has developed a need for them from previous experiences with whole language. Left to their own devices, some children will put together a very efficient system for deciphering the code. Others may not be so successful. Marie Clay writes:

> The first two years of instruction are critical for learning to read because this is the formation stage of an efficient or inefficient behavioral system.
>
> ....
>
> It is my belief that at this important time, we begin the production of our reading failures by allowing some children to build inefficient systems of functioning, which keep them crippled in this process throughout their school careers. As older readers they are difficult to help because they have been habituated in their inefficiency" (1979, p. 269).*

In the second stage of growing into reading, the goal of instruction is to help children to develop the most-efficient system for processing print. This means providing experiences and materials that will enable the child to select and attend to the most productive cues in print (graphophonic, semantic, and syntactic), to learn to combine simultaneously all three cuing systems to arrive at meaning, and to check and monitor performance to detect and correct miscues.

The instructional program for children in the second phase of acquiring literacy is not radically different from that for children in the initial phase. Many of the activities and materials remain the same, but some may now be used to serve different purposes. Language experience is one such example as shown in the description below. The teacher continues to monitor and promote children's progress in concept development and oral language. She continues to read to all children as a group and to provide a rich reading and writing environment.

*Source: Marie M. Clay, READING: THE PATTERNING OF COMPLEX BEHAVIOR (2nd ed.), Heinemann Educational Books, Auckland, 1979, p. 269. Used with permission.

Using Language Experience

Advantages of language experience. Beginning with language experience to teach children to read and write is like using a complete food to achieve good health rather than combining a number of incomplete ones. A well-planned and well-executed program based on the language-experience method provides for developing all the necessary literacy skills in a totally integrated way, and it serves a broad range of individual differences within a classroom group of children. Mary Anne Hall wrote:

> What is for some children a prereading experience is for other children a beginning reading activity. With the first stories some children will learn to read some words. Other children will be able to recognize likenesses and differences in printed words but will not be able to read individual words immediately. For some children the most important contribution the early stories can offer is helping them to see that their spoken ideas can be put into printed form. Other children may profit most from the discussion that precedes the writing of the story. For all children the meaning of the written story should be clear (1981, 17).

Language experience builds on two important elements of all learning: experience and language. Walter Loban writes, "Experience needs language to give it form. Language needs experience to give it content" (1966, 3).

Language experience enables children to learn naturally by providing a bridge from what they know from experience to the unknown elements of the language process called "reading." The content of the print is derived from the child's world; he knows the message and he, therefore, brings meaning to the printed form of that message.

Reading material is based on the natural spoken language of children. They have prior familiarity with the style and the content of what they will learn to read and are then better able to predict more accurately what individual words will be in the printed form.

The relationship between spoken and written language is easily discernible: children watch as their speech is converted to print. At the same time they can actually see a clear purpose for the use of print.

The use of language experience is highly motivating to children. The use of personal words, like the use of one's name, is a highly satisfying experience. They gain the same sense of self-esteem that adults do when seeing their own ideas in print; they are not only important to the person individually, but they are important enough to be preserved and shared with others.

A second motivational aspect to using children's own words for learning to read is that the chances of success are increased, because they bring the meaning of the message to the task. The more successful they are, the more each will enjoy reading and want to spend time with books; the more one reads, the greater the increase in reading proficiency.

Finally, language experience provides for the natural interrelationship and development of all forms of communication: listening, speaking, reading, and writing. In the process of developing a written account of an experience, children listen to others' ideas; they verbalize their own ideas; they write what they can or watch as someone else performs the task; and finally, they learn to read the printed form.

Components of the language experience process. The language-experience process consists of four main parts.

Provide a Stimulus to Generate Language.

The natural curiosity of young children and their interest in everything and everybody in the environment create almost limitless possibilities for talk. Topics may be initiated by children or by the teacher. A picture from a magazine that shows action may be discussed according to what the actors are doing, what they are wearing, what may happen, and what they are saying. Wordless picture books, or predictable books, can be used to develop orally the story told by a sequence of pictures. Discussion can follow the teacher's reading of a book, as in the previously cited example from *A Hole is to Dig*. Films and filmstrips are also sources to generate a lot of talk.

Rich oral language can also be stimulated by group activities or projects in the classroom. Making a recipe in the cooking center is always a sure winner. Objects brought into the classroom by teacher or children have numerous possibilities. One of the authors often used a coconut or a pineapple to begin a language experience. In the process, the pineapple or coconut would be discussed in terms of its looks, its feel, its color, its smell, and its taste with all children participating in each activity.

Excursions outside the classroom provide a wealth of opportunities for discussion. Trips to make plaster casts of animal tracks in the sand along a stream can initiate a whole series of animal study back in the classroom. (Check out the "track" situation before going on the trip to make sure some are available.) Take along a number of plastic bags with a cup of plaster of paris in each and water in a jar. When the tracks are located, pour a small amount of water from the jar into the bags and mash the contents around to produce a thick paste. Then, pour the paste into a depression left by the animal foot and let the plaster "set." In a few minutes the cast can be lifted out and taken back to the classroom for further use in developing any number of topics about animals.

All of the activities listed in "Expanding and Extending Concepts and Oral Language Competencies" (chapter 6) can be used for stimulating discussion and developing the remaining steps in a rich language experience. Several appendixes at the end of this text contain a number of sources for ideas to develop language experiences.

Record Children's Language

After completion of the "talking stage," compile a story or an account of what was done by recording the actual language of children. Use a large chart or chart paper to write as the children watch. (The story may be written on the board instead and later transferred to a chart.)

Read What Has Been Written

The teacher reads the chart to the children. Then they "read" along several times as she moves her hand along each line of print. This same procedure should be repeated on two or three successive days.

Follow-up with Related Reading and Writing Activities

This step provides opportunities for children to participate in activities according to their individual competencies in reading and writing. Children who are well into the second phase of reading—they are attending more to the features of print—will participate in a number of activities designed to help them focus on and use the most-productive strategies for identifying individual words and developing a larger sight vocabulary. These activities will be described in the following subsection.

Give children duplicates of the language-experience story they have helped to compile. Individual booklets can be made by adding successive language-experience stories. Some children learn to read the stories with practice in assisted reading sessions with the teacher or with other helpers. They may also take the copy home to be read with parents. The stories may be copied by some children who are more-competent writers. Others will draw pictures to illustrate a part of the story. At first these children may not write anything themselves; the teacher writes what they wish to say about their drawings.

Language experience is one approach for helping children to grow into reading and writing naturally. The child's efforts are accepted as they are in each stage—invented spelling and all. It must be remembered that children begin with gross approximations and move to finer discriminations in their development of literacy. "Children who are exposed to print in relevant, functional ways will be curious about print and will often select writing as an appealing, independent activity" (Hall 1981, 49).

Individual children will often create their own personalized versions (in reading and/or writing) of language experiences, or they will take off in other directions suggested by a particular facet of the experience. After a story about favorite pets had been written, one child produced a whole page of repeated drawings of the same dog. The next day he asked the teacher to write the word *dog* on a piece of paper, which he then used to write *dog* under each figure he had drawn the preceding day. (When he showed his work to the teacher, she replied, "Wow, but you have a lot of dogs!" The child said, "No, they're all the same one!") On the third day the child drew one very large dog picture on a page and then wrote in very large letters *D O G* under it. On the fourth day, using a number of invented symbols, he wrote what translated to "This is my dog" under the drawing he had made the day before. The teacher asked the child to read what he had written, following which she wrote under John's sentence: "This is my dog." by John. She read what she had written while pointing with her finger to the words and then returned the drawing to the child with a compliment on his work. For a short time on each of the following two days, John practiced copying the teacher's sentence and his name over and over as he slowly said the sentence to himself.

In addition to group language experiences, the same procedure can be used to work with individual children. The following example is taken from an excellent set of filmstrips and tapes describing the whole process: *Teaching Beginning Reading: Language Experience Approach to Reading,* marketed by Reading Unlimited, 2224 Glasgow Road, Alexanderia, Virginia 22307.

Using a picture to stimulate discussion, the teacher wrote the following story dictated by a kindergarten child:

> The clerk is helping the mother carry out the bags. The boy is in the bag trying to trip the clerk. He is holding the rope with a round circle in it. Maybe the boy opened and broke an apple in half when they were inside. Maybe she had to pay for the stuff he broke.
>
> by Dean

After writing the dictated story during the first session, the teacher read the story aloud. She made wording corrections suggested by the child, and then invited him to read along with her as she followed the line of print with her hand.

Activities in subsequent sessions included having the child

- read along during repeated readings;
- match whole sentences on the story by placing individual sentences cut from a second copy of the story;
- match phrases and individual words in the above manner;
- share oral reading to conclude each session;
- practice word recognition as the teacher used an adjustable "window box" card to isolate individual words and phrases;
- match words on individual cards with like words on a grid as the teacher pronounced the words on the grid;
- watch as each recognized word was entered on a card for the child's Word Bank and a sentence using the word was recorded on the backside of each card;
- point to word cards on a large pocket chart as the teacher pronounced the words in random selection;
- practice visual memory of words by closing his eyes while a card from the collection was removed from the pocket chart and then giving the missing word;
- use phonic, structural, and word meaning clues to locate specific words: point to the word that begins with *t;* the one that tells more than one bag (*bags*); the word that tells what the boy is going to do to the clerk *(trip)*;
- practice reading phrases at a glance when the teacher used a chart with flaps that covered phrases from the story.

Ideas for developing language experiences. Two examples from an excellent book of ideas and activities for using the language-experience approach are given on the following pages along with examples of the children's work in reading and writing: Ellen Cromwell, *Feathers in My Cap: Early Reading Through Experience* (Washington, D.C.: Acropolis Books, 1980).

For additional ideas around which language experiences may be developed, see the collection of activities in chapter 6 under "Expanding and Extending Concepts and Oral Language Competencies," and the list of sources given in appendix 1.

TITLE:	"Thanksgiving"
PURPOSE:	As part of an ongoing unit entitled "Preparing for Thanksgiving," this theme was directed toward life in a new land, emphasizing the contributions Pilgrims and Indians made to early America. The three-part unit included: A Voyage on the Mayflower, Pilgrims and Indians, and The First Thanksgiving. The teacher hoped that children would develop their appreciation of historical concepts, their heritage, brotherhood, and learn new words (e.g., harvest, feast, Mayflower, canoe, wampum, pheasant, deer, log cabin, freedom).
MATERIALS:	Clay, macaroni, construction paper, string, paints, and pillow cases to be used as Indian costumes (slit at the neck and fringed at the bottom).
PROCEDURE:	The teacher talked about early Indian and Pilgrim life during the week preceding her presentation, emphasizing the way the country looked to the first American settler, their first meeting with the Indians, differences in speech, appearance, and customs and how Pilgrims and Indians found ways to communicate and cooperate. She also discussed how the Indians were displaced later when the settlers moved onto their land, and how this led to conflicts which still exist today. During the week children made Indian costumes (by painting the pillow cases with Indian symbols and designs), pottery, wampum (from large macaroni shells), log cabins (from strips of construction paper), feathers, Pilgrim hats, and corn bread. During sharing time, the teacher and children acted out the story of the first Thanksgiving. As the teacher narrated the dramatization, the children went through the motions of planting and harvesting crops, hunting and fishing, and preparing for the feast. Everyone wanted to sit at the head of the table!
FOLLOW UP ACTIVITIES:	During free activity time some of the children drew pictures about their shared experience in the language center. They chose words to describe their pictures as noted under each illustration. To further develop this theme the teacher suggested that the children prepare their own Thanksgiving dinner. They decided to make vegetable soup, baked apples, corn bread, and pumpkin pie. Each child was asked to contribute a food item and to think about one thing that he/she was especially thankful for. As thank you's were shared, the teacher lit a Thanksgiving candle for this special day.

Source: Ellen Cromwell, FEATHERS IN MY CAP: EARLY READING THROUGH EXPERIENCE, Acropolis Books, Washington, D.C., 1980, pp. 71–72, 113–116. Used with permission.

"The Pilgrims are on the Mayflower. They want to go to Florida. They are good friends."

"This turkey is running into a barn. The farmer can't catch him."

Source: Ellen Cromwell, FEATHERS IN MY CAP: EARLY READING THROUGH EXPERIENCE, Acropolis Books, Washington, D.C., 1980, pp. 71–72, 113–116. Used with permission.

"This Indian chief is angry. He has lost his bow and arrow."

TITLE:	"A Nature Walk"
PURPOSE:	The teacher would like to encourage an appreciation for nature through direct observation; help children understand cause-effect relationships; develop scientific inquiry through discovery and problem solving experiences; expand visual discrimination skills, memory, and good listening habits; and provide a setting for language experience stories.
MATERIALS:	A water table, a sorting tray, shoe boxes, a magnifying glass, and items from nature.
PROCEDURE:	For teachers who have access to a park or woodland area, a walk to a pond or stream is one way to provide a firsthand experience for language development. In the process of observing water life, the teacher asks the children: "How does the water look and how does it make you feel? Let's see if we can name all the things our eyes are seeing in the water. Can you see your own reflection? Did you notice that leaf floating on the surface of the water? What would happen if we threw in this tiny stone—would it float or sink?" On a lucky day, the teacher and her friends may find some tadpoles or other little creatures to observe under a magnifying glass. When children have returned to the classroom, the teacher conducts a brief discussion about the experience while the children are resting.
FOLLOW-UP ACTIVITIES:	During free activity time, children are encouraged to draw a picture about their experience for a language experience book. At another table, some children may enjoy making a diorama

Source: Ellen Cromwell, FEATHERS IN MY CAP: EARLY READING THROUGH EXPERIENCE, Acropolis Books, Washington, D.C., 1980, pp. 71–72, 113–116. Used with permission.

(a miniature scene depicting items in a naturalistic setting). In a shoe box painted and decorated to give the appearance of a small body of water such as a stream or pond, children can add natural items such as pebbles, sticks, and rocks. They can also make little creatures—tiny fish, a snake, or a frog on a log from construction paper and clay.

When the diorama is finished, each child can claim possession by posting a sign that says "Marta's Pond" (using the name of the child).

Still other children may entertain themselves in the science center; labeling, sorting, and examining items found. The teacher may add to this experience by reading "Swimming" by Leo Lionni and "Theodore Turtle" by Ellen MacGregor (Cromwell, 1980, 71–72).

Two examples of dictated stories from the same child conclude this subsection. They were supplied by a student teacher who was supervised by one of the authors. They are remarkable examples of the rich personal meaning and feeling out of which children sometime think and of the way in which they deal with these highly personal thoughts. In the first example, the child attempts to impersonalize feelings by telling the story through animal characters; in the second story, she comes closer to personalization but still does not go all the way by using first-person reference. Note the remarkably parallel way in which both stories develop the same theme. The second story was dictated a week after the first one.

A Bug and a Rabbit
by Kari

Once upon a time there lived a bug and a rabbit. The bug lived in a tree. The rabbit lived in the downstairs of the tree. All the time they would be friends. But one time the bug always made noise so the rabbit was always angry. So the rabbit moved out. Then he saw the bug on the street one day and they made friends again. So the rabbit moved back in and they always had tea together.

The Divorced Family
by Kari

Once there was a man and a woman. They were married. They lived happily, but a few months later the man had something that he did. And the woman didn't like it. And they had a child who was very young. So they were talking about getting divorced since the woman moved away. But they didn't know what to do about the baby. So they decided that the woman should have the baby. And the man wanted to have the baby so they broke the agreement. So they had to go to court. The court man decided that the man couldn't take the baby so the woman had to take it. Then one day they decided to get married again and then they weren't angry at each other about the baby. So they lived happily ever after.

Using Assisted Reading

Participation in the activities of a reading and writing environment leads naturally to the development of reading-like behaviors, which signal heavier involvement with symbols on the page. Children begin with a focus on meaning within the whole-language context and then move gradually into paying more and more attention to the "pieces" that make up print. As they begin to watch more closely the print on pages being read, they will often correct when the reader changes expected wording, they help to turn pages at appropriate times, they ask questions about specific words (Where does it say *kitten?*) and they will begin to mumble along with the oral reading. They will "read" aloud familiar stories to themselves, their toys, or other interested listeners. Successive readings come closer to producing the printed text. David B. Doake (1979) and Marie M. Clay (1972) write that during this stage children may use a combination of "finger" and "voice" pointing. They attempt to match "speech and text word-by-word and space-by-space with accuracy using hand and voice to synchronise the matching" (Clay 1973, 151).*

> This spontaneous movement to and from contextually directed and graphophonically dependent reading appears to be a highly significant aspect of a young child's drive towards literacy. . . . Initially, when matching what is being read with the ear and the eye, the concentration required to unlock the unknown word by graphophonic means, causes the young reader to forget that the page can be "read" by using all the contextual aids available. By constantly changing from one style of reading to the other, however, the child gradually comes to learn, albeit unconsciously, that all the cues on the page can be utilized to maintain the flow of the language in a meaningful way (Doake 1979, 14).

Oral reading appears to be an important element in learning to read; it is a part of each of the assisted reading methods described below. Marie Clay has the following to say:

> Saying words and sentences aloud resulted in greater ability to recognize and understand written words and sentences among beginning readers in a research comparing oral and non-oral approaches. Oral reading is then, an aid to learning at this level and not something to be minimised lest it create slow readers.
>
> Data available on self-correction behavior suggests that young children respond, hear their errors, and correct them. As reading skill increases, this thinking aloud, after the error has been made, disappears and with it observable self-correction. The trying out, rejecting and new attempts are probably being carried on in the brain. If this hypothesis can be further supported in research then oral reading may be a necessity to get the feed-back system working. Because at an early stage errors are heard by the child and fed back into the processing activity of his brain he may become able to mentally correct his errors. Oral reading remains important as the only situation the teacher can use to observe, check and reinforce appropriate reading behavior in the first few years (1979, 262–263).†

Emergent reading behaviors signal that a child is ready to move into the second phase of reading, that in which there is an increased focus on and attending to the visual features of print. A number of methods to aid this process can be used by the teacher or other classroom helpers. All are versions of some type of direct help with reading. In the three methods described below, the child is helped to take over gradually the reading task himself.

Assisted reading. Kenneth Hoskisson (1975a, 1975b) devised a method for helping children to learn to read by reading he calls "assisted reading." He identifies the following stages:

*Source: Marie M. Clay, READING: THE PATTERNING OF COMPLEX BEHAVIOR, Heinemann Educational Books, London, 1973, p. 151. Used with permission.

†Source: Marie M. Clay, READING: THE PATTERNING OF COMPLEX BEHAVIOR (2nd ed.), Heinemann Educational Books, London, 1979, pp. 262–263. Used with permission.

> The first stage consists of reading to the children and having them repeat the phrases or sentences after the person doing the reading. The second stage begins when the children begin to notice that some of the words occur repeatedly in the stories they are reading. In this stage the readers leave out some of the words they think the children know. They have the children fill in blanks left as they read. Stage three is entered when the children do the reading and the reader fills in the words the children may not know or have trouble recognizing (1979, 494–95).

Echo reading. Echo reading is another way to give the beginning reader direct assistance. While pointing, the teacher reads by phrases or sentences, and the child then points and repeats (echoes) what has been heard. After a short reading session with the teacher, the child practices with a tape using the same procedure. When the child has learned to read the material, he then reads again to the teacher.

Shared-book experience. The shared-book experience, written about by Don Holdaway (1979), is a series of classroom procedures that closely parallel the condition and responses characteristic of preschool children in the bedtime story situation: a parent introduces the story for the purpose of the child's enjoyment; the young child requests repeated readings of a favorite story in subsequent story sessions; the child spends time alone "reading" the story.

Barbara Park noted that Holdaway and his associates used the foregoing model to devise instructional procedures to move children into reading in the same natural way that preschool children experience with parents (1982, 816). The model is based on a three-part procedure.

1. *Introduction of a favorite story for the purpose of enjoyment.* The teacher duplicates the story on large sheets of heavy paper, which are then assembled into a Big Book. John H. Shuh writes, "In order to transfer the dynamics of the bed-time story into the classroom, it is essential that there be versions of favorite books large enough so that a whole group of children can all see the print at once and follow it as it is being read to them or as they are 'reading' it" (1981, 3). The Big Book may be displayed on an easel for easy viewing.

The teacher may introduce the book in several ways to generate interest; a discussion might develop around comparisons of the Big Book with its original, smaller version. Because children are familiar with the story, they will likely respond about characters and events that they recall. The focus is kept on sharing enjoyment of the story, not direct instruction.

The teacher then leads the children in unison reading of the story while pointing to each word. Children follow along according to their individual capabilities in much the same way that young children do as parents read bedtime stories. Several Big Book story favorites may be read in a single session using this procedure.

2. *Repeated readings.* When children have been introduced to several Big Book versions of favorite stories, they will request that certain ones be reread in succeeding sessions. Each time the requested story is "read" in unison, the teacher focuses attention on words and directionality by pointing as the text is read. In the process of repeated readings, individual children begin to exhibit the same emergent reading behaviors of young preschool children in storytime sessions with parents: anticipating and supplying words coming up in the sentence being read, pointing to and asking what

specific words are, and "reading" the story from memory and/or picture cues. Their reproductions of the story gradually become closer and closer approximations of the actual text.

3. *Independent reading.* Following pleasure-focused sessions with favorite stories, Park writes that "the children are provided ample time for independent reading of their favorite stories" (1982, 816, quoting Holdaway). The Big Books are made easily accessible to children on the floor for "stomach" reading or on tables and easels for those who prefer a more conventional reading posture. The story text may also be recorded on tapes and placed in a listening center along with copies of the original book so that children can "read-along" as they are able.

Opportunities to respond to favorite stories in other ways are also provided. Some children may copy the story line by line, illustrate pages, and compile their own books. Some may "write" their own versions using invented symbols as early writers often do when they begin to experiment with producing print. Still other children may choose to act out their favorite stories in a variety of dramatic productions: role-playing a character, using puppets to tell the story, or playing out the story on a flannel board with felt-backed character cutouts.

The shared-book experience provides an excellent foundation for helping beginning readers to move to the next stage in literacy development: attending more closely to specific features of written language in order to acquire efficient reading strategies. This topic is the subject of an upcoming section in the present chapter.

There are different versions of the three methods above, but each can be changed and adapted to meet the individual needs of children in a given classroom. All use the whole-language context, focus is on the sense of the material rather than specific features of the print, repeated readings of given material is required, and learning to read by reading is the overall goal. Each method can be adapted to provide practice independent of the teacher or other helper through the use of recordings.

Using Basal Reader Materials

When children have acquired certain concepts through participation in the varied types of activities described in this text, basal readers can then be used to great advantage in furthering their growth toward reading competency. Before entry into the more formal aspects of instruction, however, children should have

1. achieved a general understanding about how the process of reading works,
2. acquired some basic concepts about print and a familiarity with the styles in which print occurs,
3. developed a conceptual store sufficient to understand most of the content in reading materials they will be using,
4. developed the oral language proficiency necessary to make the transition to the printed form without excessive difficulty,
5. begun to attend to specific features of print,
6. made attempts to use strategies for achieving meaning,
7. shown increasing interest in books and learning to read them. Now basal readers can become valuable tools for acquiring further reading proficiency.

The optimum time for beginning work in basal materials is an individual matter: it is not age related. Some five- and six-year-olds will already be reading with fluency. Most children, however, will need the whole-language readiness described in this text, and some will need to grow further through participation in language and concept development activities most of the school year before they are ready for *formal* instruction in dealing with print.

Past criticisms and present materials. A major criticism of basal reading programs in this text centers primarily on the *way* the basal- or graded-reading materials are used in instruction and on their *overuse* to the exclusion of other materials and methods that offer important assistance in children's thrust toward literacy.

The newer basal reader series on the market today have come a long way in correcting many of the deficiencies cited by critics. The content represents a broad cross-section of life-styles from many cultures and socioeconomic levels. Literature selections are included from modern authors as well as from the body of traditional literary classics, which have been popular with children for generations. The language is more natural than that of former versions; but efforts to control vocabulary, especially at preprimer through grade one, still continue to result in language that contains more repetition of words and less-interesting sentences than those found in regular storybooks.

Basal series authors have obviously made a concerted effort to include themes and topics with which young children can easily identify. The Macmillan Reading Series (1983), for example, offers several primary texts that have units dealing with feelings and development of self-confidence. In *Secrets and Surprises,* grade three, Laurence Swinburne's "A Special Kind of Help" explores how two girls feel when they are rejected by other classmates because the two are different from the others. The text describes how the girls become friends and eventually gain acceptance by their classmates.

Many basal stories have all the components of well-written, entertaining literature. Frequently the stories are adaptations from classics. In *Magic Times,* grade two, Benjamin Elkin's "Lucky and the Giant" contains well-drawn characters reacting to events that build toward an exciting climax and resolution of problems encountered.

Additional changes reflected in new basals include less stereotyping in portrayal of sex roles, more expository-writing text selections, a wide selection of supplemental materials that provides for a range of individual difference and interests, and vocabulary development within whole-language context rather than in isolation from meaning.

Current basal reading series have much potential for productive use as *one* component in a balanced-literacy-development program. Materials must be chosen to meet specific needs and interests of individual children. Used selectively in this manner and in conjunction with other materials and instructional methods, basal content can be very useful in all phases of literacy development. If the whole-language emphasis presented in this text is followed, the phonics program will be altered to teach only what children need, and many workbooks will not be completed page by page.

Appropriate use and placement of basal materials. Graded reader series may be used quite effectively with children who are at various points on the continuum of literacy development. For children who have developed few, if any, emergent reading behaviors, less structured and more general uses of basal materials are indicated. More formal work should be delayed while language is developed. For those children who have developed the insights and competencies that enable them to operate with at least a minimum level of proficiency in processing print, then basal materials may be used to provide more focused instruction.

General Uses of Materials in Early Stages of Literacy Development

Readiness materials in basal series need not be "taught" page by page as the teacher's guide suggests. When the readiness books are made available to children to explore and talk about in an informal way, young prereaders will attend to the content in much the same way they react to books such as Richard Scarry's *Best Word Book Ever* (1974). They point to the shapes, objects, and colors that make up most readiness materials, name them, and then move on to other pages to repeat the performance. In this process they are building a cognitive store of concepts and interrelated categories as the authors described earlier under cognitive development in chapter 3. The young ones will probably not discover many of the relationships for which some of the materials are intended (little/big, tall/short, first/last), but these concepts, along with many others, will develop over time as children participate in the varied activities in a primary classroom and as they continue to spend time with books.

Readiness books aids help to develop an awareness of the role of pictures and illustrations in books: they can signal meaning, and they provide clues to the sequence of events portrayed. When a series of pictures depicts familiar stories in wordless form as in "Humpty Dumpty" or "The Tortoise and the Hare," children will point to the pictures and describe the event in each frame. This is a natural reproduction of the story sense in the child's own language: "There's Humpty Dumpty sitting on the wall; there he is falling down; there he is getting broken; and there are all the pieces that's left!" or "The turtle and the rabbit are getting started; there goes the rabbit 'way ahead; there he is sleeping under the tree; look at the turtle—he's going by Mr. Rabbit and he's still asleep; and there is Mr. Turtle winning the race 'cause the rabbit can't catch up!"

Readiness through primer-level context provides materials that can be used to generate language-experience stories. Whole-page, action-packed illustrations can be selected for discussion and teacher recording of children's responses. The children's recorded language becomes the text to be read. Basal materials also contain text and pictures that can be used as "story starters." A selection from Peter Martin Wortmann's "Nan" in the preprimer *You Can* (1983 54–55) contains an illustration stretching across two pages. It shows a child standing at the end of a boat dock, her hands cupped to her mouth as she calls across the waves. The text on the second page reads, "The girl calls and calls. Why does the girl call?" A discussion of the question without reading the rest of the story and recording of individual responses provides text for group reading that reflects each child's own idea about the situation.

Selections containing a high level of predictability may be used in any one of the assited reading versions. Lynn K. Rhodes (1981, 511–18) writes that rhyme provides cues to predicting upcoming words; poems with this feature are readily available in all levels of primary basal materials. Several poems can be made into a Big Book and used as described in the section on shared-book experience. Stories based on classics with which children are already familiar may be reproduced as Big Books and developed in the bedtime story format. The following are examples of this type of story available in current primary basal texts: "Make Way for Ducklings," "The Lion and the Mouse," "The Five Chinese Brothers," "Belling the Cat," and "Four Musicians of Bremen."

Specific Use of Materials in Later Stages of Literacy Development

Children who can handle a sizeable part of the reading task without step-by-step assistance can benefit from direct instruction using selected basal-reader materials. Stories that they can process with at least 95 percent accuracy are chosen from levels above preprimer and primer; stories above these levels are more likely to contain less stilted language and more-interesting content.

The procedures for guided reading of the story are similar to those of the directed-reading lesson outlined in the teacher's edition of basal series.

> Guided reading is a form of group instruction in which we introduce children to the techniques of reading new or unseen material for personal satisfaction and understanding. It is not an oral reading situation in which individual children take their turns reading around a group. Such a procedure has many damaging features: it overemphasizes accuracy at the expense of understanding; it turns reading into a performance skill with great potential threat to some children; for the child doing the reading it makes the use of sound central-strategies during reading almost impossible; and it is grossly uneconomic in that only one child is reading at a time (Holdaway 1979, 142).

Holdaway describes three phases of a guided reading lesson:

1. *Tune in* is an introduction to the story which is designed to arouse children's interest in the content. Discussion relates the story to children's background of experiences, focuses on the central theme, uses vocabulary which may not be familiar, and raises questions to be answered during reading.
2. *Reading.* Children read the story to themselves.
3. *Follow-up* involves post-reading discussion and/or other activities growing out of reading the story. These may include discussion of answers to questions from the introductory phase, locating specific points made in the text, locating cues to word identification and meaning, dramatizing events, writing and illustrating creative stories based on a similar theme (Holdaway 1979, 142–43).

Missing from the above format are the intensively skills-focused activities in workbooks and ditto pages that invariably follow traditional directed-reading lessons. Instead, the need for using specific cues and strategies grows out of problems encountered in processing the whole-language context of the story. These difficulties are identified in the post-reading discussion of the story, and they are resolved by returning immediately to the text. The teacher directs attention to the place in the text where a problem has arisen and points out cues not perceived by the children. Suppose they had difficulty identifying the word *gigantic* in the following sentence from the story text:

> The horse made one gigantic leap to get over the fence.

Context cues to meaning before and after the word could be identified—"one," "leap," and "over the fence." Children's nonvisual store, or deep structure, would likely include the concept of height of a fence and the need to make a sizeable jump to clear it. In

Your Turn 7.1 Three methods for teaching beginning reading.

Select one of the following and prepare a lesson according to the instructions given in the foregoing section, "Phase Two: Focusing on Print": (1) language experience, (b) shared-book, or (c) basal reader. (The number of sessions required to teach the lesson you plan will vary according to which of the three methods you choose.) Prepare to teach the lesson to a small group of children (3 to 5) in a primary grade above kindergarten. Make notes on what happened as soon as possible after each session.

1. When the lesson is completed, compare your teaching experience with others in the class who selected the same method you did and with those who chose a different method.
2. Based on this assignment and readings in your text, determine with your peers how all three methods can be combined to make a comprehensive primary reading program—one which reflects many of the elements relevant to learning to read naturally.

other words, they would probably have the *meaning* for the needed word. The teacher could then suggest the synonym *giant,* which the children would likely have in their speaking vocabulary and which has a common graphophonic cue at the beginning.

Dealing in this way with solutions to problems as they arise is far more meaningful to children than focusing on the same solutions in the isolation of workbook exercises. In the former, children can actually see how the solution works; in the latter, the problem *and* its solution may be lost on them entirely. All too often, children see the problem and solution as getting through the assigned page(s) in the least-possible time and with a minimum of effort.

Components of a Balanced Program for the Development of Natural Readers

In focusing on print in the second major phase of children's literacy development, we have described methods and materials we believe can be combined into a highly motivating, creative, and effective approach to beginning-reading instruction. The approach reflects many of the elements present in the preschool experience of natural readers. The language-experience method and materials and one or more of the assisted-reading versions combine to become the basic entry into the acquisition of literacy. The basal reader materials are used selectively where they fit naturally into the total program's purposes: they are not a separate and distinct component as they have been in the past.

Figure 7.1 provides an excellent summation of the concepts in the above model of a balanced reading program.

We would expand the shared-book experience to include two other types of assisted reading; Hoskisson's version and echo reading are used where needed to meet the specific needs of individual children. We would also make selective use of graded reader materials at an earlier stage when appropriate to specific learning and instructional needs. Individualized reading is seen as a common element across all three components.

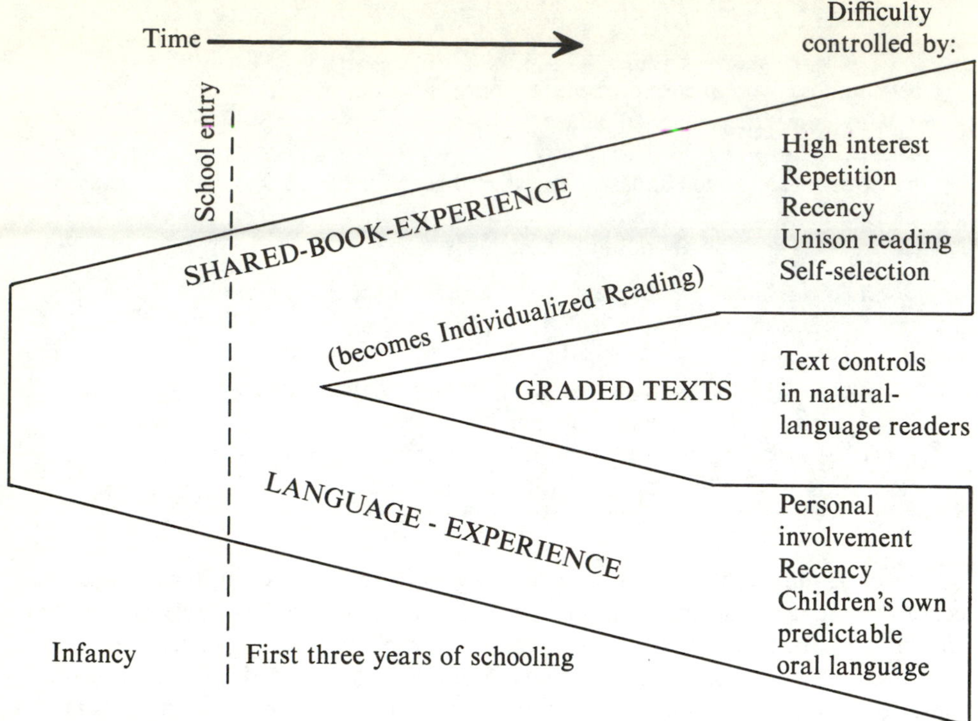

Figure 7.1. Balancing approaches and materials. Source: Don Holdaway, FOUNDATIONS OF LITERACY, Ashton Scholastic, Sydney, Australia, 1975, p. 80. Used with permission.

Participation in a program of the type just summarized, results in most children's paying closer and closer attention to specific features of written language; they can then profit from more-direct instruction aimed at helping them to attend to the most-productive cues to the meaning of written language. The materials generated out of language experience, Big Books from the shared-book experience, stories used in echo reading or Hoskisson's version of assisted reading, and selections from basal series all combine to form a rich store from which appropriate selections may be made to fit specific learning and instructional needs at any given time.

The next section describes how these various kinds of materials are used to enable children to progress farther along the learning-to-read continuum with ever-increasing independence in handling the reading task.

Focusing on the Features of Written Language

Out of early experiences with written language, many children will begin to attend more closely to the visual aspects of print as evidenced by emergence of reading-like behaviors. They are now ready for and will be receptive to instruction that will help them to determine how print works. Instruction is designed to enable them to locate and to use all three cue systems by which meanings are signaled in written language: *graphophonic, syntactic,* and *semantic.*

The content of materials used for beginning instruction must already be familiar to children. Knowing the meaning enables them to predict with greater accuracy what the printed text actually is. At the same time, they can be helped to focus on specific visual cues without becoming so distracted that meaning is lost. Therefore, all the materials described in the preceding section are appropriate for directing children's attention to the most-productive cues to meaning in print: language-experience stories; Big Books duplicating basal reader stories or poems and original stories drawn from literary classics; and text used in other versions of assisted reading.

Later, when children have learned to focus more on the cues to written language as a source for arriving at meaning, they may be given new materials and receive instruction as we described earlier in a guided reading lesson from a basal reader selection.

Developing strategies for using the cue systems of language. Begin with language experience material or a Big Books to develop a number of strategies and skills.

Graphophonic Cues

1. Directionality of print.
   - The child watches as the teacher writes a language experience story from left to right, sweeps back to the left to begin a new line, and proceeds from the top to the bottom of the chart paper.
   - In reading stories to the children and in read-along repetition, she sweeps her hand along beneath the words.
   - Hall also suggests "game-type activities with left and right directions such as 'Simon Says' and 'Lobby Loo' . . ." (1981, 107).
   - When children write, place a mark in the upper left-hand portion of the page to signify the beginning spot.
2. Visual discrimination and visual memory of print.
   - Match duplicate sentences, phrases, and word cutouts with their counterparts on the familiar story.
   - Use an adjustable window box to isolate individual sentences, phrases, words, and beginning letters in the story.
   - Use a grid on which the child places matching word cards as the teacher pronounces them.
   - Display sentences, phrases, or words on a pocket chart. Ask child to close his eyes, remove a card, and then have him look to identify the missing word.
   - Use a chart with flaps to cover sentences, phrases, or words from the story to adjust speed of exposure to each item. Practice having the child tell what he sees each time a flap is lifted. Gradually decrease the time of exposure.
   - Provide several individual letter cards. Point to words in the story and ask the child to find a letter card to match the beginning (or ending) letter in the word. Have him locate all other words that begin or end with the same letter.

Each of the above activities also contributes to a child's learning some of the metalanguage, the terms used to talk about print: *letter, word, phrase,* and *sentence.*

3. Phonics. Children can be aided in learning to associate sounds with symbols in a number of ways that grow naturally out of their experiences with whole language.

- In unison reading of language-experience and shared-book-experience materials, use some form of masking to isolate beginning consonants in selected words. An adjustable window box has already been described. Holdaway advocates the use of paper flaps to cover parts of words. the flaps may be attached to the enlarged version of the story or to the normal-sized version:

> The children then volunteer what is under the flaps. With a normal-sized book, the teacher simply pauses at predictable words, or gives crucial letter cues on a blackboard or with a felt pen. All the intricacies of phonic options (and they can be discussed honestly as options) can be taught and exemplified at the critical moment when they are needed—when they are clearly functional. Many of the classic difficulties of teaching phonics are overcome by such natural procedures (Park 1982, 819).

- To focus children's attention on beginning word cues, use sentences from the text to prepare cloze activities. Write the initial consonant(s) and omit the remaining letters. For example,

  One, two
  Buckle my sh_______ .

  Three, four
  Knock on the d_______ .

  Five, six
  Pick up st_______ .

  Seven, eight
  Lay them str_______ .

  Nine, ten
  A big, fat h_______ .

- Have children locate and pronounce other words in the story beginning with the same letter or blend.
- Have children sort words in their word banks into stacks which begin with the same letter. Have them pronounce each word, then cover all except the first letter of the word, and pronounce its sound.
- Use magazine or readiness book pictures that correspond to new words beginning with a specific letter, *w,* for example. Say to the child, "Now, let's see if you can figure out some new words that begin with *w.* You know all the words except the ones beginning with *w.* Read the sentence I write for each picture, and think of a word that makes sense in the sentence." Examples might include:

  The boy is looking out the *window.*
  The street is *wide.*
  The boy has a glass of *water.*
  The family likes to *watch* TV.

  (Hall 1981, 117)

Many variations of the procedures above can be used to teach recognition of other beginning and ending consonants, consonant digraphs, and blends.

Consonants		**Vowels**			
Single Consonants	*Consonant Combinations*	*Single Vowels*	*Vowel Combinations*	*Vowel-Consonant Combinations*	*The Schwa*
Single	Consonant	Single vowels	Vowel digraphs:	Vowels	(ə)
consonants (one	blends:	(May be long	ai in sail	A followed by	penc*i*l
phoneme):		or short):	ay day	"l" or "w":	*a*bout
	bl br sc tw		ea beat		beck*o*n
b d f h	cl cr sk scr	a e i	ea head	"aw" in bawl	lat*e*nt
i k l m	fl dr sm spr	o u	ea tea	"al" in wall	
n w y z	gl fr sn str	y (sometimes)	ee sleep	Vowels followed	
Single	pl gr sp shr		ei receive	by "r":	
consonants with	sl pr st spl		ie believe	a in arm	
two or more	dw tr sw sch		ey key	e fern	
common sounds:	wr thr		ey they	i dirt	
"c" as "k"	Consonant		oa boat	o word	
"c" as "s"	digraphs:		oe toe	u hurt	
"g" as "g"	One sound:		ow show	y martyr	
"g" as "j"			ou though	q and u	
"s" in hiss	gh, ph, sh, ck,		Vowel blends	qu in quick	
rose	ng, nk		(diphthongs):	squ squirrel	
sugar	Two or more		oi in soil		
"x" in six	sounds:		oy boy		
xylophone	th: this, thin		ue true		
exact	wh: what, who		ew in new		
	ch: chin,		ow now		
	chalet		ou though		
	choir		oa goal		

Figure 7.2. The phonic elements. From Zintz, Miles V. CORRECTIVE READING 4th ed. © 1966, 1972, 1977, 1981. Wm. C. Brown Publishers, Dubuque, Iowa. All rights reserved. Reprinted by permission.

The phonic elements of the English language are shown in figure 7.2. Through the whole-language approach, children will learn most, if not all, of these elements; thus, the need for excessive drill in workbooks and ditto sheets will be eliminated.

4. Structural analysis. Use whole sentences from familiar materials to help children identify the meaning units of words: compounds, prefixes, suffixes, roots, and inflections (the *s* in *boys,* for example, or the *ed* in *walked.*) The latter are the morphemes, or smallest meaning-bearing units of which words are composed, and their identification can help to unlock unknown words in context.

Work on structural analysis should be kept simple at this stage of a child's learning to read. The major purpose should be to create an awareness of how word meanings can be changed by adding and subtracting morphemes. The number and types of roots used should be few and, where possible, have concrete referents. All roots should be within the child's sight word repertoire before they are used with the various morphemes. Children should also have developed the concepts of *word* and *letter.*

The following are examples of structural units that may be used:

- *compounds:* grandmother, grandfather, snowman, bedroom, airplane (or other compounds out of the child's experiential background).

- *inflections:* possessives—*'s* in *boy's, man's;* plurals—*s* in *cows;* verb changes—*ed, s, ing* in *walked, walks, walking;* comparison—*er* and *est* in *taller* and *tallest.*
- *roots, prefixes,* and *suffixes:* Use roots that are already recognized on sight. The most useful prefix at this stage is probably *un;* suffixes may include *ful, less,* and *ly.*

After children are aware of how morphological features work, the teacher will use other examples of morphemes as they occur in the child's reading material.

The following procedure is appropriate for most types of structural elements:

- Present contrasting examples in pairs of sentences until children discover what is happening. For example,
  "What is the difference between these two sentences?"

  The girl was happy at school.

  The girl was unhappy at school.

  Supply other examples as necessary.

  The chair is comfortable to sit on.

  The chair is uncomfortable to sit on.

  When children understand that the pairs of sentences have opposite meanings, see if they can locate the visual feature that makes the difference. When they do, underline the prefix and show how covering it up can leave *happy* or *comfortable.*
- Provide the following practice with a pocket chart. Place appropriate individual sight word cards on the chart and have children place other prefix cards before each word to change the meaning of the root. For example:

  un able

  un willing

  un like

  Physically manipulating word parts is important because it more actively involves the child in creating changes in the word structure; by his own actions he can watch and see the change. Compounds will not fit into the contrasting element format in the above procedure. Adjust the format by presenting a sentence with a compound, and ask the children to see if they can find a word that has two words they know.

  The children built a snowman.

  Underline the word and then use a pocket chart to show the two individual roots. Provide other combinations of sight words that have a common root, and have children combine them on the pocket chart to form appropriate compounds.

  mail man

  police man

  fire man

Syntactic Cues

Syntax, a part of grammar, concerns the ordering of words within sentences and the relations shown among those words by visual cues. The rules of English prescribe the ordering of words according to the function they serve. *Hot the was stove* does not make sense because the ordering of the individual words does not place them in slots where they serve an expected function. In *The stove was hot,* the words are in the places where they serve the expected function; *the* marks the noun, *stove,* which follows; the noun, *stove,* signals an upcoming verb, *was,* which in turn signals an upcoming predicate adjective, *hot.* The interrelationship among words in a sentence is signaled in the following way: in *The boys ate their lunches,* the *s* on *boys, their,* and *es* on *lunches* all show a plural relationship among the words. This is called *redundancy,* the provision of multiple cues to the same information.

Children already possess an intuitive grasp of the rules of syntax derived from their knowledge and use of oral language. Many are able without instruction to apply this knowledge to predict successfully the syntax of the author's writing. But other children may not be so successful in applying syntactic knowledge to the new medium of print. Yetta M. Goodman and Carolyn Burke suggest that a major purpose of syntax instruction is to "build confidence in readers by making them aware of their language competence and helping them apply this competence to their reading so they will feel secure about predicting syntactic structures" (1980, 85).

The following activities are designed to achieve the above purpose:

- Have children read a sentence from a familiar experience story: *We put the stone in the soup.* Then present the words in mixed fashion on a pocket chart: *The the in put stone we soup.* Have children read the cards to see that the arrangement makes no sense. Ask them to rearrange the words to make sense. Provide other examples for children to arrange words correctly.
- Use the cloze procedure for developing awareness of which words will or will not fit in a given position within sentences.

  The cat fell into the ______.

  Have children suggest words that make sense. From sight words on cards, try examples and have them tell you which ones make sense and which do not. Use the same procedure for other examples.
- Prepare a worksheet of sentences from a familiar story that the children can now read. Delete the final word from each sentence. Supply a list of the deleted words and have children place them in the proper spaces.
- When children are familiar with cloze in these highly predictable deletions, use the procedure to focus on words serving other functions in sentences.

adjectives:	The ______ boy crossed the street.
noun markers:	______ cat climbed ______ tree.
prepositions:	The girl ran ______ the house.
	The book was ______ the table.
	The cow jumped ______ the fence.

Semantic Cues

Semantics is synonymous with *meaning;* semantic cues relate to the meanings (concepts) represented by words (vocabulary) in the text and the way in which words in a thought unit are interrelated.

Throughout this text we have cited the importance of a rich background of experience in helping children to build a large store of meanings and the oral vocabulary that stands for those meanings. Through direct experiences children develop many of the individual word meanings represented by content word classes: nouns, adjectives, verbs, and adverbs. Children have meanings and the oral labels for a multitude of these content words when they come to printed language. This vocabulary store becomes a major basis for predicting or anticipating the message from print.

Through use of oral language, children also develop an intuitive grasp of the *rules* which govern the semantic patterns of language. They acquire a sense of how individual words in a thought unit relate to produce meaning. These interrelationships form patterns in language that occur over and over, regardless of the words used to generate a message. One such pattern is subject-verb agreement. The underlying rule is that both must be either singular or plural; they do not mix. Thus we say:

The boy works in the yard.

but not

The boy work in the yard.

The boys work in the yard.

but not

The boys works in the yard.

All of this prior knowledge of the way in which meanings are made is brought to the reading situation. The task of the teacher is to help children to apply existing strengths to process written language—to match what they know with what is reflected by print.

Two types of activities can help children learn to use the semantic cues in written language: *categorizing* and *cloze* procedures in a whole-language context.

1. Categorizing activities. A number of categorizing activities will help children to bridge between the oral and printed form for which there is a common meaning known to them. Content words that have a referent in the real word are the focus of these categorizing activities because such content words usually carry a heavy meaning load. The most-elementary form of categorizing is to use pictures. Then picture/word matching may be made, followed by matching words only.

- Sort individual picture cards made from illustrations in basal series readiness books into two categories—clothing and food.
- Use a similar procedure to sort according to other categories: animals/plants, babies/adults, fruits/vegetables, and others.
- Provide a master sheet or chart for the child to use in matching word and picture cards for any of the above categories. He can then work from the chart on which the

word/picture combinations are shown to produce his own matchings. In subsequent sessions, he can first make as many word/picture matchings as he can before referring to the chart.

- Provide word cards for any two of the previous categories and have the child sort them accordingly. Again, a checksheet or card is provided for reference and/or checking as needed by the child.

2. Cloze in whole language context. The cloze procedure is an excellent context in which to focus on many features of written language. It is basically a way to predict meanings from visual and nonvisual cues. Cloze is simple to use: it requires only the deletion of a chosen element. Whole language is used so that all cues to meaning are available. The procedure can be used with all types of written language.

The cloze procedure helps the child to identify and use the cues to meaning that show interrelationships among words within the context of whole language. Knowing the meanings of words alone is not sufficient to arrive at meaning in print; individual word meanings are often determined by the context in which they are used. The meaning of the word *tear* (and also its pronunciation), for example, can only be determined by the way it is used with other words: There was a *tear* in his jacket, and there was a *tear* in his eye. (Cues to the meaning of words are also provided by context *outside* individual sentences. This feature will be developed more fully under the next subtopic.)

Instruction should begin with written materials that contain a message which is already known to the child. Language experience, Big Books, and other materials used in assisted reading and echo reading fulfill this requirement. Knowing the story message enables the child to predict more accurately what individual words in the context will be.

The following language-experience story was based on a classroom project dictated by a group of children, and they watched as the teacher wrote it on a chart.

The Baby Chickens We Hatched in Our Room

We got some eggs. We put the eggs in an incubator. One day we saw a crack in the egg. Then a baby chicken came out. It was all wet.

After the children have read the story several times with the teacher, prepare the following cloze activity to aid them in using context to identify individual words within the sentence.

We got some _______ . We put the eggs in an _______ . One day we saw a _______ in the egg. Then a _______ came out. It was all _______ .

- Point to the words as you read with the children. Wait for their response to each blank and fill in the word suggested. Read the completed sentence together. Follow the same procedure for the remaining sentences in the story. Read the entire story together.

- Prepare a number of sentences in which identification of a word in each sentence is strongly suggested by semantic cues. Have children read the sentences with you and say the word implied by the context.

  The boy put on his shoes and _______ .

  He combed his _______ and brushed his _______ .

  The dog wagged his _______ .

  Jim turned out the lights and went to _______ .

Integrating the cue systems of written language. Fluent reading requires that the reader be able to use all three cueing systems simultaneously as needed during the process of reading. This proficiency develops over a period of many years, even a lifetime. Young children make great strides toward this goal when they are helped to develop a highly efficient system of processing print; they will not be blocked by the habitual use of ineffective and wasteful strategies, such as overattending to graphophonic cues.

Left to their own devices, many children devise a highly efficient system for synthesizing the various cues of language. But some children may focus on only one set of cues to the exclusion of all others. They may, for example, try to recognize words by using only graphophonic cues. This seems to be fairly common to beginning readers for short periods of time. But if they do not achieve a balance in focusing on syntactic and semantic cues as well, their system will not work as efficiently as it must if proficient reading is to be achieved. We have mentioned examples of children who can "sound out" words and become excellent word callers but who do not arrive at meaning. These children are not readers.

In growth toward fluency in reading, children use all the cues of written language as needed to *predict* or anticipate the meaning of print on the basis of their background experiences and knowledge of the oral language system. They sample the graphic or visual cues in order to *confirm* or *correct* their predictions of meaning. Weaver provides an excellent summary of this process in figure 7.3. (See the example from McKenzie [1977] which shows how a child goes about integrating both visual and nonvisual cues to arrive at meaning from print.)

Whole written language is used for all activities designed to aid children in integrating the cue systems; only in the context of whole language are all cues present.

Prediction Strategies

- Use wordless picture books to help children predict what will happen from the picture clues.
- Use familiar nursery rhymes, folktales, jingles, or legends with highly repetitive sentence patterns. Sara M. Pickert (1978, 16–17) suggests the following from two folktales. The first is from Peter Asbjorsen and Jorgen Moe's *The Three Billy Goats Gruff* (1957).

> As the billy-goats head for green pastures by way of a bridge, each, in turn, meets the troll, and the identical dialogue occurs three times.
>
> "Trip, trap, trip, trap."
> "Who's that tripping over my bridge?" roared the Troll.
> "Oh, it is only I, the (tiniest, second, big) billy-goat Gruff, and I'm going to the hillside to make myself fat," said the billy-goat.
> "Now, I'm coming to gobble you up," said the Troll.

		READING STRATEGIES		
		Predict	*Sample*	*Confirm/Correct*
LANGUAGE CUES	*Syntactic*	✓		✓
	Semantic	✓		✓
	Grapho/phonic		✓	

Figure 7.3. Language cues and reading strategies. Source: Constance Weaver, PSYCHOLINGUISTICS AND READING: FROM PROCESS TO PRACTICE, Little Brown and Company, Boston, 1980, p. 80. Second edition will be published by Heineman, 1986. Used with permission of author.

> The increasing noise of the hooves on the bridge coupled with the changing pitch and loudness of the dialogue heightens the story's suspense while making it easy to remember.

Another use of repetition is a setting description which punctuates the story, like Wanda Gag's *Millions of Cats* (1928). Seven times in the brief twenty-nine-page book, the author pauses to describe the setting:

> Cats here, cats there, cats and kittens everywhere,
> Hundreds of cats, thousands of cats, millions and billions and trillions of cats.

In the two preceding activities, children predict meanings from picture clues and from nonvisual information—they already *know* the story sense. They should also be taught to use two types of context to identify unfamiliar words. First, context *within* a sentence can be used to predict or anticipate what individual words will be. Within sentences, the context *before* a word is used to predict what is coming next; the context *following* the word is used to confirm or correct predictions. Figure 7.4 explains this process.

Context *beyond* sentences also provides cues to individual word meanings as in the example below where Weaver describes how her young son used this type of context.

> The boy in the story was named Hap. While at a local fair, he noticed someone who was jumping high as he walked along. The boy's father explained that the person was able to jump so high because of the pack on his back. Here are the following four sentences of the story, along with my son's miscues on the word gas:
>
> "The pack has a kind of *gams* (gas) in it. The *gams* (gas) is very light. It helps the boy to jump high." "What kind of *gams* (gas) is it?" asked Hap.
>
> As you might suspect, my son was getting little meaning from this passage. But on the next page of the story, Hap's father explained to him that the gas is called helium. This explanation apparently triggered my son's understanding because the next time he came to the word *gas* his face lit up and he said "I got that wrong on the other page. It was *gas* all the time." In this case, the meaning of the word was familiar to the reader,

	Preceding Context	Following Context
Syntactic Context	Preceding syntactic context indicates the word is a noun or a noun modifier.	Following syntactic context confirms that the word is a noun.
	The cruel giant fell into the water and drowned.	
Semantic Context	Preceding semantic context suggests the word should indicate something into which one can fall.	Following semantic context shows that the word should indicate something in which one can drown.

Figure 7.4. Context within the sentence. Source: Constance Weaver, PSYCHOLINGUISTIC AND READING: FROM PROCESS TO PRACTICE, Little, Brown and Company, Boston, 1980. p. 71. Used with permission of author.

but he did not recognize the word in print until the context of following sentences triggered his own personal context, his prior knowledge of helium and its effects (1980, 78).

Activities for developing proficiency in use of context cues *within* sentences and *beyond* sentences follow. The italicized words are those that children do not recognize in print, although the words are known in oral language.

- Prepare several sentences, each with a word that requires use of context to arrive at meaning. Ask children to read each sentence and try to decide what the italicized word is. Discuss how they can tell what the word might be. Point out the cues as they respond, or show the cues they cannot identify.

  The boy got a bow and *arrows* for his birthday.

  Sam was driving *nails* with a hammer.

  The squirrel sat in the tree with his bushy *tail* over his back.

  We had *scrambled* eggs for breakfast.

  The squirrel *cracked* the nuts with his teeth.

  The little girl began to *scream* when the dog ran after her.

  The boy ate his soup with a *spoon.*

- Prepare a series of two or more sentences to teach children how to use context cues beyond the sentence to figure out unknown words. Follow the same procedure as in the preceding activity.

  The boy was playing with a hammer. He *mashed* his finger and began to cry.

  One day I was really *frightened.* I was walking along by myself. A big, black dog began to chase me.

  The bubble was very *fragile.* When I touched it with my finger, it broke.

  He was a very *wicked* giant. Everytime Jack came near, the giant hit him with a broom.

We have a lot of *instruments* to make music. Everybody brought drums and horns.

The old man and the little boy were *friends.* They played baseball and went camping all the time.

Sample Strategies

Activities are provided that help children to learn to sample graphophonic and syntactic cues to meaning. On the basis of this sampling, children are able to confirm or correct predictions.

- Read each of the following sentences with the children and ask them to supply the word suggested by the beginning of the word given before each blank. (The position of the word will also provide a cue, but children are not expected to define a syntactic cue.)

The boy fell down and cut his l_______ .

The boy cl_______ a tree.

The boy fell down and broke his ar_______ .

The w_______ was washing the cl_______ .

They rode the b_______ to school.

The bird fl_______ away.

We heard a loud cr_______ when Nan dropped the dishes.

He was ch_______ gum.

The man was ch_______ wood with an ax.

Confirmation or Correction Strategies

Highly predictable materials such as familiar nursery rhymes and experience stories are used to help children determine that the selection of a word has made sense in the context in which it is used. If the word does not make sense, they can then search for other cues to meaning to arrive at the appropriate term. The first two examples below from Goodman and Burke (1980, 192) are designed to break the habit of overdependence on graphophonic cues and to increase reliance on other cues to meaning.

- Have children read the text with you. Have them supply words for each blank; write in the words as suggested. Ask them if there are any other words that could fit. Why? Why not?

Mary Had a Little Lamb

Mary had a little _______ . Its fleece was white as _______ . Everywhere that Mary went, the _______ was sure to go.

The Three Little Pigs

Once upon a time there were three little pigs. One day the three little pigs left home. Each little pig wanted to build a _______ . The first little pig made a house of _______ . The second little pig made a house of _______ . The third little pig made a house of _______ .

Jack Sprat

Jack Sprat could eat no ________ ,
His wife could eat no ________ ,
And so between them both, you see,
They licked the platter ________ .

The Old Woman in a Shoe

There was an old ________ who lived in a ________ .
She had so many ________ she didn't know what to ________ .
She gave them ________ without any ________
And whipped them all soundly and sent them to ________ .

The Baby Chickens We Hatched in Our Room
(language-experience story)

We got some ________ . We put the eggs in an ________ .
One day we saw a ________ in the egg. Then a ________ ________ came out. It was all ________ .

Phase Three: Functioning as a Reader

Once children have participated in the activities in the first two phases of the program for developing natural readers, many will have gained the knowledge, skills, and strategies necessary to work more independently in reading. As they move into the final phase on the literacy continuum, it is crucial that extensive time be provided daily for independent reading of materials. Such practice not only sharpens budding competencies, it also provides for the acquisition of additional ones. Children do, indeed, learn to read by reading. Glenda L. Bissex confirms the need for practice in describing her son's growth into reading:

> Paul gained fluency and expressiveness by rereading favorite books—some of the books that had been read aloud to him before he could read. This kind of practice, which seemed important for both his enjoyment and his mastery of reading, is often not provided in school. Basal readers repeat words but not stories, which is quite a different thing and does not give practice with broader language structures or the satisfaction of having read challenging material really well (1980, 141).

What the teacher provides at this time is especially important because the emerging skills and strategies are like new and fragile wings, which have not yet experienced much flying. The materials read must be compatible with and support the children's capabilities.

1. The materials should be highly interesting to the child.
2. Moira McKenzie observed that the books should have a "good story element and natural language (uncomplex and uncontrived)" (1977, 322).
3. The books should "allow prediction in terms of language and meaning" (McKenzie 1977, 322).
4. The materials should be selected by the child.
5. If children tend to restrict their choices to only one type over an extended period of time, the teacher should create a purpose for the children's reading other types of materials. For example, ask children to prepare a demonstration for making a recipe in the cooking center; they must read the recipe to know how to conduct

the demonstration. Or, have a child tell a group of children about how mother cats care for their babies. A suitable book on the topic is read and the child shows illustrations while giving the information.

The materials already used in language experiences, Big Books, and other forms of assisted reading meet the foregoing criteria and should be made readily accessible. They form a natural bridge for moving into more independent reading. Initially, these are the sources children often choose to read on their own.

When they have satisfied the need to spend time with old favorites, they will begin to search out new, more-stimulating sources to satisfy their growing appetite for reading. The teacher provides basal readers at several levels from which children select stories that they are able to read pretty much on their own, stories that have been only read to them, and trade books representing modern writers and traditional literary classics. Some children will move into independent reading by way of comic books before they advance to other forms of printed materials. Others will seek out books of riddles and rhymes and poems. Still others will concentrate on materials related to a single topic. One of the authors remembers the following from an early independent reader: "I don't want to read nothin 'cept about horses. Well, I guess I *might* look at some dog pictures!" Another well-remembered episode concerned a child who was fascinated by a copy of the *Guinness Book of World Records*. He spent days looking over the text at every free-reading opportunity. One day he approached the teacher with Guinness in hand and challenged, "I'll bet you don't know what's the littlest bird in the whole world!" Before the teacher could respond with her best guess, he opened the book and read the exact words from the text: "The smallest bird in the world is the bee hummingbird." Given the opportunity, children do indeed find their way to reading by many routes.

While the main focus for children who are in the third phase is on doing their own reading, they also continue to participate in many of the activities described in the first two phases of learning to read naturally. All of the following are included:

1. Listening to stories and other types of materials to extend and expand interests in and familiarity with many types of written language.
2. Participating in developing and reading language-experience materials to enhance writing skills and competencies.
3. Participating in on-going shared-book experiences and other forms of assisted reading to expand interests and acquire additional reading skills.
4. Receiving direct instruction as needed, either individually or in small groups, designed to further refine knowledge and strategies for dealing with specific aspects of written language.
5. Participating periodically in guided reading lessons from a basal text.

Your Turn 7.2 Three phases in development of reading competency.

Refer to the data you collected when administering the "Concepts About Print Test."

1. In which of the three phases of reading competencies would you place each child?
2. Cite data from your text that you might use to support your decisions.

Summary

Three phases of growing into reading and writing naturally have been described. During each of these phases, specific activities and materials are required to enable children to move forward along the literacy continuum. We have described in detail instructional practices and materials that provide for individual differences among primary children who may be functioning at a variety of levels in the same classroom. Emphasis has been placed on building on the interests and strengths of children so that the process of acquiring literacy is an enjoyable and rewarding one. We believe this will result in children's learning to read more naturally and that they will more likely become lifelong readers.

References

Allen, Vernon L., ed. *Children as Teachers, Theory and Research on Tutoring.* New York: Academic Press, 1976.

Asbjornsen, Peter, and Moe, Jorgen. *The Three Billy Goats Gruff.* New York: Harcourt Brace Jovanovich, 1957.

Ashton-Warner, Sylvia. *Teacher.* New York: Simon and Schuster, 1971.

Baghban, Marcia. *Our Daughter Learns to Read and Write. A Case Study from Birth to Three.* Newark, Del.: International Reading Association, 1984.

Bissex, Glenda L. *GNYS AT WRK.* Cambridge, Mass.: Harvard University Press, 1980.

Butler, Dorothy, and Clay, Marie M. *Reading Begins at Home.* Auckland: Heinemann Educational Books, 1979.

Calkins, Lucy McCormick. *Lessons from a Child. On the Teaching and Learning of Writing.* Exeter, N.H.: Heinemann Educational Books, 1983.

Clay, Marie M. *The Early Detection of Reading Difficulties: A Diagnostic Survey with Recovery Procedures.* (2nd ed.) Auckland: Heinemann Educational Books, 1979.

———. *Reading: The Patterning of Complex Behavior.* London: Heinemann Educational Books, 1973.

———. *Reading: The Patterning of Complex Behaviors.* (2nd ed.) London: Heinemann Educational Books, 1979.

———. *What Did I Write?* Auckland: Heinemann Educational Books, 1975.

Cloward, R. O. "Studies in Tutoring." *Journal of Experimental Education* 36 (Fall 1967): 14–25.

Cromwell, Ellen. *Feathers in My Cap: Early Reading Through Experience.* Washington, D.C.: Acropolis Books, 1980.

De Saint Exupéry, Antoine. *The Little Prince.* New York: Harcourt Brace Jovanovich, 1943.

Doake, David B. "Book Experience and Emergent Reading Behavior." Paper presented at meeting of the International Reading Association, Atlanta, May 1979.

Durkin, Dolores. "Children Who Learn to Read at Home." *Elementary School Journal* 62 (October 1961): 15–18.

———. *Children Who Read Early.* New York: Columbia University, Teachers College Press, 1966.

Ehly, Stewart, and Larsen, Stephen C. *Peer Tutoring for Individualized Instruction.* Boston: Allyn and Bacon, 1980.

Elkin, Benjamin. "Lucky and the Giant." In *Magic Times,* rev. ed., 28–42. Second level of the Macmillan Basal Reading Series. New York: Macmillan Publishing Company, 1983.

Ellis, DiAnn W., and Preston, Fannie W. "Enhancing Beginning Reading, Wordless Picture Books in a Cross-Age Tutoring Program." *The Reading Teacher* 37 (April 1984): 692–98.

Gag, Wanda. *Millions of Cats.* New York: Coward-McCann, 1928.

Galbraith, Margery A. "Guidelines for Reading Aloud." *The Reading Teacher* 36 (December 1982): 319–20.

Gamby, G. "Talking Books and Taped Books: Materials for Instruction." *The Reading Teacher* 36 (January 1983): 366–69.

Glazer, Susan M., and Brown, Carol S., eds. *Helping Children Read: Ideas for Parents, Teachers, and Librarians.* Trenton, N.J.: New Jersey Reading Association, 1980.

Goodman, Yetta M., and Burke, Carolyn. *Reading Strategies: Focus on Comprehension.* New York: Holt, Rinehart and Winston, 1980.

Graves, Donald H. *Writing: Teachers and Children at Work.* Portsmouth, N.H.: Heinemann Educational Books, 1983.

Hall, Mary Anne. *Teaching Reading as a Language Experience.* 3d ed. Columbus: Charles E. Merrill, 1981.

Holdaway, Don. *The Foundations of Literacy.* New York: Ashton Scholastic, 1979.

Hoskisson, Kenneth. "The Many Facets of Assisted Reading," *Elementary English* 52 (1975a): 312–15.

———. "Successive Approximation and Beginning Reading." Elementary School Journal 7 (1975b): 442–51.

———. "Learning to Read Naturally." *Language Arts* 56 (May 1979): 489–96.

Johnson, Richard, and Adams, John. "Reading Aloud—Tips for Teachers." *The Reading Teacher* 36 (April 1983): 829–31.

Jolly, Thomas. "Would You Like to Read to Me?" *The Reading Teacher* 33 (May 1980): 994–96.

Kaplan, Sandra; Kaplan, Jo Ann Butom; Madsen, Sheilia Kunishima; and Taylor, Bette. *Change for Children.* Pacific Palisades, Calif.: Goodyear Publishing Company, 1973.

Kaplan, Sandra; Kaplan, Jo Ann Butom; Madsen, Shelia Kunishima; and Gould, Bette Taylor. *A Young Child Experiences.* Pacific Palisades, Calif.: Goodyear Publishing Company, 1975.

Krauss, Ruth. *A Hole Is to Dig.* New York: Harper and Row, Publishers, 1952.

Lamme, Linda Leonard. "Reading Aloud to Young Children." *Language Arts* 53 (November/December 1976): 886–88.

Lamme, Linda Leonard, ed. *Learning to Love Literature.* Preschool through grade 3. Urbana, Ill.: National Council of Teachers of English, 1981.

Lamme, Linda L.: Cox, Vivian; Matanzo, Jane; and Olson, Miken. *Raising Readers. A Guide to Sharing Literature with Young Children.* New York: Walker and Company, 1980.

Lehr, Fran. "Peer Teaching." *The Reading Teacher* 37 (March 1984): 636–39.

Lippitt, Peggy, and Lohman, John. "Cross-Age Relationships—an Educational Resource." *Children* 12 (May–June 1965): 113–17.

Loban, Walter. "What Language Reveals." In *Language and Meaning,* edited by James B. McDonald and Robert R. Leeper. Washington, D.C.: Association for Supervision and Curriculum Development, 1966.

Loughlin, Catherine E., and Suina, Joseph H. *The Learning Environment: An Instructional Strategy.* New York: Columbia University, Teachers College Press, 1982.

McCracken, Marlene J., and McCracken, Robert A. *Reading, Writing and Language. A Practical Guide for Primary Teachers.* Winnipeg: Peguis Publishers Limited, 1979.

McCracken, Robert A., and McCracken, Marlene J. *Reading is Only the Tiger's Tail.* San Rafael, Calif.: Leswing Press, 1972.

McKenzie, Moira. "The Beginnings of Literacy." *Theory into Practice* 16 (1977): 315–24.

National Geographic Society. *Creepy Crawly Things.* Books for Young Explorers Washington, D.C.: National Geographic Society, 1974.

Nevi, Charles. "Cross-Age Tutoring: Why Does It Help the Tutors." *The Reading Teacher* 36 (May 1983): 892–98.

Park, Barbara. "The Big Book Trend—A Discussion with Don Holdaway." *Language Arts* 59 (November/December 1982): 815–21.

Pickert, Sara M. "Repetitive Sentence Patterns in Childrens Books." *Language Arts* 55 (January 1978): 16–18.

Reading Unlimited. *Teaching Beginning Reading: Language Experience Approach to Beginning Reading.* Filmstrips and cassettes. Alexanderia, Va.: Reading Unlimited, 1976.

Rhodes, Lynn K. "I Can Read! Predictable Books as Resources for Reading and Writing Instruction." *The Reading Teacher* 34 (February 1981): 511–18.

Scarry, Richard. *Best Word Book Ever.* New York: Golden Press, 1974.

Sealey, Leonard; Sealey, Nancy; and Millmore, Marcia. *Children's Writing. An Approach for Primary Grades.* Newark, Del.: International Reading Association, 1979.

Shuh, John Hennigar. "The Shared Book Experience." *Journal of Education* 6 (1981): 1–6.

Sine, M. R. "Reading Practice with Read-Alongs." *Curriculum Review* 21 (December 1982): 464–66.

Smith, Carl B., and Arnold, Virginia A., sen. authors. Basal Reading Series. rev. ed. New York: Macmillan Publishing Company, 1983.

Stahlschmidt, Agnes D., and Johnson, Carole S. "The Library Media Specialist and the Read-Aloud." *Library Media Quarterly* (Winter 1984): 146–49.

Swinburne, Laurence. "A Special Kind of Help." In *Secrets and Surprises,* rev. ed., 186–201. Third level of the Macmillan Basal Reading Series. New York: Macmillan Publishing Company, 1983.

Taylor, Denny. *Family Literacy. Young Children Learn to Read and Write.* Exeter, N.H.: Heinemann Educational Books, 1983.

Temple, Charles A.; Nathan, Ruth G.; and Burris, Nancy A. *The Beginnings of Writing.* Boston: Allyn and Bacon, 1982.

Trelease, Jim. *The Read-Aloud Handbook.* New York: Penguin Books, 1982.

Weaver, Constance. *Psycholinguistics and Reading: From Process to Practice.* Cambridge, Mass.: Winthrop Publishers, 1980.

Wortmann, Peter Martin. "Nan." In *You Can,* rev. ed., 54–55. Preprimer level of the Macmillan Basal Reading Series. New York: Macmillan Publishing Company, 1983.

Zintz, Miles V. *Corrective Reading.* Dubuque, Iowa: William C. Brown Company Publishers, 1981.

8

Planning, Organizing, and Managing the Primary Reading Program

Outline

Guide Questions

1. What are classroom centers and why are they important additions to the classroom literacy-development program?
2. What experiences can be adapted to meet individual needs?
3. Why is individualized instruction crucial in classroom reading instruction?
4. Why is it important to plan and organize instruction over longer time periods (two weeks or more)?
5. How might you involve parents and other helpers in the classroom reading program?

Terminology

discovery center	adapted experiences
library or reading center	under-predictive readers
writing center	over-predictive readers
project center	time management
study center	parents as partners
listening center	

Planning an instructional program that promotes the development of natural readers and writers is a large, but not impossible, task. To provide a balanced program for all children, the teacher must successfully manage four major areas: (1) arranging the learning environment, (2) selecting activities and materials to meet particular needs, (3) grouping children for activities, and (4) managing time schedules.

The goal of the program must be kept in focus: it is to provide for the individual differences among children. These differences are not recognized when decisions are based on age/grade standards; children are simply not made that way. The one reality that relates to any age/grade mentality is that more children at kindergarten level will likely be in the first phase of literacy development. The percentage of children in each of the other two phases will increase proportionately with time spent in the program we have described. But, at any grade level or within any age group, a full range of differences among children will persist.

Planning on the basis of individual differences within a group is not as overwhelming as it may first appear. As we have already noted, it is neither necessary nor possible to plan a totally different program for each child. Many of the same activities can serve a wide variety of individual levels of competence. With appropriate assistance, most children will be able to manage their own learning quite successfully and in accordance with their own level of ability.

The program must reflect both *continuity* and *flexibility*. Continuity is achieved when today's activities are built on what was done yesterday as a bridge to what will be done tomorrow. Flexibility demands that the teacher change any part of the program to meet the changing needs of children as they grow into reading. Flexibility also means that the teacher is not so bound to lesson plans that she fails to take advantage of unexpected events, which can sometimes literally drop from the sky. A teacher shared the following anecdote:

> All was going well with plans for the day until midmorning when a large shadow floated across the room. The first graders looked outside to see a parachutist, who had overshot a nearby drop zone, struggling to control his billowing 'chute. Right in the middle of the teacher's instructions, the children arose as a body and scrambled to the windows to watch. The teacher might have eventually restored order and returned to her plans; however, she was wise and knew the ways of children. She scrapped her plans, and for the next two weeks, the children studied and learned much about parachutes, smokejumpers, forest fire fighting and conservation.

Not every learning experience will arise so dramatically, of course, but teachers must take advantage of many unplanned opportunities for learning as they occur. Children bring many interests to the class from time to time; they are already motivated to explore and learn about them. The teacher's flexibility must allow for taking advantage of these opportunities to learn.

Arranging the Learning Environment

The physical aspects of the classroom—space, equipment, and materials—should be organized to facilitate conducting a variety of activities and also to provide for effective groupings of children for participation in those activities.

The authors have found that organizing some of the space into a number of centers is an excellent way to promote proficient learning. All the materials and equipment necessary for carrying out an activity are readily available in each center. The visual effects of centers should be designed so that the area captures the interest and imagination of children. Use of bright colors, eye-catching designs and varieties in shapes, textures, and captions, and balance in organization of materials can all help to achieve this effect. For example, in the discovery center one might use the caption "Magnifying Magic" in black block-print letters mounted on red construction paper above the center. Smaller print for questions could be displayed with different objects: "What's in a rock?" "How big is sand?" "Draw the weed you see." Print questions on 3″ × 5″ cards, mount on 5″ × 7″ pieces of colored posterboard, and cover the surface with clear contact paper. (This protection extends the life of the materials.)

If centers are to be a productive learning experience, they must not only arouse children's interest, but they must also sustain it. The materials and the focus of the centers must, therefore, be changed often. One of the authors is reminded of an incident that illustrates this point perfectly. In her classroom near the door was a display of pictures and other materials depicting the life cycle of chickens. Children in classrooms down the hall passed the door each day to get to the cafeteria and the playground. One day a third-grader stuck his head in the door and asked, "Say, teacher, when are you going to get some new chickens?"

Although centers were discussed briefly in chapter 7, we develop the topic more fully below. The types of centers described and the related materials are particularly useful at the primary level.

Discovery Center

The discovery center is particularly good for concept and oral language development. It can be located on a table against a wall or set out so that easy access is provided from all sides. The purpose is to provide a collection of materials and equipment for children to explore on their own or in small groups. Placing one or more magnifying glasses with a collection of earth materials—rocks, weeds, sand, and dirt—offers many possibilities for developing concepts of shape, color, size, and weight. Materials in the center can be changed for exploring the same concepts with various types of fabrics—yarn, burlap, cotton, and velvet. At other times blocks of varying shapes may be stacked in the center, where children can experiment with stacking, designing, and sorting.

Library or Reading Center

This center provides opportunities for children to explore and read many types of print. It is best located in a corner of the room where a couple of bookcases can serve dual purposes: (1) to visually screen off the area to reduce distractions, and (2) to provide space for displaying a wide variety of printed media. Included in the center should be many books, both in narrative and expository language in a variety of formats: picture books, wordless picture books, predictable books, poems, riddles, rhymes, fairy tales, information books and books made in language-experience activity, basal reader materials (K–3), and the original and Big Book versions of stories from shared-book experiences. Also available are children's magazines, adult magazines with high picture or photographic content, mail order catalogs, newspapers, and comic books. Books should be arranged so that some titles show, and the selected display should be changed often. Equipment and its arrangement should *invite* reading and browsing: carpet and/or old bean bags and throw pillows to sit on and a painted nail keg or wooden box to hold a lamp.

Writing Center

In the writing center children can experiment with everything from creating their own symbols on paper, drawing pictures and writing captions, and composing language-experience stories to writing creative poems and stories. Each child operates at her own level. Materials include pencils, colored markers, and paper of several sizes. Examples of experience stories, printed alphabet models in lower and upper case, and labeled pictures are available. Collections of pictures and sentence starters are there for creative writing ideas. Some children like to cut out magazine pictures to illustrate their stories, so a stack is provided along with scissors and paste.

Project Center

This center is best located within easy access to water and, when possible, in an area removed from other centers so that the noise of children working together will not be distracting. As its name implies, this is a "doing" center. Children can participate in a variety of activities related to art, creative dramatics, and preparing for class productions, such as a puppet show about "The Three Billy Goats Gruff." Materials should include the following: a scrap collection of fabrics, yarn, jars of buttons, and other scrounged items; paints and brushes, scissors, paste, construction paper, tagboard, and newsprint; old clothing; boxes, jars, cans, and bottles. Shelves for storage should contain labeled boxes for keeping materials organized.

Study Center

Children need a quiet area where they may complete individual assignments or read on their own. Individual carrels for this purpose are made by using three-sided cardboard dividers on each desk to screen out the surrounding area. An area along one wall can accommodate several desk carrels. Each child brings the necessary materials to the individual study stations in this center.

Planning and Instruction Center

A table and chairs located in a corner diagonally across from the library center can serve several purposes. The center can be used for individual or small group work where the teacher provides direct instruction to meet a specific need, such as identifying and using graphophonic cues for recognizing words. The center may also be used by groups participating in a shared-book experience or developing a language-experience story with the teacher. At other times, small groups of children may gather in the center to plan a particular activity, perhaps the production of a group version of a favorite poem with illustrations and text. The teacher may, on occasion, accommodate the whole group for discussion and/or demonstration of a relevant topic.

Listening Center

This center is arranged on a table with chairs to accommodate six-to-eight children. It contains a listening unit with outlets for multiple headsets and a record and/or cassette player. Records, cassettes, and read-along materials are located in a bookcase nearby.

Figure 8.1 shows an arrangement of classroom space using the centers concept.

Teachers need not feel that the centers concept for organizing the classroom environment is "set in cement." It should not be. Center are an excellent way to organize for learning experiences, but whenever the need arises, the room arrangement or any part of it should be changed accordingly.

Teachers who are inexperienced in using centers will probably want to start with a limited number, perhaps no more than one or two, and add more as they become more experienced and confident with this arrangement.

Finally, it is important that young children be given preparation for the use of centers. They should know what centers are for, and they should know how to use, care for, clean up, and return materials to their proper places. We have found that two practices help in teaching children to use centers productively. First, have a "practice walk through" with children before they begin to work in centers. Take a small group to the discovery center, for example, and explore with them how they may use the materials. Remind them to put things back in their proper places. (They probably will not do so for awhile, so miracles should not be anticipated.) In lieu of miracles, we have found that having an older child or an adult helper in the early stages for supervision of work in centers can greatly reduce the confusion that will surely occur otherwise. Of course, the teacher can supervise some of the early work in centers. However, one of the functions of centers is to have children learn to work more independently, and as they do, the teacher is released to work with other children who need individual attention.

Teachers need to observe children "at work" and to note *traffic patterns* in movement throughout the room. If traffic jams occur, perhaps a rearrangement is needed, or a shelf of materials needs to be relocated to be more accessible to different users. (For a discussion of traffic patterns, see Catherine E. Loughlin and Joseph H. Suina 1982, 62–65, 70–72, 152–154.)

What is done with the learning environment determines to a large extent whether or not productive learning will take place. If the teacher and the environment are not organized, neither will children be. It has been our experience in working with children

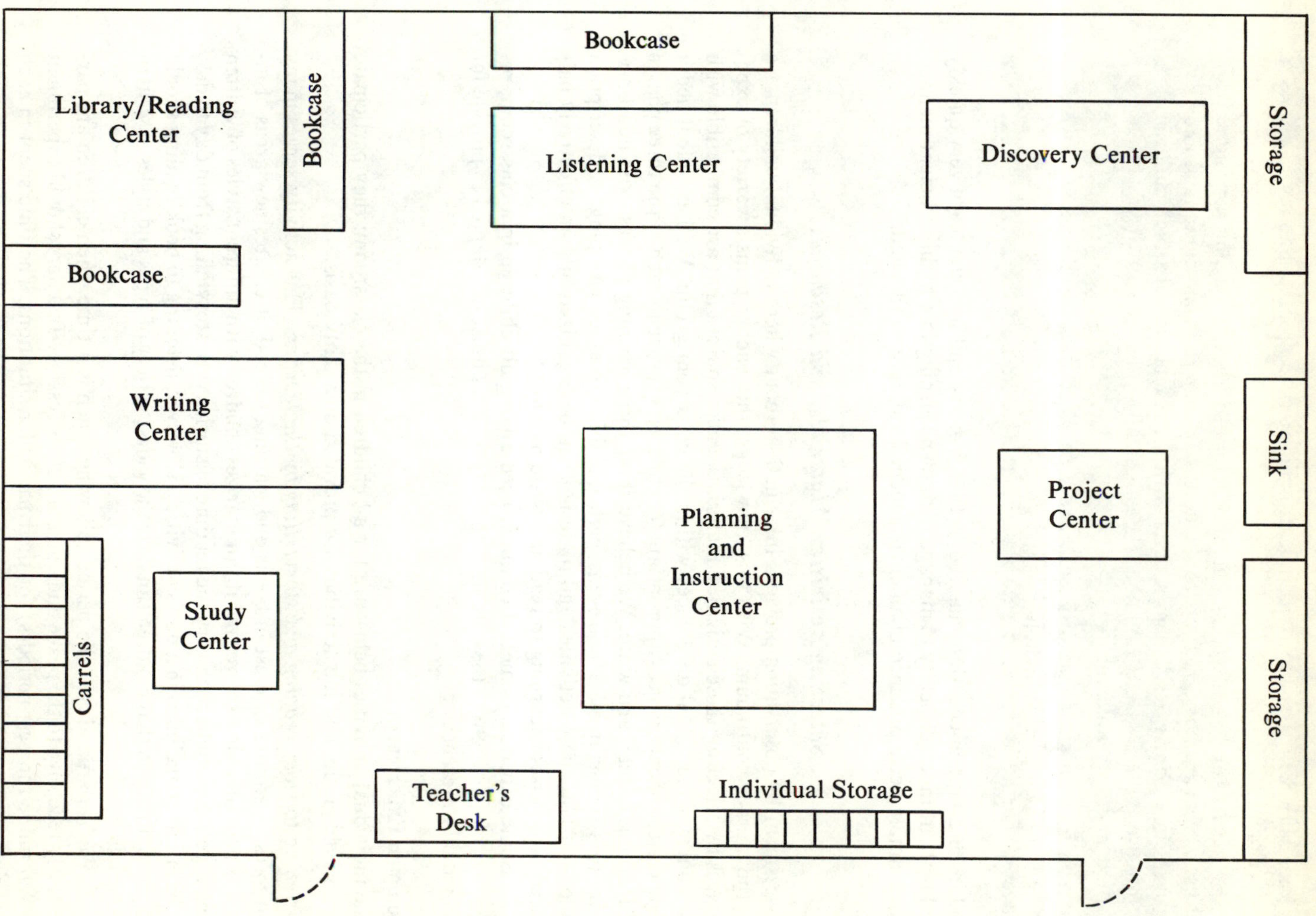

Figure 8.1. A learning center arrangement for the primary classroom.

Your Turn 8.1 Using classroom learning centers to promote literacy development.

Select one of the types of centers described in the foregoing section or one of your own design. Prepare the necessary materials and equipment and use it in a primary classroom. Confer with the teacher about which children might use the center, the number (keep it small) to participate at any given time, and a schedule for its use.

1. List what went well in the center's use. Explain why.
2. List what you would change and give reasons.

and in observing in countless classrooms that primary children can learn very quickly and without much difficulty to manage their own learning in a highly efficient manner. They simply need guidance in an environment conducive to this end.

Selecting Activities, Materials, and Resources

Assessment by observation provides information about where individual children are on the literacy continuum. With this knowledge, the teacher plans a variety of experiences by selecting those activities, materials, and resources that are compatible with the range of individual differences within the classroom group. We have identified a wide variety of experiences appropriate for children who are in each of the three phases of learning to read and write. We believe these three learning phases exist in all primary classrooms: fives, sixes, sevens, eights, and in cross-age grouping. A description follows of how these activities and materials can be organized into an effectively balanced program for learning to read and write naturally.

Some experiences meet a common need among all children in a classroom, regardless of which phase they are in. Other experiences must be adapted to provide for individual differences.

Common Experiences

The individual activities below are for all children in the classroom; they participate as a whole group, and the activities are provided on a daily basis.

Listening to story reading and storytelling by the teacher. This activity serves many purposes: it arouses interest in books and learning to read, it creates new areas of interests and topics to explore, and it familiarizes children with different styles of written language. The teacher can vary the reading of stories with storytelling from day to day, or both can be included in a day's activities. However, listening to book reading should be predominant so that children can hear the widest variety of types and styles of written materials.

We have found that the period following lunch is a time when children are particularly receptive to the peace and quiet of a story session. Teachers should experiment to determine the best period(s) for their particular situations. The time spent in each listening session also varies from group to group; again, the teacher should experiment.

Generally, the more children have participated in listening sessions, the longer they can attend with concentration. (Of course, *interest* in the story being read strongly influences attentiveness; interest should be a major criterion for selecting stories in the first place.) In the beginning, kindergarten children may listen for no more than five minutes; the time should be increased gradually as the attention span warrants. Second- and third-graders may listen up to thirty minutes. The child who is no longer interested may be excused if she finds another quiet activity.

Sustained Silent Reading (SSR). SSR serves many of the same purposes as those cited in the section above. In addition to creating an interest in books and an awareness of topics to explore, SSR provides excellent practice in using the developing skills of young children who are into the second and third phases of learning to read. The sessions may be no more than five minutes for beginners; appropriate lengthening of the time occurs as children can attend for longer periods of time. Experimenting is also necessary to determine the most-appropriate-time period during the day. SSR held before going home at the end of the school day may work well; or, the session may come after a very active period during the day when children need a change of pace.

Adapted Experiences

Some experiences are appropriate for all children to a point, but then they should be adapted in one or more ways to match individual differences and needs. All children can benefit from participation in the initial phases of language experience, but not all are ready for the third and fourth steps. Experiences are also differentiated by the number of children involved at a given time, and by the period during which they work.

Language experiences. The whole classroom can profitably participate in the first two steps of language experience; they can go on a field trip, discuss it, and then watch as the teacher records some of the childrens' dialogue. At this point differentiation begins. Because some children are not ready to learn to read the story, they move to other activities. Some children are ready to work on the reading of the experience story, and they proceed with this step. But they may not be ready for more direct instruction dealing with specific features of print. They then move to other activities, perhaps some form of assisted reading. Finally, some children will be fully capable of completing the follow-up related reading and writing activities of the total language experience. (See pp. 177–184.)

Shared-book experiences. Adaptations similar to those described for language experiences may also be made in the shared-book experience. All children can benefit by participation in the introduction and unison reading of favorite stories. However, some may not be ready for extensive repeated readings in a group. The opportunity is then provided for them to read along on a one-to-one basis with the teacher or other helper. Provision should also be made for these children to explore self-selected Big Books on their own. They will respond according to their individual level of capability; for example, telling the story from memory and/or picture clues and repeating words they can identify visually. (See Don Holdaway's *The Foundations of Literacy,* chapter 4, "A Fresh Start: Shared-Book Experience," pp. 64–80.)

Writing experiences. All children should have an opportunity to work with paper and pencil, brush, or markers each day. What they write, when they write, and where they work will all vary according to their level of capabilities. Some children will paint or draw pictures, symbols, and designs of their own creation. Some will move toward conventional writing by combining letters with invented symbols to label pictures they have drawn. Others will write whole stories using the combination of conventional and invented symbols. Still others will use the writing center to create their own stories and messages, which closely approximate conventional letter forms and more-advanced sentence structures. Some will receive direct instruction in small groups in the mechanics of writing. However, most writing assistance will be given spontaneously at the time a child has a special need.

At various times during the day, children may work individually or in small groups in the writing center, at study stations, in the listening center, or in the project center with art materials.

Exploration and discovery experiences. We discussed earlier the need for all children to expand and extend their stores of concepts and oral language competence. The need for these types of development persists through the primary level and beyond. All children participate individually, in small groups, or as a total classroom group in exploration/discovery type activities. Often these can be part of a language experience as we just described. Activities in the discovery center are, of course, appropriate. Classifying and categorizing different materials according to a given characteristic (size, shape, or color) help to develop new concepts.

When left to their own creative urges, children will quite naturally examine and explore all manner of phenomena in a stimulating environment. Marie Hughes designed "instructional kits," collections of like objects: keys, old gloves, and spoons. One of the kits would be placed in a discovery center without any instructions. As observers, we were often amazed to see what children did with them, particularly the "key" kit. Some sorted by color, by size, or by shape. Others went further to sort by type—car keys, house keys, and an "I don't know that one" pile. Once, a group of three five-year-olds spent an hour arguing and sorting all the car keys according to the make of the automobiles: Volkswagen, Ford, and Chevrolet.

Individualized Experiences

Some experiences are designed only for specific children. They are organized in the following contexts: (1) teacher-pupil, (2) teacher-small group, and (3) child alone.

Repeated readings and assisted reading. These activities are best conducted with one child and one helper (teacher, adult, or student aide). In sessions held on successive days, the helper reads the same story to a child while sweeping the hand along each line of print. When the child knows the story sense, she will begin to mumble along with the reader and gradually vocalize more closely the print as it occurs on the page. She can then practice reading assisted by read-along tapes and stories in the listening center.

Provisions for children experiencing difficulty in learning to read. (Material in this section is a summary of ideas for working with slow learners drawn largely from Don Holdaway's *The Foundations of Literacy.* The content is an excellent description of

Your Turn 8.2 Adapted experiences for meeting individual needs within a reading group.

Design a plan for adapting the lesson you used in chapter 7 to meet the individual needs of children who participated in the lesson.

1. Clearly show what the individual needs are and how you propose to adapt instruction to accommodate them.
2. Use your adapted lesson with the children.
3. How well did your adapted lesson work?

some highly successful practices that are being used to develop literacy during the early years of schooling in Australia and New Zealand. Much of the content reflects the work and research of Marie Clay, whose work has also been a major source used in developing this text.)

While most children can grow into reading quite naturally through participation in the kinds of experiences we have described in this text, a few in any given group may not make acceptable progress. "What we need is a preventive system which locates children experiencing difficulty very early before accumulating failure disorders their natural learning" (Holdaway 1979, 167). Prevention entails the following components:

1. "*Sensitive observation.* Monitoring of an individual and longitudinal kind which produces appropriate data and allows us to distinguish between healthy approximation and unproductive confusions" (1979, 167).

It is important to distinguish between reading behaviors that denote progress in learning to read and those which reveal basic confusions as to what the reading process is all about. Self-correcting miscues, when they detract from meaning, is an example of behavior that may be taken as evidence of satisfactory progress; failure to recognize when miscues have distorted meaning may indicate confusion.

2. "*Timely intervention.* Most of the intervention should be a natural part of normal teaching—it should seldom require isolated one-to-one teaching, although there will be cases where this is necessary" (1979, 168).

In an earlier discussion of the follow-up phase of a guided reading lesson (chapter 7), we suggested that the teacher should deal with difficulties and confusions as they are identified in the post-reading discussion of a story. Written text is then addressed at the point of difficulty, and the teacher directs children's attention to clues that provide solutions to the difficulty. This is, indeed, "timely intervention": it extends help when and where the problem occurs. This type of help is also given throughout the day as the teacher monitors individual and group reading activities.

3. "*Establishing self-regulation in the learner*" (1979, 170–71). The purpose of intervention, according to Holdaway, is to enable the child to develop her own unique system for processing print, which fits her learning style, and to monitor her performance. Intervention is, therefore, not prescriptive: it does not *tell* the child what to do. Rather, questions are posed by the teacher to provide a route to solution; the child must make the trip. (Ways to develop self-regulation skills in the learner are described more fully later in this section in the discussion of specific problems in processing print.)

4. "*Multi-disciplinary team work.* Most early difficulties will involve inhibiting factors such as hearing loss or emotional instability which are not specific to language development. In such matters we need the help of professional expertise beyond the competence of the trained teacher, and we should use it *early* rather than wait until failure is aggravated by secondary neurosis" (1979, 168).

Schools ordinarily provide many support services through personnel who have expertise in diagnosing learning problems and helping teachers plan instruction to deal with those problems. These sources should be consulted whenever teachers feel that the learner's problems are beyond their competencies.

One of the major problems experienced by beginning readers is faulty processing of print. Children in this category can be classified as either *under-predictive* or *over-predictive* (1979, 176–78).

Under-predictive readers attend almost exclusively to the visual features of print and neglect to demand meaning as they read. They plod through print word by word and sometimes letter by letter.

Many techniques to help children learn to predict with greater accuracy have already been included in this text. Holdaway suggests the following:

> Oral Cloze procedures in shared-book-experience. Reading favorite and familiar stories, poems, and songs. Reading own experience stories in language-experience. Read-along experiences with the listening post. Reading material with strong structural support for prediction (1979, 177).

In the shared-book experience, under-predictive readers will already have had several sessions "reading" the story along with the rest of a group while the teacher points to individual words along the lines of print. These readings familiarize the children with the story sense. They can then anticipate more accurately those words leading up to and following the "cloze" words. Knowing the preceding and subsequent context then aids in the identification of the cloze word(s). It becomes unnecessary to attend to individual words and letters.

Reading in favorite stories, poems, songs, and personal language-experience stories has the same effect for the same reasons above. The story sense, including much of the identical wording, is already in the mind of under-predictive readers. They can read along without the need to focus on every word. Meaning in the deep structure is carrying them beyond the surface structure, or the print on the page.

Reading along with a tape or record in predictable books, those with "strong structural support for prediction," also helps to reduce the need to overattend to various features of print. Children use deep structure to anticipate upcoming lines of print, particularly the highly repetitive ones.

The cassette recorder can be used to create self-awareness of the problem of overattending. Have the child tape her reading of a short passage, read the same passage with a marker under each line of print as she watches, and have her read along with you several times. Then have her read the passage alone several times until she indicates it is ready for recording; record the second reading and have her react to the differences between the two samples. After children are familiar with the foregoing procedure, provide time periodically for additional sessions with an aide, an older child, or other more-fluent reader.

Over-predictive readers have the opposite problem. Where under-predictive readers look too closely at print, over-predictive children do not look closely enough. They rely too heavily on their knowledge of content and oral competence, ignore many visual cues in print, and create their own versions of the text. They fail "to carry out proper confirmation, especially in terms of matching words or observing letter detail" (1979, 178).

These children can be helped to develop confirming skills by activities which require that they attend more closely to the visual aspects of print. Have them use a card to mark lines as they read. The card narrows their attention to smaller "chunks" of the passage and will likely increase attention to individual words and letters within that part of the text.

Different versions of masking procedures can also be used to increase the focus on specific features of print. Masking is a technique that forces attention to a given word, letter, or phrase by separating, or blocking, it out from surrounding print in a passage. (See figures 8.2 and 8.3 for examples of masking.) In order to identify a masked word(s), the over-predictive reader must attend more closely to context *before* and *after* that word. This is especially true in material not familiar to the child; for this reason, more unfamiliar materials should be used frequently with children who are prone to "create" their own versions of print.

Over-predictive readers can also use the cassette recorder to pinpoint discrepancies between what is actually in print and their personal versions. Have them record a passage and then listen while following the line of print in the text. Have them tell you where the two versions differ. Provide additional sessions of this type alternating familiar (more-predictable) text with less-familiar (more-unpredictable) materials.

These children may also be helped by writing, which by its very nature requires attention to details of print. On this point, Holdaway observes: "Their proper entry into literacy may be through writing rather than reading" (1979, 178).

In addition to the problems related to faulty processing of print, some children experience difficulty because they are too dependent on others for confirmation of the accuracy of what they read. They continually look to the teacher for validation. Still other children are distracted by what Holdaway calls the "performance syndrome": they are so intent on how they *sound* in reading that they neglect to attend to the *sense* of what is being read. Both types of readers can be helped by selection of activities already given for developing prediction and confirmation strategies in the subsection "Integrating the cue systems of written language" in chapter 7.

Independent reading. When children have made sufficient progress in dealing with print, they will be able to read more independently. They are ready for *extensive* reading practice. During the course of a day they may spend time reading in the library center, reading to each other in small groups in the sharing center, and reading alone in the study center.

Their purposes for reading will vary from session to session. They may read for pleasure or to locate information about a topic of interest or for preparing a project. Given the opportunity, children at this stage will themselves create many opportunities and purposes for reading. Their initiative should be nourished when possible by providing the time for reading when they wish to read. Time is usually available if every

Figure 8.2. Masking with an overhead projector. Source: Don Holdaway, FOUNDATIONS OF LITERACY, Ashton Scholastic, Sydney, Australia, 1975 p. 75. Used with permission.

child is not required to participate in all the activities of a given day. For example, some children will profit more from reading on their own than from working with a language-experience story. Those who are already reading fluently do not need to spend time in working on phonics or other features of language. They obviously have these skills already or they would not be reading fluently. Instead, they should be given opportunities to read a variety of language styles and/or to learn about new topics through reading about them. If we really believe in individual differences, then we will not require that all children do the same thing in the same way at the same time.

Figure 8.3. Sliding mask used with a big book. Source: Don Holdaway, FOUNDATIONS OF LITERACY, Ashton Scholastic, Sydney, Australia, 1975, p. 76. Used with permission.

Grouping Children in the Reading Program

The discussion of reading- and writing-related experiences in the preceding section implies two basic concepts relevant to grouping children: *purpose* and *flexibility*. Both are crucial, if individual differences are to be respected and nurtured.

Groups are formed for specific purposes, to meet specific needs. The purposes determine the size of the group, who will be in the group, the activities to be engaged in, the length of group sessions, the duration of the group as a working whole, and the area where activities are carried out.

Flexibility means that grouping arrangements are changed in keeping with the purposes already achieved and with new needs as they arise. Patterns of grouping change many times during a school term as old ones are dissolved and new ones are formed. The traditional three reading groups that remain static over the year are totally incompatible with the dynamic, ever-changing nature of children and their learning.

Fixed groups not only ignore individual differences to a large extent, but the idea acts as an opiate to teachers' consciousness *about* those differences. Many teachers tend to believe they have provided sufficiently for individual differences when they form

Your Turn 8.3 Overcoming prediction problems.

Ask a second-grade teacher to suggest one of the following types of readers: (a) a child who plods through reading word by word (an under-predictive reader) or (b) a child who tends to ignore many of the meaning cues in print (an over-predictive reader). Select two techniques with appropriate materials and use them with the child.

1. Did the techniques appear to be helpful in correcting the problem? Explain.
2. What other techniques and/or materials might be used in subsequent sessions?

three groups representing three different levels of competence in reading. In fact, they have only narrowed somewhat the range of differences. Within each group there continues to exist myriad differences among the individuals who constitute the group. When teachers fail to make further differentiations in activities, they are still ignoring individual differences.

Purpose and flexibility in grouping should be implicit in the types of learning experiences provided and in the groupings for participation. There is a balance in grouping arrangements—large group, small group, and individual.

Large Groups

The whole class can participate in experiences that serve a common purpose, for example, listening to the teacher read or tell a story. In SSR the class can be considered a whole group working individually on a common activity at the same time. A part of language experience and shared-book experience can be conducted as a whole-group activity; so can planning and organizing for the school day, for special projects, and for solving a common problem. Listening to announcements and teacher's directions are also whole-group activities.

Small Groups

Many needs are best met in small groups of no more than four-to-six children. If the purpose is to generate a lot of discussion and idea exchange, then the size should be kept small enough to give all children the opportunity to make contributions and to listen to the ideas of others. Marie Hughes taught that the teacher can maintain eye contact with no more than five children at a time (class lectures, 1971). Direct instruction groups would likewise be kept to no more than four-to-five children so that the teacher can closely monitor the individual child's grasp of concepts being developed. Project planning and preparation groups should also be kept small so that all children have ready access to materials and so that the noise level can be more easily controlled. Center activities are more productive when confined to individuals or small groups.

Other needs dictate even smaller numbers of participants. Repeated readings and some types of assisted reading require a one-to-one arrangement between child and helper. Tutorial-type activities are best conducted on a one-to-one basis. Reading practice in which pairs of children read together is a good arrangement. At times, the teacher will provide instruction on a one-to-one basis.

Individual Arrangements

Many needs are met outside a group context when children work alone. Reading for practice, free reading, work in the study center, and listening to and recording oral reading in the listening center are examples. Occasionally, children will choose to work alone on special projects and in exploring and working in various centers. Respecting the choice to work alone is important; while group participation meets many needs, everyone requires some private time, too.

Teachers should not only comply with a request to work alone but should provide a special place to do so. One teacher used a "think tank," for which reservations were always full. The "tank" was a large refrigerator carton with an opening in one side to crawl through; windows were cut at the top to provide light and air. But the top was left on—the children insisted! Inside was a large throw pillow on which one could sit and lean back against the side of the box which was braced securely against a wall.

Many purposes, then, are served by grouping arrangements in the classroom. In addition to those that relate to specific activities, children increase their levels of oral language competence as they listen to group talk and strive to convey their own ideas through spoken language. They acquire many social skills: considering the ideas and feelings of others, taking turns in talking, and responding to others with empathy. In a caring environment, they learn not only to value themselves but also to value others.

The skills of effective group participation are not "given"; they are *achieved* over a long period of time with patient guidance from the teacher.

Time Management: A Day in the Life of Ivan, His Class, and Mrs. Mattingly

The teacher's most challenging task is to plan each day so that all children will have the most-productive learning experiences possible as they progress along the route to becoming fluent readers and skillfull writers. Everything comes together in the course of this planning. The teacher must first assess the strengths of children to determine the level at which each can function most profitably. On the basis of this information, the teacher then makes a number of instructional decisions designed to provide for a wide range of individual differences. Appropriate activities, materials, grouping arrangements, and room areas are selected. All these components are then coordinated with specific time frames during the school day.

Four Time-Management Aids

We have found four procedures to be valuable aids in planning and time management. The first is to make a *general* plan over a period of at least two weeks. Planning for larger segments helps to keep the "forest and the trees" in proper perspective. The teacher identifies all special or "big" activities—those which are not part of the regular daily routine—and enters them as appropriate on the two-week schedule. Unless this kind of planning is done first, there is a tendency for routine activities to crowd out the bigger events. Special activities might include any of the following: a classroom demonstration of Navajo sand painting, a trip to a museum to see an exhibit of desert animals, a school production of "The Sorcerer's Apprentice," a puppet show performed for another class, a mask-making session with a local artist in the classroom, or a "junk" art exhibit to which other classes are invited.

Second, plan the daily schedule in larger time blocks and reduce the number of activities in each, if necessary, to prevent trying to "sandwich" in too much. Remember, not every child needs to participate in everything every day. For example, plan so that center activities are alternated for individual children over several days. Large time blocks also aid in more effectively combining a variety of grouping arrangements—large group, small group, and individual. Within these arrangements, children may be working on a common topic simultaneously. At other times they may be participating in a variety of activities with no common theme.

Third, vary the daily schedule as needed. Monday morning may be spent in a special activity (watching a mask-making demonstration followed by mask making). Tuesday morning could be spent in centers in individual and small groups with children writing about the masks made, looking at and/or reading materials about masks, and planning a mask display to show another class. Wednesday morning might be devoted to a variety of activities unrelated to masks. A filmstrip for the whole group might introduce the topic of *whales* in preparation for developing a language-experience story. Individuals and small groups would then participate in a variety of activities in centers—some related to whales and others not related.

Last, vary the types of activities planned for the day by alternating quieter ones with those that are more physical. One author once observed a group of first-graders being kept in their seats for an entire hour without a break—cruel and unreasonable punishment, indeed, for young, growing minds and bodies!

A sample schedule for a day in a hypothetical primary class is shown in figure 8.4. It was designed to reflect many of the foregoing points. Whole-group activities are alternated with small-group and individual activities. Also, the plan shows a concentration of centers work for a given day, but such a concentration would not be characteristic of everyday; nor would it occur when children and teacher are inexperienced with centers. Children gradually acquire the independence and self-direction necessary for productive work in centers. They should not be given more responsibility than they can handle; so, the teacher begins slowly, monitors participation continually, and schedules as capabilities indicate. Over time, young children can, indeed, learn to work with a high degree of success in these more self-directed situations.

Ivan, His Class, and Mrs. Mattingly

Ivan is one of twenty-four children in a class that has already had one year in school. Assessment of strengths shows that Ivan, along with nine other children, is within the second phase of the literacy continuum. All are attending more closely to various features of print. Eight children are in phase one; they exhibit few reading-like behaviors. Six children are already into phase three; they have a sizeable sight vocabulary and can use a variety of strategies to arrive at meaning in simple text. Two children are reading on a high third-grade level.

This spread of differences among children in Ivan's class is not exceptional; with some groups the range may be expected to be even greater. Teachers work with this reality each day as they plan for teaching. Mrs. Mattingly's schedule for the day is designed to accommodate the range of differences in Ivan's class. Where common needs

Time	Time	WHOLE GROUP	SMALL GROUP AND INDIVIDUAL		
			P1	*P2*	*P3*
9:00	9:00	Planning for day			
	9:15	Language Experience			
	9:45		Listening Center	Instruction Center	Writing Center
	10:05		Library Center	Writing Center	Study Center
	10:25		Discovery Center	Study Center	Library Center
10:45					
10:45	10:45	Movement Activity			
	11:00	Creative Activity			
	11:35	Sustained Silent Reading			
	11:45	Lunch			
	12:30	Story Listening			
12:45	1:00	Planning for afternoon			
1:00	1:20		Study Center	Library Center	Discovery Center
1:20	1:40		Instruction Center	Listening Center	Project Center
1:40	2:00		Writing Center	Study Center	Planning and
2:00	2:20		Project Center	Discovery Center	Instruction Center
2:20	2:30	Closing the Day			
2:30					

P1—Phase One Level
P2—Phase Two Level
P3—Phase Three Level

Figure 8.4. Schedule of a day's activities with focus on centers.

The legend for symbols on the schedule is as follows:

> *P1* represents Phase One Level children, those who are in the process of building a strong support system for entry into reading.
>
> *P2* represents Phase Two Level children, those who exhibit many emergent reading behaviors and are paying increasingly closer attention to specific features of print.
>
> *P3* represents Phase Three Level children, those who have developed sufficient competencies and insights about reading to be able to read some materials independently.

exist, children are grouped into a single whole across all three phases of literacy development. Then individual needs are met by scheduling children into differentiated activities in a variety of centers.

After the usual "housekeeping" chores at the beginning of the day—counting the number of children having a hot lunch, collecting milk money, and "taking up" permission notes for an upcoming field trip—the teacher discusses the plans for the day's activities. The whole group then participates in a language experience. They discuss an animal tracking trip to the park the previous afternoon, and the teacher records dialogue in an experience story. (See figure 8.5.) When the story is recorded, all children read along as the teacher follows the text with her hand. At this point, instruction is differentiated.

Phase two (*P2*) children remain with the teacher in the instruction center for further readings of the story and activities focusing on phonics and structural analysis related to the story text. Phase one (*P1*) children move to the listening center to hear story records. Four children in the group listen to teacher-recorded cassettes and follow along, as they are able, with story text.

Phase three (*P3*) children move to the writing center to read materials about different types of animal tracks and to compose their own "animal track" stories.

The times given on the schedule for centers activities are not rigid: they are estimates and should be handled accordingly. When children are working productively on an activity, there is no need to interrupt them to play "fruit basket turn over" when the schedule calls for movement to another area. Children may continue to work, and the next center activity can be rescheduled another time. The teacher looks at the situation toward the end of the first center period and adjusts as necessary. She does monitor closely the changing from center to center. Some teachers use a timer to help everybody keep track. When the timer signals the end of a period, the teacher directs the flow of traffic to new areas and then circulates among the groups to help them get started with the activities at hand.

For this day's schedule, the second center period finds *P1* children looking at wordless picture books and other materials in the library center. *P2* children work at the writing center drawing illustrations for the language-experience story just developed. Some children use a combination of invented and conventional symbols to label their drawings or to write a sentence of text. *P3* children work at a variety of individual activities in the study center. Four are reading books of their own selection; one is using a story-starter sentence to compose a story to share with a small group; the sixth child is working on a cloze activity designed to help him use context cues for identifying new words.

During the third center period in the morning, *P1* children join an older helper who has come in from another class to work in the discovery center. The shell collection is sorted, examined, discussed, and "magnified" by all participants. *P2* children move to the study center to explore a variety of materials about rabbits, dogs, and cats. Interest in the topics was generated by finding tracks of these animals during the field trip the previous day. *P3* children are looking for additional sources of information on animals in the library center. Three young ones have gone to the school library in search of other sources about the topic.

The Monster Tracks

We took our lunches to the park. There were some big tracks in the sand. They were by the pitcher's mound. They were bigger than our hands. Eight and one-half tracks were there. Sand fell in on one. We looked for pictures in a book, but we did not find the tracks. It must have been a monster, or maybe a big dog. Lupe drew some pictures of the tracks. Here they are.

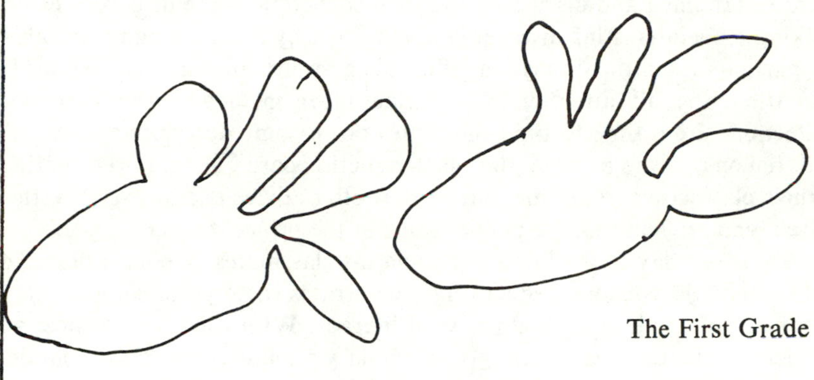

Figure 8.5. The monster tracks.

The pace changes with the completion of the first time block. Now all children join in movement activities designed to increase motor coordination. Then all participate in making individual and small-group collages from the classroom scrap collection. If time permits, this is followed by a quiet sustained-silent-reading (SSR) period before lunch. If time is not available, SSR comes shortly before the close of the day.

After lunch, children listen to a story read by the teacher. This whole-group activity is followed by individual and small-group work in centers. *P1* children work in the study center and at other quiet places in the room with their assigned student helpers in listening to repeated readings of stories. The teacher participates in *P3* activities in the discovery center. Children are examining a collection of shells and related reading materials in preparation for a whole-group development of a unit on "Shell Creatures." *P2* children explore materials in the library center; several practice reading the newest language experience story in the instruction center.

The second afternoon session in centers finds *P1* children working with the teacher at the instruction center. They are divided into two small groups around the table for participation in a concept/oral language development activity involving artifacts from the museum trunk. *P2* children practice assisted reading with read-along tapes and stories in the listening center. *P3* children are preparing puppets in the project center for an upcoming production of "Hansel and Gretel."

During the third period, *P1* children work as a group with the teacher in the writing center. They are drawing pictures generated by the earlier language-experience activity. The teacher assists in discussion of individual drawings and labels them on request. *P2* children have moved to the study center, where some practice reading easy materials while others complete individual work as assigned on phonics, structural analysis, and context clues. Worksheets have been distributed for this print-focus activity. *P3* children have moved to the planning and instruction center to discuss and plan a script for the Hansel and Gretel production.

The last period of center activity for the day finds part of the *P1* group continuing work at the writing center, where they chose to remain to complete their drawings and related writing activities. The others have moved to the project center to work on a puppet stage made from a large cardboard box. One of the *P3* children is assisting. *P2* children are examining and discussing the shell collection in the discovery center. They are making some interesting discoveries about shells by using a magnifying glass. The teacher participates in the discussion, offers suggestions, and raises questions for further exploration. She calls attention to the various labels included in the center with the shell collection. From time to time she writes down some descriptive comments from the children on cards to place on the "shell bulletin board". *P3* children continue to work on their play script; from time to time they offer advice and answer questions for *P1* children who are building the puppet stage in the project center.

This, then, is one day in the life of Ivan and his classmates. We have described how Mrs. Mattingly, their teacher, effectively orchestrates the myriad components in one small segment of children's growth toward literacy. With time, experience, and patience, we believe that the Mrs. Mattinglys of primary reading programs in countless classrooms can learn to manage and coordinate all parts within the time constraints of a day. We also believe that the task can and must be accomplished without reducing teachers to "burned out ash" in the process. Our aim has been to suggest ways to preclude this development. We hope we have been reasonably successful.

Long years of experience with young children in classrooms and outside those formal walls has taught us firsthand about many of the challenges and rewards of helping children to learn. Truly, we have found that one of the greatest delights of adult life is watching a child "discover" reading!

Parents: Partners in the Process

We began this text by describing the role of parents in promoting natural reading and writing in preschool children. The part that parents play continues to be just as important when their children begin formal schooling. In partnership with the teacher, they can do many things to reinforce all facets of the instructional program.

Getting Parents Involved

Parents can contribute to their children's developing literacy by helping both at school and at home. Not all parents will have either the time or the interest in helping at school, but most will be able to do things at home to enhance their children's school experiences.

The teacher is the key to successful parental involvement in the education of their children. Teachers should begin by sharing with parents *what* they are doing to help their children to learn to read, and they should explain *why* they are doing what they do. We have found that parents are often hesitant to take the initiative in finding out about what goes on in the life of their children at school. So, the teacher, as a regular part of beginning a new school year invites parents to meet as a group. At that time, she shares with them her ideas about the instructional program for the year. The get-acquainted session should be held after the first two-to-three weeks of school so that the teacher will have had some time to get to know the children.

We have found that having children help with preparations for the meeting by making "refreshments" and personal invitations can be an added incentive for parents to attend. Along with the children's invitations should go one from the teacher explaining briefly the purpose of the meeting.

Selection of a meeting time is one that the teacher should consider carefully. If it is held after school, many fathers and mothers who work will not be able to attend; if it is held in the early evening, it will likely have to compete with other interests and needs of the parents. So, there is no *best* time; the teacher must consider the advantages and disadvantages peculiar to the situation and choose accordingly.

Establishing rapport with parents can determine the success of the meeting and the quality of future interpersonal relations with parents. A teacher who has an understanding of children and how they best learn to read and write can talk confidently about the instructional program without appearing superior. Parents can be intimidated by a teacher who appears to be a "know-it-all" and uses a lot of educational jargon to prove it. Both teacher and parents are human first; *then* they are parents and teachers. A caring, genuine manner on the part of the teacher sets the best tone for communicating effectively with parents.

Other acts of the teacher can convey a strong sense of caring and increase the likelihood that parents will become more involved in their children's education. Arrange to make at least one home visit during the first few months of the year. The time required is small in comparison to the benefits. Once parents, teacher, and child have shared the home environment even for a brief period of time, role barriers that sometimes exist will be relaxed, and all can relate in a more human-to-human way.

Send home a message by note or by telephone telling the parents something special each child has done—once a week, if possible, or at least once every two weeks. This approach may take some getting used to by parents who have had little positive feedback from the school. One writer remembers a parent's telephone call after receiving two positive notes. "Now what is *really* the problem?" she asked.

Specific Things Parents Can Do at Home

We have already described the types of help parents can provide in the classroom. There are also many ways in which they can support at home what the teacher does at school to aid in their children's becoming successful readers and writers.

1. *Read to the child regularly.* (It is important that fathers as well as mothers participate.) Bedtime stories can be very special times for sharing not only a book but

Your Turn 8.4 Parents as partners in literacy development.

Interview a primary teacher to determine the following:

1. What parents do in the classroom.
2. What the teacher's assessment is of parental involvement.
3. How parental help is obtained.
4. What the teacher expects parents to do at home to complement literacy development in the classroom.

also tender, loving closeness as well. One state-wide program was started by Senator James H. Donovan in New York recently; it has been very successful in getting parents involved in reading to their children regularly for fifteen minutes each day. The program offers many suggestions for other ways to stimulate children's interest in books and reading. (Further information about the program is available free by writing to: Senator James H. Donovan, "Parents as Reading Partners," Legislative Office Building, Albany, New York 12247. Another excellent source for locating many types of materials to share with young children is the following: Rhodes, Lynn K., and Hill, Mary W. "Supporting Reading in the Home—Naturally: Selected Materials for Parents." *The Reading Teacher* 30 [March 1985]: 619–23.)

2. *Provide reading and writing materials in the home.* Establish the tradition of giving books for special occasions, and schedule regular trips to the public library. Have the child include a note when letters are sent to relatives and friends.
3. *Provide regular times for children to spend on their own with books.*
4. *"Unplug" children from the TV.* Television can be an excellent source for stimulating interests in new subjects and new books. However, when the time spent in viewing is excessive, too little time is left for reading. The prevention of "addiction" to this medium is much easier than trying to effect a "cure" later. Discretion and guidance by parents in their children's early years can keep television and reading in proper perspective. Neither must be sacrificed to the other.
5. *Follow up on school assignments.* See that the teacher's requests for special at-home activities are carried out by the child.
6. *Communicate with the teacher.* When concerns develop about the child's life at school, do not just hope "they will go away." Contact the teacher to discuss them.

Summary

In this chapter we have described the various components of a primary reading program and the ways and means to coordinate these components into a unified whole to best meet the individual needs of children at a variety of places on the continuum of literacy development. We have also looked at the role parents can play in concert with that of the teacher in promoting learning to read and write in a natural way for the greatest possible number of young children.

References

Donovan, James H. "Parents as Reading Partners Program." Albany, N.Y.: State Senate, 1979.

Holdaway, Don. *The Foundations of Literacy.* New York: Ashton Scholastic, 1979.

Loughlin, Catherine E., and Suina, Joseph H. *The Learning Environment. An Instructional Strategy.* New York: Columbia University, Teachers College Press, 1982.

Rhodes, Lynn K., and Hill, Mary W. "Supporting Reading in the Home—Naturally: Selected Materials for Parents." *The Reading Teacher* 38 (March 1985): 619–23.

Taylor, Denny. *Family Literacy. Young Children Learn to Read and Write.* Exeter, N.H.: Heinemann Educational Books, 1984.

9

A Whole Language Approach to Learning to Read Naturally

This text has described an instructional program that can enable children to grow more naturally into reading by building on what is known about how many children teach themselves to read. We have also documented from many sources the thesis that there are a number of traditional practices in teaching reading which need to be examined and, in some cases, changed in order to make beginning reading a more meaningful, a more enjoyable, and a more natural learning experience.

Learning to read *is* a complicated process. Contributions from many fields—psychology, sociology, neurology, speech communication, sociolinguistics, and psycholinguistics—are needed to understand the process. Edmund Burke Huey, decades ago, made this point clearly:

> And so to completely analyze what we do when we read would almost be the acme of a psychologist's achievement, for it would be to describe very many of the most intricate workings of the human mind, as well as to unravel the tangled story of the most remarkable specific performance that civilization has learned in all its history (1908, 6).

Since we have written extensively about the contribution of psycholinguistics to the understanding of how children grow naturally into reading, the impression might be that this is a psycholinguistic method of teaching reading. The terms "Learning to read naturally" or "A whole language approach to reading" sound very acceptable to us. However, we wish to remind the reader that there is more to the process than psycholinguistic theory alone. We agree with John B. Carroll when he wrote:

> I would be the first to deny that there is, or could be a "psycholinguistic method" of teaching reading, because there is much more to the teaching of reading than whatever might be contributed by psycholinguistics (1978, 11).

While *not a method* of teaching reading, psycholinguistics has, nevertheless, made valuable contributions to understanding the nature of language and how it is used to communicate meaning, both in speaking and in reading. A better understanding of the communicative process provides a stronger basis for planning and implementing more-effective methods of instruction.

After allowing each child time to learn how the process of reading works and to develop the curiosity about "what reading says," children in their own time will learn to read by reading. As readers, they will demand meaning in all the reading they do because they will not be reading if they have no purpose. This is a process of sampling and confirming or correcting ideas in the print when they make sense to the reader. We have shown how this is done by following the leads of children as they expand their curiosity, enrich their language concepts, and ask innumerable questions.

When children have become fluent in expressing *ideas* and have developed an awareness of the way print records for them the things *they have spoken,* they are ready to dictate many stories of things they already know for the teacher (1) to record, (2) to read back to them, (3)to ask them to read and reread, and (4) to preserve for future use. In producing their own books, they learn more about words, both with reference to structure and meaning, and more about how words constitute language.

This metalinguistic awareness gives them the metalanguage to talk meaningfully about letters, sounds that letters make, words, phrases, sentences, paragraphs, and stories. This progression gives children a considerable knowledge of the sounds of the English phonemes, or phonics, without the need for drills, workbooks, or ditto sheets to learn phonic elements in isolation. It is well to point out that it is the teacher who needs to *know phonics* so that he can supply the child's need at the opportune moment when meaning is the child's focus. A table of phonic elements in chapter 7 was presented as a refresher for the teacher.

When children have heard many stories read, have sat in small groups in shared-book experiences, and have read along with an adult, they will internalize the sense of story language or "the way the books say it" as contrasted with children's oral language. Shared-book experiences and their language-experience writing can extend their world view and whet their curiosities for further learning. When they have read the structure of language presented in basals, they should have no difficulties in thinking meanings in their own vernacular.

At this point, most children will likely be ready to read stories in books to extend their own horizons beyond their immediate environment. Because the basal reader is found in abundance in all schools, it will be used to enable all children to read extensively. It is hoped that children who can read the stories easily and for personal enjoyment will not be required to complete skills exercises that do not enhance their learning. Selected children's literature (appendix 9) provides additional quantities of reading that should be available to encourage children to read much and often. Jeannette Veatch has written an excellent little book, highly illustrated, to show teachers how to teach reading through the use of children's books (1968).

In any given class there will usually be a few children who do not move naturally into reading as most will. These children may profit by participation in small-group sessions of directed reading lessons from the basal reader. It would be well, however, not to follow the lesson plan in the order in which it is outlined in the guide. Rather, the teacher can give the students a synopsis of the story orally, build background to

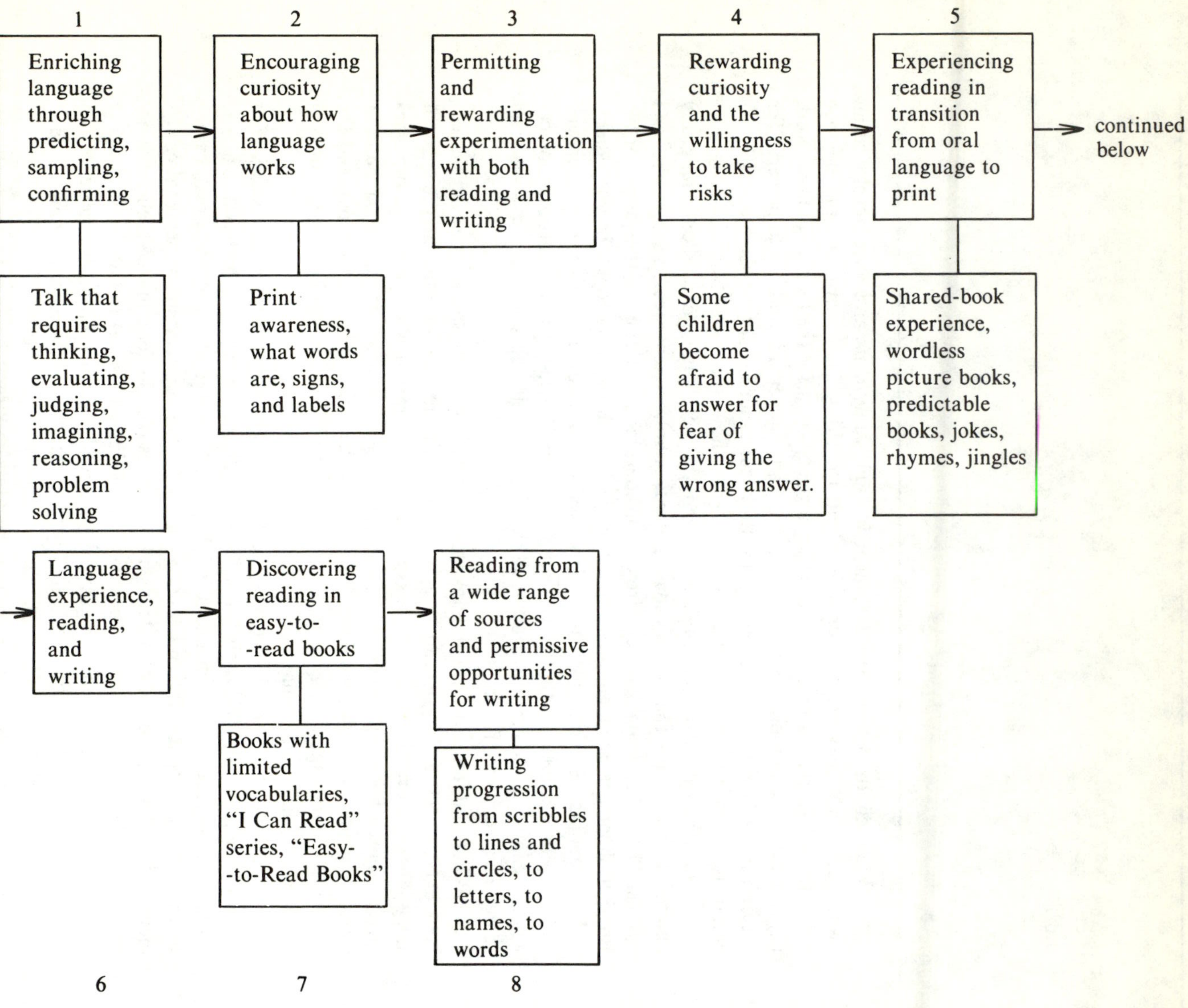

1
Enriching language through predicting, sampling, confirming
Talk that requires thinking, evaluating, judging, imagining, reasoning, problem solving
2
Encouraging curiosity about how language works
Print awareness, what words are, signs, and labels
3
Permitting and rewarding experimentation with both reading and writing
4
Rewarding curiosity and the willingness to take risks
Some children become afraid to answer for fear of giving the wrong answer.
5
Experiencing reading in transition from oral language to print
Shared-book experience, wordless picture books, predictable books, jokes, rhymes, jingles
continued below
Language experience, reading, and writing
Discovering reading in easy-to- -read books
Books with limited vocabularies, "I Can Read" series, "Easy- -to-Read Books"
Reading from a wide range of sources and permissive opportunities for writing
Writing progression from scribbles to lines and circles, to letters, to names, to words
6
7
8

Figure 9.1. Moving into reading with a whole language approach.

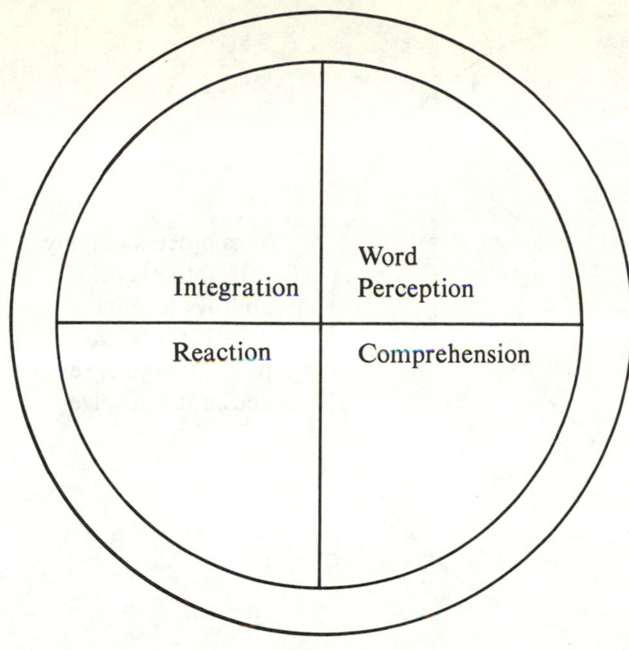

Reading is a process of thinking, evaluating, judging, imagining, reasoning, and problem solving.

Figure 9.2. Gray's definition of reading. Source: William S. Gray, ON THEIR OWN IN READING, Scott, Foresman and Company, Glenview, Illinois 1948, pp. 35–37. Used with permission.

increase understanding of the story, and ask questions answered in the story—all before beginning reading. Then if the group enjoys the reading, little follow-up will be indicated.

The flow chart in figure 9.1 depicts the progression from activities familiar to children from the first day they come to school to activities that consumate the reading act. While there are eight designated steps in the chart, the number is not significant in itself. It only suggests directions for teachers of young children to move.

We believe that the definition of reading given years ago by William S. Gray is still a complete enough definition of the process for people who do read. He wrote that reading is a four step process of the following: (1) word perception; (2) comprehension—establishing the word as a concept; (3) reaction—involving making a judgment or an emotional response; and (4) integration—putting new ideas in personal perspective. Of course, Gray emphasized that the act of reading requires thinking, evaluating, judging, imagining, reasoning, and problem solving. This definition is diagrammed in figure 9.2.

The whole language approach to reading requires a lengthy period of growth in language development and extension of concepts and experience. This is done by guiding children in questioning that leads them to predict, sample, and confirm or correct their thinking about events, places, and relationships. Figure 9.3 illustrates this process.

After this has been achieved by giving some boys and girls more time than is required by others along with opportunities to venture into reading that which interests

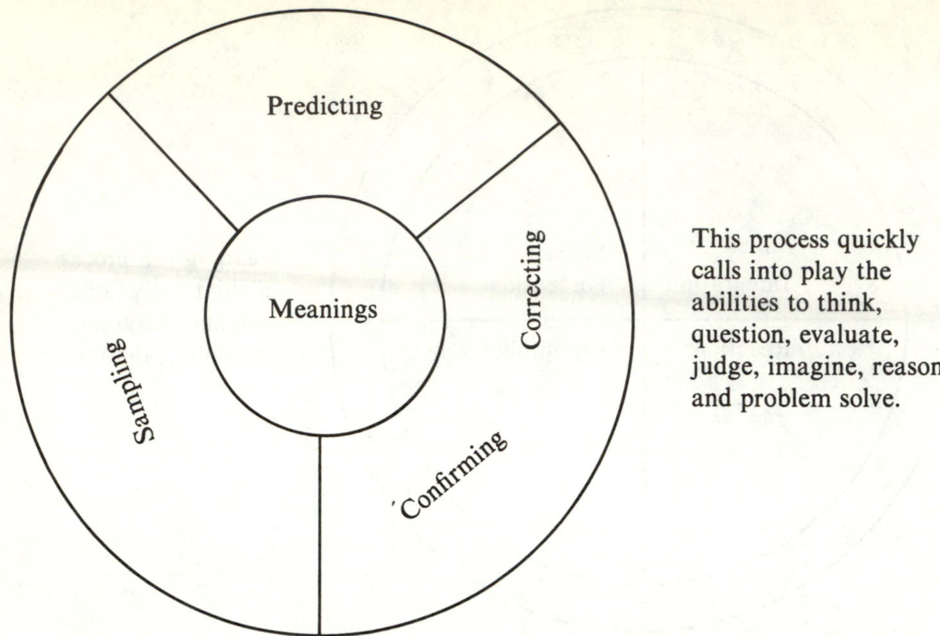
Predicting
Meanings
Correcting
Sampling
Confirming
This process quickly calls into play the abilities to think, question, evaluate, judge, imagine, reason, and problem solve.

Figure 9.3. Three key elements in the whole language approach. Based on Constance Weaver, PSYCHOLINGUISTIC AND READING: FROM PROCESS TO PRACTICE, Little, Brown and Company, Boston, 1980, p. 144. Used with permission of author.

them, then children need teachers who can come to their aid with respect to elements in phonic and structural analysis, recognizing sight words instantly, and in reading sentences and demanding meanings. However, there will be no "set sequence" for teaching all the consonant sounds or in the teacher's deciding what specific ten or twenty words need to be learned first. Children will learn most of the facets of "how to read" in the shared-book experience, in the approximating of the story after hearing it read, and in retelling wordless-picture-book stories. They will have learned most, perhaps, from their language-experience stories that they write with the teacher and preserve in books of their own. The point to be made, however, is that phonic analysis, sight words, and sentence reading—shown as elements in a beginning reading program in figure 9.4—need not be the persevering, "head-on" activities which they currently are in some basal reading programs.

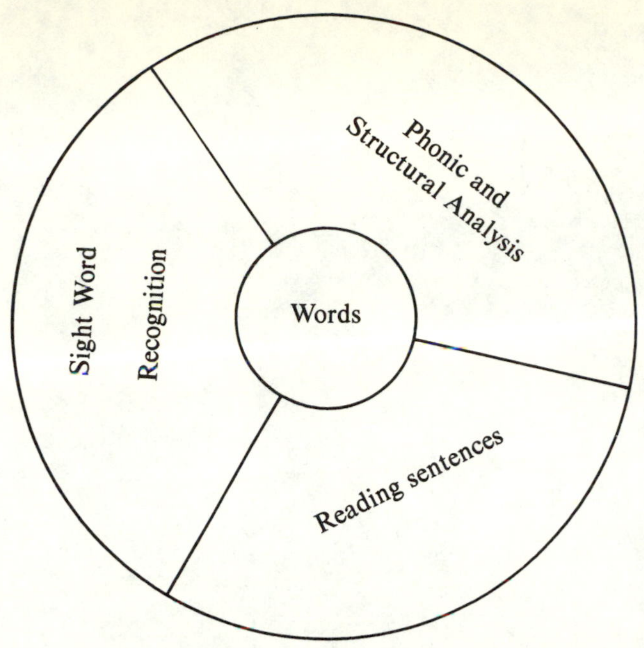

The problem in this process is that the abilities of thinking, evaluating, judging, imagining, reasoning, and problem solving may not be called into play sufficiently.

Figure 9.4. Three key elements in the traditional basal reading program. Based on Constance Weaver, PSYCHOLINGUISTICS AND READING: FROM PROCESS TO PRACTICE, Little, Brown and Company, Boston, 1980, p. 144. Used with permission of author.

References

Carroll, John B. "Psycholinguistics and the Study and Teaching of Reading." In *Aspects of Reading Education,* edited by Susanna Pflaum-Connor. Berkeley, California: McCutchan Publishing Corporation, 1978.

Gray, William S. *On Their Own in Reading.* Chicago: Scott Foresman, 1948.

Huey, Edmund Burke. *The Psychology and Pedagogy of Reading.* New York: Macmillan Publishing Company, 1908. Reprint. Cambridge, Mass.: The M.I.T. Press, 1968.

Weaver, Constance. *Psycholinguistics and Reading: From Process to Practice.* Boston: Little Brown, 1980.

Veatch, Jeannette. *How to Teach Reading with Children's Books.* New York: Citation Press, 1968. Available from Richard C. Owen, Publishers, Rockefeller Center, Box 819, New York, N.Y. 10185.

Appendixes

1 Language Experience: Sources of Information
2 Games and Activities
3 Classroom Learning Centers
4 Wordless Picture Books
5 Alphabet Books
6 Predictable Books
7 Books with Language Play
8 Jingles, Jokes, Limericks, Puns, Proverbs, Puzzles, and Riddles
9 Read-Aloud Books
10 Expository Reading with Children
11 Narrative Materials
12 Poetry Books
13 Read-Along Records and Books
14 Films and Records

The authors are indebted to Kathleen Hill, elementary school librarian, Anchorage Public Schools, for assistance in making selections of books, records, and films in the appendixes.

Appendix 1 Language Experience: Sources of Information

Allen, Roach Van, and Allen, Claryce. *Language Experiences in Reading.* Levels I, II, and III. Chicago: Encyclopaedia Britannica Corporation, 1970.

Allen, Roach Van. *Language Experiences in Communicating.* Boston: Houghton Mifflin Company, 1976.

Ashton-Warner, Sylvia. *Teacher.* New York: Simon and Schuster, 1971.

Cromwell, Ellen. *Feathers in My Cap: Early Reading Through Experience.* Washington, D.C.: Acropolis Books, 1980.

Hall, Mary Anne. *The Language Experience Approach for the Culturally Disadvantaged.* Newark: IRA, 1972.

———. *The Language Experience Approach for Teaching Reading: A Research Perspective.* 2d ed. Newark: IRA, 1978.

———. *Teaching Reading as a Language Experience.* 3rd ed. Columbus: Charles E. Merrill, 1981.

Kerfoot, James, ed. *First Grade Reading Programs, Perspectives in Reading No. 5.* Newark: IRA, 1965.

Lee, Dorris M., and Allen, Roach Van. *Learning to Read Through Experience.* New York: Appleton-Century-Crofts, 1963.

Lee, Dorris, and Rubin, Joseph B. *Children and Language.* Belmont, Calif.: Wadsworth Publishing Company, 1979.

Martin, Bill, Jr. *Strategies for Language Learning.* Tulsa, Okla.: Educational Progress Corporation, 1980.

McCracken, Robert A., and McCracken, Marlene J. *Reading is Only the Tiger's Tail.* San Rafael, Calif.: Leswing Press, 1972.

McCracken, Marlene C., and McCracken, Robert A. *Reading, Writing and Language. A Practical Guide for Primary Teachers.* Winnipeg: Peguis Publishers Limited, 1979.

Reading Unlimited. *Teaching Beginning Reading, Language Experience Approach to Beginning Reading.* Filmstrips and cassettes. Alexandria, Va.: Reading Unlimited, 1976.

Stauffer, Russell. *The Language Experience Approach to the Teaching of Reading.* 2d ed. New York: Harper and Row, Publishers, 1980.

Veatch, Jeannette, et. al. *Key Words to Reading: The Language Experience Approach Begins.* Columbus: Charles E. Merrill, 1973.

———. *Key Words to Reading: The Language Experience Approach Begins.* 2d Ed. Columbus: Charles E. Merrill, 1979.

Appendix 2 Games and Activities

Barratta-Lorton, Mary. *Workjobs: Activity-Centered Learning for Early Childhood Education.* Reading, Mass.: Addison Wesley, 1972.

———. *Workjobs for Parents.* K–3. Reading, Mass.: Addison Wesley, 1975.

———. *Workjobs for Parents.* Preprimer–2. Reading, Mass.: Addison Wesley, 1975.

Burie, Audrey Ann, and Heltshe, Mary Ann. *Reading With a Smile. 90 Reading Games That Work.* Washington, D.C.: Acropolis Books, 1980.

Cahoon, Owen W. *A Teacher's Guide to Cognitive Tasks for Preschool.* Provo, Utah: Brigham Young University Press, 1975.

Daniels, Steven. *How 2 Gerbils, 20 Goldfish, 200 Games, 2,000 Books and I Taught Them How to Read.* Philadelphia: Westminister Press, 1971.

Dorsey, Mary E. *Reading Games and Activities.* Belmont, Calif.: Pitman Learning, 1972.

Ekwall, Eldon E. *Locating and Correcting Reading Difficulties.* 2d ed. Columbus: Charles E. Merrill, 1977.

Flemming, Bonnie, and Hamilton, Darlene. *Resources for Creative Teaching in Early Childhood Education.* New York: Harcourt Brace Jovanovich, 1977.

Golick, Margie. *Deal Me In! The Use of Playing Cards in Teaching and Learning.* Guilford, Conn.: Jeffrey Norton Publishers, 1973.

Henderson, Julia K. *The Reading Box, 150 Reading Games and Activities.* N.p., 1974.

Kromer, Thomas, and Bleeker, Joyce. *Learning Can Be Fun with Michigan Games.* n.p.: Hillsdale Educational, 1980.

Marbach, Ellen S. *Creative Curriculum—Kindergarten Through Grade Three.* Provo, Utah: Brigham Young University Press, 1977.

Norton, Donna E. *Language Arts Activities for Children.* Columbus: Charles E. Merrill, 1977.

Novakovich, Harriet, and Zoslow, Sylvia. *Target on Language.* Bethesda, Md.: Christchurch Child Center, 1974.

Russell, David H. and Karp, Etta E. *Reading Aids Through the Grades.* Revised by Anne Marie Mueser. New York: Columbus University, Teachers College Press, 1975.

Russell, David H. and Russell, Elizabeth F. *Listening Aids Through the Grades.* 2d ed. edited by Dorothy Grant Hennings. New York: Columbia University, Teachers College Press, 1979.

Smith, Charlene. *Listening Activity Book.* Belmont, Calif.: Pitman Learning, 1975.

Spache, Evelyn B. *Reading Activities for Child Involvement.* 2d ed. Newton, Mass.: Allyn and Bacon, 1976.

Taylor, Barbara J. *A Child Goes Forth.* Provo, Utah: Brigham Young University Press, 1975.

———. *When I Do, I Learn.* Provo, Utah: Brigham Young University Press, 1974.

Appendix 3 Classroom Learning Centers

Bennie, Frances. *Learning Centers: Development and Operation.* Englewood Cliffs, N.J.: Educational Technology Publishers, 1977.

Crabtree, June. *Learning Center Ideas.* Cincinnati, Ohio: Standard Publishing, 1977.

Davidson, Tom, et. al. *Learning Center Book: An Integrated Approach.* Pacific Palisades, Calif.: Goodyear Publishing Company, 1976.

Forte, Imogene, et. al. *Center Stuff for Nooks, Crannies and Corners.* Nashville: Incentive Publications, 1973.

Greff, Kasper N., and Askov, Eunice N. *Learning Centers: An Idea Book for Reading and Language Arts.* Dubuque, Iowa: Kendall Hunt Publishing Company, 1977.

Johnston, Hiram, et. al. *Learning Center Idea Book: Activities for the Elementary and Middle Grades.* Newton, Mass.: Allyn and Bacon, 1978.

Kaplan, Sandra, et. al. *Change for Children.* Pacific Palisades, Calif.: Goodyear Publishing Company, 1973.

———. *A Young Child Experiences.* Pacific Palisades, Calif.: Goodyear Publishing Company, 1975.

Maxim, George W. *Learning Centers for Young Children.* Reading, Mass.: Addison and Wesley, 1977.

Nations, James E., ed. *Learning Centers in the Classroom.* Washington, D.C.: National Education Association, 1976.

NEA. *Learning Centers.* Washington, D.C.: National Education Association, 1976.

Peterson, Gary T. *Learning Center: A Sphere for Non-Traditional Approaches to Education.* Hamden, Conn.: Shoe String Press, 1975.

Appendix 4 Wordless Picture Books

Alexander, Martha. *Bobo's Dream.* New York: Dial Books, 1970.

Amoss, Berthe. *By the Sea.* New York: Parents Magazine Press, 1969.

Ardizzone, Edward. *Wrong Side of the Bed.* New York: Doubleday and Company, 1970.

Baum, Willi. *Birds of a Feather.* Reading, Mass.: Addison-Wesley, 1969.

Brinckloe, Julie. *Spider Web.* New York: Doubleday and Company, 1974.

Carle, Eric. *Do You Want to Be My Friend?* New York: Crowell-Collier Press, 1971.

DeGroat, Diane. *Alligator's Toothache.* New York: Crown Publishers, 1977.

Fromm, Kilo. *Muffel and Plums.* New York: Macmillan Publishing Company, 1973.

Fuchs, Erich. *Journey to the Moon.* New York: Delacorte Press, 1969.

Goodall, John S. *Creepy Castle.* New York: Atheneum Publishers, 1975.

Knobler, Susan. *Tadpole and the Frog.* New York: Harvey House Publishers, 1974.

Krahn, Fernando. *Flying Saucer Full of Spaghetti.* New York: E. P. Dutton, 1970.

Mari, Lela. *Chicken and the Egg.* New York: Pantheon Books, 1970.

Mayer, Mercer. *Oops.* New York: Dial Books, 1977.

Pierce, Robert. *Look and Laugh.* New York: Golden Press, 1974.

Remington, Barbara. *Boat.* New York: Doubleday and Company, 1975.

Schick, Eleanor. *Making Friends.* New York: Macmillan Publishing Company, 1969.

(Selected from Stewig 1978, 10–11)

Sesame Street. *Sesame Street Book of People and Things.* Boston: Little, Brown and Company, 1970.

Simmons, Ellie. *Cat.* New York: David McKay Company, 1968.

Sugano, Uoshikatsu. *Kitty's Adventure.* New York: McGraw-Hill Book Company, 1971.

Turkle, Brinton. *Deep in the Forest.* New York: E. P. Dutton, 1976.

Ueno, Noriko. *Elephant Buttons.* New York: Harper and Row, Publishers, 1973.

Winter, Paula. *The Bear and the Fly.* New York: Crown Publishers, 1976.

(Selected from Mason 1981, 144–45).

Appendix 5 Alphabet Books

Barry, Katharine. *A Is for Anything.* New York: Harcourt, Brace and World, 1961.

Brown, Marcia. *All Butterflies.* New York: Charles Scribner's Sons, 1974.

Brown, Marcia. *Peter Piper's Alphabet.* New York: Charles Scribner's Sons, 1959.

Falls, C. B. *ABC.* New York: Doubleday and Company, 1923.

Fujikawa, Gyo. *A to Z Picture Book.* New York: Gosset and Dunlap, 1974.

Gag, Wanda. *The ABC Bunny.* New York: Coward-McCann, 1933.
Howard, Frances. *An Illustrated Comic Alphabet.* New York: Henry L. Walck, 1967.
Miles, Miska. *Apricot ABC.* Boston: Little, Brown and Company, 1969.
Rey, H. A. *Curious George Learns the Alphabet.* Boston: Houghton Mifflin Company, 1963.
Travers, P. L. *Mary Poppins from A to Z.* New York: Harcourt, Brace and World, 1962.
Williams, Garth. *The Big Golden Animal ABC.* New York: Simon and Schuster, 1957.

Appendix 6 Predictable Books

Balian, Lorna. *Where in the World Is Henry?* Scarsdale, N.Y.: Bradbury Press, 1972.
Becker, John. *Seven Little Rabbits.* New York: Scholastic, 1973.
Brown, Marcia. *The Three Billy Goats Gruff.* New York: Harcourt Brace Jovanovich, 1957.
Carle, Eric. *The Mixed Up Chameleon.* New York: Thomas Y. Crowell, 1975.
———. *The Very Hungry Caterpillar.* Cleveland: Collins World, 1969.
Duff, Maggie. *Rum Pum Pum.* New York: Macmillan Publishing Company, 1978.
Galdone, Paul. *Henry Penny.* New York: Scholastic, 1968.
———. *The Three Billy Goats Gruff.* New York: Seabury Press, 1973.
Keats, Ezra Jack. *Over in the Meadow.* New York: Scholastic, 1971.
Langstaff, John. *Frog Went A-Courtin'.* New York: Harcourt Brace Jovanovich, 1955.
Martin, Bill. *Brown Bear, Brown Bear.* New York: Holt, Rinehart and Winston, 1970.
———. *Fire! Fire! Said Mrs. McGuire.* New York: Holt, Rinehart and Winston, 1970.
Mayer, Mercer. *If I Had. . . .* New York: Dial Press, 1968.
———. *Just for You.* New York: Golden Press, 1975.
Peppe, Rodney. *The House that Jack Built.* New York: Delacorte Press, 1970.
Preston, Edna Mitchell. *Where Did My Mother Go?* New York: Four Winds Press, 1978.
Quackenbush, Robert. *Skip to My Lou.* Philadelphia: J. B. Lippincott, 1975.
Sendak, Maurice. *Where the Wild Things Are.* New York: Scholastic, 1963.
Skaar, Grace. *What Do the Animals Say?* New York: Scholastic, 1963.
Zaid, Barry. *Chicken Little.* New York: Random House, n.d.
(Selected from Rhodes 1981, 511–18.)

Appendix 7 Books with Language Play

Alphabet Games

Brown, Marcia. *Peter Piper's Alphabet.* New York: Charles Scribner's Sons, 1959.
Sendak, Maurice. *Alligators All Around.* New York: Harper and Row, Publishers, 1962.

Patterned Language

Cameron, Polly. *"I Can't," Said the Ant.* New York: Coward-McCann, 1961.
Chwast, Seymour. *The House That Jack Built.* New York: Random House, n.d.
Einsel, Walter. *Did You Ever See?* New York: Scholastic, 1972.
Emberley, Ed. *Drummer Hoff.* New York: Prentice-Hall, 1967.
Zemach, Harve. *The Judge.* New York: Farrar, Straus, 1969.

Homonyms

Gwynne, Fred. *A Chocolate Moose for Dinner.* New York: E. P. Dutton, 1973.
———. *The King Who Rained.* New York: Windmill, 1970.

Onomatopoela

Spier, Peter. *Gobble, Growl, Grunt.* New York: Doubleday and Company, 1971.
———. *Crash Bang Boom.* New York: Doubleday and Company, 1972.

Comparisons (Metaphors, Similes, Collective Names)

O'Neill, Mary. *Hailstones and Halibut Bones.* New York: Doubleday and Company, 1961.
Reid, Alastair. *Ounce, Dice, Trice.* New York: Little, Brown and Company, 1958.
Wildsmith, Brian. *Birds.* New York: Franklin Watts, 1967.
———. *Fishes.* New York: Franklin Watts, 1967.
———. *Wild Animals.* New York: Franklin Watts, 1967.

Plays on Meaning

Parish, Peggy. *Amelia Bedelia.* New York: Harper and Row Publishers, 1963.
Raskin, Ellen. *Figgs and Phantoms.* New York: E. P. Dutton, 1974.
(Selected from Blatt 1978, 491–93)

Appendix 8 Jingles, Jokes, Limericks, Puns, Proverbs, Puzzles, and Riddles

Arnold, Arnold. *The Big Book of Tongue Twisters and Double Talk.* New York: Random House, 1964.
Bishop, Ann. *Riddle Raddle, Fiddle Faddle.* Chicago: Albert Whitman, 1966.
Bridwell, Norman. *How to Care for Your Monster.* New York: Scholastic, 1970.
Cerf, Bennett. *More Riddles.* New York: Random House, 1961.
Chrystie, Frances N. *The First Book of Jokes and Funny Things.* New York: Franklin Watts, 1951.
Cole, William. *The Book of Giggles.* New York: World Publishing Company, 1970.
Cole, William. *Oh, What Nonsense!* New York: Viking Press, 1972.
Emrich, Ducan. *Riddles and Jokes and Foolish Facts.* New York: Scholastic, 1972.
Higgins, James. *Tongue Twisters.* Boston: Houghton Mifflin Company, 1973.
Hymes, Lucia, and Hymes, James L. *Hooray for Chocolate and Other Easy-to-Read Jingles.* New York: Young Readers Press, 1960.
Kessler, Leonard. *Ghosts and Crows and Things with O's.* New York: Scholastic, 1976.
Laymon, Ritchie. *Fun with Puzzles.* New York: Young Readers Press, 1971.
Lear, Edward. *Whizz!* New York: Macmillan Publishing Company, 1973.
Miller, Albert G. *Talking Letters.* Glendale, Calif.: Bowmar, 1974.
Mosler, Gerard. *Parents Magazine Family Quiz Book.* New York: Parents Magazine Press, 1969.
Ridlon, Marci. *A Frog Sandwich: Riddles and Jokes.* Chicago: Follett Publishing Company, 1973.
Sendak, Maurice. *Chicken Soup with Rice.* New York: Harper and Row, Publishers, 1962.
Thaler, Mike. *Soup with Quackers: Funny Cartoon Riddles.* New York: Franklin Watts, 1976.
Thorndike, Susan. *The Electric Radish and Other Jokes.* Garden City, N.Y.: Doubleday and Company, 1973.
Tripp, Wallace. *A Great Big Ugly Man Came Up and Tied His Horse to Me.* Boston: Little, Brown and Company, 1973.
Van Gelder, Rosalind. *Tricky Questions to Fool Your Friends.* New York: Scholastic, 1966.
Wagner, Betty Jane. *Limericks.* Boston: Houghton Mifflin Company, 1973.
Wyler, Rose, and Ames, Gerald. *Funny Magic: Easy Tricks for Young Magicians.* New York: Scholastic, 1972.
———. *Magic Secrets.* New York: Scholastic, 1967.
(Selected from Moe and Hopkins 1978, 958–95, 1003)

Appendix 9 Read-Aloud Books

Emotional and Social Development

Brown, Margaret Wise. *The Run Away Bunny.* New York: William Morrow and Company, 1954.

Cohen, Miriam. *Will I Have a Friend?* New York: Macmillan Publishing Company, 1967. The story of a boy's first day in kindergarten.

Fatio, Louise. *The Happy Lion.* New York: McGraw-Hill Book Company, 1954.

Flack, Marjorie. *The Story About Ping.* New York: Viking Press, 1933. This book is about a duck who tries to avoid a spanking.

Heyword, Du Bose. *The Country Bunny and the Little Gold Shoes.* Boston: Houghton Mifflin Company, 1939.

Hoban, Russell. *A Baby Sister for Frances.* New York: Harper and Row, Publishers, 1964.

———. *A Bargain for Frances.* An *I Can Read Book.* New York: Harper and Row, Publishers, 1970.

———. *Bedtime for Frances.* New York: Harper and Row, Publishers, 1960.

———. *The Sorely Trying Day.* New York: Harper and Row, Publishers, 1964.

Johnson, Crockett. *Harold and the Purple Crayon.* New York: Harper and Row, Publishers, 1955.

Krauss, Ruth. *The Carrot Seed.* New York: Harper and Row, Publishers, 1945.

Piper, Watty. *The Little Engine That Could.* New York: Platt and Munk, 1954.

Rodgers, Mary. *The Rotten Book.* New York: Harper and Row, Publishers, 1969.

Scarry, Patsy. *My Baby Brother.* New York: Simon and Schuster, 1956.

Seuss, Dr. *Horton Hatches the Egg.* New York: Random House, 1940.

———. *Horton Hears a Who.* New York: Random House, 1954.

Seuss, Dr. and McKie, Roy. *My Book About Me: By Me, Myself.* New York: Random House, 1969.

Steptoe, John. *Stevie.* New York: Harper and Row, Publishers, 1969.

Yashima, Taro. *Umbrella.* New York: Viking Press, 1958.

Zion, Gene. *Harry by the Sea.* New York: Harper and Row, Publishers, 1965.

Zolotow, Charlotte. *Big Sister and Little Sister.* New York: Harper and Row, Publishers, 1966.

———. *The Bunny Who Found Easter.* Berkeley, Calif.: Parnassus Press, 1959.

———. *Mr. Rabbit and the Lovely Present.* New York: Harper and Row, Publishers, 1962.

———. *The Quarreling Book.* New York: Harper and Row, Publishers, 1963.

———. *The Storm Book.* New York, Harper and Row, Publishers, 1952.

Entertainment

Eichenberg, Fritz. *Ape in a Cape.* New York: Harcourt, Brace and World, 1952. A rhyming alphabet picture book.

Graham, Al. *Timothy Turtle.* New York: Viking Press, 1946.

Hutchins, Pat. *Rosie's Walk.* New York: Macmillan Publishing Company, 1968.

Joslin, Sesyle. *What Do You Say Dear?* New York: William R. Scott, 1958. For ages four to six.

Langstaff, John. *Frog Went A-Courtin'.* New York: Harcourt, Brace and World, 1955. Illustrations are outstanding. For ages two and one-half to six.

———. *Over in the Meadow.* New York: Harcourt, Brace and World, 1957. For ages three through five.

Mayer, Mercer. *Frog, Where Are You?* New York: The Dial Press, 1969. A small book with no words; pictures tell this lively story.

Moore, Clement C. *The Night Before Christmas.* New York: Grosset and Dunlap, 1949.

Rey, Hans A. *Curious George.* Boston: Houghton Mifflin Company, 1941. For ages four to six.

Robinson, Tom. *Buttons.* New York: Viking Press, 1938.

Scarry, Richard. *Best Mother Goose Ever.* New York: Western Publishing, 1964. A Giant Golden Book for ages four to six.

Segal, Lore. *Tell Me a Mitzi.* New York: Farrar, Straus and Giroux, 1970.
Sendak, Maurice. *Where the Wild Things Are.* New York: Harper and Row, Publishers, 1963. For ages four to six.
Seuss, Dr. *And to Think That I Saw It on Mulberry Street.* New York: Vanguard Press, 1937.
———. *Bartholomew and the Oobleck.* New York: Random House, 1949.
———. *The Cat In the Hat.* New York: Random House, 1957.
———. *The Cat In the Hat Comes Back.* New York: Random House, 1958.
———. *If I Ran the Circus.* New York: Random House, 1956.
———. *If I Ran the Zoo.* New York: Random House, 1950.
———. *Thidwick the Big Hearted Moose.* New York: Random House, 1948.
———. *Yertle, the Turtle and Other Stories.* New York: Random House, 1958.
Slobodkina, Esphyr. *Caps for Sale.* New York: W. R. Scott, 1957.
Steig, William. *Sylvester and the Magic Pebble.* New York: Simon and Schuster Windmill Books, 1969.
Turkle, Brinton. *Obadiah, the Bold.* New York: Viking Press, 1965.
Turlay, Clare. *Marshmallow.* New York: Harper and Row, Publishers, 1942. Has beautiful pictures.
(Selected from Rogers, n.d., 7–15)

Appendix 10 Expository Reading with Children

Animal Changes: Migration, Hibernation, and Camouflage

Carle, Eric. *Mixed-up Chameleon.* New York: Crowell-Collier Press, 1975. Unsatisfied with being able to camouflage by changing brownish on a branch or reddish on a crimson flower, this chameleon wants to be swift as a deer, smart as a fox, and pretty as a flamingo.

Lionni, Leo. *Fish is Fish.* New York: Pantheon Books, 1970. Minnow is lonely because his tadpole friend has *changed into a frog* and hopped out of the pond. The curious fish manages to jump out onto the bank, but learns that he *can't breathe* out of his watery home.

Most, Bernard. *If the Dinosaurs Came Back.* New York: Harcourt Brace Jovanovich, 1978. If the dinosaurs returned, a young boy humorously imagines they would be useful in mowing the lawn, rescuing kites from tall trees, and building skyscrapers. The final pages of the book illustrate the shapes and real *scientific names* of various prehistoric creatures.

Stevenson, James. *Howard.* New York: Greenwillow Books, 1980. After missing the annual fall migration south, a duck spends the winter in New York City.

Insects—Changes and Identification

Carle, Eric. *Very Hungry Caterpillar.* n.p.: Philomel, 1969. Beginning with a tiny egg laid on a leaf, this delightful story follows the growth of a caterpillar as it eats a variety of foods (making actual holes in the pages), forms a cocoon, sleeps, and *becomes a beautiful butterfly.*

Miller, Edna. *Jumping Bean.* New York: Prentice-Hall, 1979. What makes a jumping bean jump? This story explains the *metamorphosis* of the jumping bean larva (whose eggs are laid by the moth on the blossoms of the desert arrow plant) into a caterpillar (burrowed in a seed pod of the arrow plant).

Nakatani, Chiyoko. *Zoo In My Garden.* New York: Crowell-Collier, 1973. These are some of the menagerie of "animals" found in a young boy's garden: ants, beetles, a snail, a wasp, and butterflies. Appealing multi-hued pictures embellish the slight text.

Poulet, Virginia. *Blue Bug and the Bullies.* Chicago: Children's Press, 1971. Blue Bug is hampered by an assortment of insects, including a wasp, cricket, praying mantis, spider, centipede, dragonfly, and water bug. Large, colorful pictures made this a perfect *"bug" identification* book.

Light—Rainbows and Shadows

Crews, Donald. *Light.* New York: Greenwillow Books, 1981. Vibrant illustrations explore the concept of different *kinds of light* in the city and in the country: daylight, starlight, moonlight, car headlights, and neon flashing lights.

De Regniers, Beatrice. *Shadow Book.* Photographs by Isabel Gordon. New York: Harcourt Brace Jovanovich, 1960. A young child explains that his *shadow* is a constant companion that *changes* size during the day and helps him know what *time* it is. ("If it's small and you feel hungry, it's probably lunch time".)

Freeman, Don. *Rainbow of My Own.* New York: Viking Press, 1966. After trying unsuccessfully to catch the *rainbow* he admires in the sky, a child notices a tiny rainbow right on the wall of his very own room. (The *sun* was shining through the *water* in his glass *goldfish-bowl!*)

Larranga, Robert. *King's Shadow.* Illustrations by Joe Greenwich. Minneapolis: Carolrhoda Books, 1970. A king attempts to get rid of the *shadow* he fears by painting over it, nailing it to the floor, and stepping out of his shoes. In desperation he hides in a dark room until he's forced to leave in order to kill a dragon. At evening as he rides his horse, with the *sun behind him.* He keeps a watchful eye on his lengthening shadow in *front of him*—which, luckily, frightens the dragon away!

Machines, Magnets, and Tools

Branley, Franklyn, and Vaughan, Eleanor. *Mickey's Magnet.* Illustrations by Crockett Johnson. New York: Scholastic, 1956. (paperback) When Mickey accidentally drops his mother's sewing pins all over the floor, his father gives him a horseshoe magnet. Mickey happily discovers, through trial and error, that magnets pick up only *metal* (iron and steel) and that needles can be magnetized too!

Rockwell, Ann and Harlow. *Machines.* New York: Macmillan Publishing Company, 1972. Full-page multicolored drawings and brief text depict various machines: levers for lifting, wheels that turn, pulleys, gears, ball bearings, cars that use gasoline, sewing machines that work with electricity, and bicycles that require feet power!

———. *Toolbox.* New York: Macmillan Publishing Company, 1971. Inside father's toolbox is a saw, hammer, nails, a drill, screws and a screwdriver, a clamp that holds pieces of wood, a wrench, pliers, a plane that smooths wood, and a ruler. Attractive bold pictures realistically portray each item.

Moon

Fuchs, Erich. *Journey to the Moon.* New York: Delacorte Press, 1969. This wordless picture book depicts the eight-day journey of the Appollo II spacecraft of 1969—from the rocket's take off at the launch pad to the moon landing and to the splashdown in the Pacific. Explanatory notes in the preface provide capsulized information about this astronautical mission. Unusual geometric watercolor artwork in full color captures the excitement of the flight.

Preston, Edna. *Squawk to the Moon.* Illustrated by Barbara Cooney. New York: Viking Press, 1974. A silly little duck believes that the fox swallowed up the moon (actually a cloud covered it) and then thinks that the moon fell into the pond (actually he sees the moon's reflection in the water). In the end the duck outwits the fox as he tells the fox to jump in the pond and eat the delicious cheese that appears to be floating on the water.

Plants and Seeds—Growing

Hutchins, Pat. *Titch.* New York: Macmillan Publishing Company, 1971. Poor Titch had only a *tiny seed,* while his older brother, Pete, had a big spade, and his older sister, Mary, had a fat flowerpot. But guess what? Titch's tiny seed grew and grew until it was a huge lovely plant!

Krauss, Ruth. *Carrot Seed.* Illustrated by Crockett Johnson. New York: Harper and Row, Publishers, 1945. Carefully a small boy *plants* his *carrot seed,* sprinkles it with water, and pulls the weeds. And, just as he said it would, it grew into a big orange carrot!

Time and Seasons

Carle, Eric. *Grouchy Ladybug.* New York: Harper and Row, Publishers, 1977. A grouchy and greedy ladybug, wanting to eat all the aphids herself, decides to fight rather than share, but at meeting each intruder says, "Oh, you're not big enough." As each *hour* ticks away (portrayed by tiny *clocks* on each page), larger and larger creatures pass by until a whale gives ladybug her comeuppance.

Hutchins, Pat. *Clocks and More Clocks.* New York: Macmillan Publishing Company, 1970. The gentleman in this story is confused, because his hall clock reads 4:20, but when he checks the attic clock, it says 4:23, and after running to the bedroom clock, he sees it's 4:25. Which timepiece is correct? All three—because, he learns, *time constantly changes,* even as he goes from room to room.

Provensen, Alice and Martin. *A Year At Maple Hill Farm.* New York: Atheneum Publishers, 1978. Beautifully detailed illustrations and text describe what happens during the year on a farm. Signs of spring include a *baby calf* and *foal, robins hatching,* and ice melting on the pond. In summer *insects* are everywhere and *sheep graze* all day. *Migrant birds* head south in fall, along with the *harvest of crops.* Days are shorter in the *cold* winter and cows stay in the barnyard.

Weather: Clouds, Rain, Sun, Wind, Snow, and Temperature

Barrett, Judith. *Cloudy With a Chance of Meatballs.* New York: Atheneum Publishers, 1978. Just imagine the marvelous town of Chewandswallow where the weather comes three times a day—breakfast, lunch, and dinner! It *rains* soup and juice, *snows* mashed potatoes, the *wind* blows *storms* of hamburgers, and there are tomato *tornadoes!* A sheer fantasy story with a fresh twist, ideal for creating a "downpour" of children's comments and a "gale" of laughter about weather.

Burningham, John. *Mr. Gumpy's Motor Car.* New York: Crowell-Collier Press, 1973. Dark *clouds* overhead warn the animal and human friends squashed into an old car that rain is sure to come. After the shower, the dirt road gets muddy and everyone has to push the vehicle. As the sun *shines,* and it gets *hot* outside.

Elliott, Alan. *On Sunday the Wind Came.* Illustrated by Susan Bonners. New York: William Morrow and Company, 1980. Each day of the week brings weather, which is suitable for many different childhood activities. On Monday a *thunderstorm* provides puddles good for racing boats. Tuesday brings *fog* ideal for hide and seek. On Wednesday it turns *cold* enough to draw faces on fogged-up windowpanes. Thursday's *sleet and icicles* make sliding on boxes fun. Friday's *snow* is perfect for making snowballs and snow angels. Saturday the *wind* blows just right for flying kites. Sunday the *sun* comes out!

Ginsburg, Mirra. *Where Does the Sun Go At Night?* Illustrated by Jose Aruego. New York: Greenwillow Books, 1981. This fanciful story consists of questions a child asks about the sun and the answers he receives as if "he" (the sun) was human. ("What does he dream about? The moon and the stars." "What is he covered with? A wooly cloud." "Who is his grandpa? The wind.")

Himler, Ronald. *Wake Up, Jeremiah.* New York: Harper and Row, Publishers, 1979. Full color paintings capture the splendid flow of the morning sun as a small child exuberantly greets a new *day dawning.*

Hutchins, Pat. *The Wind Blew.* New York: Macmillan Publishing Company, 1974. Rhymed text tells one by one the items which the wind blew out to sea: an umbrella, hat, kite, shirt, a wig off the judge's head, the postman's letters, a flag, scarves, and a newspaper! Lively colorful illustrations enhance this humorous story.

Keats, Ezra Jack. *Snowy Day.* New York: Viking Press, 1962. Peter awakens one morning to find that a blanket of snow has covered the ground. He enthusiastically makes tracks in the snow, builds a snowman, and makes snow angels. He keeps a snowball in his pocket. Before going to bed, he checks his pocket and finds it empty!

Kessler, Ethel and Leonard. *The Day Daddy Stayed Home.* New York: Doubleday and Company, 1959. A virtual blizzard brings transportation to a halt, and daddy stays home from work, while snowplows clear *snow* off the roads. A facsimile of a real *thermometer* shows "it's *twenty degrees*"—"that means it's very cold." The children wish the snow "would never melt away."

Water: Evaporation, Floating, and Melting

Burningham, John. *Mr. Gumpy's Outing.* New York: Holt, Rhinehart and Winston, 1971. When many animals squeeze into a boat for a ride, the boat capsizes and everyone falls into the water. After swimming to the bank, the *wet* friends *dry off* in the *hot sun.* Huge lovely artwork adds color and charm.

Holl, Adelaide. *Rain Puddle.* Illustrations by Roger Duvoisin. New York: Lothrop, Lee and Shephard, 1965. A plump hen looks into the rain puddle, sees her *reflection,* and believes she has fallen in. Soon the whole barnyard of animals comes and thinks they've all fallen into the water too. When the *sun* comes out, the *puddle dries up* and the animals are so glad to have climbed out safely!

Rey, H. A. *Curious George Rides A Bike.* Boston: Houghton Mifflin Company, 1952. Curious George decides to see if his toy boats, made from the newspapers he was delivering, will *float* on the river.

Zion, Gene. *Summer Snowman.* Illustrations by Margaret Graham. New York: Harper and Row, Publishers, 1955. Henry hides his winter snowman in the refrigerator until the Fourth of July when he sets it proudly on the lawn. It quickly *melts* in the *hot summer sun.* (His brother, Pete, wonders if the moon ever gets hot and could melt a winter snowman at night.)

Appendix 11 Narrative Materials

Burningham, John. *Mr. Grumpy's Motor Car.* New York: Thomas Y. Crowell, 1973.
Burton, Virginia Lee. *The Little House.* Boston: Houghton Mifflin Company, 1943.
Feder, Paula Kurzband. *Where Does the Teacher Live?* New York: E.P. Dutton, 1979.
Freeman, Don. *Corduroy.* New York: Viking Press, 1968.
Freschet, Berniece. *The Happy Dromedary.* New York: Charles Scribner's Sons, 1977.
Haley, Gail E. *A Story, A Story.* New York: Atheneum Publishers, 1970.
Harper, Wilhelmina. *The Gunniwolf.* New York: E. P. Dutton, 1967.
Hoban, Russell. *A Baby Sister for Frances.* New York: Harper and Row, Publishers, 1964.
Hutchins, Pat. *Happy Birthday, Sam.* New York: Greenwillow Books, 1978.
Keats, Ezra. *The Snowy Day.* New York: Viking Press, 1969.
———. *Whistle for Willie.* New York: Viking Press, 1964.
Lamorisee, Albert. *The Red Balloon.* New York: Doubleday and Company, 1956.
Lionni, Leo. *Alexander and the Wind-Up Mouse.* New York: Random House, 1969.
———. *Frederick.* New York: Random House, 1967.
McKloskey, Robert. *Make Way for Ducklings.* New York: Viking Press, 1941.
Miles, Miska. *Annie and the Old One.* Boston: Little, Brown and Company, 1971.
Piper, Watty. *The Little Engine That Could.* New York: Platt and Munck, 1930.
Scott, Ann Herbert. *On Mother's Lap.* New York: McGraw-Hill Book Company, 1972.
———. *Sam.* New York: McGraw-Hill Book Company, 1967.
Sendek, Maurice. *Where the Wild Things Are.* New York: Harper and Row, Publishers, 1963.
Steig, William. *Amos and Boris.* New York: Farrer, Straus, Giroux, 1971.
———. *Sylvester and the Magic Pebble.* New York: Simon and Schuster, 1969.

Steptoe, John. *Stevie.* New York: Harper and Row, Publishers, 1960.
Taylor, Mark. *Henry the Explorer.* New York: Atheneum Publishers, 1966.
Udry, Janice. *A Tree is Nice.* New York: Harper and Row, Publishers, 1956.
———. *What Mary Joe Shared.* Chicago: Albert Whitman and Company, 1966.
(Selected from Cromwell 1980, 197–203).

Appendix 12 Poetry Books

Ciardi, John. *You Read to Me, I'll Read to You.* Philadelphia: J. B. Lippincott Company, 1962.
———. *Fast and Slow.* Boston: Houghton Mifflin Company, 1975.
———. *The Man Who Sang the Sillies.* Philadelphia: J. B. Lippincott Company, 1961.
Cole, William. *Beastly Boys and Ghostly Girls.* Chicago: Collins and World, 1964.
———. *Oh, That's Ridiculous!* New York: Viking Press, 1972.
Dunning, Stephen. *Reflections on a Gift of Watermelon Pickle.* New York: Scholastic, 1966.
Geismer, Barbara P., and Suter, Antoinette B. *Very Young Verses.* Boston: Houghton Mifflin Company, 1972.
Larrick, Nancy. *On City Streets.* New York: M. Evans and Company, 1968.
McCord, David. *Everytime I Climb a Tree.* Boston: Little, Brown and Company, 1967.
O'Neill, Mary. *Fingers are Always Bringing Me News.* New York: Doubleday and Company, 1969.
———. *Hailstones and Halibut Bones.* New York: Doubleday and Company, 1969.
Service, Robert. *The Shooting of Dan McGrew and the Cremation of Sam McGee.* Reading, Mass.: Addison-Wesley, 1969.
Silverstein, Shel. *Where the Sidewalks Ends.* New York: Harper and Row, Publishers, 1974.
Tripp, Wallace. *A Great Big Ugly Man Came Up and Tied his Horse to Me.* Boston: Little, Brown and Company, 1973.
(Selected from Halloran 1980, 63–67)

Appendix 13 Read-Along Records and Books

Disneyland Records:
Bambi, Dumbo, The Little Red Hen, 101 Dalmations, The Ugly Duckling, The Little House, Sleeping Beauty, The Gingerbread Man, Pinocchio, How The Camel Lost His Hump, and *Peter Pan and Wendy.*

RCA Records:
Dance-A-Story Records, Little Duck, Noah's Ark, Magic Mountain, Balloons, Brave Hunter, Flappy & Floppy, The Toy Tree, and *At the Beach.*

Scott Foresman Talking Story Book Box:
Ask Mr. Bear, Brownie, Goggles, The Wild Duck & The Goose, M is for Moving, Just Me, and *Joey's Cat.*

(Cromwell 1980, 209)

Appendix 14 Films and Records

Films

The film distributor for the following list of 16 mm films is Weston Woods, Weston, Conn. 06880. Sound filmstrips, books, and records are also available for most of the films selected.

Andy and the Lion, 10 minutes, Caldecott Honor Book.
Beast of Monsieur Racine, 9 minutes, animated, first prize children's category, International Animation Film Festival.
Caps for Sale, 5 minutes, ALA Notable Children's Book.

Changes, Changes, 6 minutes, animated, ALA Notable Children's Book.
Chicken Soup with Rice, 5 minutes, animated, ALA Notable Children's Book.
The Cow Who Fell in the Canal, 9 minutes.
Crow Boy, 13 minutes, Caldecott Honor Book, ALA Notable Children's Book.
Curious George Rides a Bike, 10 minutes.
The Happy Owls, 7 minutes, animated, ALA Notable Children's Book.
Harold and the Purple Crayon, 8 minutes, animated.
Harold's Fairy Tale, 8 minutes, animated, Grand Prize, Harrisburg Film Festival.
The Little Drummer Boy, 7 minutes, ALA Notable Children's Book.
Make Way for Ducklings, 11 minutes, Caldecott Honor Book, ALA Notable Children's Book.
Mike Mulligan and His Steam Shovel, 11 minutes.
Patrick, 7 minutes, animated, Gold Medal at Atlanta International Film Festival.
Peter's Chair, 6 minutes.
Petunia, 10 minutes, animated.
The Selfish Giant, 14 minutes, animated, German State Prize—Most Beautiful German Children's Film.
The Snowy Day, 6 minutes, animated, Caldecott Honor Book, ALA Notable Children's Book, Best Children's Film, Venice Film Festival.
Stone Soup, 11 minutes, Caldecott Honor Book, ALA Notable Children's Book.
The Story about Ping, 10 minutes, Award of Merit, Columbus Film Festival.
A Story, A Story, 10 minutes, animated.
Strega Nonna, 9 minutes, animated, Caldecott Honor Book, ALA Notable Children's Book.
Time of Wonder, 13 minutes, Caldecott Honor Book, ALA Notable Children's Book.
Where The Wild Things Are, 6 minutes, Caldecott Honor Book, ALA Notable Children's Book.

Rental Sources

Weston Woods
Weston, Conn. 06800

Center for Instructional Media and Technology
University of Connecticut, Film Library
Stanford, Conn. 06268

Media Library, Audio-Visual Services
University of Iowa
Iowa City, Iowa 52240

Boston University, School of Education
Krasker Memorial Film Library
Boston, Mass. 02215

Film Rental Center of Syracuse University
Syracuse, N.Y. 44240

Kent State University
Audio-Visual Services
Kent, Ohio 44242

Portland State University
Continuing Education Film Library
Portland, Oreg. 97207

University of Utah
Educational Media Center
Salt Lake City, Utah 84112

Modern Film Rentals
2323 New Hyde Park Rd.
New Hyde Park, N.Y. 11040

(Selected from Cromwell 1980, 205–207)

Records (Story Telling Albums)

Alice in Wonderland, read by Joan Greenwood and Stanley Holloway, Caedmon.
Cinderella in Story and Songs, story and lyrics by Peter Haas, Pickwick International.
Curious George and Other Stories, read by Julie Harris, Caedmon.
Hansel and Gretel, with music from the opera by Humperdink, Disneyland.
The Little Engine That Could, Disneyland.
The Little Tailor, read by Peter Ustinov, Angel Recordings.
Mary Poppins, read by Maggie Smith and Robert Stephens, Caedmon.
The Nutcracker Suite, Dance of the Hours, Disneyland.
Petunia, read by Julie Harris, Caedmon.
Puss in Boots and Other Fairy Tales from Around the World, retold by Anabel Williams-Ellis, Caedmon.
Snow White and Other Fairy Tales, read by Claire Bloom, Caedmon.
The Tale of Peter Rabbit and Other Stories by Beatrix Potter, read by Claire Bloom, Caedmon.
The Three Little Pigs, Disneyland.
The Ugly Duckling and Other Tales, read by Boris Karloff, Caedmon.
The Wind in The Willows, read by Jessica Tandy and Hume Cronyn, Pathways of Sound.
Winnie-the-Pooh, read and sung by Carol Channing, Caedmon.
The Wizard of Oz, Disneyland.

(Selected from Cromwell 1980, 208)

Glossary

Accommodation Modification of existing cognitive structure to fit new information.

Accountability Being held responsible for educational programs and practices in terms of learner progress.

Adaptation "The continuous process of learning from the environment and learning to adjust to environmental changes" (Piaget).

Adapted experience A learning activity that has been changed to accommodate individual differences. Differentiations may be made in the number of steps individual children are assigned in a given activity, in grouping size, and in room location for work.

Affect Feeling or emotion.

Affective domain The psychological field of emotional activity, as contrasted to the cognitive domain (the psychological field of knowing and understanding).

Affix Any morpheme that is not an independent word; it is grammatical only if occurring as part of a word. Example, *im-* and *-er* in *importer.*

Alphabetic principle Using alphabet letters to represent each phoneme or speech sound of oral language. English is an alphabetic language.

Alphabetic system Where graphic symbols (letters) are used to represent oral language, as in English, an alphabetic system.

Assessment Gathering information about a child's current knowledge, background, and understanding of print in order to make effective instructional decisions.

Assimilation Incorporating new ideas to make them a part of one's present cognitive store of meanings, as contrasted to *accommodation,* which requires restructuring current mental structures.

Assisted reading Help given to aid children in learning to read connected discourse; child follows along with the reader and gradually takes over the reading task itself.

Basal reader A text in a basal reading program or series.

Basal reading program or series A comprehensive, integrated set of books, workbooks, teacher's manuals, and other materials for developmental reading instruction, chiefly in the elementary and middle school grades.

Big Books Enlarged versions of story material to be placed on a stand for viewing by a group during the shared-book experience.

Body language The nonverbal signals used in spoken communication: facial expressions, eye contact, use of hands, body postures, and head movements.

Book awareness The knowledge of the basic features of a book: front, back, top, bottom, beginning, middle, and end.

Bottom-up processing Theory that comprehension in reading consists of attending first to the smallest units of print (letters) and then combining these into words and sentences. Comprehension as text driven: it is built up and governed by the text only and does not involve the reader's nonvisual store of meanings. Reading as deriving meaning *from* print contrasted to *top-down* processing, which is seen as bringing meaning *to* print.

Category A class or a group whose parts are related by one or more common criteria. A category is a division of a larger classification system. Example, *dog* is a category of *animal.*

Classroom center An area in the classroom that contains all materials, equipment, and instructions for conducting specific learning activities, often independent of the teacher.

Cloze procedure Way of supplying missing portions of an oral or written message. Reading activities which involve deletion of words from text so that reader must supply the word implied by the written message.

Cognitive clarity The understanding that printed text is a form of language, that is, that it has a communicative purpose and that features of spoken language are represented by written signs; cognitive clarity as essential in learning to read.

Cognitive structure The organization of thinking into a consistent system. Changes in cognitive structure are a product of learning.

Compound word A word formed by combining two or more words, such as in *snowman, mailman.*

Comprehension In reading, the process of getting the meaning of a message in print; understanding the writer's message.

Concept A meaning derived from experience that becomes part of one's cognitive store; usually has a word referent associated with it.

Concepts about print Those meanings that describe the various features and conventions peculiar to the written form of language; meanings that aid children in learning to read. For example, English has small and large letters.

Concrete operations (Piaget) The first organized system of logical thought in mental development, usually from 7 to 11 years; it is dependent on direct interaction with the real, concrete world. The child who can develop a hierarchy of classes of objects that he can see, but cannot do so for absent objects, is using concrete operations.

Confirmation In reading or listening, the verification of predictions using information about a writer or speaker's meaning or use of language.

Connected discourse The form of language in books; whole language in sentences.

Connotation An implied, suggested, nonliteral meaning of a word or group of words.

Conservation (Piaget) The logical thinking ability to keep an invariant property of something in mind under changing perceptual conditions. Seeing that the quantity of a substance remains constant even though its shape changes.

Content words Those having lexical meaning; those classes of words that carry the heaviest meaning load (nouns, verbs, adjectives, and adverbs); usually have referents in the world.

Conventions of writing Includes the symbols used to record language in meaningful representations and the ways in which these recordings are organized on a page. Example, left-to-right progression across a page, spacing between words, and punctuation.

Correction strategy Use of reader's or speaker's knowledge of language and the context in which it is used to correct errors; self-correction.

Cross-age helpers Children in an older age group who act as tutors to children in a younger age group: a fourth-grader assists a first-grader in reading.

Cumulative sequence In language, adding a new episode and then repeating all that went before: "This is the House That Jack Built" is based on cumulative sequencing of language.

Decode To get the intended meaning of a printed message by an analysis of graphic symbols.

Deep structure The meaning to which the surface structure (speech and print) refers; the meaning that exists in the mind of the users of language; a nonobservable feature of communication.

Deficit model Concentration on the weaknesses that children bring to given learning situations; views teaching as basically a process of eliminating the deficiencies of a child; deficiencies defined as not reaching a preset standard of performance.

Denotation The direct, explicit meaning of a word or phrase, as contrasted with connotation or implied meaning.

Discovery center A classroom area with a collection of materials and equipment selected to stimulate exploration of the many phenomena of the physical world.

Disequilibrium (Piaget) Existence of a state of mental confusion occurring when new information does not fit with existing concepts.

Distinctive feature A distinguishing characteristic of a speech sound or a written symbol that differentiates it in meaning from other sounds or symbols: the letter forms *A* and *O* differ in distinctive features; *K* and *k* do not.

Echo reading A form of assisted reading in which the child imitates or repeats another's reading.

Egocentric speech Talking to and with oneself; characteristic of early language development.

Egocentrism (Piaget) The child's *inability* to take another's point of view; differs from adult egocentrism in which adult *could* but *will not* see another's viewpoint.

Embedding A sentence-combining process in which one clause is contained inside another: *The boy was my brother* combines with *He won a prize* to form *The boy who won the prize was my brother.*

Emergent reading behaviors Behaviors reflecting attention to the specific visual features of print: asking about specific words, pointing to words, retelling a story while turning pages at appropriate places, and "talking like a book" in storytelling.

Encode To change a message into symbols, such as encode oral language into writing and encode an idea into words.

Environmental print The print that occupies the everyday world in the form of labels, signs, and slogans; print outside that of regular connected discourse characteristic of books, magazines, and newspapers.

Experimentation/testing/feedback The processes by which a child learns the rules of language; trying out certain ways to say things and then receiving responses from others that confirm or disconfirm whether the spoken language is compatible with the rules.

Expository language A form of language used to explain, to convey information, as contrasted to narrative language, which gives an account or tells a story.

Features of print Those characteristics that describe the conventions of written language. Examples: shapes of letters, front of book, left-to-right arrangement, top-to-bottom processing of page.

Formal operations (Piaget) An organized system of logical thinking, which usually appears in mental development between ages 11 and 15, involving abstract reasoning and setting up and testing of verbal hypotheses.

Grapheme A written representation of a speech sound. In English, the letters of the alphabet are graphemes.

Graphophonic Referring to the relationship between a grapheme (letter) of writing and a phoneme (sound) of speech.

Graphophonic cues Using letter/sound correspondence to recognize words in print.

Guided reading A form of group instruction similar to that of a directed-reading lesson from a basal series; introduces children to techniques for reading new material including introduction to materials, reading, and follow-up (Holdaway).

Holophrastic speech The use of a single word to express the meaning of a sentence; applies to an early stage in language development during which a child may say *milk* to mean several things: I want more milk. I want milk. I want it in a hurry!

Hypothesis testing In reading, the use of language cues in print to check anticipated meaning.

Illustrated books Books that use illustrations to break up long passages of print.

Inflection Changing the form of a word to express a different meaning, such as in adding *un* to happy or *s* to boy.

Informal assessment Evaluation of ability or performance by any nonstandardized means. Example: observation of behaviors for a specific purpose.

Integration process In reading, the simultaneous processing of the cue systems of written language to arrive at meaning.

Intonation The melody of a spoken language; the rise and fall of pitch in speech.

Invented spelling Children's versions of written language in the early stages of literacy development; versions may include shapes and combinations that do not conform to adult standards.

Juncture Pauses of varying lengths in speech production that contribute to the meaning of words, phrases, and sentences.

Kernel sentence A simple declarative sentence that can be changed into more complex sentences by transformation rules. Example, *boys play*.

Key words (Ashton-Warner) Words that have a high level of personal meaning; derived from the child's own experiences. Used to form the text for the child's reading.

Language cues *See* phonological, semantic, and syntactic cues.

Language-experience method An approach to learning to read in which the child's own words or oral compositions are written down and used as materials of instruction for reading, writing, speaking, and listening.

Learning center Specific location in a classroom that contains all the necessary materials for accomplishing given tasks in either small groups or individually.

Learning disabled Having difficulty in learning; inability to learn at a normal rate.

Learning-to-read continuum Progression along a course from emergent reading behaviors to reading proficiency.

Library or reading center An area in the classroom where materials and equipment are provided for children to explore and read many types of print.

Linear mock writing A kind of writing occurring early in writing skills development: scribbles along a line of a tablet, which may stand for any number of possible things to the child, but which do not convey a particular message.

Listening center An area in the classroom equipped with a listening unit which has multiple headsets and record player and/or cassette recorder; tapes and records are also available.

Literacy continuum The range between nonreading and fluent reading along which a child moves in the acquisition of literacy.

Literate Able to read and write.

Metalanguage A language *about* language. The words used to talk about written language (*word, letter, sound,* and *sentence*).

Miscue An oral reading response that differs from the expected response to the written text: reading *man* for *mean*.

Mock letters (Clay) An early writing stage; beginning to produce writing that has some of the characteristics of conventional forms; connecting lines, writing along a line on the page.

Modeling behavior Engaging in activity that may be copied by the child. Example: a parent's reading which is imitated by the child.

Morpheme The smallest meaning unit in a language; may be a complete word (*boy*) or a unit that has no meaning in and of itself (*s*); thus, *boys* would consist of two morphemes: *boy* and *s*. (A *free* morpheme is one that represents meaning when used alone, such as *boy;* a *bound* morpheme must be combined with another morpheme to have meaning, such as *s* in *boys*.)

Narrative language A form of composition in speech or writing that describes, gives an account of, or tells a story, as contrasted to the expository form which explains. Story language is narrative.

Natural readers Children who learn to read without formal, systematic instruction; some do so before entering school. In essence, they have taught themselves to read.

Nonverbal Communication without speech (words); the unspoken signals of body language that accompany speech.

Nonvisual information That which the reader brings to print; the meanings derived from experience.

Object permanence During the early stages of mental development when a child comes to understand that objects can exist even though they are removed from his sight.

Orthography The writing system of a language, particularly that which has to do with spelling conventions.

Over-predictive readers Readers who do not pay sufficient attention to the visual features of print; rely heavily on knowledge of content and oral language facility and create their own versions of a passage.

Parents as partners Parents who engage in mutual effort and support with the teacher to further the advancement of the child's learning.

Perception Deriving information through the senses; an understanding.

Phases of literacy development *See* phases one, two, and three.

Phase One Literacy The first stage in the development of reading competence during which the child builds *a support system* for learning to read (becoming familiar with books and written language, developing a more extensive conceptual store and expanding oral language competence). During this phase, the child begins to exhibit some emergent reading behaviors, such as focusing more on the visual aspects of print.

Phase Three Literacy The child functions as a reader: she has developed a sufficient sight vocabulary and strategies for attending to the features of print so that she can read easy material independently.

Phase Two Literacy The stage during which the child attends closely to the visual aspects of print. She gradually develops competence in knowing which cues of language to pay attention to, and how to use the cues to recognize words and arrive at meaning in processing print. She is not yet an independent reader, but she is acquiring the basic foundation for becoming so.

Phoneme The smallest unit in spoken language that makes a difference in meaning; for example, the *b* in *bit* and the *p* in *pit*.

Phonics An approach to the teaching of reading that stresses symbol-sound relationships.

Phonological cues Signals to meaning provided by the sounds, sound patterns, and intonations of spoken language.

Phonology The study of speech sounds and their functions in a language. The relation of the surface structure of a sentence to its actual physical representation.

Picture storybooks Books in which the illustrations play an integral part in the story; they help to tell the story.

Pitch The rise and fall of the voice in an utterance that helps the listener to understand the intended meaning of the speaker.

Predictable books Books written to enable children to anticipate quite accurately what message is upcoming in a passage.

Prediction strategy A reader's use of knowledge about language and the context in which it occurs to anticipate what is coming in print.

Prefix A morpheme that precedes the root word, such as in *un*happy.

Prelinguistic stage The first stage of oral language development in which the child experiments with making sounds; meaning is not yet associated with the sounds made.

Preoperational (Piaget) Stage in which thought is representational rather than logical, usually from 2 to 7 years; characterized by egocentrism, centering, and nonreversibility.

Primer A beginning reading book; usually preceded by one or more readiness books and/or preprimers in a basal series.

Print awareness Knowing that print has meaning associated with it, has an audio/visual correspondence, is written from left to right and from top to bottom, and is composed of individual symbols (letters) combined to form meaning units (words), which are then combined to form complete thought units (sentences).

Project center An area in the classroom equipped with everything children need to create a variety of objects related to art, creative dramatics, and other curriculum areas; a hands-on, doing environment.

Psycholinguistics Interdisciplinary field of psychology and linguistics in which language behavior is studied; includes inquiry into language acquisition and use.

Read-along tapes Tapes with stories recorded that a child may listen to while following print in a text.

Readiness books One component of a basal series used at primary level (usually K–1) to provide prereading activities.

Reading environment The condition of being surrounded by print in various forms, the modeling of reading as a valuable activity, and the sharing of reading on a continuing basis.

Recode To change information from one code to another. Example: changing written language into oral speech.

Redundancy A convention of language in which multiple cues are given for the same information. In the sentence *Boys eat peanuts,* there are three separate cues to the plural relationship among the words—*s* on boys, the plural verb, *eat,* and *s* on peanut.

Repeated readings Reading the same story over and over to a child until he gradually begins to match meaning with individual words and finally takes over the reading himself. The type of reading parents engage in with bedtime story reading.

Repetitive sequence Story language in which the same episode with identical wording is repeated several times: "I looked in the closet. It was not there. I looked in the refrigerator. It was not there," and so on.

Reversibility (Piaget) Awareness that for every operation there is a counter operation to cancel it; what is done can be undone; addition and subtraction.

Risk taking Willingness to chance mistakes in reproducing print or oral language.

Root word A morpheme to which affixes may be added to form new meanings. In *walked, walk* is a root.

Sample To focus on the most productive cues in a line of print for the purpose of confirming (or correcting) one's predictions about meaning.

Schema An understanding held, a conceptual system for understanding something; a schema for reading, a schema for dog, and others.

Schemata The plural form of schema.

Semantic cues Evidence from the general sense or meaning of a written or spoken communication that aids in the identification of an unknown word.

Semantics Having to do with meanings—of individual words or the relationship of meaning to syntax and phonology.

Sensory-motor intelligence Prelogical representation of meaning by acting and doing rather than by thinking.

Sensory-motor schemata The store of mental images derived from physically acting on the environment during the first stage of development; the base on which later meanings are developed and given language labels.

Sensory-motor stage (Piaget) The developmental period from birth to approximately two years during which intellectual development relies primarily on sensory input and motor activity prior to attaining symbolic functioning and representational thought.

Shared-book experience Use of an enlarged version of familiar reading material to teach reading to an entire group; technique includes reading along in unison as teacher points and masks to focus attention on specific aspects of print.

Situational context The environment surrounding oral exchanges between participants and their familiarity with the topic(s) of conversation.

Skill A product of a process: in reading, a word recognition skill would be to recognize and use beginning consonants to identify words; a comprehension skill would be to use all visual cues in print simultaneously to arrive at meaning.

Sociolinguistics Study of the relationships between language behavior and other aspects of social behavior; the influence of the social environment on language development.

Spatial egocentrism The tendency to view an object from only one perspective—one's own.

Strategy A systematic way of solving a problem. In reading, one uses the strategies of predicting, sampling, confirming and/or correcting to arrive at meaning.

Strengths model Concentration on the strong qualities that children bring to school learning situation; view teaching as the process of capitalizing on what children already know and can do.

Stress In speech, the emphasis placed on certain words, or parts of words, to convey meaning.

Structural analysis One of the subskills of the word recognition category, which focuses on larger units of print—roots, morphemes, and compounds.

Structure (function) words Words that have no lexical meaning; they function to show certain types of relationships between and among words in an utterance or text; included are prepositions, conjunctions, verb auxiliaries, and noun determiners.

Study center An area in the classroom designed for children to complete teacher-assigned or self-selected work.

Subskills Those lesser skills comprising a larger category of skills, such as *identification of beginning consonants* is one subskill of the word recognition category of skills.

Successive approximations The process by which children's reading comes closer and closer to reproduction of the actual printed version during repeated readings of same material.

Suffix A morpheme attached to the end of a base or root word, such as in walk*ed*.

Suprasegmentals Pitch, stress, and juncture in the stream of speech—all of which influence meaning.

Surface structure The observable features of language; the sounds heard in speech, and the print seen in written language.

Sustained silent reading (SSR) Reading in which everyone of a group participates during a given period of time.

Syntactic cue Evidence from a knowledge of the rules and patterns of language that aids in the identification of an unknown word by the way it is used.

Syntax "The arrangement of words into grammatical phrases and sentences" (Hodges and Rudorf 1972, 233).

Systems approach In reading instruction, the sequential ordering of skills teaching, skill by skill in a test-teach-test-reteach pattern.

Telegraphic speech Stage in language development in which all but the essential words of an utterance are omitted, such as *Give cookie* for *Mother give me a cookie.*

Theory of the world The accumulated meanings derived from experiencing the environment which form one's outlook or point of view (Frank Smith).

Top-down processing View of reading as a process of using one's experiences and expectations in order to react to text and arrive at comprehension; comprehension is seen as reader driven rather than text driven; reader brings meaning *to* print rather than getting meaning *from* print, as in the bottom-up view.

Transformation The changing from one linguistic construction to another according to syntactic rules, such as in *It is raining* to *Is it raining?*

Under-predictive readers Readers who overattend to the specific features of print to the neglect of the message; failure to anticipate upcoming meanings.

Unnatural language Text language that is unlike the language used by the child in everyday speech. Basal reader language is an example of unnatural language.

Verbal communication The use of words to send and receive messages.

Very-own words Those words that have highly personal meanings for a child; those words are used to compose text for that child's reading, as in a language-experience activity (McCracken and McCracken).

Visual discrimination The process of perceiving likeness and differences in the printed features of language that make a difference in meaning. For example, the *p* in *pit* and the *b* in *bit.*

Visual information The cues in a printed passage that can be seen as contrasted to nonvisual information which the reader brings to print in the form of concepts derived from experience.

Visual memory The retention, recall, and/or recognition of something seen; for example, in reading, the recall of a word that has been removed from a list of words.

Voice language The nonverbal aspects of speech that accompany the saying of words in a stream of oral language. Use of stress, pitch, and juncture to convey meaning, which may or may not match the message of the words spoken.

Whole language Sentences, phrases, clauses, or any combination of these elements, as contrasted with individual words that have no interrelationships.

Word bank In language experience, a collection of words on individual cards made for a particular child; form the basis for study in building a sight vocabulary.

Wordless picture books Books without words in which pictures carry the story plot.

Writing center Area equipped with materials and ideas to arouse and sustain children's interests in recording their own thoughts and practicing a variety of writing skills.

Writing environment Surroundings that provide an abundance of materials and stimulations to promote interests and participation in writing activities.

(Glossary compiled with the aid of Theodore L. Harris and Richard E. Hodges, coeditors, *A Dictionary of Reading and Related Terms* (Newark, Del.: IRA, 1981).

Bibliography

Allen, Roach Van, and Allen, Claryce. *An Introduction to a Language-Experience Program.* Levels 1–3. Chicago: Encyclopaedia Britannica, 1970.

Allen, Vernon L., ed. *Children as Teachers, Theory and Research on Tutoring.* New York: Academic Press, 1976.

Applegate, Mauree. *Easy in English.* New York: Harper and Row, Publishers, 1960.

Artley, A. Sterl. "Reading: Skills or Competencies?" *Language Arts* 57 (May 1980): 546–49.

Asbjornsen, Peter, and Moe, Jorgen. *The Three Billy Goats Gruff.* New York: Harcourt Brace Jovanovich, 1957.

Ashton-Warner, Sylvia. *Teacher.* New York: Simon and Schuster, 1971.

Baghban, Marcia. *Our Daughter Learns to Read and Write. A Case Study from Birth to Three.* Newark, Del.: International Reading Association, 1984.

Bettelheim, Bruno, and Zelan, Karen. *On Learning to Read. A Child's Fascination with Meaning.* New York: Random House, Vintage Books, 1982.

———. "Why Children Don't Like to Read." *The Atlantic Monthly* vol. 248 (November 1981): 25–31.

Bissex, Glenda L. *GNYS AT WRK.* Cambridge, Mass. Harvard University Press, 1980.

Black, Janet K. "Those 'Mistakes' Tell Us a Lot." *Language Arts* 57 (May 1980): 512.

Blatt, Gloria T. "Playing With Language." *The Reading Teacher* 31 (February 1978): 487–93.

Brown, Roger. *Words and Things.* New York: Free Press, 1958.

———. *A First Language: The Early Stages.* Cambridge, Mass.: Harvard University Press, 1973.

Brown, Roger, and Bellugi, Ursula. "Three Processes in the Child's Acquisition of Syntax." *Harvard Educational Review* 34 (1964): 133–151.

Bruner, Jerome. "Schooling Children in a Nasty Climate." *Psychology Today* vol. 16, no. 1, (January 1982): 57–63.

Burie, Audrey Ann, and Heltshe, Mary Ann. *Reading With a Smile, 90 Reading Games That Work.* Washington, D.C.: Acropolis Books, 1980.

Butler, Dorothy, and Clay, Marie. *Reading Begins at Home.* Auckland: Heinemann Educational Books, 1979.

Byers, Paul, and Byers, Happie. "Nonverbal Communication and the Education of Children." *Functions of Language in the Classroom,* edited by Courtney B. Cazden, Vera P. John, and Dell Hymes. New York: Columbia University, Teachers College Press, 1972.

Cahoon, Owen W. *Cognitive Tasks for Preschool.* Teacher's Guide. Provo, Utah: Brigham Young University Press, 1975.

Calkins, Lucy McCormick. *Lessons from a Child: On the Teaching and Learning of Writing.* Exeter, N.H.: Heinemann Educational Books, 1983.

Carroll, John B. "Psycholinguistics and the Study and Teaching of Reading." In *Aspects of Reading Instruction,* edited by Susanna Pflaum-Connor. Berkeley, Calif.: McCutchan Publishing, 1978.

Carson, Rachel. *The Sense of Wonder.* New York: Harper and Row, Publishers, 1956.

Cauley, Lorinda Bryan. *Pease-Porridge Hot: A Mother Goose Cookbook.* Illus. by author. Lindhurst, N.J.: G. P. Putnam's Sons, 1977.

Cazden, Courtney. *Child Language and Education.* New York: Holt, Rinehart and Winston, 1972.

Chan, Julie M. T. *Why Read Aloud to Children?* IRA micromonograph. Newark: International Reading Association, 1974.

Chomsky, Carol. "After Decoding: What?" *Language Arts* 53 (March 1976): 288–96, 314.

Chomsky, Noam. *Aspects of the Theory of Syntax.* Cambridge, Mass.: The MIT Press, 1965.
———. *Language and Mind.* New York: Harcourt Brace Jovanovich, 1968.
———. *Reflections in Language.* New York: Random House, 1975.
Clark, M. M. *Young Fluent Readers.* London: Heinemann Educational Books, 1976.
Clay, Marie M. *The Early Detection of Reading Difficulties: A Diagnostic Survey with Recovery Procedures* (2nd ed.). Auckland: Heinemann Educational Books, 1979.
———. *Reading: The Patterning of Complex Behavior.* London: Heinemann Educational Books, 1973.
———. *Reading: The Patterning of Complex Behavior* (2nd ed.). London: Heinemann Educational Books, 1979.
———. *What Did I Write?* Auckland: Heinemann Educational Books, 1975.
Cloward, R. O. "Studies in Tutoring." *Journal of Experimental Education* 36 (Fall 1967): 14–25.
Cohn, Margot. "Observations of Learning to Read and Write Naturally." *Language Arts* 58 (May 1981): 549–56.
Combs, Arthur. *Professional Education of Teachers.* Boston: Allyn and Bacon, 1965.
Cromwell, Ellen. *Feathers in My Cap: Early Reading Through Experience.* Washington, D.C.: Acropolis Books, 1980.
Cummins, James. "Educational Implications of Mother Tongue Maintenance in Minority Language Groups." *Canadian Modern Language Review* 34 (February 1978): 395–416.

Dechant, Emerald, and Smith, Henry. *Psychology in Teaching Reading.* 2d ed. Englewood Cliffs, N.J.: Prentice-Hall, 1977.
De Saint-Exupéry, Antoine. *The Little Prince.* New York: Harcourt Brace Jovanovich, 1971.
DeStefano, Johanna S. "Research Update: Demonstrations, Engagement and Sensitivity: A Revised Approach to Language Learning—Frank Smith." *Language Arts* 58 (January 1981): 103–12.
Doake, David B. "Book Experience and Emergent Reading Behaviors." Paper presented at meeting of the International Reading Association, Atlanta, May 1979.
Donovan, James H. "Parents as Reading Partners Program." Albany, N.Y.: State Senate, 1979.
Douglas, Malcolm C. "Stop Trying to Teach Reading." *Los Angeles Times,* 25 February 1973.
Downing, John. *Reading and Reasoning.* New York: Springer-Verlag, New York, 1979.
———. "Reading—Skill or Skills?" *The Reading Teacher* 35 (February 1982): 534–37.
Durkin, Dolores. "Children Who Learn to Read at Home." *Elementary School Journal* vol. 61, (October 1961): 15–18.
———. *Children Who Read Early.* New York: Columbia University, Teachers College Press, 1966.
———. *Getting Reading Started.* Boston: Allyn and Bacon, 1982.
———. "Phonics: Instruction That Needs to Be Improved." *The Reading Teacher* 28 (November 1974): 152–56.
———. *Strategies for Identifying Words.* 2d ed. New York: Allyn and Bacon, 1980.
———. "What Classroom Observations Reveal about Reading Comprehension Instruction." *Reading Research Quarterly* 14 (1978–1979): 481–533.
———. "What is the Value of the New Interest in Reading Comprehension?" *Language Arts* 58 (January 1981): 23–43.
Dyson, Anne Haas. "Oral Language: The Rooting System for Learning to Write." *Language Arts* 58, no. 7 (1981): 776–84.

Eastman, Phillip D. *Are You My Mother?* New York: Random House, 1960.
Edge, Nellie, (comp.) *Kindergarten Cooks.* Port Angeles, Wash.: Peninsula Publishing, 1975.
Ehly, Stewart, and Larsen, Stephen C. *Peer Turoring for Individualized Instruction.* Boston: Allyn and Bacon, 1980.
Elkin, Benjamin. "Lucky and the Giant." In *Magic Times,* rev., pp. 28–42. Second-grade level of the Macmillan Basal Reading Series. New York: Macmillan Publishing Company, 1983.
Elkind, David. "The Curriculum Disabled Child." Paper presented at the University of Florida, Gainesville, 15 May 1978.

Ellis, DiAnn W., and Preston, Fannie W. "Enhancing Beginning Reading, Wordless Picture Books in a Cross-Age Tutoring Program." *The Reading Teacher* 37 (April 1984): 692–98.

Flemming, Bonnie Mack, and Hamilton, Darlene Softley. *Resources for Creative Teaching in Early Childhood Education.* New York: Harcourt Brace Jovanovich, 1977.

Furth, Hans G. *Piaget for Teachers.* Englewood Cliffs, N.J.: Prentice-Hall, 1970.

Gaarder, A. Bruce. "Bilingualism and Education." In *The Language Education of Minority Children, Selected Readings,* edited by Bernard Spolsky. Rowley, Mass.: Newbury House Publishers, 1972.

Gág, Wanda. *Millions of Cats.* New York: Coward-McCann, 1928.

Galbraith, Margery A. "Guidelines for Reading Aloud." *The Reading Teacher* 36 (December 1982): 319–20.

Gamby, G. "Talking Books and Taped Books: Materials for Instruction." *The Reading Teacher* 36 (January 1983): 366–69.

Gardner, K. "Early Reading Skills." In *Reading Skills: Theory and Practice,* 18–23. London: Ward Lock Educational, 1970.

Genesee, Fred; Tucker, G. R.; and Lambert, Wallace E. "An Experiment in Trilingual Education." *Canadian Modern Language Review* 34 (1978): 621–43.

Glazer, Susan M., and Brown, Carol S., eds. *Helping Children Read: Ideas for Parents, Teachers and Librarians.* Trenton, N.J.: New Jersey Reading Association, 1980.

Glovach, Linda. *The Little Witches Black Magic Cookbook.* Englewood Cliffs, N.J.: Prentice-Hall, 1972.

Golding, William. *Lord of the Flies.* New York: G. P. Putnam's Sons, 1954.

Golub, Lester. "Evaluation Design and Implementation of a Bilingual Education Program, Grades 1–12, Spanish/English." *Education and Urban Society* 10 (1978): 363–84.

Goodman, Kenneth S. "Acquiring Literacy is Natural: Who Skilled Cock Robin?" *Theory Into Practice* 16 (1978): 309–14.

———. "Breakthroughs and Lock-outs." *Language Arts* 55 (November/December 1978): 919–20.

———. *Reading: Process and Program.* Champaign, Ill.: National Council of Teachers of English, 1970.

———. "Reading: A Psycholinguistic Guessing Game." *Journal of Reading* 6 (1967): 126–35.

———. "Viewpoints: From a Researcher." *Language Arts* 57 (November/December 1980): 846–47.

Goodman, Mary Ellen. *The Culture of Childhood: Child's Eye View of Society and Culture.* New York: Columbia University, Teachers College Press, 1976.

Goodman, Yetta, and Burke, Carolyn. *Reading Strategies: Focus on Comprehension.* New York: Richard C. Owen Publishers, Inc.

Goodman, Yetta, and Goodman, Kenneth. "Twenty Questions about Teaching Language." *Educational Leadership* Vol. 38 (March 1981): 437–42.

Goodman, Yetta, and Watson, Dorothy J. "A Reading Program to Live With: Focus on Comprehension." *Language Arts* 54 (November/December 1977): 868–79.

Graves, Donald H. *Writing: Teachers and Children at Work.* Portsmouth, N.H.: Heinemann Educational Books, 1983.

Gray, William S. *On Their Own in Reading.* Chicago: Scott Foresman, 1948.

Greer, Margaret. "Affective Growth Through Reading." *The Reading Teacher* 25 (January 1972): 336–41.

———. "The Effects of Studying the Structure of Concepts and Cognitive Emphasis Social Studies Units on Selected Cognitive Processes of Fifth-Grade Children." Unpublished doctoral dissertation. In Zintz, Miles V. *The Reading Process.* 3rd ed. Dubuque, Iowa: William C. Brown Company Publishers, 1980.

Hacker, Charles. "From Schema Theory to Classroom Practice." *Language Arts* 57 (November/December 1980): 866–71.

Hall, Mary Anne. *The Language Experience Approach for Teaching Reading.* 2d ed. Newark: International Reading Association, 1978.

———. *Teaching Reading as a Language Experience.* 3rd ed. Columbus: Charles E. Merrill, 1981.

Halloran, Bill. *Thoughts, Word and Promises.* Tulsa, Okla.: Educational Progress Corporation, 1980.

Harris, Theodore L., and Hodges, Richard E., eds. *A Dictionary of Reading and Related Terms.* Newark: IRA, 1981.

Harste, Jerome C., and Burke, Carolyn L. "Toward a Socio-Psycholinguistic Model of Reading Comprehension." *Viewpoints in Teaching and Learning* 54 (July 1978): 9–34.

Hittleman, Daniel R. *Developmental Reading: A Psycholinguistic Perspective.* Chicago: Rand McNally, 1978.

———. *Developmental Reading, K–8, Teaching from a Psycholinguistic Perspective.* 2d ed. Boston: Houghton Mifflin Company, 1983.

Hodges, Richard E., and Rudorf, E. Hugh. *Language and Learning to Read: What Teachers Should Know About Language.* Boston: Houghton Mifflin Company, 1972.

Hoffman, Stevie, and Fillmer, H. Thompson. "Thought, Language and Reading Readiness." *The Reading Teacher* 33 (December 1979): 290–94.

Holdaway, Don. *Foundations of Literacy.* Sydney: Ashton Scholastic, 1979.

———. *Stability and Change in Literacy Learning.* Exeter, N.H.: Heinemann Educational Books, 1984.

Holl, Adelaide. *Adventures in Discovery.* Teacher's Guide. New York: Western Publishing Company, 1970.

Hoskisson, Kenneth. "Learning to Read Naturally." *Language Arts* 56 (May 1979): 489–96.

———. "The Many Facets of Assisted Reading." *Elementary English* 52 (1975): 312–15.

———. "Successive Approximation and Beginning Reading." *Elementary School Journal* 7 (1975): 442–51.

Huey, Edmund Burke. *The Psychology and Pedagogy of Reading.* New York: Macmillan Publishing Company, 1908. Reprint. Cambridge, Mass.: The MIT Press, 1968.

Hughes, Marie M. "Language—Function of Total Life Situation." Mimeographed paper, Seminar, The University of New Mexico, 1970.

Ireton, Judy; Meinema, Jay; Miller, Shirla; Morse, Luella; Peck, Sandra; Thomas, Mary Jo; and Wilson, Diane. *Kindergarten Activities Resources Book.* Anchorage: Anchorage School District, 1976.

Johnson, Richard, and Adams, John. "Reading Aloud—Tips for Teachers." *The Reading Teacher* 36 (April 1983): 829–31.

Jolly, Thomas. "Would You Like to Read to Me?" *The Reading Teacher* 33 (May 1980): 994–96.

Kaplan, Sandra; Kaplan, Jo Ann Butom; Madsen, Shelia Kunishima; and Taylor, Bette. *Change for Children.* Pacific Palisades, Calif.: Goodyear Publishing Company, 1973.

Kaplan, Sandra; Kaplan, Jo Ann Butom; Madsen, Shelia Kunishima; and Gould, Bette Taylor. *A Young Child Experiences.* Pacific Palisades, Calif.: Goodyear Publishing Company, 1975.

Kavale, Kenneth, and Schreiner, Robert. "Psycholinguistic Implications for Beginning Reading Instruction." *Language Arts* 55 (January 1978): 34–40.

Klein, Marvin L. "Key Generalizations About Language and Children." *Educational Leadership* 38 (March 1981): 446–48.

Krauss, Ruth. *A Hole is to Dig.* New York: Harper and Row, Publishers, 1952.

Kubie, Lawrence S. *Neurotic Distortion of the Creative Process.* New York: Noonday Press, 1961.

Lambert, Wallace E. "Cognitive and Sociocultural Consequences of Bilingualism." *Canadian Modern Language Review* 34 (1978): 537–47.

Lamme, Linda L.; Cox, Vivian; Matanzo, Jane; and Olson, Miken. *Raising Readers: A Guide to Sharing Literature with Young Children.* New York: Walker and Company, 1980.

Lamme, Linda Leonard. "Reading Aloud to Young Children." *Language Arts* 53 (November/December 1976): 886–88.

———. *Learning to Love Literature.* Preschool through Grade 3. Urbana, Ill.: National Council of Teachers of English, 1981.

Lass, Bonnie. "Portrait of My Son as an Early Reader." *The Reading* Teacher vol. 36, no. 1, (October, 1982): 20–28.

Lee, Dorris, and Allen, Roach Van. *Learning to Read Through Experience.* New York: Appleton-Century-Crofts, 1963.

Lehr, Fran. "Peer Teaching." *The Reading Teacher* 37 (March 1984): 636–39.

Lippitt, Peggy, and Lohman, John. "Cross-Age Relationships—an Educational Resource." *Children* 12 (May-June 1965): 113–17.

Loban, Walter. "What Language Reveals." In McDonald, James B., and Leeper, Robert R. *Language and Meaning.* Washington, D.C.: Association for Supervision and Curriculum Development, 1966.

Loughlin, Catherine E., and Suina, Joseph H. *The Learning Environment: An Instructional Strategy.* New York: Columbia University, Teachers College Press, 1982.

McCracken, Marlene, and McCracken, Robert A. *Reading and Writing Language. A Practical Guide for Primary Teachers.* Winnipeg: Peguis Publishers, 1979.

McCracken, Robert A., and McCracken, Marlene. *Reading is Only the Tiger's Tail.* San Rafael, Calif.: Leswing Press, 1972.

McDonell, Gloria M., and Osburn, E. Bess. "New Thoughts About Reading Readiness." *Language Arts* 55 (January 1978): 26–29.

McKenzie, Moira. "The Beginnings of Literacy." *Theory into Practice* 16 (1977): 315–24.

McNeill, David. "Developmental Psycholinguistics." In *The Genesis of Language,* edited by Frank Smith and George A. Miller. Cambridge, Mass.: The MIT Press, 1966.

Malstrom, Jean. *Understanding Language: A Primer for Language Arts Teachers.* New York: St. Martin's Press, 1977.

Martin, Bill, Jr. *Strategies for Language Learning.* Tulsa, Okla.: Educational Progress Corporation, 1980.

Mason, George E. *A Primer on Teaching Reading.* Itasca, Ill.: F. E. Peacock Publishers, 1981.

Matthews, Virginia H. "Adult Reading Studies: Their Implications for Private, Professional and Public Policy." *Library Trends* 22 (October 1973): 159.

Menyuk, Paula. *The Acquisition and Development of Language.* Englewood Cliffs, N.J.: Prentice-Hall, 1971.

Miller, George A. "Some Preliminaries to Psycholinguistics." *American Psychologist* 20 (1965): 15–20.

Milstein, Elinore. *Language Arts Can Be Creative.* Washington, D.C.: National Education Association, 1959.

Modiano, Nancy. "A Comparative Study of Two Approaches to the Teaching of Reading in the National Language." Doctorial Dissertation. New York University School of Education, 1966.

Moe, Alden J., and Hopkins, Carol J. "Jingles, Jokes, Limericks, Poems, Proverbs, Puns, Puzzles and Riddles: Fast Reading for Reluctant Readers." *Language Arts* 55 (November/December 1978): 957–65.

Morris, R. Darrell. "Some Aspects of the Instructional Environment and Learning to Read." *Language Arts* 56 (May 1979): 497–502.

Murphy, Marilyn, and Zintz, Miles V. "Classroom Teachers, Let's Write." *The Reading Teacher* 35 (October 1981): 4–6.

Myers, R. E., and Torrance, E. Paul. *For Those Who Wonder.* Boston: Ginn and Company, 1966.

National Geographic Society. *Creepy Crawly Things*. Books for Young Explorers. Washington, D.C.: National Geographic Society, 1974.

Nevi, Charles. "Cross-Age Tutoring: Why Does It Help the Tutors." *The Reading Teacher* 36 (May 1983): 892–98.

Newman, Katherine K. "Do You Eat Potato Chips When You Read?" *Language Arts* 55 (November/December 1978): 977–79.

Page, William D., and Pinnell, Gay Su. *Teaching Reading Comprehension.* Urbana, Ill.: National Council of Teachers of English, 1979.

Park, Barbara. "The Big Book Trend—A Discussion with Don Holdaway." *Language Arts* 59 (November/December 1982): 815–21.

Paul, Aileen. *Kids Cooking Without a Stove*. Garden City, N.Y.: The Seabury Press, 1973.

Pearson, Craig. "The Main Event: Reading vs. Reading Skills." *Learning* 9 (November 1980): 26–30.

Pearson, David P., and Johnson, Dale D. *Teaching Reading Comprehension.* New York: Holt, Rinehart and Winston, 1978.

Piaget, Jean. *The Child's Conception of the World.* Totowa, N.J.: Littlefield, Adams and Company, 1965.

———. *The Origins of Intelligence in Children.* New York: W. W. Norton and Company, 1963.

Piaget, Jean, and Inhelder, Barbel. *The Psychology of the Child.* New York: Basic Books, 1969.

Pickert, Sara M. "Repetitive Sentence Patterns in Children's Books." *Language Arts* 55 (January 1978): 16–18.

Pilulski, John. "Readiness for Reading: A Practical Approach." *Language Arts* 55 (February 1978): 192–97.

Plessas, G. P., and Oakes, C. R. "Prereading Experiences of Selected Early Readers." *The Reading Teacher* 17 (1964): 241–45.

Price, Eunice. "How Thirty-Seven Gifted Children Learned to Read." *The Reading Teacher* 30 (October 1976): 44–48.

Reading Unlimited. *Teaching Beginning Reading Language Experience Approach to Beginning Reading*. Filmstrips and cassettes. Alexandria, Va.: Reading Unlimited, 1976.

Rhodes, Lynn K. "I Can Read! Predictable Books as Resources for Reading and Writing Instruction." *The Reading Teacher* 34 (February 1981): 511–18.

Rogers, Norma. *What Books and Records Should I Get for My Preschooler.* Newark: IRA, n.d.

Root, Shelton. "What Place Pleasure in the Reading System?" Paper presented at the International Reading Association Conference, New Orleans, 1981.

Satre, J. P. *Words*. London: Hamish Hamilton, 1964.

Scarry, Richard. *Best Word Book Ever.* New York: Golden Press, 1974.

Sealey, Leonard; Sealey, Nancy; and Millmore, Marcia. *Children's Writing. An Approach for Primary Grades*. Newark, Del.: International Reading Association, 1979.

Sebesta, Sam. "Why Rudolph Can't Read." *Language Arts* 58 (May 1981): 545–48.

Shuh, John Hennigar. "The Shared Book Experience." *Journal of Education* 6 (1981): 1–6.

Sine, M. R. "Reading Practice with Read-Alongs." *Curriculum Review* 21 (December 1982): 464–66.

Singer, Dorothy G., and Revenson, Tracey A. *A Piaget Primer: How a Child Thinks.* New York: International Universities Press, 1979.

Slobin, Dan I. "Comments on Developmental Psycholinguistics." In *The Genesis of Language,* edited by Frank Smith and George A. Miller. Cambridge, Mass.: The MIT Press, 1966.

———. "Grammatical Transformations and Sentence Comprehension in Childhood and Adulthood." *Journal of Verbal Learning and Verbal Behavior* 5 (1966): 219–27.

Smith, Carl B., and Arnold, Virginia A., sen. authors. *Basal Reading Series*. rev. New York: Macmillan Publishing Company, 1983.

Smith, E. Brooks; Goodman, Kenneth S.; and Meredith, Robert. *Language and Thinking in School.* 2d ed. New York: Holt, Rinehart and Winston, 1976.

Smith, Frank. "Comprehension." *Language Arts* 54 (November/December 1977): 866.

———. *Comprehension and Learning.* New York: Holt, Rinehart and Winston, 1975.

———. "The Learner and His Language." In Hodges, Richard, and Rudorf, E. Hugh. *Language and Learning to Read.* Boston: Houghton Mifflin Company, 1972.

———. *Psycholinguistics and Reading.* New York: Holt, Rinehart and Winston, 1973.

———. *Reading Without Nonsense.* New York: Columbia University, Teachers College Press, 1979.

———. *Understanding Reading: A Psycholinguistic Analysis of Reading and Learning to Read.* 2d ed. New York: Holt, Rinehart and Winston, 1978.

Stahlschmidt, Agnes D., and Johnson, Carole S. "The Library Media Specialist and the Read-Aloud." *School Library Media Quarterly* Vol. 12 (Winter 1984): 146–49.

Stauffer, Russell G. *The Language Experience Approach to the Teaching of Reading.* New York: Harper and Row, Publishers, 1970.

Stewig, John Warren. "Alphabet Books: A Neglected Genre." *Language Arts* 55 (January 1978): 6–11.

Strange, Michael. "Instructional Implications of a Conceptual Theory of Reading Comprehension." *The Reading Teacher* 33 (January 1980): 391–97.

Strickland, Ruth. *The Language Arts in the Elementary School.* Boston: D. C. Heath and Company, 1951.

Swinburne, Laurence. "A Special Kind of Help." In *Secrets and Surprises,* rev., 186–201. Third level of the Macmillan Basal Reading Series. New York: Macmillan Publishing Company, 1983.

Taubenheim, Barbara, and Christensen, Judith. "Let's Shoot 'Cock Robin'! Alternatives to 'Round Robin' Reading." *Language Arts* 55 (November/December 1978): 975–77.

Taylor, Barbara J. *A Child Goes Forth.* Provo, Utah: Brigham Young University Press, 1975.

Taylor, Denny. *Family Literacy. Young Children Learn to Read and Write.* Exeter, N.H.: Heinemann Educational Books, 1983.

Taylor, Nancy E., and Vawter, Jacquelyn M. "Helping Children Discover the Functions of Written Language." *Language Arts* 55 (November/December 1978): 941–45.

Teale, William H. "Positive Environments for Learning to Read: What Studies of Early Readers Tell Us." *Language Arts* 55 (November/December 1978): 922–32.

Teale, William H., and Sulzby, Elizabeth, eds. *Emergent Literacy: Writing and Reading.* Exeter, N.H.: Heinemann Educational Books, 1985.

Temple, Charles A.; Nathan, Ruth G.; and Burris, Nancy A. *The Beginnings of Writing.* Boston: Allyn and Bacon, 1982.

Torrey, J. W. "Learning to Read Without A Teacher: A Case Study." *Elementary English* 46 (1969): 550–58.

Trelease, Jim. *The Read-Aloud Handbook.* New York: Penguin Books, 1982.

Veatch, Jeannette, et al. *Key Words to Reading: The Language Experience Approach Begins.* Columbus: Charles E. Merrill, 2d ed., 1979.

Wadsworth, Barry J. *Piaget for the Classroom Teacher.* New York: Longman, 1978.

Weaver, Constance. *Psycholinguistics and Reading from Process to Practice.* Cambridge, Mass.: Winthrop Publishers, 1980.

Weir, Ruth. *Language in the Crib.* The Hague: Mouton, 1962.

White, Burton L. *The First Three Years of Life.* New York: Avon Books, 1978.

White, Robert. "Motivation Reconsidered: The Concept of Competence." *Psychological Review* 66 (1959): 297–333.

Woodruff, Asahel D. *Basic Concepts of Teaching.* concise ed. San Francisco: Chandler Publishing Company, 1961.

Wortmann, Peter Martin. "Nan." In *You Can,* rev., 54–55. Preprimer level of the Macmillan Basal Reading Series. New York: Macmillan Publishing Company, 1983.

Wylie, Joanne, coordinating ed. *A Creative Guide for Preschool Teachers.* New York: Western Publishing Company, 1969.

Zintz, Miles V. "Are You Attending to the Affective Domain in Your Classroom Reading Program?" Presentation at the Nineteenth Annual Reading Conference, The McLean County ISU Reading Council, University Union, Illinois State University, Normal, Illinois, September 1975.

———. *Corrective Reading*. 4th ed. Dubuque, Iowa: William C. Brown Company Publishers, 1981.

———. *The Reading Process*. 3rd ed. Dubuque, Iowa: William C. Brown Company Publishers, 1980.

Zintz, Miles V., and Maggart, Zelda R. *The Reading Process*. 4th ed. Dubuque, Iowa: William C. Brown Company Publishers, 1984.

Zweifel, Frances. *Pickle in the Middle and Other Easy Snacks*. Scranton, Pa.: Harper and Row, Publishers, 1979.

Index